P9-DIF-870

THE
BATTLE HISTORY
OF THE
U. S. MARINES

ALSO BY JOSEPH H. ALEXANDER

Utmost Savagery: The Three Days of Tarawa

Storm Landings: Epic Amphibious Battles in the Central Pacific

Sea Soldiers in the Cold War (with Merrill L. Bartlett)

THE
BATTLE HISTORY
OF THE
U. S. MARINES

A
FELLOWSHIP
OF VALOR

COL. JOSEPH H. ALEXANDER, USMC (RET.)

WITH DON HORAN AND NORMAN C. STAHL

Foreword by Brig. Gen. Edwin H. Simmons, USMC (Ret.),
Director Emeritus, Marine Corps History and Museums

THE HISTORY CHANNEL®

A Lou Reda Book

HarperPerennial
A Division of HarperCollins Publishers

Lou Reda Productions

Maps on pages 36, 56, 90, 114, 140, 166, 192, 208, 230, 253, 269, 284, 319, 333, and 379 drawn by Mary Craddock Hoffman.

A hardcover edition of this book was published in 1997 by HarperCollins publishers under the title *A Fellowship of Valor*.

THE HISTORY CHANNEL ® is a trademark of A&E Television Networks and is registered in the United States and other countries.

THE BATTLE HISTORY OF THE UNITED STATES MARINES: A FELLOWSHIP OF VALOR. Copyright © 1997 by Lou Reda Productions, Inc. All rights reserved. Printed in the United States of America. No part of this book may be used or reproduced in any manner whatsoever without written permission except in the case of brief quotations embodied in critical articles and reviews. For information address HarperCollins Publishers, Inc., 10 East 53rd Street, New York, NY 10022.

HarperCollins books may be purchased for educational, business, or sales promotional use. For information please write: Special Markets Department, HarperCollins Publishers, Inc., 10 East 53rd Street, New York, NY 10022.

First HarperPerennial edition published 1999.

DESIGNED BY JOEL AVIROM AND JASON SNYDER

The Library of Congress has catalogued the hardcover edition as follows:

Alexander, Joseph H., 1938–
  A fellowship of valor / by Joseph H. Alexander with Don Horan and Norman C. Stahl; foreword by Edwin H. Simmons.
    p.   cm.
    Includes index.
    ISBN 0-06-018266-0
    1. United States. Marine Corps—History. 2. United States—History, Military. 3. Battles—United States—History. I. Horan, Don. II. Stahl, Norman. III. Title.
  VE23.A94   1997
  359.9'6'0973—dc21   97-18578

0-06-093109-4 (pbk)

00 01 02 03 ❖/RRD 10 9 8 7 6 5 4 3 2

FOR DON HORAN
AND FOR EVERY UNITED STATES MARINE
WHO EVER EARNED THE TITLE

*There is a fellowship of valor
that links all U.S. Marines,
past, present, and future.*
—From the Prologue

CONTENTS

LIST OF MAPS

ACKNOWLEDGMENTS

This book culminates a dream nurtured for the past decade by our friend and associate, the late Don Horan. Don, a double Emmy Award–winning director and author, served as Executive Director for the Reda Group during the production of more than 100 historical documentaries for national television. Over the years he developed a special affinity for the United States Marines. It was his zealous desire to produce a comprehensive book that cut to the bone—a unique volume that would chronicle the twin themes of the Marines' matchless combat valor and their metaphysical sustaining spirit of *Semper Fidelis*. In his words, "I want this to be the John Wayne version, not the Henry James version."

Our book follows his vision—maximum emphasis on battles and *esprit*, minimum coverage of organization charts or grand strategy.

In the year's work of pulling these two themes together, we received invaluable assistance from more people than we can possibly list here. Among the most helpful of all were:

Mr. Lou Reda, of Lou Reda Productions, for his encouragement and coordination. Also Mr. Mort Zimmerman and Mr. Sammy Jackson of Lou Reda Productions for sharing their superb battle photo archives.

The United States Marine Corps, especially Brigadier General Edwin H. Simmons, USMC (Ret.), Director Emeritus of Marine Corps History and Museums; Mr. Benis M. Frank, Chief Historian of the Corps; Mr. Danny J. Crawford and Mr. Robert V. Aquilina, research historians; Ms. Lena M. Kaljot, photographic archivist, and Mr. John T. Dyer, Jr., Combat Art Director, Marine Corps Historical Center; Brigadier General Terrence P. Murray, USMC, Brigadier General Clifford L. Stanley, USMC, Colonel Fred Peck, USMC, and Lieutenant Colonel Patricia Messer, USMC, the sequential Directors of Public Affairs and their deputies; Mr. Kenneth L. Smith-Christmas of the Marine Corps Air-Ground Museum in Quantico; and Chief Warrant Officer Joseph Boyer, USMC, of Marine Barracks, Washington.

The community of retired and former Marines ("and others") who provided personal interviews and special insights: Lieutenant General Victor H. Krulak, USMC (Ret.) (particularly his poignant, extemporaneous remarks during the taping of our Okinawa documentary); Lieutenant General Bernard E. Trainor, USMC (Ret.); Major General J. Michael Myatt, USMC (Ret.); Dr. (former Corporal) Eugene B. Sledge; Mr. (former Lieutenant) Joseph R. Owen; Colonel Robert J. Putnam, USMC (Ret.); Major General John P. Condon, USMC (Ret.); Mr. (former Navy Lieutenant) Eddie Albert; Major General Michael P. Ryan, USMC (Ret.); the Honorable (former Private First Class) J. T. Rutherford; Major Norman T. Hatch, USMC (Ret.); Mr. (former Pri-

vate First Class) Fred K. Fox; Mr. (former Captain) William T. Ketcham, Jr.; Mr. (former Sergeant) Martin Russ; Colonel John W. Ripley, USMC (Ret.); Colonel John G. Miller, USMC (Ret.); Colonel William H. Dabney, USMC (Ret.); Mrs. (former Naval Flight Nurse Lieutenant) Norma Crotty; Lieutenant General George C. Axtell, Jr., USMC (Ret.); Major General Frederick P. Henderson, USMC (Ret.); Major General James L. Day, USMC (Ret.); Mr. (former Private First Class) Win Scott; Mr. (former Corporal) Wayne Queen; Colonel Richard T. Poore, USMC (Ret.); Lieutenant Colonel James C. Hitz, USMC (Ret.); Mr. (former Gunnery Sergeant) Kenneth B. Wheeler; and Mr. Henry E. Colton, nephew of Lieutenant Johnnie Overton, USMC (killed at Soissons).

The source of several battlefield quotes and sidebars deserves special mention. Private First Class Carl A. Brannen's observations of WWI combat were first published by Major J. F. Holden-Rhodes in "Private Brannen's War," *Marine Corps Gazette*, November 1983. Our description of the Christie seagoing tank in Chapter 4 is based on the paper presented by Dr. George F. Hofmann, "Technology, Ideas, and Reality: The U.S. Marine Corps and the First Assault Amphibian Tank," at the 1992 Meeting of the Society for Military History. Lieutenant General Anthony Zinni's comments about the future of expeditionary warfare in Chapter 20 appeared in his essay "It's Not Nice and Neat," in the August 1995 issue of *Naval Institute Proceedings*. All quotes by Joseph Owen are from his book *Colder Than Hell: A Marine Rifle Company at Chosin Reservoir* and are used with permission of the Naval Institute Press. And nothing better captured the spirit of *Semper Fidelis* than the essay "Two Marines Die in Oklahoma Blast" by Chief Warrant Officer Robert C. Jenks, USMC, in the June 1996 *Leatherneck*. His interviews provided the basis for our Epilogue.

The book's illustrations were greatly enhanced by the contributions of former Marine David Douglas Duncan, Colonel Charles R. Waterhouse, USMCR, and Sergeant Charles G. Grow, USMC. Mary Craddock Hoffman designed the maps. Sharon Stahl provided complete TV interview transcripts. Anne R. Gibbons created the index.

Finally, we are grateful for the artful editing and guidance of the staff of HarperCollins Publishers, especially M. S. ("Buz") Wyeth, Jr., editor-at-large; designers Joel Avirom and Jason Snyder; and copy editor Estelle Laurence.

Notwithstanding all this magnificent advice, we alone are responsible for the contents and comments that follow.

Joseph H. Alexander
Asheville, NC

Norman C. Stahl
Bay Shore, NY

FOREWORD

U.S. Marines have appropriated the term *esprit de corps* as their

own—their e*sprit*, their *Corps*. The personal ties between a Marine and his Corps are strong. Marines believe in their Corps. They also believe that they are the best. They insist that the "M" in "Marine" be capitalized. The highest accolade they can bestow on a member of another service is "He would make a good Marine."

Part of that *esprit*, perhaps the very root, is that Marines are much aware of their history and traditions. In recruit training, enlisted Marines get a good dose of both in "boot camp" at Parris Island or San Diego. So do the new lieutenants, who after pursuing one of the several pathways to a Marine commission, go to The Basic School at Quantico. "TBS" is well titled; it is where *the basics* are taught, and history and traditions form a basic foundation for belief in the Corps. And injections of traditions and customs, even language, continue for the rest of their time in the Corps.

Through the pages of *The Battle History of the U. S. Marines : A Fellowship of Valor* march most of the somewhat larger-than-lifesize heroes of the Corps, among them Presley O'Bannon, Archibald Henderson, Tony Waller, "Handsome Jack" Myers, Smedley Butler, John Lejeune, Dan Daly, Herman Hanneken, Chesty Puller, Lem Shepherd, Cliff Cates, Brute Krulak, Manila John Basilone, Lou Wilson, Lew Walt, Bob Barrow, the several General Smiths, including Howlin' Mad, and many more.

Marines should be forgiven if they assert a bit too aggressively that Washington might not have succeeded at Princeton if it had not been for a small battalion of Continental Marines. Or that the great frigate duels of the War of 1812 might have ended differently if it were not for the Marine sharpshooters and grenadiers in the fighting tops of such as *Old Ironsides*.

Marines can talk sagely about their forerunners chasing Indians through Georgia and Florida in the Seminole Wars with their Commandant of the time, Archibald Henderson, leading the regiment. They believe quite sincerely that Winfield Scott would not have taken Mexico City in 1847 except for the work of his Marine Battalion at Chapultepec and San Cosme Gate. They are apt to be silent about the Civil War. Fratricide is not to their taste. They prefer to do their fighting on foreign shores.

There are fond tribal memories of expeditionary duty in such places as China, Panama, Cuba, Nicaragua, Santo Domingo, and Haiti. When Marines on guard at Guantanamo look across the wire into Castro's Cuba they know that other Marines have been on post there for a hundred years.

Then there are the big wars. Marines know that other Marines went to France in the First World War. They will tell you that the Marine Brigade

stopped the German army on the road to Paris with aimed fire from their Springfield rifles, then counterattacked through Belleau Wood, went forward to Soissons, and pushed on until they had cracked the Hindenburg Line.

They will tell you that the Second World War, as fought in the Pacific, was particularly well suited to Marine Corps ship-to-shore talents. From their grandfathers (the tendency to join the Marines is remarkably hereditary) they have heard of such epic battles as Guadalcanal, Tarawa, Iwo Jima, and Okinawa.

They have been told of that bitter war in Korea where the fire-brigade defense of Pusan, MacArthur's master stroke at Inchon, and the glory of the stubborn fallback from the subzero Chosin Reservoir faded into a War of the Outposts, while the wrangling went on over an armistice at Panmunjom.

There are still Marines on active duty who were in the northern five provinces of South Vietnam. They fought in the big scraps such as Hue City and Khe Sanh and in thousands (yes, there were *thousands*) of nasty little fights in the rice paddies and the mountains to the west. The Marine Corps bought more than its share of that war.

Marines know the importance of the Marine air-ground team. A quarter or more of today's Marines are in Marine aviation. Marines can tell you that Marine aviation got its start early, in 1912, that four squadrons were sent to France in the First World War, that the Banana Wars gave opportunities for experimentation in close air support and dive-bombing. They like to talk of the World War II aces, among them Joe Foss, Marion Carl, John Smith, and Pappy Boyington. They know that Marines did as much as anyone to make helicopter flight practical and that Marine helicopter pilots still fly the President of the United States and his entourage. They know also of the Harrier, a remarkable aircraft that can take off and land vertically, which the Marines brought into the U.S. Armed Forces.

There are plenty of Marines around, Regulars and Reserves alike, who went to the Persian Gulf. They can tell you that General Schwarzkopf gave the Marines the task of attacking frontally against the forbidding Saddam Hussein line, while U.S. Army and Allied mechanized and armored forces made that great swinging attack around the Iraqi right flank. They will go on to say that the Marines cracked the line so deftly that the schedule for the flanking attack was advanced a day.

Before and since the Persian Gulf there have been other expeditions and interventions, most of which were "humanitarian," among them: Lebanon, Panama, northern Iraq, Bangladesh, Liberia, Somalia, and a bit of Bosnia. These adventures get rehashed wherever Marines gather in the evening. Marines are not noted for their modesty. Tales get more brightly colored as they are told and retold. History becomes legend and legends can become myths, but threaded through it all is that business of *esprit*.

Joseph Hammond Alexander and Norman C. Stahl are a well-matched pair of writers.

Joe Alexander was a career Marine, with nearly twenty-nine years of active duty, coming in as a midshipman from the Naval ROTC at the University of North Carolina and going out as a colonel. He has been where the bullets fly—two combat tours in Vietnam. He now lives on a ridge overlooking Asheville, North Carolina (a

good Marine always seeks the high ground), and here he writes articles and books and does an occasional video bit. His string of publications is long. Readers of this book might find most interesting his *Sea Soldiers in the Cold War: Amphibious Warfare, 1945–91* (co-authored with Merrill L. Bartlett; 1994), *Utmost Savagery: The Three Days of Tarawa* (1995), and *Storm Landings: Epic Amphibious Battles in the Central Pacific* (1997), all published by the U.S. Naval Institute Press.

Norm Stahl, while not a Marine himself, has been infused with the Marine Corps spirit as the principal script writer and editor of numerous television documentaries for Lou Reda Productions, including *Death Tide at Tarawa; Iwo Jima: Hell's Volcano; The Bloody Hills of Peleliu; Imperial Sunset at Saipan; Okinawa: The Last Battle; Flying Marines;* and *Pageantry of the Corps.*

Together they have written a vivid telling of the story of the Marine Corps' battles and heroes. They sift through the myths and get to the truth, as they know it (history has no absolute truths), and still keep the verve and color of the tale. Marine readers will have their faith in the Corps (remember, the motto is *Semper Fidelis*, "Always Faithful") reaffirmed. Other readers will be led to a better understanding of that line in *The Marine Hymn:* ". . . proud to claim the title of United States Marine."

The authors have dedicated the book to the late Don Horan, a double Emmy Award–winning TV director and lifelong Leatherneck enthusiast (among his more notable productions: *The Gallant Breed* and *Korea: The Forgotten War* in the 1980s).

Edwin H. Simmons
Brigadier General, U.S. Marine Corps (Ret.)
Director Emeritus, Marine Corps History and Museums
Dunmarchin
Mount Vernon, Virginia
August 1997

PROLOGUE

Retired Marine General Victor Krulak isn't called "Brute" for nothing. He is a fighting man, not given to excess sentiment. But there is a catch in his growl when he talks about the long line of Marines he fought beside through three bloody wars. "War after war, year after year, battle after battle . . . they're always the same" he says in wonder. And that same is something awesome.

Kuwaiti Border, Northeast Saudi Arabia, 0300, February 24, 1991

Eighty thousand United States Marines lay waiting, tensely, impatiently, in darkened assembly areas along the threatened border, or in aircraft cockpits on ready alert in nearby expeditionary airfields.

Along the banked sand defenses known as The Berm, combat troops of the storied 1st and 2d Marine Divisions waited to take their chances against enemy minefields, razor wire, and long-range field guns. They wore bulky protective outerwear, fully expecting the Iraqis to release poison gas.

"We're going to go fast and go violently!" said their commanding general quietly. "Our next stop is Kuwait." The ground war to liberate Kuwait from Saddam Hussein's Iraqi invaders would finally begin—just before daybreak.

Beyond The Berm, each Marine knew, lay two belts of sophisticated obstacles, minefields and fire pits, all designed to channel attackers into pre-

"Waiting for H-Hour" (sketch by Charles Waterhouse)

registered "fire traps" saturated by artillery barrages. In this manner the Iraqis had slaughtered their Iranian enemies in the most recent Gulf War. The Marines would be attacking into the teeth of these defenses, endeavoring to distract the focus of the Iraqi high command from the more celebrated "End Run" assault by the "Combined Force" farther west.

A special hour in a great war. But nothing special in the two-centuries-long battle saga of the United States Marine Corps. They had been here many times before, and in the same magnificent company.

There is a fellowship of valor that links all U.S. Marines, past, present, and

future. The assault troops preparing to stream through the freshly dug gaps in The Berm shared a common bloodline with those who had fought the earlier battles.

They were one and the same with that handful of Continental Marines who lay shivering in the snow at Princeton, waiting for the signal from General George Washington to attack Lord Cornwallis's veteran British Redcoats. They were inheritors of the same grim determination of Captain Charles McCawley's "forlorn hope" Marines of 1863, preparing to launch the suicidal night assault on Fort Sumter. And they were blood brothers to Lieutenant Colonel Raymond Davis's 1st Battalion, 7th Marines, executing one of the most daunting night marches in military history, crossing the ridges above "Frozen Chosin" in North Korea in subzero cold to rescue their fellow Marines defending Toktong Pass.

Marines have executed many improbable missions in their centuries of service to America. They have suppressed riots, rescued hostages held by prison inmates, guarded the U.S. mail from train robbers, and arrested seal poachers in the Arctic. But Marines mainly exist to fight—on sea, on land, in the air.

General Charles C. Krulak, the thirty-first Commandant, said: *"The Marines really provide only two essential services to our nation: We make Marines; we win battles."* These two themes provide the essence of this book.

Here is the full sweep of Marine Corps combat history, more than 220 years of blood and valor, tragedy and triumph. This is the Corps in terms of battle and heroes, free of the numbing inventory of encyclopedic works.

Shining through is the special *esprit de corps* that stamps Marines of all ages as a distinct breed apart and fosters the characteristic brash confidence that so irritates fellow warriors of other services—yet remains so essential to the Marines' traditional propensity for close, offensive combat.

This spirit combines unmatched fighting ferocity with loyal devotion to the "band of brothers"—the haunting immortality of *Semper Fidelis*.

WARRIORS FROM THE SEA

H-Hour on a hot beach is the loneliest place on earth. Being the first Marine to splash ashore from an eighteenth-century surf-boat—or from a twentieth-century air-cushion landing craft—demands a certain fortitude and downright impatience. Naked impulse and tactical necessity coincide—*get your ass off the beach, charge ahead, throttle that sonofabitch shooting at you.* This collective impatience pervades the amphibious assault, spurs the urgency to press on, accelerate, advance by shock action, bypass the pockets, pierce through to the objective— *"Let's finish the job and get outa here!"* Other U.S. services, bigger, heavier, more fully armed and equipped, more methodical, fight their battles differently. Sometimes it takes both kinds to win a sustained battle.

That Marine doctrine is shock doctrine, imbued with the offensive, needs no apology. "Hi-diddle, straight up the middle," epitomizes the attitude of an amphibious breed that doesn't like to wait around. Even when it's safer.

1: THE LEATHERNECKS

(1775–1859)

The first amphibious assault. Continental Marines under Captain Samuel Nicholas storm Fort Montague, New Providence Island, British West Indies, on March 3, 1776.
(Donald L. Dickson, Marine Corps Combat Art Collection)

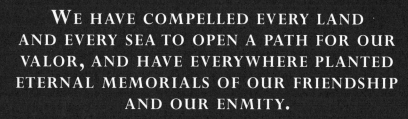

> WE HAVE COMPELLED EVERY LAND
> AND EVERY SEA TO OPEN A PATH FOR OUR
> VALOR, AND HAVE EVERYWHERE PLANTED
> ETERNAL MEMORIALS OF OUR FRIENDSHIP
> AND OUR ENMITY.
>
> *Pericles, Funeral Oration over the Athenian Dead, 431 B.C.*

In times of peace the Marines have always represented an imperfect fit—rough-hewn square pegs in round organizational holes, neither soldiers nor sailors, but a special breed, amphibians, Soldiers of the Sea. Fortunately for the nation and its Corps, the Marines established a distinctive pattern of combat usefulness from the onset in 1776. Always few in number and of necessity lightly armed, America's Marines rather quickly built a tradition on the cornerstones of readiness, discipline, marksmanship, and *esprit*—topped by the brash swagger of those who have leapt onto an enemy quarterdeck in a boarding party brawl and lived to boast of it.

U.S. Marine,
War of 1812
(Charles Waterhouse)

The Revolutionary War (1775–1783)

On a blustery February morning in 1776, during the tenth month of the American Revolution, Commodore Esek Hopkins led a squadron of eight extemporized warships out of the ice-clogged Delaware River below Philadelphia. In this, the first deployment of the Continental Navy, Hopkins's force included 236 newly recruited Continental Marines, commanded by Captain Samuel Nicholas, a thirty-two-year-old former Philadelphia innkeeper. They were the vanguard of two battalions of Marines authorized by the Second Continental Congress on November 10, 1775 (traditionally celebrated as the birthdate of the Corps).

Nicholas's group differed from other so-called "marines" already serving in state navies and on board Yankee privateers. The new contingent, patterned after the British Marines, was a separate adjunct of the regular American Navy, recruited for service as sharpshooters and boarding-party fighters during close combat at sea. Congress also expected the Continental Marines to conduct seaborne landing operations and help maintain discipline among the polyglot Navy crews.

On March 3, 1776, in the company of fifty sailors, Samuel Nicholas and his men conducted the first amphibious landing in Marine history when their surfboats touched shore at New Providence Island in the Bahamas. The Marines and sailors seized undefended Fort Montague and, the next morning, advanced on nearby Fort Nassau.

The undermanned garrison fired a few cannon shots in defiance, then surrendered. To Captain Nicholas went the honor of raising the Grand Union flag over the captured fort. The American Revolution had for the first time spread beyond its borders.

This unimpressive force of seagoing musketeers had executed one of the most difficult maneuvers in all military science—an amphibious assault launched from Naval ships at sea against a hostile shore.

Primitive and obscure, the seizure of Fort Nassau in 1776 served as the progenitor of epic amphibious landings to come.

In late 1776, however, the British Army launched a series of attacks that sent the Continental Army reeling across New Jersey.

Responding to General Washington's call for assistance, Samuel Nicholas, now a major, organized and trained a new battalion of Marines, then adjoined them with Colonel John Cadwalader's Pennsylvania militia.

Washington led his patchwork forces back across the Delaware River to strike a surprise blow against Lord Cornwallis's overconfident veterans at Princeton. This was a desperate battle for the Americans. At the height of the confused fighting, Washington personally rallied the Marines and Pennsylvanians for yet another charge against the Redcoats. It turned the tide. Cornwallis had to modify his otherwise promising campaign.

For all their pains, the Marines were assimilated into the regular Army, most serving as artillerymen.

Continental Marines
storm the clifftops
during the difficult
amphibious assault
at Penobscot Bay
in 1779.
(Charles Waterhouse,
Marine Corps Combat Art
Collection)

Thereafter, the Marines would do their fighting afloat, or storming ashore, with the Navy. But Nicholas had set a valuable precedent. His "sea soldiers" had fought inland admirably with the Army.

As the Revolution raged on, Continental Marines saw Naval action as far east as the British Isles.

There they served with distinction with Captain John Paul Jones, executing the first amphibious landings in European waters at Whitehaven and St. Mary's Isle in the Irish Sea.

In September 1779, Jones's Marines manned the fighting tops of his flagship, the *Bonhomme Richard*, when she squared off against the fifty-gun British frigate HMS *Serapis* in the North Sea. As the thundering, burning ships grappled together, the Marines aloft responded magnificently, first shooting their counterparts out of their towering crow's nests, now just yards away, then raining a deadly fusillade against every British attempt to launch a storming party below. The British soon struck their flag.

The year 1779 saw the fortunes of the Marines swing to extremes, including the disaster at Penobscot Bay.

"LEATHERNECKS"

The Marines' oldest and most colorful nickname came from the characteristic black leather stock worn around the necks of all enlisted Marines (and many officers) for the first hundred years of the Corps. The neck stock served two purposes: improved posture on parade, and protection of the throat from a slashing cutlass during boarding party melees. The troops hated the uncomfortable accessory. To them, the best defense against a cutlass was the fourteen-inch steel bayonet on the end of their five-foot musket. But they did like the name, and it has stuck for a couple of centuries.

The British established an advanced Naval base in Penobscot Bay in current-day Maine. To uproot the base, Commodore Dudley Saltonstall led forth an amphibious force of ships, privateers, and Marines, reinforced by several thousand militia.

The Marines stormed ashore under fire, scrambled up a steep cliff at the water's edge—a hell of a landing place—and overcame the stouthearted British Marines and Highlanders defending the rocky crags at the top. Then, re-forming their battle line, they prepared to charge the unfinished fort just inland. The British commander had the halyards to his colors in his hands, prepared to haul them down in surrender.

Then, inexplicably, Commodore Saltonstall got cold feet.

The blistering attack fell off to a halfhearted siege, allowing time for the British fleet to fall upon the hapless American ships, sinking or capturing every one.

The suddenly stranded landing force barely had time to melt into the woods—then had to work their way back through the Maine wilderness in an epic of "escape and evasion." The Marines and sailors were furious . . . .

Commodore Saltonstall received his just deserts when a court-martial found him "unfit for future command," but the long, negative shadow of Penobscot Bay—like Gallipoli 136 years later—cramped the growth of American amphibious operations for half a century. Not until the Mexican War would the United States risk another large-scale, opposed amphibious assault.

When the Treaty of Paris finally ended the eight-year-old Revolutionary War in 1783, an economy-minded Congress gradually disbanded its plucky Marines and sold off the nation's warships. Marine numbers dwindled until finally there were none.

Marine marksmen and grenadiers cut loose at close range on a British frigate during the Revolutionary War.
(Charles Waterhouse, Marine Corps Combat Art Collection)

It took Congress another fifteen years to officially establish the United States Navy and Marine Corps (as opposed to the *Continental* Marines).

On July 11, 1798, Congress passed "An Act for Establishing and Organizing a Marine Corps."

The wording of this legislation reflected unusual forethought. The Marine Corps was to be a separate and distinct armed force "in addition to the present Military Establishment." Further, the Corps would ever thereafter hold the special mission, in addition to service afloat, of conducting "any other duty on shore, as the President, at his discretion shall direct." This blanket proviso became the so-called "wild card" among the Marines' roles and missions, leading to joint adventures with the Army in such diverse places as New Orleans, the Everglades, Mexico City, Belleau Wood, and Okinawa.

Congress established the U.S. Marine Corps with an authorized strength of 33 officers and 848 "non-commissioned officers, musicians, and privates."

The first privates earned six dollars a month; sergeants drew nine; second lieutenants twenty-five.

President John Adams selected forty-year-old William Ward Burrows, a Charleston attorney with combat experience in the Revolutionary War, as Major Commandant. Burrows got the new Corps off to a quick start with intelligent recruiting, strong leadership, and fierce discipline.

The Tripolitan War

The four Barbary states of North Africa—Morocco, Algiers, Tunis, and Tripoli—exacted galling tribute, bribes, and ransoms from unescorted American merchantmen plying the Mediterranean. Then the Basha of Tripoli burned the American flag and declared war on the United States.

President Thomas Jefferson tested the constitutional limits of his powers by deploying most of the Navy and Marines to the Mediterranean without a declaration of war.

The Barbary states were no weak sisters compared to the tiny American fleet. Their port cities were formidable citadels and their swift corsairs were manned with daring and pugnacious seafarers.

The American Naval "presence" got off to an embarrassing start on October 31, 1803, when the fast frigate *Philadelphia* went hard aground on a Tripolitan reef. Captain William Bainbridge tried his damnedest to free his ship—even rolling his precious cannons overboard—to no avail. The Tripolitans captured ship, captain, and crew—over 300 Americans, including 43 Marines.

The ensuing diplomatic impasse bore an uncanny resemblance to future events involving the United States and its Marines in the Mideast in the late twentieth century. A petty tyrant held hundreds of Americans hostage, demanded exorbitant ransoms, and threatened to burn them alive.

THE MAMELUKE SWORD

Legend has it that Lieutenant O'Bannon returned from the Barbary Wars with a jeweled Mameluke scimitar, a gift from a grateful desert chieftain. The Mamelukes were fierce and renowned desert warriors of North Africa; their unique scimitars held a special attraction for Marine officers, who soon began to wear their own imported versions. By 1825, Marine Corps regulations mandated Mameluke swords for all officers. With the exception of a brief period during the Civil War, all subsequent Marine officers to this day have worn the distinctive Mameluke sword, recognizable by its ivory grips, straight brass guard, curved blade, and silver scabbard.

An angry President, under intense pressure to take action by the press and the public, found himself blocked on one side by a hostile Congress disputing his war-making authority, and on the other by his own parsimonious Cabinet. Naval forces, finally deployed, were shackled by changing missions and restrictive rules of engagement. Meanwhile the hostages languished in captivity....

On the night of February 16, 1804, Sergeant Solomon Wren and seven other Marines joined Navy Lieutenant Stephen Decatur in a volunteer raiding party. They boarded *Philadelphia*, surprised and cut down the enemy crew, and burned the great ship to the waterline without losing a man.

The raid enraged the Basha of Tripoli, who soon had other concerns.

With equal daring, Marine Lieutenant Presley O'Bannon led his handful of Leathernecks in support of Naval agent William Eaton and a few hundred mercenaries during a bold, cross-country strike against the coastal stronghold of Derna. Their 600-mile march across the Libyan Desert from Alexandria, Egypt, was the stuff of legend.

On April 27, 1805, Tripolitan sentries manning the fortified gates of Derna could scarcely believe their eyes. Like a mirage, a ragged band of armed men suddenly appeared out of the trackless desert and formed a line of battle.

Eaton, leading, demanded the city's surrender. The governor, summoned to behold the phenomenon, was not impressed.

"Your head or mine!" he replied.

Implausibly, Eaton's force, led by O'Bannon and his Marines, surged forward in a lusty charge.

The invaders breached the walls; the fighting became hand-to-hand and vicious. Three of the eight Marines went down. American warships entered the harbor and opened a hot distracting fire.

The dazed governor surrendered. And Marine First Lieutenant Presley Neville O'Bannon became the first American military officer to raise the Stars and Stripes over a captured fortress in the Old World.

Maddeningly, President Jefferson, unaware of these great achievements and his Marine's newfound capabilities, had despaired of the eighteen-month impasse and paid the ransom to free the American hostages.

Yet the sheer heroics of the seven-week forced march to Derna and the bold assault had captured the imagination of the American public.

Lieutenant O'Bannon received a ceremonial sword from the state of Virginia. And forever more "the Shores of Tripoli" would herald the emergence of the United States Marines.

The War of 1812

The brief period of peace that followed the Tripoli misadventures ended with a military confrontation between the United States and its former adversary, Great Britain.

When diplomatic efforts failed, the U.S. Congress declared war against England on June 18, 1812.

The Marine Corps, now under the leadership of Lieutenant Colonel Commandant Franklin Wharton, a forty-five-year-old Philadelphian, commenced the war with 493 officers and men, most assigned to the fast frigates.

In December of 1812, USS *Constitution*'s Marines swayed a key naval battle when *Old Ironsides* locked alongside HMS *Java* in mortal combat. As the British captain tried to lead his boarding party against the *Constitution*, an American Marine marksman shot him down. Other Marine sharpshooters aloft, now armed with the more accurate Model 1808 U.S. musket, tumbled British officers and petty officers into writhing piles along the scuppers.

Naval action, War of 1812. U.S. Marines deliver a galling fire from the rigging of the frigate USS *Wasp* against British officers and Royal Marines of HMS *Reindeer* as the two ships grapple for close combat.
(John Clymer, Marine Corps Combat Art Collection)

The Marines in the fighting tops had organized themselves into six-man teams—five men reloading while the sixth, the best shot, methodically raked the opposite decks with rapid, well-aimed fire. Meanwhile, *Java*, shot to pieces, surrendered.

The Americans by no means won the majority of battles in this ragged war, and the Marines suffered the same defeats. On June 1, 1813, the American frigate *Chesapeake* clashed with HMS *Shannon* off Boston. When British broadsides splintered the *Chesapeake*, its inexperienced crew panicked and abandoned their guns. *Shannon* quickly closed for the kill.

A British boarding party took the fight to the American deck. As *Chesapeake*'s mortally wounded captain, James Lawrence, was carried below, he issued his now-famous order, "Don't give up the ship."

Only a handful of Marines and sailors stood firm, battling valiantly, swinging clubbed muskets, until overwhelmed by *Shannon*'s swirling, slashing boarders. Thirty-two of Lieutenant James Broome's forty-four Marines went down fighting; fourteen died, Broome among them.

The Final Stand at Bladensburg. With the British at the very gates to the nation's capital in August 1814, a small band of Navy flotilla men and Marines from the nearby barracks fired their twelve-pounder field guns to bloody the enemy advance for a glorious hour. Then, outnumbered and outflanked, the sea-service troops withdrew in good order toward Baltimore.

(Charles Waterhouse, Marine Corps Combat Art Collection)

The final land battle of the War of 1812 took place before news of the earlier armistice could reach American and British troops facing each other just below New Orleans. Here, in January 1815, Captain Daniel Carmick's 300 Marines defended a key segment of Andrew Jackson's defensive line against repeated charges by British veterans of the Napoleonic campaigns. Although Carmick would die of wounds received in the fighting, the Battle of New Orleans remains one of the most lopsided victories in America's military history.
(Charles Waterhouse, Marine Corps Combat Art Collection)

In late summer 1814, a confident, combined-arms British force under Vice Admiral Alexander Cockburn and Major General Robert Ross advanced on Washington, brushing militia forces aside contemptuously.

President Madison and his Cabinet fled Washington. So, to his later disgrace, did Lieutenant Colonel Commandant Wharton, taking the payroll with him.

But Wharton's adjutant, Captain Samuel Miller, stayed to fight, along with 110 Marines from the new Barracks. Miller attached his small force to the disembarked sailors commanded by Commodore Joshua Barney near the hamlet of Bladensburg.

General Ross's Redcoats and Royal Marines received an unpleasant shock from the small, resolute naval brigade opposing them on the heights. Barney held his fire until the British were uncomfortably close, then blasted their lead columns with well-served artillery, fired in naval broadsides.

A fierce little battle ensued. The British had the numbers and the experience; the Marines and sailors had grit and the high ground. At length, out of ammunition, and with Barney and Miller both down with wounds, the Americans withdrew in good order.

Ross and Cockburn burned much of Washington but spared the Marine Barracks and the Commandant's quarters at "8th and Eye," some say out of respect for the valiant Marines who had stung their advance force so sharply at Bladensburg.

9

Most red-blooded Marines tend to chafe under political restrictions ("Rules of Engagement"), which proliferated during the limited wars of the late twentieth century. Yet similar political constraints afflicted the Old Corps as well. During a secret, filibustering expedition to seize Spanish East Florida in 1812, such precautions proved fatal to the troops. "I wish someone could find the reason why U.S. troops are being kept in this province without the liberty of firing a gun unless we are fired upon," fumed Marine Captain John Williams to his Commandant. One week later, in a dark swamp outside of St. Augustine, Williams and his men ran into an ingenious ambush set by paramilitary forces of the Spanish governor. Williams rallied his terrified troops and prevented a massacre, but he took eight musket balls in the skirmish. His subsequent death influenced President James Madison to abort the ill-conceived invasion.

Capturing Washington represented the apogee of British military action in America. The Treaty of Ghent, signed on Christmas Eve 1814, essentially ended the war. But rudimentary communications kept word of the war's end from reaching the combatants until more blood had been spilled.

In January 1815, Major General Sir Edward Pakenham, brother-in-law to the legendary Lord Wellington, led 9,000 veterans against New Orleans. There General Andrew Jackson assembled a hodgepodge force.

Captain Daniel Carmick's 300 Marines joined frontiersmen, pirates, adventurers, and Army regulars in one of the greatest underdog victories in American military history, cutting down half the invading force and slaying its major general. Carmick, shot in the head, later died of his wounds.

A month after the Battle of New Orleans, still oblivious to the war's end, USS *Constitution* engaged HMS *Cyane* and HMS *Levant* in four hours of short-range dueling in which the aimed musketry of the Marines contributed significantly to victory. Commanding the Marine detachment on *Old Ironsides* was Captain Archibald Henderson, a thirty-two-year-old Virginian.

Earlier, bored with marginal assignments that kept him away from the action, Henderson had threatened to resign the Corps and join the Army. Now, in the war's extended final hour, he gained both fame and a brevet promotion to major.

Five years after his heroics on the high seas, Archibald Henderson became the youngest officer ever selected to become Commandant of the Marines. He would emerge as one of the most dynamic Commandants in the Corps' storied history, serving in that post nearly thirty-nine years—"the Henderson Era."

Of the many legends that surrounded Henderson, the most familiar has the redoubtable Colonel Commandant leaving his Washington headquarters for field duty with this apocryphal note upon the door: "Gone to fight the Indians. Will be back when the war is over."

If the ensuing Creek and Seminole Wars in the summer of 1836 proved less than exemplary for America's green military establishment, few political leaders would ever forget how Henderson mustered from a dozen scattered posts a fully armed and equipped force of 400 regulars ready to board the

troopships within ten days. This fifth Commandant was the last of the lot to be able to leave Washington and personally lead his Marines in battle.

The Seminole War presaged America's involvement in the Vietnam War 120 years later—an endless guerrilla campaign against an elusive foe, one that quickly lost public support. Most of Henderson's Marines remained in Florida for five miserable years.

Marine Lieutenant Colonel John Marshall Gamble, commanding the Marine Barracks, Brooklyn Navy Yard, about 1830. During fleet action in the War of 1812 in the Pacific, Gamble became the only Marine officer to command a Navy ship (a prize crew of a captured British sloop). The painting is one of the earliest portrayals of the newly adopted Mameluke sword, still worn by Marine officers today.

(A. de Rose, Marine Corps Combat Art Collection)

Mexican War, 1847.
Following the fierce
battle for the citadel
of Chapultepec,
Army General John A.
Quitman leads his
division in triumph
into the Grand Plaza
of Mexico City. The
Marine Battalion,
showing the effects
of the fighting, which
cost them thirty-nine
casualties, marches
in just behind
Quitman.
(Tom Lovell,
Marine Corps
Combat Art Collection)

The Mexican War: 1846–1848

At the outbreak of the Mexican War, Henderson again tendered the services of a provisional battalion of Marines for quick deployment with the Army. President James K. Polk accepted the offer and ordered the Marines to join General Winfield Scott's army in its campaign against Mexico City.

This time Henderson, now sixty, did not take the field. There was another difference. Unlike the regulars mobilized to fight the southern Indians the previous decade, most of the Marines who deployed to Mexico were untrained recruits (the best regulars were already serving with the fleet).

Lieutenant Colonel Samuel E. Watson commanded the Marine battalion; Major Levi Twiggs served as second-in-command. Both officers had served in the War of 1812 and were now long in the tooth.

In the crucial assaults on Chapultepec Castle in Mexico City on September 13, 1847, Twiggs was killed and Watson showed no initiative. Lacking senior leadership on the scene, many Marines missed the crucial action, waiting in defilade for attack orders that never came.

Only a handful of officers—notably Captain George Terrett and Lieutenants John Simms and Charles Henderson (the Commandant's oldest son)—took the bit in their teeth and fought with conspicuous valor. The

Marines who sprang up to follow these officers attacked in the highest traditions—battering down the gates to the ancient citadel, coolly shooting onrushing Mexican lancers out of their saddles, even raising the American flag. But on balance Chapultepec was not a shining moment for the Marine Battalion.

Back in Washington, however, Henderson emphasized the positive contributions of his Marines to the victory. When the citizens of Washington presented Henderson with a commemorative flag inscribed with the words "From Tripoli to the Halls of Montezuma" the legend was immortalized. A rousing song would soon follow.

Main mission or not, Marines conducted fully a half hundred armed landings "under conditions short of war" during the Henderson Era. These small landing excursions occurred all around the globe, from the Falkland Islands to Liberia, and from Sumatra to Uruguay.

In fact, Marines splashed ashore at far distant places called Tarawa and Okinawa in this era, islands to which they would bloodily return nearly a century later.

Archibald Henderson may have lacked a vision for amphibious warfare, but in his steadfast way he did worlds to establish formal legitimacy and informal legacy for his small Corps. He accorded special status to Marine noncommissioned officers, many of whom would command Marine detachments on the smaller ships of war without benefit of an officer's rank or privilege. He made Marine NCOs the heart of the Corps, a hallmark of its success.

AWAY ALL SURFBOATS

On March 9, 1847, the U.S. Navy executed a virtually flawless, large-scale amphibious assault on a hostile shore, landing some 12,000 troops including Marines in surfboats just below Veracruz, Mexico. Unlike the long-ago disaster at Penobscot Bay, this amphibious assault contained all the right ingredients—unity of command, bold leadership, effective naval gunfire support, and no lapses in offensive momentum.

The "amphibious task force commander," Commodore Matthew Perry, thereafter assumed command of the Gulf Coast Squadron, promptly formed a naval brigade around the nucleus of Captain Alvin Edson's Fleet Marines, and executed razor-sharp amphibious seizures of Alvarado, Tuxpan, Frontera, and San Juan Bautista, all within ten weeks. Naval commanders in the Pacific also used their Marines in amphibious landings along the California coast effectively.

It would still take the Marines another eighty years to adopt amphibious assault as its main mission.

THE NCO WEAPON

The command responsibilities routinely given United States Marine NCOs would be entrusted to lieutenants or captains in the Soviet Army. Marine officers recognize the NCOs' special abilities and accord them respect and room to operate on their own. New Marines principally learn Marine Corps values and traditions from their NCOs. It's why in the heat of battle, with officers dead and units fragmented, Marines have found formidable fighting leadership at any level. That's why the legendary Colonel Lewis "Chesty" Puller reacted so calmly during the battle for Peleliu's Bloody Nose Ridge when an excited subordinate reported, "We've had such heavy losses we have nothing better than sergeants to lead our platoons!" "Let me tell you something, son," replied Puller quickly, "in the Marines, there *is* nothing better than a sergeant!"

2: MANIFEST DESTINY

(1859–1914)

> THE APPEARANCE OF MARINES ON FOREIGN SOIL
> HAS ALWAYS IN THE PAST INDICATED
> THE BEGINNING OF EXTREMELY DANGEROUS
> MILITARY ADVENTURES.
>
> *Red Star, 1963*

RIGHT: Marines in the Civil War
(Charles Waterhouse)

OPPOSITE: The Battle of Drewry's Bluff, May 15, 1862, featured an attempt by Union Navy ironclads to force a river passage to Richmond. At close range occurred a deadly duel between Confederate Marine sharpshooters and U.S. Marine riflemen on the ships. Here Corporal John F. Mackie, virtually the last man standing on the starboard gundecks of USS *Galena*, returns fire resolutely. Corporal Mackie became the first U.S. Marine to receive the Medal of Honor.
(Charles Waterhouse, Marine Corps Combat Art Collection)

While the combat role for fighting Marines on warships declined, the Marines still proved useful in battle. In declared wars, the nation always found need for an instantly available, rigorously trained force of relentless fighters. But in the "extra-curricular" fighting of the imperial age they were especially handy, presenting a powerful national military presence in something of a seagoing constabulary role, always politically easier to commit than the Army.

The Marines had a pivotal role in a crucial moment in the countdown to the Civil War.

When abolitionist John Brown seized the federal arsenal at Harpers Ferry with an insurrectionist force, took hostages, and barricaded himself in an engine house as he sought a general uprising of slaves, the situation represented a national tinderbox. The Marines got there first.

It was November 1859. Lieutenant Israel Greene mustered a full company of regulars from Marine Barracks Washington in short order—armed, equipped, and aboard the first train to Harpers Ferry in three hours. Greene then made ready to execute that most delicate of military operations, the rescue of civilian hostages held by desperate armed men.

Greene led two columns of his Marines in a storming attack against the barricaded engine house at daybreak. Using a ladder to knock down the doors, the Marines scrambled inside, reeling momentarily from a volley of point-blank carbine fire.

Two Marines fell. Greene flattened John Brown with a back-handed slash of his sword. His troops killed or captured the other kidnappers with deadly efficiency. All hostages survived.

Nice work. But the Corps faced deep problems.

General Archibald Henderson had died in office in 1859, succeeded as Commandant by sixty-one-year-old Colonel John Harris, the last active Marine veteran of the War of 1812. Harris, once dashing, had grown stale

and hidebound; he would be subsumed by the enormous pressures of the Civil War.

While all armed services suffered the loss of Southern officers resigning their commissions, the Marine Corps arguably lost its best and brightest. Lieutenant Israel Greene, a national hero after Harpers Ferry, "went South" to fight for the Confederacy. So did half of all captains and lieutenants, as well as John Simms and George Terrett, legitimate heroes of Chapultepec.

The U.S. Marines also missed a ripe opportunity to provide the spearhead in forcible amphibious assaults along the entire Southern coast, as well as in thousands of miles of inland rivers. Instead, Harris clung mutely to the old ways, providing "penny-packets" of Marine detachments for outdated 1812-era functions on the major warships. His few attempts to organize larger fighting forces were disastrous.

The earliest of these debacles occurred during the first battle of Manassas on July 21, 1861. The Secretary of War, seeking to stiffen General Irvin McDowell's raw-boned Union Army with regulars, asked for a battalion of Marines.

Colonel Harris could barely assemble a makeshift outfit of green recruits and a handful of veterans from the various Naval stations.

Major John G. Reynolds led the Marine Battalion to join McDowell's Army south of Washington. Reynolds was undeniably a fighter, but he still smarted from whispered rumors about his sluggish performance at Chapultepec. Now, finally, along the obscure creek called Bull Run, Reynolds sought redemption.

Reynolds's Marines had the mission of supporting Captain Charles Griffin's West Point Battery, artillerymen of the Regular Army. As the confused fighting of Manassas ebbed and flowed, Griffin and Reynolds found themselves defending the crest of Henry House Hill, the battle's epicenter.

When a blue-clad infantry regiment emerged from a nearby wood line on the battery's flank, the artillerymen and Marines breathed a sigh of relief, sensing reinforcements at hand. Too late they saw the muskets being leveled their way. The 33d Virginia, as yet too proud of their original blue uniforms to adopt Confederate gray, unleashed a point-blank volley that devastated Griffin's battery and the Marines beyond. The fight for the guns became desperate.

Three times the Marines fell back under a hail of minié balls; three times their NCOs and officers led them back to the crest. The battle hung in the balance until a late Confederate cavalry charge swept the Union forces from Henry House Hill.

The exhausted Marines joined the retreat, which began in orderly fashion, then became a formless rout when Rebel artillery shelled the one bridge across the creek. The troops of all units flowed back to Washington, terrified, exhausted, and resentful.

Colonel Harris forwarded Major Reynolds's action report to the Secretary of the Navy with a heavy heart, noting that "the battle represented the first instance in Marine Corps history where any portion of its members turned their backs to the enemy."

Harris could have provided a more positive endorsement had he left his office to observe his Marines in action firsthand. Green as they were, the Leathernecks had fought with considerable bravery. And John Reynolds had redeemed himself under fire.

But Reynolds's luck remained snake-bit. Given command of another Marine battalion, he trained and embarked his Leathernecks for what would have been a major amphibious campaign in South Carolina. But his troopship foundered and sank in a Cape Hatteras storm, another disaster. Most of the Marines escaped, barely, but the loss of all their equipment knocked them out of the campaign.

Fort Sumter, squatting in Charleston Harbor as a symbol of Southern armed insurrection, remained a defiant monolith throughout most of the war, withstanding repeated efforts by the Union Fleet to obliterate it with heavy gunfire. But at midnight on September 8, 1863, the Union commodore would launch a boarding party of 500 Marines and bluejackets to storm the bulwarks and overrun the sleeping garrison.

Captain Charles McCawley, veteran of Chapultepec and a future Commandant, led the Marines. The landing party planned to attack the fort from thirty-five converging rowboats.

The plan, unrehearsed and poorly coordinated, unraveled tragically. Slowed by the ink-black night and a punishing headwind, the boats became separated; the noise of their oarlocks alerted Confederate sentries, who opened fire. The appearance of two small enemy gunboats anchored in the shadows behind the fort surprised the attackers.

The gunboats, augmented by the giant guns of the fort, blew several Union rowboats completely out of the water. Those men who scrambled ashore along the debris-strewn footing of the battered fort found their way up to the parapets blocked by massive chunks of masonry and intense rifle fire from the garrison.

The Marines and sailors returned fire desperately. A vicious battle raged in the darkness for an hour, with Confederates showering the attackers with grenades and bricks, and the Marines clambering up the rocks to stab their tormentors with bayonet lunges. But Fort Sumter would not fall to cold steel.

McCawley and some of the others reembarked and pulled for the fleet anchorage. Behind them lay a full third of the raiding force—killed, captured, or drowned.

The fighting heart of the Corps continued to beat, quietly and effectively, in a thousand close-range naval engagements. At Drewry's Bluff on the James River below Richmond, Confederate Marines and Union Marines dueled each other with muskets while the forts and the federal ironclads swapped thundering broadsides. Hardest hit was USS *Galena*, whose gun decks quickly ran red with blood. Through all the death and destruction strode U.S. Marine Corporal John Mackie, who pulled the wounded to shelter and matched his

Rebel counterparts round for point-blank round until *Galena* could extricate herself from the firestorm.

Mackie's actions may have escaped the attention of his deskbound Commandant but not his President. Abraham Lincoln personally awarded John Mackie the Medal of Honor, the first such award ever earned by a Marine.

More Marine citations followed. Eight Marines earned the Medal of Honor for extraordinary bravery under fire during the Battle of Mobile Bay with its close encounters with the mammoth Confederate ironclad *Tennessee*.

Other Marines were frittered away in valiant but disorganized operations which achieved little but casualties. The worst of these occurred during the Union assault on Fort Fisher, North Carolina, on January 15, 1865.

Major General Alfred Terry would land 8,500 seasoned infantrymen ashore just north of the bastion. In a diversion, Marine Captain Lucian Dawson's 400 Leathernecks, collected from Admiral David Porter's warships offshore, would provide covering rifle fire as some 1,600 sailors armed with pistols and cutlasses launched a "boarding party" surge against the huge fort.

Everything went wrong. The exuberant sailors did not wait for the Marines to take up firing positions, but charged forward through the loose sand with a great shout, followed by the irate Leathernecks. Confederate gunners and marksmen slaughtered them wholesale.

Tactically, the plan succeeded. Terry's soldiers invested Fort Fisher's northern palisades virtually unopposed while the sailors and Marines fell by the hundreds on the opposite side. The surviving Marines joined Terry's forces and fought with a vengeance the remainder of the day and night.

But the Navy, keenly embarrassed by this very visible failure, blamed the Marines, and the concept of amphibious assaults against opposed beaches incurred another black eye, another half-century setback.

The Civil War for the U.S. Marines thus began and ended on frustrating notes in the bookend disasters of First Manassas and Fort Fisher.

At no time during the war did Marine Corps strength exceed 4,000 men, truly a drop in the bucket compared with the hundreds of thousands who served in the Union Army or Navy.

The Marines suffered 138 killed in action—brave but inconsequential losses amid the great slaughter.

SEMPER FI

Jacob Zeilin recognized that *esprit* was worth whole battalions to the Marines. He equipped Marine NCOs with their own sturdy saber, restored the officers' Mameluke sword, and convinced the Secretary of the Navy to adopt a distinctive Marine Corps insignia portraying a spread eagle, the western hemispheric globe, and an anchor—tying the Marines' seagoing roots and wide-ranging deployments to national fealty. Five years later, the Corps established its motto with the Latin phrase *Semper Fidelis*—"always faithful"—to further bond Marines to country and Corps. John Philip Sousa, celebrated director of the Marine Band, gave wide popularity to the motto with his stirring march of the same name, the only march officially authorized for a designated armed service by Congress. "Semper Fi" has grown to be the irreverent, beloved all-purpose greeting and benediction of the U.S. Marines.

The Battle of Mobile Bay, August 1864. U.S. Marines man the center gun on Rear Admiral David G. Farragut's flagship *Hartford* in this close encounter with the Confederate ironclad ram *Tennessee*.
(W. H. Overender, Marine Corps Combat Art Collection)

In truth, the only shining achievement for the Corps during this cataclysmic war was the enhancement of its tradition of strong NCO leadership. These men proved to be highly responsible, technically proficient, tough-as-nails fighters. And they carried the Corps through its doldrums.

Fifteen of the seventeen enlisted Marines to receive the Medal of Honor during the Civil War wore the stripes of corporals or sergeants.

Jacob Zeilin, brevetted for gallantry during the amphibious raids along the California coast in the Mexican War, wounded at First Manassas, became Commandant in 1864. Zeilin would preserve the Corps and in fact become its first fully appointed general officer (Henderson had held a brevet rank), but the Marines would not flourish in the decades that followed the Civil War.

Small detachments of Marines, led by junior officers and NCOs, continued to spearhead landing parties around the world: China in 1866; Formosa, Japan, and Nicaragua in 1867; Japan again and Uruguay in 1868; Mexico in 1870. "A ship without Marines is like a garment without buttons," said a grateful Admiral David Dickson Porter.

In 1871, Commodore John Rogers's Far Eastern Squadron launched a battalion-sized landing party to seize a series of forts from pugnacious Salee River pirates in a land that the Marines would visit again for mortal combat—Korea.

Captain McLane Tilton commanded the composite Marine force in this "Weekend War" with the Koreans.

Naval gunfire paved the way for the landing. Marines and sailors lugged field pieces through the mudflats, charged with abandon, scaled the walls, overwhelmed the garrison, and came away with huge Korean flags as sou-

venirs. Six enlisted Marines earned the Medal of Honor in the spirited, hand-to-hand struggle.

The Marines rode into the new century on the bow-wave of public enthusiasm for imperialism.

On the evening of February 15, 1898, the proud new armored cruiser *Maine*, moored in Havana harbor to "show the colors" during Spain's unpopular repression of its Cuban colony, erupted in a violent explosion and sank, killing 260 Americans, among them 28 Marines.

"Remember the Maine" became the national cry. Congress soon recognized Cuba's independence and authorized military action against Spain.

MARINE MARKSMANSHIP

Although Commodore Rogers cited his Marines for their superior marksmanship during the forcible capture of the Salee River forts, Captain Tilton complained to Commandant Zeilin about having to use "the blasted old Muzzle Fuzzels" in the action. Tilton had a good point. Even the Korean "barbarians" proved to be better armed than the Marines with their pre–Civil War, muzzle-loading muskets. Years earlier Tilton had served on Marine ordnance boards which favorably endorsed such new breech-loaders as the Remington Navy Rolling-Block rifle. In fact, the Commandant in 1870 had approved the so-called "Allin Conversion" breech-loading Springfield for issue to all fleet Marines. But the new rifles failed to arrive before Tilton's squadron sailed for the Far East the following year—a situation not unlike the 1st Marine Division landing in Guadalcanal in 1941 still armed with the M–1903 ("03") bolt-action Springfield, years after the M–1 semiautomatic Garand had gained approval. Small wonder that Tilton's Marines so quickly resorted to hand-to-hand fighting against the well-armed Koreans.

Lieutenant Colonel Robert Huntington, a bearded, bristling Marine with an unpleasant memory of the Battle of First Manassas, assembled a large, well-armed battalion of troops from posts and stations throughout the east. The Marines mobilized with a speed that would have made the ghost of Archibald Henderson smile approvingly, Huntington had his 647-man First Marine Battalion embarked and underway for Key West in two-days' time.

With most of the Spanish fleet holed up in Santiago Harbor, Admiral William Sampson ordered the forcible seizure of the eastern Cuba harbor of Guantanamo Bay as an advance naval base and coaling station. The nod went to Huntington's impatient Marines.

Eight thousand Spanish troops occupied the rugged hills around Guantanamo, but none opted to oppose Huntington's landing on June 10, especially after a pelting bombardment by the cruiser *Marblehead*.

Huntington soon realized that Guantanamo's fate remained inextricably linked to access to fresh water. Spaniards and Marines alike had their eyes on Cuzco Well, several miles away.

Huntington sent two Marine rifle companies under Captain George Fielding Elliott to seize the well. Supporting fire would come from the gunboat *Dolphin* steaming along the coast.

Elliott maneuvered into position and launched his attack. Spanish riflemen of the 6th Barcelona Regiment returned a brisk fire.

Dolphin, lying offshore, began dropping shells into the Marine lines. Hot shrapnel whickered through the underbrush, and Marines went down painfully wounded. In the middle of this unwelcome chaos, Sergeant John H. Quick scrambled to an exposed overlook to wave an emphatic semaphore message to *Dolphin*. The ship abruptly shifted its fire to the nearby Spaniards, as directed by Quick, and the Marines resumed their advance with a growl.

Intense fighting ensued in the thick vegetation, but the Marines had the advantage of momentum and the corrected fire of the gunship. The Spaniards yielded the precious well.

Elliott reported the loss of six Marines killed, sixteen wounded, to Huntington. Elliott, a future commandant, also nominated Sergeant Quick for the Medal of Honor.

Later that month, the U.S. Army's 5th Corps landed east of Santiago. Soon

Spanish-American War, 1898. Marines of Huntington's Battalion repel an early-morning attack by Spanish regulars against their encampment at Guantanamo Bay, Cuba.
(F. C. Yohn, Marine Corps Combat Art Collection)

21

Samoa, 1899. Marines from the USS *Philadelphia* guard the residence of the American consul in Apia during bloody tribal uprisings. For several years during the close of the nineteenth century the Marines adopted the spiked dress helmet of the Prussians—smart-looking when worn on a ship's quarterdeck, but patently impractical in combat operations ashore. Note the Navy corpsman on the right of the steps. (U.S. Marine Corps)

"CIVILIZE 'EM WITH A KRAG!"

The Marines deployed to the Philippines better armed than usual. Captain Tilton's "old Muzzle Fuzzels" of 1871 had been replaced in rapid order, first with the breech-loading Allin Conversion Springfield, then by the durable single-shot Springfield Model 1884 caliber .45–70, with its "trapdoor" breech and folding-leaf rear sight. To that point, however, the Marines still utilized the same angular steel bayonet wielded by their ancestors in the Continental Marines. Then for the Spanish-American War, the Marines first adopted the Navy-issue Lee "Straight-Pull" 6mm rifle, whose short, knife-shaped bayonet had a variety of field and combat uses. By the time the Marines splashed ashore into Samar's green jungles, they carried the same Krag-Jorgensen Model 1898 .30 caliber rifles as the U.S. Army. The troops generally liked their Krags, which had more stopping power than the Lees and used smokeless powder. "Civilize 'em with a Krag!" became the troops' cynical response to antiwar protesters at home. The Krag came with three bayonets: a standard knife-point, a lovely but fragile Bowie blade, and a bolo blade. The realities of jungle fighting soon made the troops abandon the fancy blades and pick up long-shanked bolos from dead guerrillas, vicious weapons for close combat. But for all its advantages, the Krag proved to be a marginal weapon for jungle fighting. It was too damned heavy and its low muzzle velocity made the rounds too easily deflected by underbrush. The Marines were still four years away from adopting the fabled Springfield "03" rifle.

Philippine Insurrection, 1901. A rifle company of the 1st Marine Battalion takes a break during a conditioning hike outside of Olongapo in the Zambales region of Luzon.
(U.S. Marine Corps)

Teddy Roosevelt's Rough Riders battled their way into history at San Juan Hill, and the "Splendid Little War" petered out.

But America was suddenly an imperial nation, with overseas colonies or protectorates in Puerto Rico, Guam, Midway, the Philippines, and Hawaii. And the Marines, back in favor, abruptly had a lot of Uncle Sam's dirty work to do.

Commodore George Dewey, victor over the Spanish fleet in the Battle of Manila Bay, later confessed to Congress that many of the subsequent problems of the Philippine Insurrection (1899–1902) could have been avoided "had I had five thousand Marines embarked with my Naval force."

Dewey inadvertently aided the seeds of rebellion by bringing from exile the impassioned Filipino guerrilla chieftain Emilio Aguinaldo to fight against the Spaniards. When hostilities ended, Aguinaldo expected nothing less than full independence for his country. When it was not forthcoming, Aguinaldo turned his guerrilla army against his former ally.

The violent Philippine Insurrection foreshadowed the American war in Vietnam sixty years later: a jungle war against shadowy guerrillas—a protracted, brutal campaign increasingly unpopular on the American home front.

Washington responded to the guerrillas' challenge by sending overseas the Army's VII Corps and an entire regiment of Marines, the largest organized body of Leathernecks to take to the field in their history.

Emilio Aguinaldo's capture by U.S. Army forces in March 1901 led to an uneasy peace throughout the Philippine Islands, except for Samar in the southeast. There, six months later, rebel tribesmen attacked an outpost of the 9th U.S. Infantry at breakfast, killing forty soldiers, mutilating their bodies obscenely.

The Marines had fought side-by-side with the 9th Infantry in China and actively sought the mission of seeking retribution against the Samar insurgents.

By this time the Navy Department had deployed nearly a fourth of the entire Marine Corps to the Philippines, organized for the first time in brigade strength.

Major Littleton Waller Tazewell Waller—short, stout, and fierce—commanded the provisional brigade to "pacify" Samar.

Waller's orders from Army Brigadier General Jacob Smith, commanding the Sixth Separate Brigade in the region, seemed unequivocal: "Kill, burn, and take no prisoners."

By mid-November, Waller's scouts located the rebel jungle headquarters in a series of fortified caves in a 200-foot cliff over the Sohoton River.

Waller executed a brilliant three-pronged attack against the heavily jungled cliffside caves. He himself led a flotilla of pole-boats upriver, towing a three-inch Fletcher field gun on a bamboo raft. Two columns of riflemen disappeared into the jungle at different points downstream, cut north, then linked up in the trackless wilderness just adjacent to the stronghold on the opposite side of the Sohoton. Their stealthy approach yielded total surprise.

The guerrillas had prepared a devilish defense—nets full of boulders to

25

be released on climbing assailants, plus dozens of fire-hardened bamboo cannon packed with black powder and lead bolts. Fortunately the Marines had taken pains to drag along through the jungle the one weapon most feared by the insurgents.

THE "POTATO DIGGER"

The Colt-Browning M–1895 6mm automatic rapid-fire gun was the first true machine gun used by the Marines. Its ungainly operating lever flailed awkwardly in a half arc beneath the barrel—hence "Potato Digger"—but the weapon was steady, reliable, and deadly. Army troops in an earlier firefight in Luzon had marveled at the Marines' skill with this machine gun, reporting one guerrilla found dead with "five holes in his body that could be covered by one hand."

No Marine was more proficient with the Potato Digger than Gunnery Sergeant John Quick, hero of the fight at Cuzco Well, Cuba, three years earlier.

Quick opened the Battle for Sohoton Cliffs with disciplined bursts of well-aimed 6mm fire at the clusters of rebels taking their ease outside the caves across the river. The guerrillas were extremely tough fighters but no match for the torrents of fire that lashed them unmercifully, tumbling their lacerated bodies down the cliffs.

Now all the Marines on the east bank of the river opened up. Under cover of this fusillade, Corporal Robert Leckie swam across the surging Sohoton, untied a native boat, and recrossed the river, paddling furiously. Many rebel sharpshooters thought they had the Marine NCO in their sights, but each time one leaned forward to squeeze off a shot he was nailed by preemptive fire from the Marines on the opposite bank.

With a great yell the Marines ran down the bank, boarded Leckie's boat, and hurried across. More boats shuttled back and forth. The guerrillas tried to counterattack during the crossing, but then Waller arrived around the bend and began blasting the cliffs with his field gun. The assault force scaled the heights, met the surviving insurgents bolo-to-bolo, and cut them down.

The insurrection on Samar effectively ended with this battle.

But there was another enemy on Samar: the lethal jungle. Three weeks after his resounding victory at Sohoton Cliffs, Waller foolishly led an expedition west from Lanang in monsoon season, trying to find the old Spanish trail across the island for a telegraph line.

The fact that the Army had tried and failed to find this passage may have been an incentive. Waller had been known to stake his own men in such interservice rivalries. While in China the previous year, Waller had bet his Army counterparts he could march his Marines the 120 miles from Peking to Taku in less than three days without losing a man. He won the bet, if not necessarily the hearts of his men.

Waller took off from Lanang on December 27, 1901.

The disaster began when monsoon rains raised jungle rivers twenty feet or so overnight. As Waller described New Year's Eve in his journal: "Followed a stream bed up a slope so steep it was almost like climbing a waterfall." One of his enlisted Marines wrote: "Climbed mountain all day; raining torrents and very cold; no shelter; no food."

The nightmare continued for three weeks. Waller, Quick, and the stronger ones eventually straggled out of the wilderness, totally exhausted. But other Marines began to die along the trail. One went stark mad. Nine others died of starvation and exposure. Their bodies were never recovered, a keenly galling consequence for Marines.

The Philippine "guides," of mixed loyalties at best, turned on the weakened Marines with bolos. From his hospital bed Waller ordered ten of these Filipino turncoats tried by drumhead court-martial, then executed.

When the Marines returned to Luzon from Samar, fully expecting to be lionized for their victory at Sohoton, a general court-martial awaited Waller. Although acquitted, he forever bore the stain of "The Butcher of Samar" from the anti-imperialism press and Congress.

The Marines were more forgiving of "Tony" Waller. Over the years, whenever Waller or one of his Marine survivors entered an officers' mess, the command was heard, "Stand, gentlemen! He served on Samar."

Unknowingly, the Marines had commenced a full century of combat in the Pacific. The first of several conflicts to come with the Chinese began in 1900 with the so-called Boxer Rebellion. Marines fought in north China to rescue Western diplomats from the murderous, xenophobic "Society of the Righteous Harmonious Fists," the Boxers.

In late May 1900, Captain John "Handsome Jack" Myers led a contingent of U.S. Marines to Peking to help protect the legations. Marching his men past hordes of scowling Boxers, and purposefully displaying his wheeled Potato Digger machine gun, Myers and his men took up positions at the Legation Quarter, inside the walled Tartar City. Within hours, Marines and Boxers began exchanging fire.

On June 5, Britain's Sir Edward Seymour led a multinational force, including 112 U.S. Marines and sailors, north by train from Tientsin to relieve the beleaguered legations at Peking. Heavily armed Boxers stopped Seymour's advance, then surrounded him in an arsenal at Hsiku.

On June 18, Major Waller led ashore at the Chinese port of Taku a battalion of Marines, fresh from the fighting in Luzon. Joining with a battalion of Russian infantry, Waller's Marines set off for Tientsin. The Boxers greeted Waller with heavy fire, stopping him cold.

On June 24, a more muscular international force rescued Waller and pushed through the outskirts of Tientsin to relieve Seymour's encircled group at the Hsiku Arsenal.

Meanwhile, the famous "Fifty-five Days at Peking" began with the Boxer siege initiated on June 20. Thousands of foreigners, mainly noncombatants, jammed the besieged Legation Quarter, an area less than three quarters of a mile square. There was little food or water, and the Boxers kept the enclave under constant bombardment.

Marines under Captain Myers held the Tartar Wall, a critical position at the southern end of the Quarter. Tired of being bombarded, the Marines slith-

27

ered over the wall at night to assault enemy gunners with rifles and bayonets. Myers went down with a Chinese spear in his leg during one of these sorties; his troops pulled him to safety.

Nowhere did the Marines take a backward step along the perimeter. They were indeed in their element: helpless women and children depending on them, professional counterparts from a dozen nations eyeing them critically, a savage, implacable enemy to fight.

Back at Tientsin, with even more U.S. Marines swelling its ranks, the International Army launched its attack against the towering walls.

Feisty Lieutenant Smedley Butler fell wounded as he led his Marines against the fortified city's gates. Tientsin finally fell.

The International Army commenced a ten-day overland march to Peking, arriving in force before the massive gates on August 14. The next day, after a brief bombardment, the Marines led the attack, scaling the wall south of the Tung Pien Gate to open fire on the Boxers inside.

Smedley Butler, newly promoted to captain for his heroism at Tientsin and barely healed from his first wound, received another bullet wound in a repeat performance at Peking, climbing the wall to open the main gate to the British compound. Thousands of fighting men, their various uniforms now a quilt of different colors, swarmed inside. The fifty-five-day siege had been broken.

The light of national publicity shone with unaccustomed brightness

Boxer Rebellion, 1900. The Marine
contingent of an international relief
force prepares for the final assault on
the beleaguered city of Peking.
(U.S. Marine Corps)

Veracruz, 1914.
Marine corpsman
attends a Mexican
soldier wounded
during street fighting
for the port city.
(National Archives)

around the Marines following their heroics in China. American newspapers
began a long love affair with the Leathernecks. And the Marines, after all the
disappointments and doldrums of the past half-century, did not shy away from
the limelight.

In 1914, in a final period of naïveté before the monstrous world war, President
Woodrow Wilson asked Congress for approval to employ armed force in
Mexico for "affronts and indignities committed against the United States." The
target, first Tampico, shifted to Veracruz.

   The Marines mobilized half the entire Corps to deploy five provisional
regiments at Veracruz within the first ten days. They raced to the scene in anything that would float—transports, warships, coal ships, a target ship, even a
chartered commercial liner. They stormed ashore in surfboats, launches, tugs,

or scows. And they gleefully beat the more heavily laden Army to the fight by a full week.

"Five hundred Mexican troops with five three-inch field pieces occupy Veracruz," warned Lieutenant Colonel Wendell ("Whispering Buck") Neville, commanding the Marine assault force.

Neville's Marines streamed ashore throughout a very hot June afternoon, fanning out to seize the customs house and cable office.

Organized Mexican forces pulled back, but sufficient militia, cadets, and armed civilians remained to put up a stiff resistance. Marines and sailors under Neville, Albertus Catlin, and the ubiquitous Smedley Butler had to root them out door-by-door. Strongholds required the Marines to fight through the houses with picks, shovels, and bayonets to gain the tactical edge. It was exhausting, confusing, dangerous work.

A day and a half of this close-range fighting cost the Americans nineteen dead and seventy-five wounded. Hundreds of Mexicans died. President Wilson recoiled in horror at what his show of force had wrought—there would be no "On to Mexico City" culmination of this little catfight.

Now Wilson agreed to mediation, and the Mexican crisis would go away, to be replaced very shortly by a war where desperately fighting Marines would lose more men in an hour than they had lost in all of these far-flung forays on behalf of "Manifest Destiny."

3: "DEVIL DOGS"

(World War I)

I AM UP FRONT AND ENTERING BELLEAU WOOD WITH THE U.S. MARINES . . .

Dispatch from war correspondent Floyd Gibbons, June 6, 1918

The fighting in the last year of WWI—the American year—was everything the Marines were created not to do. Their expeditionary doctrine was thwarted. The immobility of bogged-down, mud-slogging trench warfare negated all hope of surprise and slashing maneuver. Barbed wire, the machine gun, and massed artillery turned shock tactics into mass graves.

Yet, the savage three-week Battle of Belleau Wood in that war eclipsed everything the Marines had achieved in their first 143 years. And that was just the beginning. The price in flesh and lost innocence was hideous, but it was the making of the Marine Corps as a lethal, murderously tenacious weapon in the big-unit battles of modern, protracted war.

In the summer of 1914, with the U.S. military still smug about its lopsided victory at Veracruz, a war of unimaginable proportions exploded in Europe. Touched off by an assassin's bullet in the Bosnian capital at Sarajevo, what began as a dispute between Austria-Hungary and Serbia quickly spread across the continent as a war of giants, pitting Germany and her allies against Britain, France, and Russia.

After months of sweeping offensives and counteroffensives, the war in Europe calcified into a gruesome three-and-a-half-year stalemate. The opposing armies faced each other along a 400-mile front extending through France and Belgium, a jagged scar of trench lines and shell holes dominated by relentless machine guns and the heaviest artillery ever seen in warfare. Isolated America reacted with abhorrence, and the nation reelected President Woodrow Wilson in 1916 largely on the slogan "He kept us out of war."

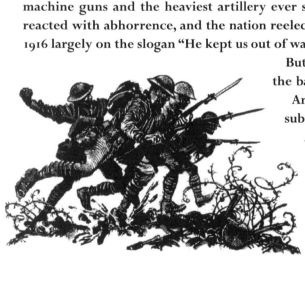

But foundering Allied fortunes on the battlefield, coupled with the loss of American lives in Germany's Atlantic submarine offensive, gradually eroded America's antiwar sentiment. By the spring of 1917 the nation had resigned itself to fighting "The War to End All Wars."

BELOW: Belleau Wood, June 1918. German machine gun crews were among the deadliest in the war; the Marines were adept with small arms and bayonets. Both sides lost heavily in the desperate, three-week battle for the small patch of shell-torn woods along the Paris-Metz highway. (Marine Corps Combat Art Collection)

OPPOSITE: Marines in World War I (Charles Waterhouse)

None of the nation's military services were prepared to fight a war so mammoth in scale or so advanced in lethal technology. United States Marines, soldiers and sailors, had not fought a major land war since the Civil War over a half-century before. How could any American ground force face the battle-honed German juggernaut with any prospect of victory?

An alarmed Congress did its part, expanding the bare-bones military even before Wilson's request for a Declaration of War on April 6, 1917. The Marine Corps, riding a minor crest of public acclaim following its achievements in the Spanish-American War, the Boxer Rebellion, and the Veracruz adventure, fared well in the allocation of new resources.

America went to war with Germany with an unprecedented 22,000 Marines under arms; the total would double before year's end.

The Army, still smarting over the perceived Marine publicity coup in beating their soldiers to the beach (and fleeting glory) at Veracruz, notified Major General Commandant George Barnett that there would be no room for any Marines on their dedicated transports. No problem, replied Barnett, anticipating the ploy; the Marines would go to France aboard a trio of Navy transports, including the brand-new USS *Henderson*, launched in 1916.

Army Major General John Pershing, commanding the newly organized American Expeditionary Forces (AEF), realized his dilemma. He needed regular troops—and the Marines were offering a huge brigade of infantry and machine-gunners—but damned if he wanted a group of glory hounds grabbing headlines and screwing up his fragile logistics systems with their peculiar uniforms and weapons.

THE MARINES AS GLORY HOGS

Maybe it was the dashing green coats and the ability to grab headlines in the early single-ship naval victories. Or maybe it was the tingling toot and rattle of Marine fifes and drums as they signaled frigates into action. Whatever the reason, the Marines from the first seized the imagination of the public as the Army and Navy never did. The Marines got named glamorous things like Leathernecks and Devil Dogs, while their equally valorous compatriots ended up as doughboys, dogfaces, and swabbies. While jealousy among the services is unbecoming, it is real. The Army's General Pershing could not have been pleased to pick up the May 20, 1917, issue of the *New York Times* to read a headline trumpeting, "2,600 MARINES TO GO WITH PERSHING." The article mostly forgot to mention the 95 percent of Pershing's force that were soldiers.

A compromise ensued. Marines would trade their greens for Army olive-drab, accept anonymity, and—later—forgo their beloved Lewis guns for the unpopular French Chauchats.

The Leathernecks who sailed for France on June 14 with Pershing were the 5th Marines, led by Colonel Charles Doyen. But when they arrived at St. Nazaire, Pershing assigned Doyen's regiment the decidedly unglamorous task of rear-area security and labor details. It would take months of top-level intervention to get Pershing to relent and commit the Marines to the same pre-combat training being given Army troops by French veterans.

More Marines deployed to France: the 6th Marines under Colonel Albertus Catlin, and Major Edward Cole's 6th Machine Gun Battalion. Now the 4th Marine Brigade was formed, nearly ten thousand strong. In size alone, the

brigade equaled many of the shot-up French and British divisions.

Doyen, promoted to brigadier general, assumed command; Colonel "Buck" Neville took over the 5th Marines. Pershing assigned the brigade to the U.S. 2d Division, a first-rate outfit whose Army components consisted of two infantry regiments, three of field artillery, and one of engineers.

Among the salty Leathernecks were storied staff noncommissioned officers like Gunnery Sergeant Dan Daly, First Sergeant Daniel "Beau" Hunter, and Sergeant Major John Quick. Marines tend to perpetuate legends of their sergeants and corporals, especially when those legends are earned with great daring and colorful profanity.

One "high-hearted volunteer" was captain of the Yale track team and holder of the world's indoor record for the mile run, twenty-two-year-old Lieutenant John "Johnnie" Overton. Overton, like so many of the best and brightest of his generation, sacrificed his college graduation to enlist in the Marines.

A year in France would weld these disparate "old breed" and "new breed" Marines—the Dan Dalys and the Johnnie Overtons—into a lethal fighting machine when the ultimate test finally came.

At the threshold of glory, General Doyen's health could not withstand the rigors of field duty, and in May 1918 he had to be shipped home, terminally ill. Back in Washington, Commandant Barnett decided to send his heir apparent, Brigadier General John Lejeune, to France to take command of the brigade, but Pershing could not wait.

THE OLD BREED

The Marines who first went to France in 1917 comprised a rich amalgam of experienced veterans and idealistic recruits. Captain John W. Thomason, an officer as adept with pen and brush as he was with ordnance and expeditions, left an indelible description of one essential component:

"There were also a number of diverse people who ran curiously to type, with drilled shoulders and a bone-deep sunburn, and a tolerant scorn of nearly everything on earth. Their speech was flavored with navy words. . . . Rifles were high and holy things to them and they knew five-inch broadside guns. . . . They were the Leathernecks, the Old Timers . . . the old breed of American regular, regarding the service as home and the war as occupation; and they transmitted their temper and character and view-point to the high-hearted volunteer mass which filled the ranks of the Marine Brigade."

German General Erich Ludendorff had launched a massive new offensive, and the AEF would soon be called to play its first major role. Pershing assigned his chief of staff, Army Brigadier General James Harbord, to take command of the Marines, saying sternly, "Young man, I'm giving you the best brigade in France—if anything goes wrong I'll know whom to blame."

Harbord took command of the 4th Marine Brigade with some trepidation. He was a National Guard cavalry officer, a temporary brigadier, and somewhat intimidated by his two regimental commanders, Catlin and Neville, hard-boiled Marines, both recipients of the Medal of Honor. But Harbord proved to be worthy of all the respect and support they could give him. "They never failed me," he said later, and they felt the same about him.

35

Now came time to fight. Ludendorff's May 27 offensive against the Aisne Heights proved too much for the French forces holding that line. Faced with specially trained "shock units" that spearheaded the German drive, the French reeled backward. When Ludendorff reached the Marne at Chateau Thierry, he stood just fifty miles from the French capital.

There was never a war hungrier for men. The British and French generals whose troops had manned the trenches for most of the war were commanding divisions bled white. The prospect of fresh foreign troops to feed into the fray, under their own command for their own battle aims, was appetizing. But not to Pershing or the United States Marines.

General Ferdinand Foch, Commander-in-Chief of Allied Forces in France, had little confidence in the largely untested American military. Foch and Pershing had clashed over the initial combat assignments of the AEF. Foch wanted to feed small units of American forces piecemeal to reinforce the shattered French and British divisions; Pershing fought to preserve the tactical integrity of the AEF, demanding to fight as an American army.

But the crisis at the Marne demanded quick action. Pershing reluctantly released his five American divisions to Foch.

On May 30, 1918, Pershing ordered the U.S. 2d Division to join French General Joseph Degoutte's Sixth Army in desperate fighting along the Marne

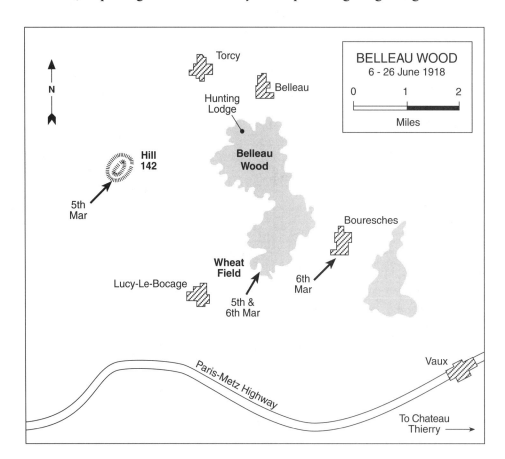

front. The Marines boarded *camions*—covered French trucks with seats along either side—and raced toward Chateau Thierry for their first major confrontation with the German Army and the greatest crossroads in their battle history.

Ahead, the Germans had seized a line of villages—Vaux, Bouresches, Torcy—and in this sector the 461st Imperial German Infantry, a 1,200-man regiment reinforced with plentiful Maxim machine guns, occupied a wooded area for a brief rest before resuming their drive on Paris.

The mile-square region, a game preserve, was known as Bois de Belleau, Belleau Wood.

The *camions* screeched to a halt, discharging thousands of stiff-legged members of the 2d Division along the shoulders of the crucial Paris-Metz highway. Sergeants ordered their men off the exposed thoroughfare and into positions along both sides. The Leathernecks assumed responsibility for a long stretch of line to the north, the 5th Marines on the left, the 6th Marines on the right.

A half-mile away, through a ripening wheat field, lay Belleau Wood, dark and brooding. The few French pickets out front seemed overmatched.

On June 2, Ludendorff resumed his attack with a new fury. The already battered French Sixth Army began falling back.

The Marines watched in silence as the demoralized soldiers retired through their lines. A passing French officer suggested that they join the retreat. Captain Lloyd Williams answered for every Marine when he said, "Retreat, hell! We just got here."

By early afternoon of June 3, an eerie stillness settled over the field. In their shallow fighting holes—they nicknamed them "foxholes"—the Marines suffered in the heat and kept watch on the rolling fields before them. The incessant enemy shelling increased.

At last, the German infantry appeared, long lines of men approaching rapidly across the fields, shoulders hunched, weapons low. The rookies in the Marine lines swallowed hard at the sight; the veterans smiled grimly, adjusted the folding-leaf rear sights on their Springfield "03's," and settled into steady firing positions. Never again in this bloody war would the Marines have such lucrative targets.

The brigade opened sustained rifle fire at 800 yards, more than three times the accepted combat range. The Springfield's 30–06 bullet impacted like a mule's kick, even at that extended range, and German soldiers spun and tumbled with the fusillade.

Incredulous, the survivors wavered, then went to ground. Their officers harangued them into resuming the attack; another hail of rifle bullets struck the exposed men with sickening thuds. Cole's massed machine guns began raking the lines. A third advance fared little better, and the Germans, no fools, flowed back into the shelter of the woods. There would be no breakthrough along the Paris-Metz highway this day.

37

While Harbord's Marines celebrated their turkey shoot, the Germans licked their wounds and wondered how the French Sixth Army had suddenly developed such prowess in long-range marksmanship. Early in the day's fighting, the Germans had swept up a few advance pickets of the 2d Division. Soon they realized they were facing American regulars. The news had a galvanic effect on the Imperial high command.

General Ludendorff knew that the Americans would eventually assemble an enormous, well-armed, fully equipped, and irresistible army against his own war-weary forces.

Germany's only hope, Ludendorff believed, was to cause the premature deployment of the initial American forces—which he had just done—and then defeat and demoralize them so badly that President Wilson would lose heart about squandering American lives in this far-off European meat-grinder.

"American units appearing on the front should be hit particularly hard," Ludendorff ordered. Across from the U.S. 2d Division, the commander of the German 28th Division announced, "We are not fighting for ground—for this ridge or that hill. It will be decided here whether or not the American Army will be equal to our own troops." The Marines would not give him the answer that he wanted.

There were many roads to Paris. The objective for the Germans in Belleau Wood became that of spoiling the Americans' combat debut—convincingly, bloodily.

The assault of the 4th Marine Brigade against Belleau Wood would resemble the exposed, bloody landing of the 2d Marine Division against fortified Japanese positions on Tarawa twenty-five years later.

At Belleau Wood, with field artillery brave but ineffectual, infantry was forced to undertake a very long haul through the wheat fields in the face of a terribly relentless machine-gun fire. The Marines had not faced such a formidable force of combat veterans since Bladensburg and New Orleans in 1814–15. There they had delivered a hot defensive fire against advancing troops in the open. Now the tables were reversed.

General Degoutte ordered the U.S. 2d Division to counterattack the German positions on the sixth of June.

The 1st Battalion, 5th Marines were the first to "go over the top," spilling out of their foxholes for a dawn attack against Hill 142, an intermediate objective on the left flank.

Leaving an increasing hemorrhage of dead and wounded in the wheat behind them, the Marines clawed forward against the disciplined, grazing fire of the German machine gunners. Advancing the half-mile to their hill, and wresting it from the German defenders, took until noon and cost 410 casualties, a sobering first step in the prolonged battle to come.

Harbord launched the main assault at 5 P.M. on June 6. Two battalions of

the 6th Marines and one of the 5th fell into line forward of their foxholes, dressed their ranks, deployed skirmishers, then advanced forward at a fast walk—exactly as they had been taught for the past year by their veteran French instructors. Only one thing was wrong. The French had not really used this vulnerable formation since 1915.

Now German machine gunners feasted on the massed targets, enjoying a turkey shoot of their own. The first ranks of Marines fell in appalling numbers. The others hit the deck and, in the dubious shelter of the wheat, continued the advance on their hands and knees—junking their French training with the same cynical adaptability which would help them seize Pacific atolls in the war to come.

The assault became fragmented and confused; neither the German commander nor Harbord ever again knew for certain the status of the battle as irregular pockets of Marines and Prussians fought to the death throughout the fields and woods.

This improvised assault—one small group popping up to blaze away with rifles while another rushed forward a few dozen yards—also had its price. The veteran German machine gunners had the range and deflection—and plenty of ammo. Bands of interlocking Maxim machine gun fire scythed down wheat and Marines alike. The final 50 yards seemed impassable.

War correspondent Floyd Gibbons lay surrounded by the dead, pinned down and terrified. At this critical point, one of the Old Breed Leathernecks leapt to his feet with a curse. Gibbons stared in awe as Gunnery Sergeant Daniel Daly, the double Medal of Honor awardee from the Boxer Rebellion and Haiti, swept by. "The sergeant," Gibbons reported in his dispatch, "swung his bayoneted rifle over his head with a forward sweep, yelling at his men, 'Come on, you sons-of-bitches, do you want to live forever?'" With a roar, the survivors in the wheat surged forward and overran the first line of German machine gun nests in the woods.

At last the Leathernecks had a toehold in the tree line, and Major Thomas Holcomb's men had actually cut through to the village of Bouresches. But the assault had taken a hideous toll. Marines looking backward at the trampled wheat field, strewn with bodies, could only shudder in horror.

June 6, 1918, had become the bloodiest single day in the Corps' history. The 4th Marine Brigade had suffered 1,087 casualties, losing more men in a single day than in all preceding 143 years combined.

Invaluable men were down: Colonel Catlin of the 6th Marines, who had survived the blowing up of the *Maine* in Havana back in 1898, shot through the lungs; First Sergeant "Beau" Hunter, shot to death in the assault on Hill 142.

Several companies reported the loss of all officers. Marine NCOs filled in the gaps as the surviving troops dug in to repel German night counterattacks.

One old-timer who seemed to live a charmed life in combat was Sergeant Major John Quick, the NCO who had fought with such conspicuous bravery at Cuzco Wells and the Sohoton Cliffs years earlier. Hearing that Lieutenant

Clifford Cates had a desperate need for ammunition in his fight to hold onto Bouresches, Quick commandeered a Model "T" truck, filled it with grenades and small-arms ammo, and hightailed it under constant fire directly to Cates, a godsend. Quick opted to stay and join Cates's fight, admitting he was safer in fire-swept Bouresches than moving about the battlefield at night in a truck with every gunner on both sides taking dead aim at him.

The Leathernecks proved surprisingly adept at bayonet fighting; the German infantry, once vaunted as the premier close combat fighters of the world, had grown too dependent on their machine guns. Once the Marines got close enough to charge the machine gun nests, the fight was usually over.

During the night and into June 7, the Marines inside Belleau Wood repeatedly challenged the German defenders in savage, close-in combat. But closing to bayonet range took countless Marine lives. They had few grenades, no signal flares, and little experience coordinating with division artillery, and were still unhappy with their overweight Chauchat automatic rifles.

"A Sprinkling of Old-Time Marines" (Lt. Col. John W. Thomason, USMC)

The battle for Belleau Wood dragged on. Lieutenant Colonel Fritz Wise led his battalion of the 5th Marines through the long axis of the shredded woods from the 8th through the 12th of June, out of sync with Harbord and disoriented, but methodically attacking German positions.

Then, just when it appeared the Germans were on the ropes, Ludendorff ordered a major counterattack.

At dawn on the thirteenth of June, the Germans clobbered the American positions with heavy artillery fire, saturated Bouresches with mustard gas, and sent fresh storm troops into the smoldering ruins. The arrogant newcomers had much to learn about these unknown American Marines.

German infantry approaching the embattled woods began to drop by the score to uncannily accurate long-range rifle fire. The 2d Division's field artillery, rapidly gaining combat proficiency, shredded the ranks of the survivors with hot shrapnel.

In the reeking woods, Major John "Johnny the Hard" Hughes and his 1st Battalion, 6th Marines withstood the loss of 450 casualties to poison gas and high explosives, then rose up to greet the attackers with a fury, their bayonets bristling like the quills of an enraged porcupine.

When German shellfire killed Captain John Francis Burns, a former first sergeant and beloved company commander, the intense fire of his men literally tore the attackers limb from limb.

"Johnny the Hard" (another Medal of Honor awardee from Veracruz) held the bloody ground, his eyes swollen shut by the gas. His laconic message

to Harbord at the height of the counterattack should have given the Germans pause: "Have had terrific bombardment and attack . . . everything is OK . . . Can't you get hot coffee to me?"

At one point, General Degoutte replaced the depleted 4th Marine Brigade with a new Army outfit and a French regiment. The bearded, exhausted Marines, having already suffered dreadful losses, took a grateful rest amid the barns and haystacks just beyond cannon range. But Ludendorff infiltrated a new German regiment into the woods, and the situation turned critical again.

Soon the Marines were back in Belleau Wood in force, fighting as desperately as ever. The woods, never tactically significant, now took on a psychological importance of unparalleled dimensions. Who would prevail?

The Germans tasked with the fighting, however, were beginning to have second thoughts about this unusual band of sea soldiers. One opposing trooper wrote that the American Marines were "terribly reckless fellows." A commander opined that these Marines would make "very good storm troopers." Legend has it that the survivors of the 461st Imperial German Infantry, who had fought the Marines tooth and nail since the third of June, had a more fitting, one-word description of their relentless foe: *Teufelhunden* or "Devil Dogs."

In the end, the Devil Dogs triumphed. On June 26, twenty days after his battalion had stormed across the terrible wheat field to begin the battle, Major Maurice Shearer of the 5th Marines wiped out the final German strong point and sent a crackling message: "Woods now U.S. Marine Corps entirely."

Victory at Belleau Wood came at a sobering price: more than 5,100 Marines killed or wounded, greater than half the entire brigade. Some rifle companies had been virtually shot to pieces.

The grateful French, convinced the Marines had removed the threat against Paris, renamed the mile-square wood *Bois de la Brigade de Marine.*

The battle's practical significance, however, was its rejection of Ludendorff's objective of demoralizing the new American Army before it could come of age. Belleau Wood, together with the U.S. Army's stirring victories at Cantigny and Vaux, showed convincingly to Germans and Allies alike that the Americans could fight with heart and lethality. Ludendorff lost not only his last best shot at Paris but his one opportunity to discredit the greatest threat to Imperial Germany on the battlefield.

Belleau Wood gave the Marines invaluable confidence and experience. Among the survivors were men who would lead the Corps in distant battles for the next four decades, including future Commandants Neville, Holcomb, Cates, and a lionhearted young lieutenant named Lemuel Shepherd.

For the Corps, however, the greatest casualty of Belleau Wood was the loss of goodwill with their Army counterparts over the unexpected windfall of publicity that emerged from the battle. All of it was a fluke.

Rumors had circulated in rear echelons during the confused opening day of the battle to the effect that Correspondent Floyd Gibbons had been

killed in action. The AEF censor, under strict orders from General Pershing not to identify individual units, felt compassion for the fallen Floyd and allowed his final dispatch, so laudatory of the Marines in action, to pass untouched.

Floyd, as it turned out, lived through his ordeal, despite three wounds and the loss of an eye. But for an American public desperate for firsthand war stories, Floyd's reports were consumed with gusto.

As Gibbons had written it, the United States Marines had single-handedly stopped the Hun, saved Paris, and reversed the course of the war. Pershing and the soldiers were furious. Marines would never again be mentioned in official communiqués.

General Barnett's considerable efforts to deploy to France an all-Marine division, with its organic USMC artillery regiment, were stonewalled by Pershing. Even efforts to deploy a Marine seven-inch naval battery to France died stillborn.

Brigadier General John Lejeune arrived in the theater of war just after the battle of Belleau Wood to a cool reception—despite his earlier graduation from the Army War College and professional reputation. Pershing initially assigned Lejeune to command a National Guard brigade.

The Marines' war pressed on. General Ludendorff launched one final German offensive on July 15, 1918. This time the Marines fought as part of the French XX Corps. Harbord, promoted to major general after Belleau Wood, took command of the 2d Division; "Whispering Buck" Neville, a tower of strength in the first fight, assumed command of the Marine Brigade.

Ludendorff's offensive created a huge bulge in the Allied lines. General Foch decided to counterattack in the Aisne-Marne region, near a place called Soissons.

The 2d Division Marines joined the XX Corps veterans—Moroccans, Senegalese, Foreign Legionnaires—in the Forest of Retz. The roads were clogged with primitive tanks, resplendent cavalry units, and horse-drawn artillery. It was urgent that the Americans reach their line of departure before daybreak. The Marines executed a nightmare of a forced march in a driving rainstorm—some rifle companies having to double-time the last mile to kick off the assault on time.

Soissons was two days of desperate fighting. The 5th Marines, under Colonel Logan Feland, led the way the first day; the 6th Marines, now commanded by Colonel Harry Lee, took over the second. In effect the attack forcibly throttled the final offensive spasm of the Imperial German Army. Both units fought bloody, exhausting battles.

Two Marine sergeants helped the 5th Marines fight clear of the tangled forest on the first day—Serbia-born Louis Cukela and Austrian-born Matej Kocak. Both maneuvered behind German machine gun nests, stormed them single-handedly, fiercely brandishing bayonets and trench knives. Both would receive the Medal of Honor. An inordinate number of Marines have won that medal with weapons that can be hung on a web belt.

A squadron of French tanks accompanied the 5th Marines' advance into the open, attracting a hellacious fire. The tanks exploded and burned fiercely, Marines giving them a wide berth.

Beyond the woods lay yet another wheat field, sprinkled almost symbolically with red poppies. Taking increasingly heavy casualties, the troops secured Beaurepaire Farm and tried to reorient their advance to the southeast. German artillery never stopped pounding them. By dark, the 5th Marines were spent.

The 6th Marines and their supporting tanks ran into an even greater buzz saw the next day.

At Soissons, Private First Class Carl Brannen, a replacement in the 2d Battalion, 6th Marines after the Belleau Wood brawl, experienced the terror of his first combat this hot July day in the wheat fields. "The Germans turned loose everything they had," he said. "It seemed to rain shells."

Out in front of the faltering formation in this maelstrom was Lieutenant Johnnie Overton, the Yale track star. Brannen did his best to follow his leader across that field of high explosives:

> The last glance I had of Lt. Overton he was walking backward and trying to shout something back to us. He carried his cane in the left hand and his .45 in the right. The din and roar was so terrific that I didn't have any idea what he was saying, but interpreted it from his expression to be some words of encouragement. He was soon down, killed. The gunnery sergeant was killed . . . all the men around me were shot down.

Brannen eventually linked up with Lieutenant Clifford Cates, but the incessant shelling and machine gun fire had ripped the 6th Marines to fragments. Cates refused to give in to despair. In a message since immortalized in Marine Corps legend, Cates reported, "I have only two men left out of my company and twenty out of others. . . . I have no one to my left and only a few to my right. I will hold."

Hold Cates and his Marines did, and the 2d Division and the XX Corps drove the Germans from the field. Other Allied units launched a general offensive which would bring unrelenting pressure on the German Empire. The Allies would never again relinquish the initiative.

But the Marines at Soissons paid another fearsome price for their part in this victory, sustaining 2,000 more casualties. Occurring so shortly after Belleau Wood, this meant that the original 4th Marine Brigade, which had hurried up the Paris-Metz Highway in such high spirits on June 1, had lost in seven weeks just about its total original number.

Replacements would pour in, but there would be no replacing men like the gifted Johnnie Overton. "That was a bad day," recalled Thomas Holcomb of the 6th Marines' savage battle on July 19.

General Pershing gave John Lejeune command of the 2d Division, with its depleted 4th Marine Brigade, on July 29.

Lejeune's first combat operation in France was the two-corps assault against the German salient at St. Mihiel. While Army troops spearheaded the attack, the Marines rushed forward on the second day to take out a powerful series of fortifications along the Hindenburg Line. Doing so took four days of stubborn fighting. The salient fell. So did 700 Marines.

Lejeune's 2d Division now supported the French Fourth Army, commanded by General Henri Gouraud. The Germans retreated sullenly, taking full advantage of the rugged terrain and excellent observation afforded by their prepared defenses along the heights above both sides of the Meuse River.

By late September they had slowed the French advance to a crawl. The strongly fortified position at Blanc Mont ("White Mountain") blocked further progress.

Gouraud knew the Germans had been fortifying Blanc Mont since 1914 and ordered Lejeune to assign components of the 2d Division as reinforcements for the

Marine 37mm gun crew in action during the Meuse-Argonne offensive, 1918. This is the best surviving photograph of Marines in combat during "The Great War." (U.S. Marine Corps)

The Marines Grow Wings

From the first, the Marine Corps had a different notion about its air arm. It had the revolutionary idea that instead of glory-hawking on its own, Marine aviation should as its first duty support the ground component.

On July 30, 1918, the 1st Marine Aviation Force arrived in France under the command of Major Alfred Cunningham, the first Marine to win his wings (1912). Cunningham's small force had to borrow used aircraft and assume marginal missions, but the aviators quickly saw action. The Marines flew the British-designed DH–4 bomber, nicknamed "The Flaming Coffin" for its spectacularly vulnerable fuel tank, for the balance of the war, dropping bombs on German submarine pens, railway yards, and airfields.

Lieutenant Everett Brewer and Gunnery Sergeant Harry Wersheimer shot down the Marines' first enemy aircraft on September 28 over Belgium, both men being severely wounded in the dogfight.

On October 14, a dozen German fighters intercepted eight USMC bombers returning from a mission at Thielt, Belgium, and ganged up on the DH–4 piloted by Second Lieutenant Ralph Talbot. Talbot's observer, Corporal Robert Robinson, a gifted gunner, shot down one Fokker D-VII, then suffered several wounds from other fighters at close range. Talbot then swung back toward his attackers and downed a surprised German pilot with his fixed guns. With Robinson critically wounded and more Fokkers swarming to the attack, Talbot dove for the deck, swooping across the German lines at fifty feet, and landed safely at a Belgium airfield. Both Marines received the Medal of Honor.

Marine aviators flew fifty-seven bombing raids, sustained four combat deaths, and shot down twelve enemy planes in World War I. Audacious new aviation commanders like Captains Roy Geiger and Francis Mulcahy gave rise to a long, hot line of epic Marine dogfighters.

The first Marine aviator, Lieutenant Alfred A. Cunningham, USMC, at Pensacola in 1915, twelve years after the Wright Brothers' first flight at Kill Devil Hills, North Carolina. *(U.S. Marine Corps)*

smaller Allied divisions. Lejeune refused. "Keep the division intact and let us take that ridge," he offered. Gouraud raised his eyebrows, stared at Lejeune appraisingly, then nodded assent.

On October 3 the 2d Division demonstrated to the skeptical Allies that its replacements had been imbued with the same fiery vigor as their fallen predecessors at Belleau Wood, Vaux, and Soissons.

Following a violent, five-minute bombardment by 200 guns, the division surged forward on the run, the 3d Infantry Brigade on the right, the 4th Marine Brigade on the left. Harry Lee's 6th Marines claimed the crest of the dominant ridge by noon; the soldiers swept the right shoulder. On the left, with the French flattened by German defenders in the Essen Hook, the 5th Marines of Logan Feland wheeled and took the position from the flank.

General Gouraud whistled in amazement. The Marine assault had been a model of professionalism—but the Germans would not relinquish the Blanc

Mont complex without a fight, and tomorrow there would be hell to pay on the reverse slopes and fire-swept valleys.

Private John Kelly had been every first sergeant's worst nightmare in garrison, a rebellious, insubordinate hard case. But in combat, the Chicago native found his element. Operating independently in the swirling assault of the 6th Marines that morning, Kelly had streaked through the artillery barrage, "yelling like an Indian," scourged the nearest German machine gun nest with a well-placed grenade, shot another defender with a pistol at point-blank range, and scared the hell out of the eight survivors who promptly surrendered to this madman. Kelly would receive the Medal of Honor from the Marines—and the Army—for his morning's work.

The following day, October 4, proved to be one of the bloodiest in Marine Corps history. The 5th Marines took the lead, advancing briskly toward the village of St. Etienne, just as the Germans launched a fierce counterattack. The Marine regiment soon came under galling fire from three sides, topped by the fiercest artillery bombardment they ever experienced in the war.

One battalion of a thousand Marines charged through a fire-storm of enormous explosives to drive the enemy back to the town. Nine hundred men fell in this endeavor. By day's merciful end, 1,100 Marines lay killed or wounded.

The Marines were getting grimly used to leaving a thousand men a day fallen on this new kind of battlefield.

Four days of bitter fighting followed before St. Etienne was taken and the area secured. In the action, the Marines had suffered more than 2,500 casualties; one company lost 90 percent of its men. Even the seemingly indestructible Gunnery Sergeant Dan Daly fell wounded.

Buck sergeants commanded the remnants of many companies. In one such case, Sergeant Aralzaman Marsh rallied the survivors of his rifle company like an old salt to reject a terrifying German night attack.

By the tenth of October the Germans were in full retreat.

The French government awarded the 5th and 6th Marines (and the 6th Machine Gun Battalion) their third citation for gallantry, thereby entitling members of those outfits to wear the scarlet and green *fourragère* on the left shoulders of their uniforms. (This distinction, won at such a painful cost, continues today among the Marines of those historic regiments.)

John Lejeune's 2d Division rejoined the American First Army and assumed a two-kilometer front in the center of the line.

Imperial Germany was clearly on the ropes. Politicians frantically negotiated to attain an armistice. But the killing continued. The German field armies, now fighting on pride alone, made the Marines pay for every ridge and crossroads.

Fighting proved particularly bitter in the Argonne Forest and along the Meuse, the river of death. On November 1, 1918, Black Jack Pershing's First Army surged forward, the Marines with them.

The 4th Marine Brigade by this time was a combat-cagey outfit, despite its heavy losses and constant replacements. The Marines assaulted, expertly hugging a "rolling barrage" of heavy artillery, and hit the Germans in their trenches just as they began lifting their heads from the bombardment.

Maxim machine guns still ruled the battlefield, however, and Marine veterans and rookies alike went down to this relentless fire whickering through the smoke.

Private First Class Brannen commented, "Sometime in the afternoon we lost Captain Green and all the lieutenants. The top sergeant was commanding the remnants of the company."

The battalions leapfrogged forward, helping each other smother the German strong points, and maintained the assault. By mid-afternoon Marines

Marine Major General John A. Lejeune, commanding the U.S. 2d Division, decorates veterans of the 4th Brigade of Marines for combat heroism, France, 1918. Two years later, Lejeune would emerge as one of the most dynamic Commandants of the Corps. (U.S. Marine Corps)

swarmed over the dominant Barricourt Heights. The Germans bailed out, abandoning the Hindenburg Line, scuttling across the Meuse, blowing the bridges behind them.

Lejeune's division included a first-rate regiment of Army engineers. These men took awful casualties trying in vain to launch floating footbridges across the Meuse. Turned back above Mouzon, the engineers tried again to the south, near Letanne. There, on the night of November 10, 1918, the one hundred and forty-third birthday of the U.S. Marine Corps, the 5th Marines stormed across successfully floated bridges and prepared to assault the Germans along the high ground beyond.

The rest of the Marines took a deep breath the next morning and prepared to make their mad dash across the narrow spans, when—in a final spasm of artillery fire—the armistice went into effect. It was eleven o'clock on November 11—the war was over.

Less than 32,000 Marines served in France. More than 12,000 of those given the opportunity to fight in France became casualties; 3,284 died. The survivors had given their country and their Corps a legacy of courage, *esprit*, and ferocity which would remain the standard of combat excellence for the remainder of the violent century.

The U.S. Marines in World War I experienced a seven-fold expansion to nearly 79,000, including, for the first time, reservists and Women Marines (277 women joined the Corps, beginning with Opha Johnson in August 1918).

The Marines fulfilled many armed missions during the period, serving on board every Navy capital ship, along the Texas border (prepared to protect the Mexican oil fields near Tampico), in Cuba, Haiti, Santo Domingo, and Siberia. Many who deployed to France never made it beyond port security duty, including the entire 5th Marine Brigade and its double Medal of Honor awardee Brigadier General Smedley Butler (to his everlasting chagrin).

But, fittingly, the glory went to those who so stubbornly fought, held, bled, and scrambled "over the top" to continue the offensive.

The great Army historian, General S. L. A. Marshall, provided a fitting salute to those ghosts of Belleau Wood, Soissons, and Blanc Mont: "The Marine Brigade because it was unique—a little raft of sea soldiers in an ocean of Army—was without doubt the most aggressive body of diehards on the Western Front."

4: "SKILLED WATERMEN

The Interwar Years (1919–1941)

Haiti, 1919. Marines and native guides on patrol for caco bandits. (U.S. Marine Corps)

OPPOSITE: Disarming Guerrillas, Nicaragua
(Charles Waterhouse)

AND JUNGLE FIGHTERS, TOO"

IT IS NOT ENOUGH THAT THE TROOPS BE
SKILLED INFANTRY MEN OR ARTILLERY MEN
OF HIGH MORALE; THEY MUST BE SKILLED
WATER MEN AND JUNGLE FIGHTERS WHO
KNOW IT CAN BE DONE—MARINES WITH
MARINE TRAINING.

*Lieutenant Colonel Earl Ellis, USMC,
Operations Plan 712, 1921*

The Marines returned from Europe after World War I to national acclaim for their sacrifices and valor. Yet the Corps would very soon be in dire straits because they still lacked a unique warfighting mission, a distinctive role that would satisfy national security interests without unduly competing with the Army.

In the doldrums ahead, a shadowy prophet would illuminate the path—the brilliant and doomed Lieutenant Colonel Earl "Pete" Ellis.

Ellis had earned his spurs in combat in France (Navy Cross, 1918), and he had both the ear and the sponsorship of General John Lejeune.

In the immediate postwar years, when most Marines envisioned their future role simply as renewed service in another continental campaign, Pete Ellis perceived a radically different *naval* mission.

Ellis foresaw a major war in the Pacific with Japan and projected the use of Marines as amphibious shock troops to forcibly seize advanced naval bases along the island stepping-stones leading to Japan. His extraordinary *Operations Plan 712: Advanced Base Operations in Micronesia, 1921*, published two decades before the Japanese strike against Pearl Harbor, proved an eerily accurate prophecy of the coming war.

Ellis died under mysterious conditions (acute alcoholism? poisoned?) two years later in the Japanese-held Palau Islands while conducting a "fact-finding" journey through the strategic islands of the Central Pacific. Yet his clarion call for a *naval assault* mission could not have been more timely for his floundering Corps.

THE TANK THAT WENT TO SEA

The Christie amphibious tank was an early concept that helped save the Marine Corps. The hybrid vehicle was a bold idea with the potential to break the logjams obstructing amphibious assault.

Automotive engineer J. Walter Christie designed a revolutionary vehicle capable of propulsion by tracks, wheels, or propellers. Christie mounted a 75mm gun on the prototype, tested it successfully in the Hudson and Potomac rivers, and called it an amphibious tank. The proposal intrigued John Lejeune, who authorized a field test of the Christie tank during the 1923–1924 fleet landing exercises at Culebra.

The Marines watched intently as the battleship *Wyoming* lowered the strange vehicle onto the deck of a submarine alongside. The sub proceeded toward the beach, submerged enough to float the prototype, then steered clear. So far so good. The tank continued shoreward on its own power until it reached the surf zone. There the unseaworthy prototype nearly swamped, and with it swamped the early hopes of a vehicle that would one day transform the Marines.

Neither Christie nor the Marine Corps had the money for a major engineering redesign, and the experiment folded. It would take another twenty years before the United States could field a legitimate "amphibious assault vehicle"—the turreted, armored amphibian ("LVT-A")—which would spearhead landings from the Marshalls to Okinawa in 1944–1945. But the Christie concept would survive.

Glorious as their service in France had been, the Marines had fought as a "second army," and U.S. Army officers, more than a little resentful of Leatherneck headlines, were quick to spotlight the duplication.

The Marines had also drifted away from the Navy. A promising Navy plan in early 1918 to launch a landing force of 20,000 Marines against German submarine bases along the Sabbioncello Peninsula in the Adriatic Sea died stillborn with Ludendorff's first great offensive on the Western Front. The Marines went instead to Belleau Wood.

Many postwar Marines still thought more in terms of field armies and river crossings than landing parties or advanced bases.

Then came the nine-year commandancy of John Lejeune in the 1920s. Very much akin to his nineteenth-century predecessor Archibald Henderson, Lejeune managed to return the Corps to its naval roots and ensure his officers and NCOs gained meaningful combat experience around the world.

Lejeune proposed the principal future focus of his fighting men as "a mobile Marine Corps force adequate to conduct offensive land operations against hostile Naval bases." The key and distinguishing word in this concept: *offensive*.

At Lejeune's insistence, the Navy and Marines conducted experimental fleet landing exercises in the Caribbean in the winter of 1923–1924. The results were not pretty.

Offensive landing operations turned out to demand the solution of significant problems that Marines were far from ready to handle. These involved command and control, communications, fire support, and—desperately—the challenge of moving men and their major weapons ashore.

Getting a regiment of troops and their light artillery and tanks into small craft from transports was tough enough. Negotiating the heavily laden small craft through a plunging surf and offloading them onto the beach was a challenge of a much higher magnitude.

"Chaos ruled the beach," glumly declared chief observer Colonel Dion Williams. Not promising for the new role the Marines needed for survival as a service.

Lejeune was hamstrung in conducting further amphibious tests in his tenure because he had virtually no field forces left at home. The Marine Corps, reduced to less than one third of its WWI strength, became heavily committed for years in "limited wars" in Haiti (1913–1934), the Dominican Republic (1916–1924), and Nicaragua (1926–1933). These were the so-called "Banana Wars," unpopular at home and among the native populations. The fighting, small in scale, savage in execution, was ugly and relentless.

Although no strangers to intervening in Haitian upheavals, the U.S. Marines returned in force in 1919 when the dynamic Charlemagne Peralte led a major revolt of the *cacos* (a *caco* was either a bandit or a counterrevolutionary, depending on one's political view).

A light brigade of Marines came ashore, many of them WWI veterans, reinforced by an aviation squadron equipped with Curtiss patrol flying boats and the ubiquitous JN–4b "Jennies," the two-seater biplanes with bantam 100-horsepower engines.

The Marines would need every bit of their experience and firepower. Charlemagne Peralte proved as formidable a jungle fighter as he was a resistance leader. The Marines fought an average of twenty firefights a month against the *cacos*, who were adept at assembling several hundred men at the point of attack, only to dissolve into the jungles when reinforcements arrived—a tactic the Marines would meet again one day in similar terrain in Southeast Asia.

The Marine-trained local *gendarmes* were helpful but did little to gain the confidence of the people among whom Peralte hid and operated.

When Peralte led a bold strike against Port-au-Prince on October 7, the Marines realized that the situation demanded an exceptionally daring plan of their own. The resulting subterfuge would be the stuff of modern fiction or result in congressional hearings today—but, in the world of 1919, it worked.

The Marines established a bogus band of dissident *gendarmes* who gradually convinced Peralte of their allegiance. Two enterprising Marine NCOs, Sergeant Herman Hanneken and Corporal William Button, joined with a *gendarme* "deserter" on the dark night of October 30 in the effort to penetrate Peralte's concentric security rings.

By sheer bluff and boldness the three men traversed six successive checkpoints, Button displaying a "captured" Browning automatic rifle, Hanneken with a pair of Colt .45s hidden under his poncho. Astonishingly, before daybreak they were escorted to the great *caco* chieftain himself, sitting by a campfire. Peralte stared at Hanneken, then at eternity as the sergeant fired two quick rounds into his chest. Button leveled the Browning and methodically cut down the bodyguards. Silence returned to the clearing. The Marines loaded Peralte's body on a mule and moved swiftly through the jungle—the very hounds of hell on their heels—to Cap Haitien. There they buried the

guerrilla leader in a block of cement to avoid any *caco* resurrection ploys. Both Button and "Hard Head" Hanneken received the Medal of Honor.

The death of Peralte caused the *caco* revolt to flicker but not perish. Benoit Batraville emerged to continue the hit-and-run raids, including a good-sized strike against Port-au-Prince in early 1920. In the sharp fighting that followed in the hills, Marine aviation lent an impressive tactical hand.

Marine pilots in the heavily jungled terrain of the Caribbean could at first contribute little more than observation and resupply. They wanted more of the action.

Lieutenant Lawson Sanderson began experimenting with what aviators worldwide now call "dive-bombing." He found he could vastly increase bombing accuracy over the customary horizontal, high-altitude approach by "pushing her over to a steep dive of 45 degrees, aiming the nose at the target, and releasing the bomb from about 250 feet." Biplanes could perform this tricky maneuver without wing flaps or diving brakes because their "built-in headwind" of struts, wires, and fixed landing gear kept airspeed under 400 mph, even in such a steep dive. (Among the interested students of this Marine innovation would be officers of the rebuilding German air forces, whose observers would study it carefully and one day present it in *blitzkriegs* led by the infamous Stuka dive-bomber.)

Sanderson's pilots used these revolutionary new tactics against a large force of Batraville's *cacos*, drove them in disarray into the cross fire of converging Marine patrols, and accounted for hundreds of casualties.

Thus was born the long-standing fraternity between Marine aviators and infantrymen.

Benoit Batraville sought revenge. In April his men ambushed a Marine patrol and captured its wounded lieutenant alive. Batraville cut the man open with his machete and ate his heart and liver. The news enraged the Marines, who hunted him grimly with unaccustomed care and patience.

Six weeks later, on May 18, a Marine patrol found his camp. In the ensuing firefight Batraville fired wildly at the screaming Marines running toward him from the bush. Sergeant William Passmore shot him down with his Browning automatic rifle. When Batraville struggled to his feet, Sergeant Albert Taubert, with hard satisfaction, shot him in the head with his service revolver. Taubert recovered the pistol that spun from the guerrilla chief's bloody hand. It had belonged to the butchered patrol lieutenant.

The *caco* revolt died down, but the State Department wanted the Marines kept on the troubled island to train the *gendarmes* and preserve stability. This assignment would last another fourteen years.

Long before it commanded the headlines of the 1980s, Marines engaged the "Sandanista movement" and the tough little man who spawned it.

The Marines returned to Nicaragua in October 1925 after a twelve-year absence to help the pro-American government of Adolfo Díaz resume power.

But persistent pressure from rebel elements led by the luminary guerrilla Augusto Cesar Sandino required a major buildup of Marine strength.

By early 1927, after landings at Bluefields, Corinto, and other sites, Marines under Brigadier General Logan Feland had garrisoned fourteen Nicaraguan towns. Eventually, 3,300 men of the 2d Marine Brigade, reinforced by two air squadrons, were in place supporting Díaz's shaky government.

Sandino, who refused to support the "American puppet" Díaz, took his rebels to the northern hills along the Honduran border to continue the fight.

Augusto Sandino, even more than Charlemagne Peralte, would prove a formidable foe for the U.S. Marines. They would pursue Sandino in the Nicaraguan jungles for five frustrating years, engaging in their bitterest guerrilla fighting since the Seminole War in the Everglades. He would elude every pursuit, dodge every ambush.

Sandino differed from Peralte. He had international support in the form of money and weapons. Although physically frail, he was a fiery demagogue and ruthless fighter. Many liberal Americans idolized him, and they criticized the mean Marines who so constantly harassed him. He was the first modern counterrevolutionary in Central America. And certainly not the last.

The Marines, for their part, tried to stabilize a civil war, allow open elections, train a local constabulary (the *Guardia*), and protect U.S. citizens. None of this was possible without going after Sandino in his mountain strongpoints. It still looked like bullying to many, but the other guy did have an awful lot of guns.

Santo Domingo: A dismounted Marine patrol (note the spurs) searches house-to-house for guerrillas. (U.S. Marine Corps)

SEND IN THE MARINES

While the "Banana Wars" in Central America were neither numerous nor widespread, they made colorful headlines and gave the United States Marines a reputation not intended and, finally, not necessarily shunned. They became, in effect, "State Department Troops." Where an Army landing would have seemed an invasion, a Marine landing, with its seaborne roots, appeared less internationally severe if not less belligerent. It came to be an unspoken threat that if elements in countries behaved in ways unbecoming to the United States, Uncle Sam would quite quickly, "Send in the Marines." It wasn't the world's greatest job, but for a while it was the only one they really had. And it earned the Corps a "rapid response" reputation that it has preserved and enhanced

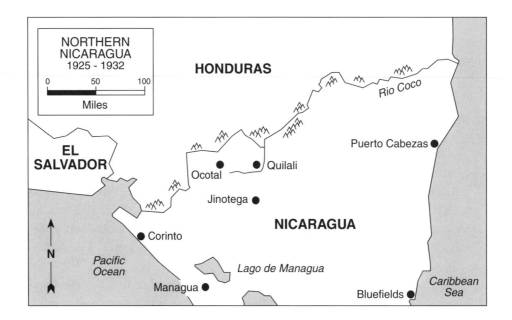

The Nueva Segovia district of northern Nicaragua contains some of the most difficult terrain in the Western Hemisphere. During the rainy season the gorges and rivers became as tough for the Marines to negotiate as "The Green Hell of Samar" a quarter-century earlier.

Marines and their *Guardia* counterparts penetrated these tangled highlands from both coasts by foot, boat, and pack mule. Their weapons of choice continued to be handheld—the reliable Springfield ".03" rifle, the Browning automatic rifle, and the mule-borne Lewis machine gun. Sandino's guerrillas had Russian rifles, machetes, plenty of machine guns, and dynamite bombs—crude hand grenades.

Ambushes inevitably occurred during river crossings, yet the rivers had to be crossed—many of them again and again during the course of a day's march. One Marine patrol followed a tortured trail that led them across the Rio Conjojas seventy-two times between dawn and sunset of a single, endless day.

It was in Nicaragua that the Marine Corps air-ground tactical team truly matured after the pioneering work of the expeditionary forces in Haiti and the Dominican Republic had paved the way.

The Marines in Nicaragua benefited from a stellar lineup of lionhearted aviators willing to try anything. Major Ross E. "Rusty" Rowell's Marine observation squadrons would in effect write the first chapter of close air support for ground troops. In the years to come, it would be Rowell's tactics studied by German *Luftwaffe* pilots.

While chasing Sandino, a combined force of about 100 Marines and *Guardias* occupied a barracks in Ocotal, the provincial capital of Nuevo Segovia, dangerously near the chieftain's operating base. On July 15, 1927, Sandino infiltrated 500 guerrillas into the town. The fight broke out at 1:15 A.M.

and raged through the night. The Marines withstood three charges, but they were surrounded and in grave danger. At dawn, Sandino sent in a flag of truce and demanded the defenders surrender. Replied Captain Gilbert Hatfield, "Marines don't know how to surrender." With that, volleys of rifle fire swept through the building's boarded-up windows and doors, the bullets ricocheting wildly around the rooms.

Hatfield prepared for the worst. The nearest reinforcements were, at best, a week away.

At mid-morning Hatfield heard a sound that must have brought a smile to his grimy face: the drone of a Liberty 400-horsepower engine. Marine De Havilland overhead! Sure enough, two DH–4Bs from Rowell's squadron in Managua circled above the town.

Hatfield, besieged in the barracks, had no way to communicate with the aviators (in other circumstances, when radios failed or were lacking, Marines took off their undershirts to lay as signal panels on the ground). No problem here. While one De Havilland strafed the rebels in the streets, the other landed in a nearby field, got the situation from local farmers.

Both planes then carried the word, flying for help at top speed to Managua, 125 miles away.

Learning of the crisis at Ocotal, Rusty Rowell loaded five De Havillands and Boeing O2-B1s for bear—600 rounds of machine gun ammo per gun, plenty of seventeen-pound bombs—and took off.

Looming thunderheads prevented a direct route, but by mid-afternoon the Marine squadron roared over the smoking town. Rowell sized up the situation on the first pass. Sandino's men, mostly mounted, crowded the streets around the barracks. A ring of scattered bodies marked the limit of their advance. The town was ripe with targets.

Rowell exultantly led the assault, diving from 1,500 feet, firing front machine guns all the way in, dropping the first fragmentation bomb at 300 feet, then pulling up steeply to let his rear gunner rake the streets.

Pandemonium struck the rebel formations; their horses stampeded in fright; scores of men fell from the bombing and strafing. Some took refuge in houses along the main street. These Rowell's dive-bombers blew to kindling wood. Some guerrillas rallied to open fire on the biplanes. Hatfield's men sortied to catch them in a cross fire. The streets became strewn with the dead and dying.

The aircraft banked and climbed through the smoke for repeat diving attacks. Rowell ripped Sandino's forces for forty-five minutes until the survivors fled the town, then, dangerously low on fuel, the planes wheeled over the southern hills and disappeared (having to make a forced landing well before Managua).

For leading this daring operation, Rowell became the first Marine to receive the Distinguished Flying Cross.

Captain Hatfield realized his beleaguered force had been saved by the

5 7

first miracle of Marine air. Sandino had launched a perfect surprise attack at Ocotal and had every expectation of a glorious victory. Instead, Ocotal became the most critical loss Sandino ever suffered.

Sandino learned from it. The diving war birds of the Marines could cause great damages any time he concentrated in the open in daylight. Henceforth he would seek concealment for his forces and train his machine gunners in anti-aircraft fire—another enemy tactic to be repeated one day in Southeast Asia.

Three months later Sandino gained partial revenge for his setback. His men shot down a Marine patrol aircraft and captured the two-man crew. In the process Sandino learned a peculiar trait about the United States military: Even in those early years, Americans would risk everything to rescue their downed aviators.

Observing the many Marine patrols beating the bush near the crash site, Sandino set a series of crafty ambushes which stung his enemies. Then he executed the aviators.

The Marines, incensed at this news, launched a major campaign to capture Sandino in his mountain fortress at El Chipote.

Two well-armed columns of Marines and *Guardias* converged on the strong point, well covered by tactical aircraft. But the Marines had telegraphed their punch and underestimated Sandino's strength. The guerrilla leader had time to prepare more ambushes, which bloodied the advance of both columns. Sandino then counterattacked in great force.

In a week-long running battle, he hammered the Marines back to the small town of Quilali. The Leathernecks hunkered down for a desperate siege, but they worried about their numerous wounded men, many critically hurt. The acting troop commander asked for medical evacuation by air "if humanly possible."

Rowell's aviators were willing enough, but there was no airstrip at Quilali, not even a suitable pasture near the mountain town. Time for Marine improvision.

A plane swooped over the town and dropped a bundle of tools. The infantry went to work converting the "main street" into an expeditionary runway—filling shell holes, leveling buildings, cutting back the jungle. Soon enough they had carved a 500-foot strip through the heart of town, ending abruptly in a sharp cliff.

Thirty-two-year-old Lieutenant Christian Schilt, a former aviation racer, volunteered for this mission, selecting one of the squadron's new Vought O2U–1 Corsairs for the job. Concerned with the extreme conditions, Schilt modified the snub-nosed biplane with oversized wheels to absorb the abrupt descent—and he flew without weapons or even a parachute in order to maximize his payload.

Schilt's chances were slim. The plane's thirty-six-foot wingspan would demand deft steering among the buildings lining the narrow street. And the Corsair had no brakes. Unless Marines posted along the street could grab the

Nicaragua, 1928: Marine First Lieutenant Christian F. Schilt stands beside his Vought O2U–1 Corsair, which he flew in and out of besieged Quilali ten different times. Schilt's sustained heroics—flying without weapons or a parachute to maximize his payload, landing precariously on the streets of the town without brakes, taking off with desperately wounded Marines while under heavy fire by Augusto Sandino's troops in the hills—resulted in a Medal of Honor. (U.S. Marine Corps)

wings as the plane roared past on its landing approach and slow it down like so many rodeo bulldoggers, the craft would whiz over the cliff.

Incredibly, this scheme worked—again and again. On three memorable days, January 6–8, 1928, Schilt made ten heart-stopping landings in "downtown Quilali," delivering 1,400 pounds of medicine, food, and ammo, then evacuating the most critically wounded Marines, two at a time.

Each landing required Schilt to make a steel-nerved approach, stalling his engine ten feet above the dusty street, then fluttering down in a series of bone-crunching bounces—Marines chasing along to grab the wings and dig in their boots like the old Keystone Kops. The Corsair would somehow shudder to a halt each time about 200 feet from the cliff.

Takeoffs were easier—except for Sandino's riflemen peppering the plane from the hills.

A few months later President Calvin Coolidge presented Lieutenant Schilt with the Medal of Honor at the White House. Schilt's bravura performance entered Marine legend and exemplified a Marine habit of one stubborn, hard-nosed man turning a battle.

The besieged Marines, now unfettered by their critically wounded, broke through Sandino's cordon and continued the pressure against El Chipote.

But Augusto Sandino, though deprived again of a rich bag of U.S. Marines and their weapons, continued to operate out of the trackless interior of Nueva Segovia.

Thinking of other ways of "skinning the cat" led Captain Merritt "Red Mike" Edson, the thirty-year-old commander of the Marine detachment on USS *Denver*, to propose a series of aggressive patrols up the Coco River, along the wild border between Nicaragua and Honduras. Gaining approval, he executed three "Coco River patrols" during 1928–1929, each sequentially longer, deeper, and bloodier. The effort hounded Sandino unmercifully, providing invaluable lessons in counterinsurgency. It even gained the grudging respect of the media.

At first glance there was little about Red Mike Edson to indicate his future emergence as one of the greatest combat leaders in the history of the Corps. The redheaded Vermonter seemed physically unimpressive until one noticed the baleful, ice-blue eyes of a gunfighter. His eyes never smile, people noted.

Edson's patrols survived grueling setbacks in the penetrating 350 miles through the unmapped region. Boats capsized in the rapids or were swept away in torrential floods; malaria struck each Marine; shoes rotted to pieces in the jungle muck; rations gave way to monkey meat and bananas. Edson was in his element. "This is a man's job if there ever was one," he wrote home, but "in spite of it all, I like it."

Edson had qualified as a Marine aviator earlier and knew the capabilities of that supporting arm.

Rusty Rowell's pilots always managed to find the small patrol in time for a critical resupply mission, the amphibians landing on a quiet stretch of the river or on a sandbar, the patrol craft dropping packages of food and weapons. And every day that they could get aloft, the aviators helped Edson search for Sandino's forces. "Pilots fly around houses at altitudes that permit the observers to look into windows and doors," reported Rowell.

By now, the Corps had adopted several Fokker tri-motor transports, good for delivering fresh troops—even fresh mules—to crude strips cut out of the jungle to keep Edson on the move.

Red Mike Edson went deep into the bush and stayed there for months, living off the land as necessary, relentlessly tracking Sandino's confederates. Firefights were vicious and point-blank. Many times the first ambush proved simply a ruse to lure the attackers into a larger killing zone. Edson's Marines, increasingly jungle-smart, rarely came out short on these exchanges.

A perhaps apocryphal story had a reporter asking if the prolonged operation didn't make the famously headlong Marines impatient. The laconic reply was said to be, "Shit, we don't live long enough to get impatient."

Sandino bitterly began pulling his forces away from the Coco, his main line of communications. Edson then decided to scrap his boats and follow the rebels inland. His report at that point tells much about the man:

> I have a territory some 200 miles long by 50 miles wide to cover with a
> force of 60 men. There are no supporting troops within 100 miles in any
> direction. The territory to be covered is that in which it is certain
> Sandino has concentrated his whole force. . . . If you can supply me with

food and clothing by air, I believe that my command can make it decid-
edly uncomfortable for the outlaws. There will be several casualties,
probably, but we hope the results will justify them. If approved, I shall
cut loose from boats, and using captured animals, move by trails.

Edson's eventual reassignment from Nicaragua (with a Navy Cross) must have come as a great relief to Augusto Sandino. But other promising Marine combat leaders arose to take his place.

The no-quarter fighting in these nasty little undeclared jungle wars had as their sole undisputed reward the training and hardening of many superb Marine officers who would command significant forces in the Pacific War to come. Among them were Julian Smith, Keller Rockey, and Harry Schmidt. But Sandino was particularly vexed by a hard-boiled pair of counterguerrilla fighters whose names had already achieved the status of legend in the American military: Gunnery Sergeant William "Iron Man" Lee and Lieutenant Lewis "Chesty" Puller.

Like Edson, Puller had learned early on the value of roving patrols in jungle warfare. In September 1932, Puller and Lee led their forty-man mounted company north of Jinotega, following a newly discovered guerrilla trail that led into the heart of Sandino's territory.

On September 26, after fighting their way through one ambush while crossing Agua Carta, Puller's force encountered a main enemy force of 150 men flanking them along two looming ridges. Gunnery Sergeant Lee, wounded twice in the initial outburst of firing, wrestled desperately with his one good hand to untie his Lewis gun from a terrified pack mule. Puller, dispatching forces up the higher ridge, covered him. Lee finally slashed the Lewis free with his knife—at no small cost to the mule—and swung the weapon to bear along the crest of the ridge.

Lee was a world-class shot with the whole family of military weapons. His cool shooting with the Lewis gun that afternoon made the difference. Puller's men gained the first ridge, then turned and fired down at the opposite ridge. The rebels broke contact, leaving a number of crumpled forms among the tree trunks and grassy slopes.

Puller paused to bury his dead in concealed graves, attended Lee and his other wounded men, then began a fighting return toward Jinotega.

The guerrillas, already hurting from the first encounter with these insane *gringos*, followed like wolves, hoping for a complete kill. But Puller paused at every defensible fold of ground to surprise and sting his pursuers with well-aimed, long-range rifle fire.

The patrol returned to Jinotega intact, having covered 150 miles, destroyed two dozen enemy camps, and killed at least thirty rebels.

For this savage running battle, both Puller and Lee received the Navy Cross, the second for Puller (who would retire with an unprecedented *five* Navy Crosses after the Korean War).

61

Sandino would outlast the assaults of enterprising combat leaders like Edson and Puller, but not by much. A year after the Marines left Nicaragua for good, the U.S.-trained *Guardia* lured Sandino to Managua and executed him.

The Marines might have known a moment of professional sadness to see their redoubtable old foe fall to trickery instead of a brisk Leatherneck assault.

The Marines' new role as suppressors of unfriendly unrest didn't end with the tiny nations. Most Marines in the interwar years rotated between overseas duties in not only Haiti and Nicaragua but also China, another nation rent by civil disorder and threatened by strong neighbors.

Although not involved in combat, the Leathernecks assigned to the Legation Guard at Peking or to the 4th Marines in Shanghai learned the ways of the Orient, which would prove invaluable in World War II.

Both Chesty Puller and Red Mike Edson scrutinized the Imperial Japanese military forces that occupied Shanghai and other major cities after the outbreak of the Sino-Japanese War in 1937. Edson was particularly interested in the *rikusentai*, the Special Naval Landing Forces.

Captain Evans Carlson, who with Edson would soon form the first Marine raider battalions, learned to speak Chinese, then boldly asked permission from Mao Tse-tung to spend a winter learning guerrilla warfare tactics from the masters of the art, the Communist Chinese Army in Yenan.

Another China Marine who developed combat instincts in the interwar years was First Lieutenant Victor Krulak. While assistant intelligence officer of the 4th Marines in 1937, Krulak observed a Japanese amphibious assault conducted against Liuho near the mouth of the Yangtze River. The amphibious expertise displayed by the Japanese impressed and alarmed "The Brute." "What we saw was that the Japanese were light-years ahead of us in landing craft design," he said.

Krulak photographed the Japanese's sturdy, bow-ramped landing craft and telegraphed a full report to the Navy's Bureau of Ships. (Two years later, puzzled at the lack of response, he visited the bureau and found his report in a dead file, annotated with the comment that it had been submitted by "some nut out in China.")

Krulak's experience with the Naval bureaucracy notwithstanding, the Marines and the Navy in the 1930s were finally merging along a similar path leading toward amphibious warfare.

Several conditions contributed. Lejeune's successors, especially Generals Ben Fuller and John Russell, continued to reconnect the Corps

A mule-mounted Marine patrol prepares to head into the jungled mountains along the northern Nicaraguan border in pursuit of Sandino's forces. (U.S. Marine Corps)

with the Navy. Russell almost single-handedly created the Fleet Marine Force in 1933, a naval "type command" responsive to the fleet commander.

By fortunate coincidence, this milestone coincided with new President Franklin Roosevelt's announcement of the Good Neighbor Policy in Latin America, at which the Marine brigades in Haiti and Nicaragua were at long last returned for more meaningful work with the fleet.

Fuller and Russell continued Lejeune's insistence on a combined arms force. The original Fleet Marine Force included aviation, engineers, light tanks, antiaircraft, and field artillery units as well as the infantry.

Then, in two remarkable years, the Marine Corps Schools at Quantico dropped everything to focus on the knotty issue of amphibious warfare.

The central, fundamental question: Could a fleet in this day and age launch a landing force from the sea against a beach defended by sophisticated weaponry and determined men and hold any chance for successful execution?

The Marines and several Navy officers examined the problem in microscopic detail, coldly, unblinkingly. The first step in answering the question was

Peiping, China, 1937. End of an era. The mounted detachment (known as "Horse Marines"— although they rode Mongolian ponies) of the Legation Guard prepares to pass in review against a backdrop of Chien Men and the Tartar Wall.
(U.S. Marine Corps)

to determine whether the amphibious debacle at Gallipoli in World War I marked the end of forcible assaults launched against opposition from the sea—or whether Gallipoli was somehow a bridge to the future.

THE LONG SHADOW OF GALLIPOLI

There were no United States Marines present at the battle that would haunt them as much as any in which they had fought: In 1915 the British War Cabinet had agreed to a bold plan proposed by Winston Churchill, First Lord of the Admiralty, to drive Turkey out of the war by forcing passage of the Dardanelles. Allied leaders decided to land ground troops to secure the Gallipoli Peninsula to permit naval passage through the adjoining straits. On April 25, a joint landing force of 78,000 English, French, Australian, and New Zealand troops struggled ashore on three primary beaches along sixty miles of coastline. The troops—ill-equipped and ill-trained for this mission—landed without benefit of intelligence, aerial bombing, specialized landing craft, or very much naval gunfire. German-trained Turkish troops slaughtered them in great numbers. Those who made it ashore clustered in miserable enclaves, mere toeholds, where they endured months of incessant shelling and rampant dysentery. Command was fragmented and halting. The campaign was an unmitigated disaster. The military world, watching this huge expedition unravel, reached the near-universal conclusion that modern weaponry had rendered large-scale amphibious landings downright suicidal in the twentieth century. The battle was waved in the face of every Marine attempt to establish their credibility with the amphibious weapon.

The study group concluded that, to hell with conventional wisdom, *Gallipoli could have been assaulted successfully*.

Amphibious warfare, they discovered, had certain inviolable principles. Of these, unity of command was paramount. There could only be one man, naval or ground, in command at any one point in time. There was a logical sequence of transfer of this command from sea to shore as the assault progressed. Also, there had to be at least temporary command of the seas—and the air and the subsurface—in the objective area for the assault to proceed. Good communications would be absolutely vital.

The most galling challenge was how to overcome the amphibious assault's inherent weakness, the fact that the whole affair begins with a single man—the first man ashore—facing the combined might of the defenders. There was a crying need for specialized landing craft to get great bunches of men, in tactical order, through the surf and on the beach as quickly as possible.

Tanks and howitzers would have to land right behind the assault troops. Solving the vulnerability of the ship-to-shore movement would prove the greatest hurdle.

Having digested all these corollaries and believing there was a future for amphibious warfare after all, the Navy and Marines resumed their annual fleet landing exercises.

But each exercise from 1934 to 1941 simply proved the point that amphibious landings are the most difficult of all military operations to execute.

Whatever could go wrong, went wrong. Boats landed on the wrong beaches or spilled their troops in the breakers. Experimental tank lighters went belly-up in the surf. Battleship gunners couldn't hit the target islands. Admirals and Marine or Army generals bristled at each other.

A caustic, scowling figure emerged from these annual nightmares of chaos and recrimination—Marine Brigadier General Holland M. (soon to be

nicknamed "Howlin' Mad") Smith, the nation's leading authority on amphibious assault.

As Smith struggled to teach amphibious warfare to the Army, Navy, and his own Marines, he vented his sulfurous spleen against the snail's pace of the Bureau of Ships in developing suitable ship-to-shore craft for the landing force. Holland Smith began to look elsewhere.

The search for the ultimate landing craft finally brought the Marines to Andrew Higgins. Higgins, an enterprising New Orleans boat designer, modified his proven, flat-bottomed, shallow-draft Eureka boat, used in bayou waters by oil-drillers and trappers, to include a retractable bow ramp and a protected propeller. It would be a world-shaking innovation, one that would defeat Germany and Japan as ineluctably as any other technology.

Neither Higgins nor the Marines suffered bureaucratic fools lightly. The competing "Bureau Boats"—top-heavy and unseaworthy—became laughing-stocks. Getting the Higgins boat accepted still took political infighting, but it was done in time to get adequate numbers of the thirty-six-foot craft to the fleet for the opening amphibious assaults in both theaters of war.

The enterprising Higgins also produced for the amphibious Navy a medium tank lighter, fifty feet in length, that could deliver a thirty-ton tank onto the beach via a retractable bow ramp.

The Higgins boats broke the gridlock on the ship-to-shore movement. It is impossible to overstate the tactical advantages his craft provided U.S. amphibious commanders in World War II. But Andrew Higgins would stand alone as a hero of amphibious boat design.

Inventor Donald Roebling's "Swamp Gator," a tracked amphibian designed to rescue downed aviators in the Everglades, caught the Marines' eye just before the new war erupted. Roebling's "Gator" could surf, climb reefs, negotiate marginal terrain, carry a large payload—ideal characteristics for amphibious warfare. Roebling modified his prototype to meet naval specs, leading to production of the ubiquitous LVT (Landing Vehicle Tracked). Known almost universally as "Alligators," they would serve all over the world, initially as logistics haulers, then—beginning with Tarawa—as the troop-carrying cutting edge of the amphibious assault.

The so-called "dead" years between the world wars had been anything but that for the Marines. They had bled and learned prodigiously, developed their unique role, and prepared with amazing foresight for the Pacific cauldron ahead.

Thanks to Roebling and Higgins and Holland Smith—and the visionary leadership of Pete Ellis and John Lejeune—the Marine Corps entered World War II with a promising new mission of forcible amphibious assault.

And thanks to Rusty Rowell and Christian Schilt—and Lejeune— Marine aviation had earned its rightful place in the Fleet Marine Force, in full and unique partnership with the infantry.

In the meantime, the Marines had shown the nation they still knew close

combat. The guerrilla skirmishes in Haiti against Charlemagne Peralte and in Nicaragua against Augusto Sandino had furnished a proving ground for a new generation of officers and NCOs, men who learned firsthand the rigors of hard campaigning, and the special discipline needed to break an enemy ambush.

In mid–1939 the Corps numbered slightly more than 18,000 Marines, roughly the size of the New York Police Department. But these few Marines now had a mission, and an organization, and a doctrine with which to help the nation fight a major naval war. Chasing Sandino had made the Marines the "skilled jungle fighters" envisioned by Pete Ellis. They were soon to become "skilled watermen," too.

Culebra Island, Puerto Rico, 1924. Marines wade ashore from a grounded, experimental landing craft, modeled after the armored "Beetle" boat used in the Gallipoli landings of 1915. The fifty-foot craft could carry sixty troops and—with great difficulty and under ideal conditions—disembark a 75mm field gun. The craft proved too large, cumbersome, and unseaworthy to meet the Marines' burgeoning amphibious needs. (U.S. Marine Corps)

5: ISSUE IN DOUBT

(World War II, 1941–1942)

COURAGE DISDAINS FAME AND WINS IT!

Inscription, Memorial Hall, Yale University

The United States Marine Corps, in effect, fought two WWIIs.

The first as an outmanned, outgunned, sorely underequipped force whose audacious attacks and defenses could reasonably hope to do little more than sting the relentless onslaught of an overpowering foe.

The second as a juggernaut of tactics, courage, and technology against which the most heavily defended bastions in the Pacific could not stand.

Yet it was this second stage of the Pacific amphibious war that produced the most shocking casualties for the Corps. The Marines landed, again and again, into the teeth of massive defensive forces that had used long months to tunnel and fortify strategic islands of terrifying terrain. They faced every defensive weapon, structure, and stratagem that a seasoned, cunning enemy could devise.

Wake Island, 1941. The pride of Wake's desperate defenses lay in the squadron of new Grumman F4F Wildcats flown with great élan by Marine Fighting Squadron 211. As VMF–211 battled daily against overwhelming Japanese aerial attacks, their dozen Wildcats dwindled down to a precious few. Marine mechanics cannibalized these wrecks from "The Boneyard" to keep the final planes airborne. At the end, out of planes, the squadron took up arms to fight as infantry. (U.S. Marine Corps)

No one would ever attempt to decide in which of these stages of a deadly war the Marines exhibited a more reckless and magnificent bravery.

For once the nation would go to war with plenty of Marines to go around. The Corps grew from 25,000 to 65,000 in the two-year grace period between the Nazi invasion of Poland and the Japanese surprise attack on Pearl Harbor.

Congress, the Roosevelt administration, and Major General Commandant Thomas Holcomb had taken prudent measures after the outbreak of war in Europe in 1939 to beef up the Corps toward wartime strength.

The Marines were able to mobilize their reserves, form the first two divisions and the first two aircraft wings in their history, and provide amphibious training (albeit still primitive) to all hands.

By November 30, 1941, the Marines already had 18,000 troops deployed overseas, including a provisional brigade in Iceland; five defense battalions strewn among Hawaii, Wake, Johnston, Palmyra, Samoa, and Midway; and the main body of the 4th Marines just completing their move from Shanghai to the Philippines.

But the widespread commitments took their toll. Both divisions were that in name only, their regiments scattered to hold the line.

"Issue in Doubt."
(Charles Waterhouse)

Pearl Harbor, Sunday Morning, December 7, 1941

The Marines' first bitter taste of death and defeat came only minutes into the opening of Japanese hostilities against the United States.

The main body of the Japanese strike force hit the sprawling naval base at Pearl Harbor at exactly 7:58 A.M. An American wireless operator tapped out the chilling alarm: "Air raid Pearl Harbor—This is no drill."

The Marine airbase at Ewa Mooring Mast Field, four miles west of Pearl Harbor, received the first Japanese air attack on that fateful Sunday. The surprise attacks caught the Marines just as flat-footed as the other services.

The attacking Japanese air squadrons struck Pearl Harbor two minutes after their first raid on Ewa Field. At the Navy Yard, a three-man Marine Color Guard stood poised to raise the colors at 0800. With two minutes to go, all hell broke loose. Let the record show that the Color Guard did execute "Colors" that awful morning, perhaps a bit hurriedly, but with proper flair and decorum. Then they dashed for the ammo lockers.

At Ewa all forty-seven planes of Marine Aircraft Group 21 (MAG–21) had been concentrated in the middle of the field, wing-to-wing, in obedience to the island commander's orders to "avoid sabotage." Japanese pilots streaking low over Ewa could not have asked for more lucrative targets. Within minutes the Zeros had destroyed or damaged every plane.

But one Japanese pilot observed a strange event that revealed the real nature of his otherwise hapless enemy.

As Lieutenant Yoshio Shiga, Imperial Japanese Navy, made a low-level firing run past the blazing wreckage, he saw a lone Marine standing upright beside a disabled plane, defiantly firing a pistol at Shiga's Zero. Intrigued, Shiga banked steeply and made a return sweep, this time aiming his machine guns at the erect Marine.

The man did not budge, just stood his ground and kept pinging away with his service automatic pistol. As Shiga later admitted: "This was the bravest American I ever encountered."

Lieutenant Shiga's confrontation with the lone *pistolero* represents a microcosm of the Marine Corps at the advent of World War II: brave-hearted but outgunned.

Marine shipboard contingents rushed into action as Kate torpedo bombers and Val dive-bombers commenced their thoroughly rehearsed destruction of "Battleship Row" along the southeast shore of Ford Island. The great ships desperately sounded General Quarters, and sailors and Marines struggled to distribute live ammo to their AA mounts, but most vessels were in their death throes in the first five minutes.

On the flagship *Arizona*, Marine Major Alan Shapley, a former quarter-back at the Naval Academy, had been relieved as commander of the Marine Detachment the day before, but had stayed around for a final intramural base-ball game on the seventh. Now he joined the patchwork teams of sailors and Marines trying to rescue trapped survivors.

Terrible explosions wracked the mighty ship. One blast blew Shapley overboard, into water filled with burning oil and struggling men. Shapley grabbed one of his wounded Marines and barely managed to "dog-paddle" them both to safety on Ford Island. There, exhausted but furious, he watched with sickened fascination as the Japanese naval air arm methodically destroyed the United States battle fleet.

Raging—and stark naked—Major Shapley limped across the fire-swept airfield searching desperately for a machine gun, any weapon. It was a miser-able way to start a war.

The *Arizona*'s Battle Division Marine Officer, Lieutenant Colonel Daniel Fox, had received the Navy Cross as an enlisted man at Blanc Mont in 1918 and survived the worst of the Nicaraguan patrols. Now Fox and the admiral he served, Isaac Kidd, both lay dying on board the flagship.

Other Marines in the eye of the storm on the burning, sinking ships gamely tried to save lives and return fire.

Sergeant Thomas Hailey escaped from *Oklahoma* just before she rolled over, swam to the battleship *Maryland*, and joined an antiaircraft gun crew blazing defiantly back at the waves of dive-bombers overhead. Evacuated to Ford Island—and still in his oil-stained skivvies—Hailey grabbed a rifle and went aloft on a patrol plane searching for the Japanese fleet. He was one of four Marine NCOs who would win the Navy Cross that morning.

The fiery Sunday morning seemed an eternity. Japanese fighters kept pounding Ewa Field on every passage to and from Pearl.

73

A strafing Zero wounded Lieutenant Colonel Claude "Sheriff" Larkin, commanding MAG–21, as he raced to the field from his quarters.

Master Technical Sergeant Emil Peters and Private William Turner climbed into the shattered rear cockpit of a shot-up dive-bomber and struggled to get the machine gun operational. Japanese pilots took sport in strafing their exposed plane, until Peters and Turner cut loose with a stream of well-aimed fire, downing a Val bomber. Their luck couldn't last. The Japanese swarmed around the pair, killing Turner, wounding Peters. But the Marines had drawn their first blood of the new war.

Machine gunners at the nearby Marine Barracks also made kills. While the Japanese aircraft concentrated on the Pacific Fleet ships in the harbor, the Marines at the Navy Yard had time to issue machine guns and ammo. Shooting at high-performance aircraft from a pedestal mount requires exceptional gunnery, but the Barracks Marines managed to down three Japanese dive-bombers.

Major Harold Roberts, acting commander of the 3d Defense Battalion, coolly broke out his entire panoply of antiaircraft weapons and deployed them around the parade ground of the barracks. The great din of the battle prevented normal fire-control communications, so Roberts positioned an improvised early-warning team in the middle of the field, accompanied by field musicians of the battalion band. The musicians would provide crude azimuth indicators by musical warnings: one blast for north, two for east, and so forth.

Effective as the system proved to be, Roberts's gunners were limited in their firing because they had no shells available for their 3-inch AA guns. Bitterly, all of the Marines' first rounds fired in anger in World War II came from handheld weapons—machine guns, rifles, pistols.

At last it was over. Pearl Harbor and much of the Pacific Fleet lay in smoking ruins. Among the dead were 112 Marines—108 from the ships' detachments, four at Eva Field. Many more were wounded or burned. More than 2,000 Americans had died; over 1,100 were wounded.

Marines fought elsewhere on that day of infamy. As the Japanese pilots departing Pearl Harbor sped toward their carriers, the destroyers *Akebono* and *Ushio* covered the fleet's withdrawal by shelling Midway Island. The two Japanese ships came close enough in the darkness of December 7–8 for the 6th Defense Battalion to open fire with not only their coast defense guns but their .50 caliber machine guns as well.

The Marine garrison, this time forewarned by virtue of the underwater telephone cable to Oahu, stood ready at full alert, but could do little better than at Pearl.

The Japanese proved to be better gunners. A well-aimed Japanese shell entered the air vent of Midway's concrete communications center, critically wounding First Lieutenant George Cannon and disrupting the garrison's switch-

board. Cannon refused medical evacuation until all other wounded Marines had been attended to and the switchboard restored to full operation. By then it was too late for Cannon; he had lost too much blood and died of his wounds.

The Japanese ships, damaged but not crippled, withdrew before light. Four Americans died, and nineteen lay wounded in the near point-blank duel. Cannon's family received a posthumous award of the Medal of Honor for his conspicuous bravery; he became the first Marine so honored in World War II.

Midway, Hawaii's principal outpost a thousand miles farther westward, assumed a role of enormous importance for the next half year. Her Marine defenders guessed correctly that the inevitable battle for the island would be a turning point in the war.

The huge Japanese armada had seemed to disappear in the Pacific mists. Stunned and incredulous, the Americans had no clue as to where the next blow would fall, but they now knew—painfully—how vulnerable their Hawaiian bastion was to Japanese carrier air strikes.

The immediate order of business was to get tactical aircraft to Midway. With the few available carriers committed to getting aircraft to the even more vulnerable Wake Island to the west, the only alternative in the emergency was to fly the small planes directly from Oahu.

Ten days after the Japanese attack, Marine Major Clarence Chappell led his squadron of seventeen SB2U Vindicator dive-bombers in a risky, ten-hour flight from Pearl to Midway—setting the world's record for the longest mass overwater single-engined flight.

But isolated, exposed Midway would require many more and much better aircraft than the miserably obsolescent Vindicators to have a fighting chance when the Japanese fleet returned.

The last weeks of 1941 would present a disheartening series of hopeless defenses for the Marine Corps. American islands far into the Western Pacific stood in the middle of a Japanese lake. There was no fragment of the ravaged United States Pacific Fleet that could stand against a full-strength Imperial Navy flushed with victory. Island defenses were frail, only partially in place, and with hardly the faintest possibility of reinforcement.

Allied forces gave way at all points. Swept up in this tidal wave were the small detachments of United States Marines in China and Guam.

In China, the Legation Guard in Peking and Tientsin never had a chance. Surprised and surrounded, the senior Marine ordered his men to capitulate, expecting repatriation with the other embassy personnel. It was not to be. The Japanese sent the diplomats home but threw the Marines in prison for the duration of the war.

In the port city of Chinwangtao, the rear echelon of the 4th Marines was within a day's labor of completing its embarkation aboard a transport, when the Japanese seized the ship and the Marines.

THE *RIKUSENTAI*—
"JAPANESE MARINES"

Two elite sea services, the U.S. Marines and the Japanese Special Naval Landing Forces, called *rikusentai,* would clash often and bloodily throughout the Pacific War.

The *rikusentai*—naval infantry trained for combat both afloat or ashore—formally appeared in 1886. Japanese recruiters traditionally selected young men of exceptional physical fitness and initiative.

At the onset of WWII, the *rikusentai* spearheaded amphibious campaigns in China, Java, Rabaul, and the Solomons. By mid–1942, the *rikusentai* numbered 50,000 men, one-eighth the Imperial Navy.

The *rikusentai* and U.S. Marines first squared off against each other at Guam and Wake in December 1941.

The Kure 3d Special Naval Landing Force would fight to the last man against the 1st Marine Division at Tulagi and Gavutu.

The greatest slugfest between the two forces occurred at Tarawa in November 1943, a Pyrrhic American victory that still stands as the bloodiest daily casualty rate any Marine division ever experienced.

Finally, in one of the last violent encounters of the war, the 6th Marine Division crushed Rear Admiral Minoru Ota's Naval Guard Force on the Oroku Peninsula of Okinawa. Ota, the last of the old-time *rikusentai,* had fought against the Marines two years earlier in the jungles of New Georgia. In the Okinawa fighting, Ota and his 5,000 sailors died hard in the ten-day battle, inflicting 1,600 casualties upon the attacking Marines.

Needless to say, respect among the elite foes was grudging but mutual.

The only spark of resistance flared briefly at the nearby railhead, where legendary Marine Gunner "Iron Man" Lee of Nicaragua fame issued his men automatic weapons and prepared to take on a Japanese regiment. Lee's commander averted the inevitable massacre by ordering the diehards to lay down their arms. These men joined the Legation Guard in captivity.

American forces on Guam were doomed in advance by two events that occurred years before the outbreak of war.

Much earlier, the League of Nations recognized Japan's participation on the winning side in World War I by mandating to her all of Germany's island possession in the Pacific. This capricious windfall gave the Japanese possession of such strategic island groups as the Marshalls, Marianas, Carolines, and Palaus. In the Marianas, Japanese possession (and illegal militarization) of the neighboring islands of Saipan, Tinian, and Rota made American Guam terribly vulnerable.

Then, in the late 1930s, a tightfisted Congress, fearful of provoking the unpredictable Japanese, voted against upgrading Guam's meager defenses, despite earnest testimony to the contrary by Navy and Marine officers. Japanese war planners thus viewed Guam as a peach ripe for plucking.

Within hours of the Pearl Harbor raid, the Guam garrison, which included 153 Marines, came under air attack from Saipan-based Japanese aircraft. The Japanese had planned their invasion intelligently. Among the first targets for the bombers was the Americans' heaviest "weapon" on the island, a single pathetic 3-inch antiaircraft gun on the minesweeper *Penguin,* berthed in Apra Harbor. The first thunderous explosions erased that capability.

Defending themselves with nothing larger than .30 caliber machine guns, the Guam Marines, assisted by naval personnel and a stouthearted detachment of native police, endured several days of punishing aerial bombardment.

Their futile predicament reached a climax on December 10 when 5,500 Japanese soldiers made a successful predawn landing at Tumon Bay, southwest of the capital at Agana, while 400 Japanese naval infantry, the storied *rikusentai*, stormed ashore at Dungcas Beach to the north.

Marine Lieutenant Charles Todd led a small force of native troops that twice repelled the invaders from Agana with well-aimed fire, but this was little more than a hopeless delaying action. Soon Guam's governor, Navy Captain George McMillan, ordered the fruitless resistance to end.

Among the nineteen dead were four Marines. Twelve others were wounded in the brief but spirited defense of the island outpost. The survivors spent the remainder of the war in a particularly brutal prison camp in mainland Japan.

Like the doomed defenders of the Alamo, looking for relief that never came and having no idea that their defense would have any long or resounding memory, the Marines of Wake Island dug in for the worst the enemy could throw.

The small sand spit, lightly garrisoned and remote from relief by the now-crippled U.S. Fleet, would provide the Empire with one more outpost in the north-central Pacific, a stepping-stone to Midway.

Just before the war began, Admiral William "Bull" Halsey had delivered Marine Major Paul Putnam's squadron of twelve F4F Wildcats to the island. The ground forces, commanded by the 1st Defense Battalion's fiery Major James Devereux, possessed an uncommon amount of gall and grit.

Quickly, Japanese long-range bombers from the Marshalls and the freshly captured Gilberts were bombing the island with relative impunity. Eight of the dozen Marine fighters were caught on the ground and destroyed. The damaged remainder were glued together with parts scavenged from the wrecks.

On December 11, the day after they steamrollered Guam, a Japanese invasion force approached Wake, expecting another easy conquest.

But Wake Island would not die easily.

The Marines ambushed the Japanese invasion force with a scorching fire from their handful of 5-inch and 3-inch coast defense guns. Devereux made his gunners wait until the ships had steamed into the "can't miss" range.

Every round splattered Japanese steel and blood into the Pacific. The destroyer *Hayate* went down, the first Japanese surface craft to be sunk by Americans in this enormous Pacific War.

As the Japanese ships steamed away in disarray, Major Putnam's stitched-together Wildcats chased them with 100-pound bombs. Captain Henry Elrod planted one squarely on the fleeing destroyer *Kisaragi*, a beautiful shot, which exploded with great violence, sending the ship to the bottom.

Suddenly in gloomy, fearful America, there came news of a great victory by the outnumbered, outgunned force on tiny Wake against the Imperial Japanese Navy. The Wake garrison and its Marines, under the overall command

of Navy Commander Winfield Scott Cunningham, had sunk two ships, damaged several more, shot down three bombers, and in all killed 500 Japanese without a single casualty. A glorious American victory after a dismal string of humiliations.

Now Wake became a matter of national pride on both sides. The Japanese, stung and embarrassed by this setback, doubled their air raids and dispatched a larger assault force for Wake.

From Pearl Harbor sailed a small American relief force. Spirits were high. But the naval high command was in disarray. The Pacific Fleet commander had been relieved of command in disgrace. The new designee, Admiral Chester Nimitz, was still en route, and the temporary commander was unwilling to risk his three remaining carriers at extreme range against unknown Japanese threats.

To the utter disgust of all hands, the American relief force turned back. The Wake garrison was doomed. But the Marines would go down fighting.

By now, the Americans on Wake had spotted carrier aircraft taking part in the Japanese air raids and realized a new invasion force had closed the range.

No matter. Major Putnam's aviators took off in their patched-up Wildcats to fly in the face of every approaching Japanese air strike. One by one, the Wildcats went down for good. On December 21, the twelfth and last Grumman crashed, and the survivors of Marine Fighter Squadron 211, less than a third of their original numbers, reported to Major Devereux as auxiliary infantrymen.

At 2:35 A.M. on December 23, the Japanese *rikusentai* poured out of their landing craft onto the island. U.S. Marines, sailors, and civilians opened up a hot fire. The fighting ashore raged for hours. In one sector, the remaining aviators fought off several hundred Japanese until every pilot fell to the overwhelming fire. Among the slain: Captain "Hank" Elrod, whose sustained bravery in the air and on the ground would make him the first Marine aviator to receive the Medal of Honor in this war.

Just before dawn, Commander Cunningham sent a taut message to Pearl: "Enemy on island; issue in doubt."

The Marines fought on desperately beyond hope. Small groups of defenders launched impromptu counterattacks which surprised the Japanese and drove them back at certain points. Marines and *rikusentai* engaged in particularly violent brawling, setting the tone for the coming bloodbaths in the later war. The dunes became dotted with clumps of bodies of both sides—frequently locked together in death.

Unwilling to preside over the wholesale slaughter of his exhausted garrison—and now aware that the relief expedition had turned back—Cunningham ordered his men to surrender. This took some doing. Small bands of defiant Marines kept knocking off Japanese sailors with rifle fire for hours. Major Devereux had to walk the entire line with a white flag to compel his men to surrender. Many wept in rage and frustration.

Forty-nine Marines, three sailors, and about seventy civilians died in the fight for Wake Island. The garrison inflicted about 1,100 casualties against the Japanese invaders. Marines had gotten their first chance to show what they could do, and it had been magnificent.

The defense of Wake had been a national inspiration, but its fall was a disaster for its defenders. The Japanese shipped the Marines and other military personnel to the same prison camp in Shanghai as the North China Marines (after beheading five POWs en route).

The hunger for vengeance would persist like a collective toothache among the Leathernecks. Each Marine who shipped out for the Pacific after December 23 hoped to be among the landing force that would someday recapture Wake and avenge the gallant 1st Defense Battalion and VMF–211.

The 44 officers and 728 men of Colonel Samuel Howard's 4th Marines had leapt from a bonfire into a volcano. Having evacuated Shanghai (minus their now imprisoned rear echelon) in late November, they now arrived in the Subic Bay area of the Philippines a week before the war swept them up. In limbo at first, the regiment swung into action after December 20 when General Douglas MacArthur, commanding the defense, requested their transfer to his command.

The Marines were due to take part in another of the hopeless fights that were becoming a depressing American specialty. If the American defense of Wake Island illuminated the darkness on the home front like a bolt of lightning, the five-month battle to hold on to the Philippines was more like a lingering sunset—breathtakingly spectacular, full of hope, but doomed as well.

MacArthur would prove his brilliance in the years to come, but his defense of the Philippines reflected little of his later military forethought or decisiveness. His bomber force caught on the ground, MacArthur swiftly faced a confident, veteran, invasion force advancing from five directions.

Having been defeated on all fronts, MacArthur declared Manila an "open city" and funneled his forces southward into the narrow, more-defensible Bataan Peninsula for a final stand.

The Marines' first role was destruction, but, to their furious frustration, not of the enemy. They torched the U.S. Naval bases at Olongapo and Cavite, then moved to Mariveles, at the southern tip of Bataan, and crossed to Corregidor, the island fortress guarding the mouth of Manila Bay.

Colonel Howard left one battalion behind on Bataan to protect the Mariveles base and guard against Japanese amphibious assaults along the peninsula's flanks.

In late January 1942, when 900 men of the Japanese 20th Infantry landed behind the American lines at Quinauan Point, the Marines at Mariveles joined the counterattacks.

Providing a brief lift to sagging morale, the GIs, Marines, and Filipinos actually thwarted the imperial landings, winning the so-called "Battle of the

"Out of the frying pan . . ."
The 4th Marines left Shanghai for the Philippines just before the war began. Here a machine gun company uses hand carts to transport their weapons from Subic Bay to join forces with General MacArthur's force trying to hold the Bataan Peninsula in late 1941. Ahead lay Corregidor, the death march, years of brutal captivity.
(U.S. Marine Corps)

Points" and throwing the invaders back into the sea—something the Japanese were never able to do to the Marines.

On March 12, President Roosevelt ordered General MacArthur to leave Corregidor for Australia, there to undertake the rebuilding and reorganizing of Allied forces in the Southwest Pacific.

The Marines left behind on Luzon bitched much less about MacArthur's leaving than they did about the government which seemed to have written them off without making any significant attempt to reinforce or resupply. They couldn't comprehend that the Japanese destruction of much of the proud Pacific Fleet that they were part of had rendered the Philippines out of reach for untold months.

On April 3, as Japanese forces launched a renewed offensive on Luzon, the weakened American-Filipino line crumbled.

Bataan fell six days later. There were 105 members of the 4th Marines among the 75,000 defenders who stumbled northward on the infamous Death March toward the POW camps.

Meanwhile, the Japanese quickly turned the full force of their field artillery and tactical aircraft against Corregidor. The small island now contained an interservice concentration of 11,000 Americans and Filipinos, survivors of the mainland fighting, all of them sickly, half-starved, and grim-faced.

Colonel Howard's 4th Marines, reinforced by stalwarts of every service, braced for the inevitable. For twenty-seven dreadful days, the garrison sustained a terrible pounding from Japanese gunners and aviators. The Marines dug in, scanning the bay for signs of the invasion force, almost welcoming the chance for one last grapple with the enemy. The emaciated survivors resembled walking skeletons.

The Japanese now called all the shots. On May 5 they commenced their most fierce bombardment of the campaign. Tiny Corregidor trembled and smoked. After dark, a Japanese battalion landed at North Point. A second battalion arrived before midnight.

The Marines greeted each landing party on the beach, and the battle raged all night at extremely close range.

Platoon Sergeant William "Tex" Haynes led one counterattack, emptying a pair of pistols at the swarming invaders, then manhandling a .30 caliber machine gun to hose down the beachfront.

Startled Japanese screamed and tumbled; survivors hit the deck and lobbed grenades at the fearsome "human tank." One exploded at Haynes's feet, and he went down for good. The Japanese leapt past his body and hastened forward. Soon they had machine guns positioned on the hogback near Malinta Hill, shooting every counterattack to pieces.

Two "Old Corps" veterans, Sergeant Major Thomas Sweeney and Quartermaster Sergeant John Haskin—combining fifty years of experience between them—led desperate attempts to outflank the enemy guns. By sheer audacity Sweeney and Haskin destroyed one machine gun crew, but nearby Japanese riflemen popped up and shot both men to death, ending the last counterattack.

By noon, the battle for Corregidor was over. Two Marines carried General Jonathan Wainwright's flag of truce into the Japanese lines. The surviving Leathernecks smashed their rifles and machine guns against rocks.

A distraught Colonel Howard ordered his regimental colors burned, exclaiming, "My God, and I had to be the first Marine officer ever to surrender a regiment."

In a painful midnight broadcast, Wainwright ordered his forces to lay down their arms. The heroic defense of the Philippine Islands passed into history. The war was five months old.

Marine casualties on Corregidor totaled nearly 700 in killed and wounded. At battle's end, Colonel Howard led 1,282 Marines into captivity. Of that number, 239 would not survive their harsh, years-long detention.

On May 2, 1942, Admiral Nimitz flew out to Midway to inspect the defenses and talk to the local commanders, among them Lieutenant Colonel Harold Shannon, commanding Marine forces on the atoll.

Nimitz had been generous in building up Midway's defenses from the beginning of his command. The squadron of Vindicator dive-bombers that had made the record-setting hop to Midway had been reinforced by a squadron of Brewster F2A–3 Buffalos, and a battery of seven-inch guns had arrived there on Christmas Day. But Nimitz and Shannon both knew that the obsolescent Vindicators and Buffalos would not stand a chance against Japanese carrier aviation; and the seven-inch guns had been taken from pre–World War I battleships and stored for decades.

When Nimitz asked Shannon what he needed to defend against the coming invasion, the Marine officer ticked off a list of basic necessities: modern fighters and torpedo bombers, more and better coast defense and AA guns, better radars, more ground forces, more fortification material.

Nimitz came through. Three weeks later the Midway Marines received sixteen SBD–2 dive-bombers and seven Grumman F4F–3 Wildcat fighters. Then came a ship loaded to the gunwales with antiaircraft guns, pallets of barbed wire, a platoon of light tanks, and two companies of Marine Raiders.

Shannon put all hands to work improving the defenses. He installed double-apron barbed wire, antiboat obstacles, and crude mines of boxes filled with dynamite and twenty-penny nails along the beaches. He trained his reinforced garrison endlessly in emergency drills.

There was no time to waste, Nimitz warned the Marines. A great Japanese armada could be expected in early June. Low-lying Midway hunkered down, anticipating the vast, Japanese typhoon approaching from the western horizon. It was a killer typhoon.

Imperial forces controlled the air and seas throughout an enormous arena ranging from the Kuriles to the Gilberts to the Solomons and on past Southeast Asia into the Indian Ocean. They had succeeded beyond their wildest dreams of conquest. But now Japan's top military and naval leaders succumbed to "Victory Disease," believing themselves invincible in any distant theater.

Thus was born the ambitious plan to seize Midway and the Aleutians and threaten Hawaii. Admiral Isoroku Yamamoto, the gifted Commander-in-Chief of the Japanese Combined Fleet, expressed confidence that this complex plan would draw the still-crippled U.S. Pacific Fleet into decisive action, where he would overwhelm the surviving carriers.

And with the American carriers gone, the thin line of Marines ashore on Midway would be the last, slim line of defense before Hawaii and the U.S. West Coast. The audacious Marines, seeming destined to fight a whole war of glorious last stands, rooted fervently for their equally beleaguered sister service on the waves.

Luckily for the Marines, Admiral Nimitz, rich in codebreaking intelligence, commanded the Pacific Fleet with a brilliant mixture of nerve and common sense, engineering a masterful carrier ambush. But it would be a near thing.

The small atoll suffered the brunt of the early action of the ensuing Battle of Midway (June 3–6, 1942), even though the crucial fighting took place between opposing carrier forces hundreds of miles to the northwest.

On the morning of June 4, the approaching Japanese carriers launched 108 planes to strike the atoll. Alerted by radar, the fighters of Marine Aircraft Group 22 streaked aloft and met the raiders head-on.

It was a turkey shoot for the skilled, veteran Japanese Navy pilots flying against Marine fighters that ranged from obsolescent to antiquated. The hapless Brewster Buffalos and even the newer Wildcats were no match for the Zeros flown by the cream of the Imperial Fleet Air Wing. Marine Fighter Squadron 221 lost fifteen aircraft and its squadron commander in this dogfight.

The Japanese formation continued, although now disorganized and behind schedule. Midway's patient Marine antiaircraft gunners knocked several bombers spinning into the sea, but the island sustained a terrific pounding. Fires raged at all points. Yet through the smoke and flames came the steady throb of AA batteries seeking targets among the enemy formations.

Ground fire was so spirited, in fact, that a Japanese flight officer radioed, "There is need for a second attack wave." The fateful decision to execute that strike would lead to the turning point of battle.

While the Japanese were rearming and refueling their planes for this unplanned second attack, the carrier planes of Admiral Raymond Spruance caught them flat-footed, sinking four fleet carriers and changing the balance of power in the Central Pacific.

As the great battle raged, Midway's Marines continued to pay a ghastly price. Major Lofton Henderson led his squadron of SBD dive-bombers against the Japanese carriers, but swarms of Zeros flying over the fleet intercepted the Marines just as they began peeling off to attack. In the one-sided melee Lofton and seven other dive-bombers went down in flames.

On June 5, Captain Richard Fleming led six of the old Vindicators in a dive-bombing attack against the slightly crippled cruiser *Mikuma*. Ferocious antiaircraft fire riddled Fleming's plane. He held course and deliberately crashed his flaming Vindicator into *Mikuma*'s after-gun turret, setting fire to the starboard engine room, slowing her to the point that Spruance's pursuit planes found and sank her the following day.

Captain Fleming, the forty-ninth and final Marine to die during the Battle of Midway, received the posthumous Medal of Honor.

On June 14, 1942, five weeks after the fall of the Philippines and barely a week after the Battle of Midway, the 1st Marine Division arrived in New Zealand

from its stateside training bases. Major General Alexander Vandegrift, a veteran of combat at long-ago Veracruz, held command.

The division was not, in Vandegrift's considered opinion, fully trained or equipped for offensive combat (in fact, the 7th Marines had been detached for defense of Samoa), but he hoped that six more months of intensive field training in New Zealand would provide the necessary boost.

Vandegrift and many apprehensive fellow officers knew that the role of the Corps in the coming years would require a revolution in the art of amphibious warfare. That was why several key Marines had been conspicuously absent from Pearl Harbor on December 7. They had been on board the cruiser *Indianapolis* conducting amphibious tests at Johnston Island. Their objective had been to determine whether a loaded Higgins boat could cross a coral reef.

The results had been sobering: The workhorse landing craft required nearly four feet of water over a reef to clear the obstacle safely. At lower tides, something else—as yet undefined—would be needed. That would take time to develop, likely a good deal of time.

But just eleven days after arriving in New Zealand, Vandegrift got the shock of his life. An emergency in the Solomons would require his understrength division to execute an amphibious assault within the next six weeks, ready or not.

His objective was a strange-sounding place he had never heard of—*Guadalcanal.*

Midway, June 1942. A brave flight crew in a Vought SB2U–3 Vindicator, an obsolete, fabric-covered dive-bomber, takes off from Midway to attack the Imperial Navy's carrier force 150 miles to the northwest. Major Lofton R. Henderson led his Marine Scout Bombing Squadron 241 in a series of uneven attacks against the enemy fleet, losing eight aircraft and his own life. Two months later the Marines would name the captured Japanese airstrip on Guadalcanal in his honor. (U.S. Marine Corps)

GOD FAVORS THE BOLD
AND THE STRONG OF HEART.

Major General Alexander Vandegrift to the 1st Marine Division
before D-Day at Guadalcanal and Tulagi, August 1942

The first terror of even the boldest landing force is not the enemy entrenched before it, but the thought that it might be cut off, left behind to wither and die on a hostile beach without reinforcement or sustenance. When the vitally interlocked support from air and sea that is essential to any landed amphibious operation vanishes in the middle of a closely fought battle, courage and sacrifice will count for nothing as bullets, food, and men melt away. Even the threat of such disaster might demoralize the best. But the Marines facing such on Guadalcanal would prove themselves better than the best.

Dead Japanese soldiers of the Ichiki Detachment lay half-buried in the sands of the river delta after the twenty-four-hour battle of the Tenaru in August 1942.
(U.S. Marine Corps)

A bomber strip!

As General Vandegrift studied his crude maps of the area, he could vividly see the emergency that prompted the Joint Chiefs of Staff to order an amphibious assault so precipitously. New aerial photographs revealed ominous evidence of Japanese construction troops busily carving a long runway out of Guadalcanal's jungles.

Japanese bombers flying out of Guadalcanal would jeopardize tenuous American positions for hundreds of miles, from New Caledonia to New Guinea. Such a forward base would create a giant "bulge" in the vital sea-lanes between the United States and Australia, further constricting the flow of war materials being shipped to the South Pacific. This would be a helluva fight, and it had to be made.

Guadalcanal is a good-sized, jungle-covered island in the southern Solomons, lying just north of the Coral Sea off Australia. Already, the Japanese Navy operated a seaplane base at Tulagi, nineteen miles north of Guadalcanal across Sealark Channel. A new base would nail the coffin shut.

Vandegrift's plea for six more months of work-up training fell on deaf ears. While there were five U.S. Army divisions in the region, only the 1st Marine Division possessed amphibious prowess. His division would comprise the landing force for Operation Watchtower, the amphibious seizure of Guadalcanal and Tulagi from the Japanese.

If August 1, 1942, was impossible, D-Day could be slipped to August 7—but no later.

Vandegrift took a deep breath and went to work. One consolation came to mind: No one, including the Japanese, expected the first U.S. offensive in the Pacific before 1943.

Vandegrift's initial "enemies" proved not to be the Japanese but frustrating local issues of inadequate resources, scant time, and fuzzy command relations. There were by no means sufficient amphibious ships and landing craft on hand to do the job right. The few available transports had been loaded "administratively" because the division had sailed from the States without a tactical mission. They needed "combat loading," the critical supplies positioned for early offload—and to hell with efficient use of space.

In very short order, the Marines had to devise a landing plan and scheme of maneuver ashore; then they had to empty each ship and carefully reembark their gear to support the tactical plans.

Compounding the problem was the fact that not even the Marines had been able during the austerity of peacetime to practice loading and landing their logistics tail, the humongous, space-eating herd of trucks and tractors and generators—plus a month's worth of "bullets, Band-Aids and beans."

The reembarkation was not pretty. Each day it rained. The Wellington piers became a nightmarish scene of disarray as the inexperienced Marines attempted to restuff their dangerously misloaded transports.

Vandegrift's division, the cutting edge of the Fleet Marine Force, would

Marine Raider,
Guadalcanal
(Charles Waterhouse)

go into combat equipped with World War I weapons and equipment—the same Springfield "03" rifles, tin hats, and crude gas masks that their fathers may have worn at Belleau Wood.

Then there was the chain of high command. Guadalcanal lay squarely along the fault line between the two powerful and competing theater commanders: Douglas MacArthur and Chester Nimitz. The Joint Chiefs dodged the issue, first by tinkering with the boundaries to give Guadalcanal to Nimitz, then by establishing under Nimitz a separate subtheater, the South Pacific Area, under Vice Admiral Robert Ghormley.

Ghormley was a reluctant commander. His flagship remained moored to a pier in New Caledonia.

He gave tactical command of the Guadalcanal invasion to Vice Admiral Frank Fletcher, whose perceived priority would be the protection of his three carriers.

Rear Admiral Kelly "Terrible" Turner would command the amphibious force and interact most closely with the Marines. Turner proved to be as tempestuous and arbitrary as he was brilliant and fearless. In his initial view, the Marine landing force comprised merely another naval unit that he could diddle with at will, even after the main body had stormed ashore.

This left many ragged edges for Vandegrift to grapple with. At one point during the campaign he would have to seek intervention from Nimitz and Commandant Holcomb. (Only later, when Nimitz began pairing "Terrible" Turner with General "Howlin' Mad" Smith, did true unity of command in amphibious operations evolve.)

The Imperial Navy had suffered an irreversible defeat at Midway, but the Combined Fleet still commanded the sea and air in the South Pacific. Attaining strategic surprise in launching the attack would be crucial to the Marines' success since the unsuspecting Japanese currently maintained only modest forces in Guadalcanal and Tulagi.

The problem was this: The islands could be reinforced rapidly by Imperial Navy forces steaming down a line of islands (The Slot) from the great Naval fortress at Rabaul. Likewise, from its well-developed circle of tactical airfields around Rabaul, the Japanese air arm could launch day and night attacks throughout the Solomons.

Rabaul also served as headquarters for the Seventeenth Japanese Army, commanded by Lieutenant General Haruyoshi Hyakutake. The Seventeenth Army contained many veterans of the conquests of Malaya and the Dutch East Indies, currently the best jungle fighters in the world. The understrength Watchtower task force would be entering the edge of a hornet's nest.

The 1st Marine Division in August 1942 included about one man in ten who had seen previous combat, typically in Central America. The great majority of the Marines were green recruits or newly commissioned lieutenants who had joined the Corps in the wave of patriotism that swept the nation at the news of Pearl Harbor.

89

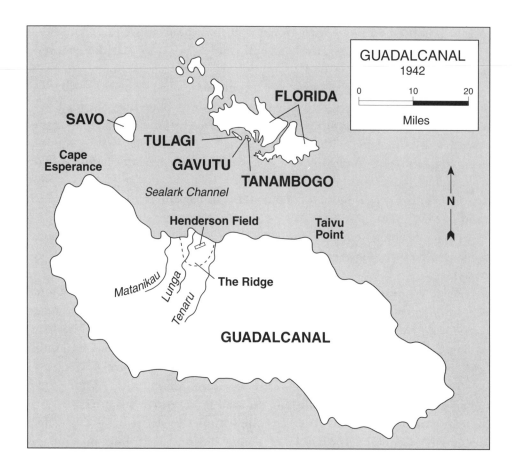

Vandegrift and his commanders had little time to harness the enthusiasm of the new men to the field savvy of the veterans. The 1st Division was a conglomerate—missing the 7th Marines but reinforced by the 2d Marines, plus three new units, the 3d Defense Battalion, the 1st Parachute Battalion, and Lieutenant Colonel "Red Mike" Edson's 1st Raider Battalion.

Vandegrift figured to divide his landing force on D-Day. The 1st Marines and most of the 5th Marines would seize Guadalcanal's airfield. The raiders, parachutists, the 2d Marines, and the remainder of the 5th Marines would capture Tulagi and the nearby islets of Gavutu and Tanambogo.

The airfield became the first and final key to the battle for Guadalcanal, and Vandegrift never wavered in his appreciation of its operational value. He would hold on to the grassy strip against the howling forces of hell.

In the blackness preceding the Pacific dawn of August 7, the Allied invasion convoy eased past Cape Esperance, entered Sealark Channel (soon and forever to be known as "Ironbottom Sound"), and split into the two elements attacking north and south of brooding Savo Island.

Shortly after 6 A.M. the cruisers and destroyers opened a noisy fire against both sets of landing objectives. Navy carrier planes streaked overhead. From the Japanese on Tulagi came this astonished, plain-language message to

Rabaul: "Enemy task force of twenty ships attacking Tulagi, undergoing severe bombings, landing preparations underway; help requested."

This flash report came as a thunderbolt to every Japanese officer in the South Pacific. Surely this was a raid, a mere diversion! Tulagi's final message slammed home the reality: "Enemy troop strength overwhelming. We will defend to the last man." The Japanese airfields around Rabaul began to throb with frenzied activity.

Eight months to the day after Pearl Harbor, the United States Navy and Marines had launched a major amphibious offensive against the startled Japanese garrisons in the southern Solomons.

Turner and Vandegrift actually executed five landings that day—one, the main effort, on Red Beach, near the mouth of the Tenaru River, at Guadalcanal, and four in and around Tulagi.

The 5th Marines led the way at Guadalcanal, splashing ashore at 9:09 A.M. from their hodgepodge assortment of landing boats. They dashed across the sand to the high-water mark, then hit the deck in prone firing positions—each man gasping in the heat, braced against the expected enemy fusillade. And . . . nothing. An eerie silence prevailed. So total had been the surprise that only a handful of *rikusentai* guarded the whole island.

The 5th Marines, hardly trusting their good fortune, pressed on, crossed the river by means of an improvised bridge thrown along the broad backs of a trio of LVT–1 Alligators, then headed guardedly toward the airfield.

The 1st Marines soon landed, crossed the bridge, and followed in trace. "Hot damn—a cakewalk!"

Things were much different to the north across Sealark Channel. Edson's Raiders had landed smoothly on Tulagi, but soon the shocked *rikusentai* of the 3d Kure Special Naval Landing Force began a grim defense, fighting the Marines with all they had. Edson required the help of two infantry battalions to finish the job in forty-eight hours. The Kure sailors died hard, shooting down 150 Marines in the process.

Gavutu and Tanambogo proved even harder nuts to crack. Because the landing force lacked sufficient boats to launch all five assaults simultaneously, the 1st Parachute Battalion's assault on Gavutu had to wait until afternoon. By that time, the *rikusentai* defending the twin islets (joined by a 300-yard causeway) had settled deep into their caves and pillboxes.

The Marines and Navy could have seen the terrible future of Tarawa, Saipan, and Peleliu in the obscure assault on Gavutu and Tanambogo.

Coral reefs channeled the landing boats into one predictable approach. Naval gunfire proved inadequate and insufficient. The Japanese allowed the first wave to touch down to mask the supporting shipborne fires, then cut loose on the succeeding waves.

The commander of the parachute battalion went down with a Nambu bullet in his lungs; two staff officers died beside him. The parachutists scrambled ashore and bravely took the fight uphill to the fortified caves, but this was

91

THE BATTLE HISTORY OF THE US MARINES

a small, lightly equipped battalion, and the job was too much for them. Reinforcements from the 2d Marines helped, but the Japanese machine guns still swept the beaches and ravines.

Calls for support from Navy carrier planes proved counterproductive. Twice they bombed and strafed concentrations of U.S. Marines. A hastily organized night attack against Tanambogo failed miserably. It took another battalion of the 2d Marines and point-blank fire from destroyers before the landing force could overwhelm the diehard defenders on the second day.

The savage fighting on Tulagi and the islets contrasted markedly with the quiet progress experienced by the bulk of the 1st Marine Division on Guadalcanal. By the second day the 5th Marines had seized the airfield intact. Alerted by friendly Coast Watchers up the island chain, the amphibious force sustained the first swarm of Japanese bombers with acceptable losses. Vandegrift worried about the haphazard offload of supplies, still stacked precariously on Red Beach because the shore party lacked the numbers and the expertise to disperse the mountains of gear inland. He also worried about the inadequacy of his maps. What the Marines called the Tenaru River was really the Ilu. The dominant terrain feature, Mount Austen, was not at all adjacent to the beachhead but several miles inland through very heavy jungle.

Admiral Fletcher had greater concerns. The first day's dogfights with the experienced Japanese Zero pilots escorting the bomber raids had cost him dearly in planes and pilots. He worried—some would say obsessively—about the vulnerability of his carriers.

On the second day he startled the amphibians by announcing his decision to withdraw his force out of range "to refuel." Turner and Vandegrift protested. Debarkation of the Marines and their combat cargo was still far from complete—the thin-skinned amphibious ships were terribly exposed in their anchorages. Fletcher reminded them that the Marines still had the protection of the four large cruisers (three American, one Australian) in Sealark Channel.

That night of August 8–9, a Japanese naval force under Vice Admiral Gunishi Mikawa moved undetected down The Slot, caught the American screening force by surprise, and launched a violent attack.

Mikawa's deadly, oxygen-powered Long Lance torpedoes, far superior to anything in the Allies' inventory, did their lethal work. Within half an hour, all four of the Allied cruisers sank in flames. Savo Island would rank as the worst defeat ever sustained by the United States Navy.

Nothing stood between the victorious Japanese task force and the defenseless amphibians but inky darkness. Mikawa failed to realize that he was that night within a hair's breath of ripping out by its roots the first American offensive. But at the moment of potential glory, mistakenly believing the American carrier force to be still in place, he withdrew his ships before dawn to avoid the expected enemy aerial counterattacks.

Daybreak on August 9 revealed to the Marines ashore on Guadalcanal a

grim seascape of oil-blackened waters and bobbing American corpses. The view got worse. Sealark Channel, filled with American warships just two days earlier, was abruptly empty. Admiral Turner, now truly defenseless, had no choice but to evacuate his amphibious ships hundreds of miles to the southeast, out of harm's way, his transports still holding thousands of troops and tons of critical materiel. The Marines were ominously alone.

Vandegrift swiftly took stock. He had 16,000 Marines ashore on both sides of the channel, but he now lacked all sea and air protection, and his men were dangerously short of ammunition, rations, earth-moving equipment, and heavy weapons.

The troops had already nicknamed Watchtower "Operation Shoestring" for its threadbare allocation of combat equipment. Shortly, reduced to two rations per day (including the soon-detested rice-and-dried-fish Japanese rations captured on the island), the troops would rename Guadalcanal, "Starvation Island."

The situation demanded a major reorientation of landing force objectives. Instead of pushing aggressively through the jungle to expand the beachhead perimeter, Vandegrift would conserve his thin forces along the ridges and beaches surrounding the airfield.

The 1st Marine Division that was meant to spearhead a strategic offensive at Guadalcanal now had to assume the tactical defensive and hold the airfield—their last link to the outside—to the last man.

Vandegrift recognized a few positive aspects of his predicament. At least he had managed to get ashore the big 90mm antiaircraft guns of the defense battalion. These soon made the daily waves of Japanese bombers seek much higher altitudes before delivering their deadly payloads on the perimeter. And the ranks of the 1st Marine Division contained a number of free-spirited, imaginative NCOs who could work wonders out of nothing. The story was, "Give those guys two hundred pounds of steel wool and they can knit you a stove."

When a fringe of towering trees seemed to prohibit the use of the airstrip by anything heavier than fighters, one sergeant cheerfully went to work with captured Japanese dynamite and "deforested" the area in two days.

Vandegrift's engineers worked night and day to make the 2,000-foot grass strip suitable for flight operations.

The advance force of aviators beseeched Vandegrift to let them name the field "before some rear-echelon staff pogue gets the notion." The general agreed. In a simple flag-raising ceremony, the captured and dearly guarded airstrip became "Henderson Field," in honor of Major Lofton Henderson, USMC, killed while leading his dive-bombers against the Japanese carriers at Midway.

Henderson Field soon had its first flying occupants, much to the joy of the infantry. Less than two weeks after D-Day, two squadrons of MAG–23 flew ashore to stay: Captain John Smith's fighter squadron of Grumman F4F–4 Wildcats and Major Richard Mangrum's scout-bombing squadron of Douglas

93

SBD–3 Dauntless dive-bombers. They would cover the island with Marine glory.

Within a day Captain Smith had downed the group's first Zero. Captain Marion Carl, a Midway veteran, trumped this feat the same week, knocking down three Zeros in violent dogfights over the embattled island. Marine pilots had learned that the sturdy Wildcat's best tactic for coping with the more maneuverable Zeros was to climb high and wait—helped immeasurably by the early warnings of the Coast Watchers—then dive on the approaching Japanese formations from above.

Some help started to trickle in for the tireless Marine aviators.

Army Air Force P400 Bell Air Cobras reinforced the Marine squadrons on August 22. The sluggish Army planes were of little use in dogfights against Zeros, but they were excellent for attacks on enemy shipping and providing close air support to Marines. Assorted Navy fighters came ashore, many "orphaned" when their carriers were sunk in the great sea battles taking place all around Guadalcanal. Soon Army medium bombers and more fighters arrived.

Soon, too, inspired air leadership arrived in the person of Marine Major General Roy Geiger, a seasoned aviator with combat experience in World War I and Central America.

"Cactus," the radio call sign for the island, led the aviators to dub their interservice *ad hoc* group the Cactus Air Force.

"The Unsinkable Aircraft Carrier." Marine F4F Wildcats line the fighter strip at Guadalcanal's Henderson Field. Allied Coast Watchers closer to the main Japanese airfields at Rabaul usually provided early warning of impending air raids, allowing time for Marine pilots to scramble aloft to avoid being caught on the strip in such an exposed area. (U.S. Marine Corps)

The Cactus Air Force did not take long establishing its composite lethality in the air. The number of Japanese day raids dropped drastically. So did the willingness of Imperial Navy surface commanders to approach Guadalcanal in broad daylight.

An interesting stasis developed. Since the Americans lacked night-fighter assets early in the war, the Japanese heavy bombers would harass and pound Guadalcanal at will every night. Surface task forces would race down The Slot to seek battle with U.S. ships, or, finding none, they would lay off the island and pummel Henderson Field in the darkness. But, like vampires, they had to exit the scene by dawn when Henderson Field sprang to life.

At the first hint of light, Marine riflemen would watch the patched-up Wildcats roar aloft, the pilots' heads bobbing vigorously as they cranked up their landing gears by hand, the planes climbing steadily to search the seas for Imperial Navy stragglers.

As recalled by General Merrill ("Bill") Twining, the former operations officer of the 1st Marine Division at Guadalcanal, the Cactus Air Force "transformed our miserable little strip into an unsinkable aircraft carrier. Their deeds were legendary."

The Japanese at Rabaul soon recognized that Henderson Field represented an unholy thorn in their side. When nightly pounding by air and surface units failed to take it out, they concluded that an amphibious counterlanding would have to do the job.

The fighting in Guadalcanal's thick jungles against Japanese soldiers and naval infantrymen exacted a daily cost. Here a stretcher detail brings in a wounded buddy.
(U.S. Marine Corps)

General Hyakutake had many experienced divisions qualified for this mission. But the Army commander unwittingly based his decisions on faulty intelligence. He thought only 2,000 U.S. Marines defended the airstrip, an easy assignment for a single veteran regiment.

Hyakutake selected the crack 28th Infantry, commanded by Colonel Kiyono Ichiki, to recapture Henderson Field. Ichiki, then occupying Guam, sailed in two increments. He accompanied his assault force of about 900 men equipped with light weapons and minimal rations. His follow-on echelon of 1,200 men would join him on turnaround shipping.

Battle-seasoned and arrogant, Colonel Ichiki had prevailed over every European or Chinese force in his path. Nothing he had heard about the Americans gave him cause for concern. Landing twenty-five miles east of the airfield's perimeter at night from a half-dozen destroyers, Ichiki quickly led his advance force into the jungle. He saw no need to wait for his second echelon. His hand-picked veterans would make short work of the green Americans.

THE GRUMMAN IRONWORKS

Fighter pilots have an affinity for planes that bring them back alive after they have been hit with a pile of hostile ordnance. So they loved the stubby, clunky, chunky Wildcat with its pounds of armor and an airframe you could use to drive nails. The Marines referred fondly to its builder's plant as "The Grumman Ironworks," and managed to work around the plane's general lack of grace and nimbleness with team tactics like the "Thach Weave." Decades later, when a film crew asked the prickly Guadalcanal Marine Ace Joe Foss to pose in front of a rakish Corsair rather than a homely Wildcat, he pointed at the 'cat and snapped, "That's the ugly son-ofabitch that brought me home and it's getting in the goddamn movie." It did.

The truncated 1st Marine Division was about to face its first major trial by fire. Engaging Ichiki's veterans would reveal a great deal about the suitability of the Fleet Marine Force for fighting this kind of war.

The Marines had never fought as a division unto themselves. While their leaders were tough men with wide experience and professional training, very few had any practical mastery of the essentials of division-level combat: large-scale fire support coordination, field communications, tactical intelligence, or logistics support.

The World War I veterans—like Col. Clifton "Lucky" Cates, commanding the 1st Marines—had seen enormous battlefields and great slaughter, but there were few of these old-timers still in the field. (Cates himself had been wounded six times in WWI.) Only those who had survived the "Banana Wars" were well versed in ambushes, scouting, and patrolling.

The jungle battles of Guadalcanal would be won or lost by the overwhelmingly new men in the ranks, learning by doing, making the most of their antiquated weapons and short supplies—and undergirded to the man by traditional Marine training and discipline.

One tragic example of the division's early inexperience occurred just before the Ichiki Detachment landed.

Lieutenant Colonel Frank B. Goettge, the division intelligence officer and a widely popular, former All-American football player, personally led a twenty-five-man patrol beyond the perimeter in a misguided effort to receive the surrender of the Imperial Navy forces still on the island. It was a trap. The Japanese ambushed the patrol. Goettge went down early. Only three terrified men escaped. Other Marines would find dismembered corpses of the Goettge Patrol scattered in the jungle.

News of this butchery enraged the division, fueling the cold hatred Marines would feel toward the Japanese in what now became a no-quarter war.

Vandegrift had lost not only Goettge but most of his intelligence section at the worst possible moment. Already some of his patrols had picked up Imperial Army stragglers, ominous evidence that the campaign was about to enter a new phase.

At this critical point a commotion erupted along one section of the perimeter. Marine sentries brought in a Solomon Islander in awful shape—beaten, impaled by bayonets, tortured. It was retired Sergeant Major Jacob Vouza of the British Constabulary. Soldiers of the Ichiki Detachment had tortured the native chief for hours, interrogating him about the Marine positions, then left him bound to a tree to die. But Vouza would gain his revenge and outlive his tormenters by several decades.

Chewing through his rawhide bonds, Vouza freed himself and staggered toward the Marine lines around Henderson Field. His message was chilling. A thousand Japanese soldiers were stealthily advancing behind him.

Vouza had given the Marines the edge. The division stood on full alert. The jungle adjacent to the mouth of the Ilu (still the "Tenaru" to the troops at the time) seemed noisier than usual. Then it grew quiet.

At 1:30 A.M. the silence turned to sheer bedlam as Ichiki's veterans came screaming out of the night with fixed bayonets.

The brunt of the assault fell on Lieutenant Colonel Edwin Pollock's battalion of the 1st Marines. Pollock's men stood their ground, cutting loose with everything they had.

Nobody had to teach a Marine how to lay fields of fire for machine guns. The Brownings stitched the night in measured bursts, the tracers intersecting in a vicious killing zone to the immediate front. The charging Japanese collapsed in droves. Others pushed on. Those that survived the fiery gauntlet closed among the foxholes with bayonets forward, expecting to sweep the ter-

THE MAGNIFICENT ORPHANS

The Marine ordnance of the Pacific war often had little to do with what was used in Europe. Several pieces of "popgun" equipment like the M3A1 37mm antitank gun and stumpy 75mm pack howitzer, hopelessly outmoded against rapidly thickening Axis armor and fortifications, were all but disowned across the Atlantic. But for the heavy going of muddy, steaming, vegetation-choked Pacific islands, the little guns with light ammunition could be transported and manhandled with always-available bicep power, and were godsends to the Marines. Shells that couldn't penetrate a German concrete pillbox or Panther tank could wonderfully well through Pacific jungle tangles.

9 9

rified Marines before them. But the Marines had trained hard for this moment.

With a yell of their own the Leathernecks rose up with bayonets at the guard, parried the thrusts, smashed rifle butts across bared teeth, stabbed home the long Springfield blades. This was primeval close combat, an art the Japanese warriors had excelled in for centuries. Some prevailed, skillfully dispatching their younger opponents, but many others went down hard—brained, shot, or impaled. Very few of the first wave of attackers survived this charge.

Colonel Ichiki screamed at his troops, directed a barrage by his 70mm howitzers and 50mm "knee mortars" (technically: grenade throwers) against the Marine lines, then ordered out his next assault force. These soldiers fared worse than the first wave. The Marine machine guns maintained their disciplined fire, now reinforced by their M3A1 37mm antitank guns, versatile little weapons that proved ideal for Pacific combat. This night the gunners used canister rounds against Ichiki's clustered attackers, blowing great holes in their ranks.

When Ichiki attempted to turn the Marines' left flank by charging across the river mouth, then shoreward through the surf, Cates called for field artillery support from the 75mm pack howitzers of Colonel Pedro del Valle's 11th Marines.

Del Valle, the first of a long line of gifted Marine artillerists to fight in the Pacific War, delivered a devastating fire along the threatened sector. The slaughter was awesome.

At daylight, Colonel Cates sent another battalion across the Ilu upstream to catch the Japanese in the flank. And above them came a cloud of Marine Wildcats, roaring over the treetops and raking Ichiki's positions with a terrible fire. This was the full circle of Rusty Rowell's long-ago air strikes in support of the beleaguered Marines at Ocotal.

It would be another year before Marine fliers could again scorch the treetops in support of Marine riflemen in the Pacific, but on this morning the bond of Marine "ground-pounders" and "airdales" was renewed forever.

Colonel Ichiki must have realized with a great shock at this point that he had stepped into something over his head. Instead of surprising and piercing the Marine perimeter, seizing the airfield, and scattering the Americans into the jungle, he was now badly bloodied and in great danger of being surrounded and annihilated.

Late in the afternoon Vandegrift sent five Stuart light tanks across the river. The remnants of Ichiki's force knocked out two of the attacking vehicles, but on their heels came hundreds of yelling Marines. Colonel Ichiki could only shake his head at this inexplicable disaster, burn his regimental colors, and shoot himself in disgrace.

In the two-day Battle of the Tenaru, the Americans had virtually annihilated his force, killing 800, capturing 15, scattering the stragglers into the jungle.

The convincing victory cost the Marines 34 dead, 75 wounded. For this price, the inexperienced Marines had taken the measure of one of the best infantry outfits in the Japanese Seventeenth Army.

Vandegrift penned a quick, understated note to Commandant Holcomb: "These youngsters are the darnedest people when they get started you ever saw."

Vandegrift relished this victory, but he knew his Marines were still isolated and vulnerable. Kelly Turner did his best, taking advantage of every rain squall to hustle in another cargo ship to unload ammo, rations, and aviation fuel before deadly darkness returned.

Vandegrift strengthened his thin lines around Henderson Field by transferring Edson's raiders, the parachutists, and the detached battalion of the 5th Marines back from Tulagi.

These reinforcements proved critical. General Hyakutake, baffled at the fate of the Ichiki Detachment, ordered another, larger, veteran outfit, the Kawaguchi Brigade, to recapture the aggravating Henderson Field. But the Japanese were still underestimating the size and the growing combat proficiency of the Marines guarding the perimeter.

General Kiyotaki Kawaguchi's 36th Infantry Brigade, based at Truk in the western Carolines, had seen heavy fighting in the jungles of Borneo. The brigade embarked within a matter of hours and set sail for the southern Solomons. On the night of August 31 they landed undetected at Taivu Point, the same location where Ichiki had come ashore so arrogantly less than two weeks before. There Kawaguchi assimilated the recently arrived (but now leaderless) second echelon of Ichiki's regiment, and took off into the jungle.

Kawaguchi had two excellent moves open to him. He opted for a disastrous third.

The Marines were strongest on either flank close to the shoreline. Southward, the lines thinned markedly. With 5,200 well-armed troops, Kawaguchi had the numbers and firepower to penetrate the perimeter at the nearest gap, less than a mile inland from Ichiki's defeat. Or he could mass his entire force at the southern border, smash the skimpy defenses there, and capture both the airfield and the Marine command post in one master stroke. Instead, he squandered his combat power by dividing the force into three columns and assigning them objectives at points along the east, south, and west.

He himself would lead the largest force, some 3,000 men, against the vulnerable southern perimeter of the Marines. But now the whole thing was keyed on intricate coordination between three forces, each out of contact with the others, attacking simultaneously.

Borneo should have taught Kawaguchi more about jungle fighting. The dense vegetation slowed and splintered his columns badly. The rough terrain

made it nearly impossible to drag along his landing guns or support material. Progress proved both excruciatingly slow and unprofessionally noisy. Vandegrift's scouts knew of the approach—but not the exact destination.

Vandegrift worried most about his weak southern perimeter and placed Red Mike Edson in charge of a composite force of raiders and parachutists. Edson deployed his meager forces along a grassy ridge south of the airfield and waited for night. Japanese destroyers made things lively with a sharp bombardment of the ridge just after dark.

This lively spot was about to take a permanent place in Marine fighting history as "Bloody Ridge," although some would prefer "Edson's Ridge" after the battle machine who would lead the defense.

Shortly before 10 P.M. on September 12, Kawaguchi's howling infantry surged forward in a massive charge. The Raiders and parachutists, their backs to Henderson Field and under terrific stress, opened fire at the thousands of oncoming Japanese. All knew that loss of the ridge would doom Guadalcanal.

This night and the next would represent for the U.S. Marine Corps an epic of desperate defensive fighting. Much of it would evolve around the cool, commanding presence of Red Mike Edson.

Edson's left flank took the first blow, wavered, then fought back, often at bayonet point. The battle dissolved into hundreds of individual duels and skirmishes. These Marines were hardly rookies. Already well trained by Edson, they had learned quickly about night-fighting on Tulagi when the Kure *rikusentai* had emerged out of nowhere to rush their lines.

Heeding Edson's calm assurances, the Marines stayed low, teamed up, and drove the attackers back. Twice more Kawaguchi's men came boiling up the slopes. Each fight seemed more desperate than before. But by 2:30 A.M. Edson advised Vandegrift that he thought he could hold. Kawaguchi pulled back to regroup.

Edson knew Kawaguchi would try again the next night. He rallied his exhausted men, asked Vandegrift for reinforcements from the 5th Marines, and tightened the line. And he worked closely with Colonel del Valle to register the 11th Marines' howitzers along the grassy slopes and the dark jungle down below the ridge.

At 6:30 P.M. on the thirteenth, Kawaguchi's main force swept forward in a renewed, more powerful assault. This was a near-run thing.

Wave after wave of frenzied Japanese fell upon the Marine lines. Edson was magnificent. So was Major Kenneth Bailey, commanding one of Edson's most exposed companies. Both men scuttled along the ridge, shouting defiance, somehow grabbing one more handful of troops to throw into an overrun gap at the last minute.

The Japanese lapped near, through, and sometimes over the Marines on the ridge like a tidal wave. Some spilled down into Vandegrift's command post (where division Marine Gunner Sheffield Banta shot one unwelcome intruder with his pistol). Vandegrift committed his reserves and the combat support troops. The larder was empty.

A Marine stands watch with his Browning .30 caliber M1917 water-cooled machine gun while 1st Marine Division troops scrub themselves clean of jungle rot in Guadalcanal's Lunga River.
(U.S. Marine Corps)

102

Marine ground
crewmen
struggle to douse
a blazing fighter
after a Japanese
air raid on
Henderson Field.
(U.S. Marine Corps)

Del Valle's artillery fired throughout the hellish night, delivering such devastating fire that the surviving Japanese marveled at the Marines' "automatic artillery."

Through all the bedlam Edson and Bailey stood like rocks, directing fire, rallying the troops to yet another hot corner of savage fighting. Both would receive the Medal of Honor for their combat leadership on "Bloody Ridge" these two nights. (Bailey's would be posthumous; he died in heavy fighting along the Matanikau two weeks later.)

Kawaguchi had lost well over half his main force in the desperate fighting, but Bloody Ridge remained in Marine hands. Two uncoordinated Japanese supporting attacks became sideshows—but so thinly were the Marine lines stretched that both nearly broke through in their sectors.

On the east, the provisional Kuma Battalion of Ichiki's second-echelon troops had the best opportunity against a very tenuous line manned by King Company of the 1st Marines. In particularly vicious hand-to-hand combat, a Japanese officer leaped at Captain Robert Putnam, his samurai sword extended at full backswing, reaching to decapitate him. Putnam, defenseless because of the artillery radio in his hands, looked death in the face. Private Marion Peregrine, sixteen years old, coolly shot the Japanese officer just in time.

King Company prevailed. Daylight revealed more than sixty dead Japanese along their widely dispersed line of foxholes.

But the shattered Kuma Battalion could still sting, and the Marines would pay a frightful price for having not yet learned the basics of tank-infantry coordination.

When six Marine Stuart tanks tried to flush the survivors out of the edge of

the jungle the next evening, the Ichiki remnants unveiled a section of 37mm guns and opened a hot fire. The Kuma gunners knocked out two tanks, drove another into the Tenaru, where it capsized, drowning the crew, then attacked one of the stricken tanks with flamethrowers to burn the crew alive. No Marine along the entire perimeter would ever forget the grisly battles of September 12–14.

As ferocious as were the irreplaceable combat losses, the troops were suffering just as badly from the effects of malaria and malnutrition and exhaustion. They needed reinforcements as badly as any Marines ever had.

Then, at last, Kelly Turner boldly managed to run in a small convoy with the 7th Marines, finally relieved from Samoan defense duties. Even this small bright spot had its cruel cost. The Imperial Navy attacked the covering force, sinking the carrier *Wasp*, and severely damaging the battleship *North Carolina*. But the gaunt Marines ashore were pleased to see the full-strength 7th Marines.

Two fabled "Banana Warriors" commanded battalions in the regiment, Lieutenant Colonels Chesty Puller and Herman Hanneken, who as a sergeant had so boldly slain Charlemagne Peralte in Haiti in 1919.

Vandegrift would need all the fighters he could get. Intelligence sources advised that General Hyakutake had finally realized the nature of the American Marines defending Guadalcanal and was now committing his major combat force, the elite Sendai Division. Indeed, Hyakutake took to the field himself, landing on Guadalcanal by barge on October 7.

The advent of October brought the full weight of the Imperial Navy as well. Amid a series of colossal sea battles, they boldly deployed two battleships to attack Henderson Field and destroy the Cactus Air Force, the Marines' indispensable air shield.

The battleships *Kongo* and *Haruna* steamed into Ironbottom Sound the night of October 13, anchored leisurely, and for the next eighty minutes delivered hundreds of fourteen-inch shells against the field, its workhorse planes, and the troops in their bunkers and foxholes.

These were the worst eighty minutes of hell any American landing force ever endured in the Pacific War, the huge, flat-trajectory shells splintering trees, planes, vehicles, men. The noise alone was deafening; the concussive force bloodied every nose and ear.

The bombardment represented a terrifying introduction to the soldiers of the 164th Infantry, the advance guard of the Americal Division, which had just landed that very day.

Yet somehow, Marines and soldiers endured, survived, and rose up with the dawn to shake it off and strike back. General Roy Geiger had only a handful of operational aircraft left, but these he dispatched with a vengeance to catch and punish the Japanese ships still delivering the Sendai Division up the coast.

Japanese bombers came overhead in broad daylight, figuring the blasted field now only needed the *coup de grâce*. Newcomer Major Harold "The Coach" Bauer, whose Marine fighter squadron arrived for duty at the most opportune

moment, paused only to refuel before roaring aloft in his F4F. "The Coach" promptly shot down four Japanese bombers to celebrate his first day with Cactus.

As the battles continued, Marine fighter pilots of the Cactus Air Force continued to earn their spurs the hard way, wrestling the utmost performance from their tubby Wildcats, respecting but not fearing the vaunted Zeros.

An astonishing five Marine pilots would garner the Medal of Honor for their aerial combat bravery during the Guadalcanal campaign: Major or "Coach" Bauer, posthumously, Captain Joseph Foss, Major Robert Galer, Major John Smith, and First Lieutenant James Swett.

Many pilots qualified as aces; some began to attain super ace status, especially the skinny captain from North Dakota, Joe Foss, who racked up twenty-six confirmed kills, tying the nonpareil Eddie Rickenbacker's record from World War I (and Rickenbacker's kills included several tethered barrage balloons). The cumulative effect of these increasingly lethal dogfighters was the gradual attrition by flaming death of hundreds of the most gifted and experienced Japanese airmen. Five Marine fighter pilots—John Smith, Marion Carl, Jim Swett, Bob Galer, and Coach Bauer—would between them shoot down seventy-seven Japanese planes over Guadalcanal.

Yet Henderson Field still wasn't secure.

Now the Sendai Division landed with 150mm guns. These had the range to punish the Marine and Army perimeter around the clock. More Japanese cruisers and destroyers steamed in at night to pound the field. The U.S. Navy was still fighting for its life. Ironbottom Sound claimed more victims each week.

Politicians in Washington wondered publicly whether the cause at Guadalcanal was lost.

Admiral Chester Nimitz stepped in quickly. He flew to Noumea, sacked Admiral Ghormley from command of the South Pacific Area, and replaced him with the aggressive "Bull" Halsey. Marines on "the Canal" whooped for joy at the news.

Three weeks later Halsey himself flew into Henderson Field (something Ghormley never did). The pugnacious admiral toured the lines, visited the sick, slapped Marines on the back—pumped them up. Meanwhile, his admirals and captains steamed more frequently in harm's way, in a much tighter orbit around Guadalcanal.

The great sea battles of October and November 1942 were bloody and costly and not altogether victorious for the Americans, but Halsey kept the pressure on his Imperial Navy counterparts. Ultimately they could not match his fiery willingness to risk every ship in his fleet to protect the strategic island.

The fighting ashore grew in intensity as the whirlwinds of sea and air battles swept nearby. The Sendai Division proved an abler opponent than the Ichiki and Kawaguchi forces. General Hyakutake, observing the situation firsthand, rued his earlier piecemeal attacks. Now Halsey's ships and Geiger's

planes made the delivery of reinforcements to Guadalcanal extremely hazardous. Thousands of Imperial Army troops drowned; many more straggled ashore minus their heavy weapons or rations. "Starvation Island" now applied more to the attackers than the "Raggedy-Ass Marines."

General Hyakutake, under tremendous pressure now from his own political and military superiors, raged at the setbacks and hustled the scattered Sendai elements through the jungle to attack the south and west sections of the perimeter.

The Sendai troops were seasoned combat veterans, and the battles that raged in late October were as bloody and desperate as those of the preceding assaults. Red Mike Edson, now commanding the 5th Marines, continued his cool-as-ice battle leadership. Chesty Puller, in his first combat in World War II, revealed the same fiery, fearless, up-front magnetism that earned so many legends in Nicaragua. Even more legendary was his fury at being temporarily knocked out (ten days) by a spray of hot shrapnel into his most delicate lower extremities.

The climax of the ground battles for Guadalcanal occurred during October 24–26. This was jungle night-fighting at its most brutal.

Major General Masao Maruyama chose to lead the bulk of his Sendai Division, some 7,000 strong, against the same distinctive landmark that had broken the back of the Kawaguchi

DELAYED ACTION

A third machine gun section leader, Corporal Anthony Casamento of Edson's 5th Marines, had to wait thirty-eight years for his Medal of Honor. In a particularly bloody battle along the Matanikau River on November 1, Casamento manned his weapon throughout a night of ceaseless Japanese assaults despite the loss of all twenty-nine of his men and crippling wounds to himself. Most of his Marines died of their wounds in the action. Only much later did two wounded survivors come forth to document the corporal's bravery in protecting them throughout the endless night. President Jimmy Carter presented the award to Casamento in 1980.

Brigade in September—Edson's Ridge. Now the 7th Marines guarded that sector—specifically the battalions of Puller and Hanneken—plus the new but gutsy 164th Infantry.

Like Kawaguchi before him, Maruyama made his troops hack a trail through the jungle and lug their heavy antitank and landing guns along by hand. The tortuous process took days; many of the guns never made it to the battlefield. Despairing of the pace, Maruyama vowed to take the airfield by cold steel.

The Sendai troops sprang out of the jungle in the pitch black of night during a driving rainstorm. Puller's men swept away the first attack with steady marksmanship, but the battalion commander could tell by the discipline and numbers of his attackers that he was in over his head.

Puller did not hesitate to call in the National Guardsmen of the 164th Infantry, whose rifle squads integrated quickly with their Marine counterparts along the fire-swept crest of the ridge.

Soldiers and Marines fought with equal tenacity, the Marines more than

a bit envious of the GIs' new M–1 Garands—this was a night when a clip of eight rounds fired semiautomatically proved far superior to the five-round, bolt-action Springfields of the Marines.

Maruyama continued these sudden, large-scale assaults against the strategic ridge for two bloody nights. The Marines of Hanneken's and Puller's battalions, ably joined by the Army infantrymen, fought with raging tenacity.

In several threatened sectors the thin margin of victory came only through superhuman exertions of rock-steady Marine NCOs, who simply refused to retreat in spite of all the furies of hell.

Bravest of all the brave were two machine gun section chiefs who distinguished themselves on successive nights. Sergeant "Manila John" Basilone of the 1st Battalion, 7th Marines, proved to be the unshakable anchor of Puller's sector the first night. Then it became the turn of Platoon Sergeant Mitchell Paige of Hanneken's battalion. Virtually the last man alive at his post, Paige kept firing, then climaxed the night by cradling the red-hot weapon in his bare arms to lead a charge down the slope to clear the last toehold of Sendai troops.

Both Basilone and Paige would receive Medals of Honor; Paige, a battlefield commission to boot.

General Maruyama had to retreat back down his jungle trail, now missing half his assault force, nearly 3,000 slain. The Marines and soldiers lost but a tenth that number.

Guadalcanal abounded with heroes, not all of them operating along the established front lines. Among the most fearless and controversial was Lieutenant Colonel Evans Carlson, the Marine who had sojourned with the Chinese Communist Route Army before the war. Carlson led his 2d Raider Battalion ashore near Koli Point in November, then cut loose in the trackless jungle for a month, applying the guerrilla tactics he had learned in China.

Carlson hounded and confounded the Japanese, beating them badly at their own game of jungle warfare, night action, and ambushes. During his extended patrol, living off the land (complained one husky Raider: "Goddammit, Colonel, we're *hungry!*"), and moving constantly, Carlson fought dozens of skirmishes, killed 500 Japanese, terrorized many more, and suffered less than 35 casualties.

The Japanese were now on the ropes, but so was the 1st Marine

The Japanese Seventeenth Army underestimated the size of the U.S. Marine enclave holding Guadalcanal and discounted the fighting spirit of the untested Leathernecks. This led to piecemeal counter-landing attempts like this failure against Marine positions west of Alligator Creek and great slaughter of valuable Imperial veterans. (U.S. Marine Corps)

Sergeant Manila John Basilone, USMC, legendary machine gunner in Chesty Puller's 1st Battalion, 7th Marines, received the Medal of Honor for extraordinary heroism during the fight against the Sendai Division in late October 1942. Sent home after Guadalcanal, Basilone later volunteered to return to combat duty and died in action on D-Day at Iwo Jima.
(C. C. Beall, Marine Corps Combat Art Collection)

Division. On December 9, after four months of constant combat, the "Old Breed" stood down.

General Vandegrift relinquished command of the island to General Alexander Patch of the Army's Americal Division. After visiting the jungle-shrouded cemetery known as Flanders Field, where more than 1,200 of his men lay buried, Vandegrift took his emaciated Marines off the deadly, pestiferous island—took them to cool, clean Australia for an extended period of rest and rehabilitation.

A well-earned Presidential Unit Citation was quickly approved and presented to the division's survivors. Similarly, the 1st Marine Aircraft Wing received the Presidential unit award for its heroic action in the skies over "Starvation Island" and Ironbottom Sound.

General Patch received reinforcements from the Army's 25th Division and additional elements of the 2d Marine Division (the 2d Marines had been there since D-Day; the 8th Marines arrived from Samoa on November 2; the 6th Marines from extended duty in Iceland on January 4, 1943).

Hard fighting lay ahead. Hyakutake still had his Nagoya Division to throw into the cauldron, but no longer was the issue in doubt. On January 10, Patch launched the largest American offensive of the campaign.

Nothing came easy on Guadalcanal, even at the end. When a strong Japanese emplacement held up the advance of one element of the 8th Marines, Captain Henry "Jim" Crowe, a "Mustang" (former enlisted) officer and former coach of the Marine Rifle Teams, shamed them into action by striding forward

with the challenge: "You bastards'll never get a Purple Heart hiding in a fox-hole—*Follow Me!*" It may have been the ghost of Gunnery Sergeant Dan Daly from Belleau Wood, but the 8th Marines rose up behind Crowe and stormed the position.

Early in February 1943, after a dogged pursuit, Army and Marine patrols reached the western end of the island to find that General Hyakutake and 11,000 of his soldiers had been spirited away by the resourceful "Tokyo Express." A nighttime extraction of troops from a threatened shore is a tremendously complex maneuver—an amphibious landing in reverse—but the Imperial Navy pulled it off without a glitch. The well-executed epilogue, however, could hardly mask the national disaster that Guadalcanal represented for the Japanese.

The American victory at Guadalcanal, dangerously risked and dearly bought, was more of a turning point in the Pacific War than even Midway.

At Midway, the Japanese could blame the fates for their carriers being caught while rearming the air groups. But at Guadalcanal, in a half-year campaign, the best of the Empire's veteran soldiers, sailors, and aviators had been fought to a standstill and eventually overwhelmed by the inexperienced American forces.

For the United States, and its corps of Marines, the victory affirmed some bright truths: The Japanese were tough but not invincible. And the Marines had shown they had something priceless to offer this war: not just amphibious expertise and fierce esprit, but also a certain distinctive valor which could transcend deprivation and be passed on, like a flaming torch, from veterans to rookies.

But the road across the Pacific that the Marines had begun to march would be numbingly long, dangerous, and . . . yes, glorious.

7: STRANGLING RABAUL (1943)

TARAWA, IWO JIMA, AND OKINAWA WOULD
HAVE FADED TO PALE PINK IN COMPARISON
WITH THE BLOOD THAT WOULD HAVE FLOWED
IF THE ALLIES HAD ATTEMPTED AN ASSAULT
ON FORTRESS RABAUL.

Samuel Eliot Morison, Breaking the Bismarcks Barrier

1st Marine Division troops struggle to push a jeep ashore
through the soft sands of Cape Gloucester. Tank landing ships
(LSTs) had now appeared in all theaters of the Pacific War (this
one was commanded and crewed by U.S. Coast Guardsmen). LSTs
were invaluable during the unopposed landing at Cape
Gloucester—beaching early on D-Day for direct, rapid offloading
of combat vehicles for the landing force. (U.S. Marine Corps)

Parachute Marine
(Charles Waterhouse)

Easily a hundred thousand Japanese occupied Rabaul in 1943. Rabaul, capital of the Bismarcks, whose looming mountains protected superb harbors and airfields, crouched like a medieval dragon on New Britain, readily reinforced from Truk to the north and fiercely defended by a circle of strong positions on New Ireland, Bougainville, and New Georgia.

MacArthur wanted to conquer Rabaul directly; Halsey had huge doubts. The Joint Chiefs of Staff decided for them: Neutralize and eventually bypass Rabaul in 1943 by a series of low-budget half-steps—working sequentially "up the ladder" of the Solomons and Bismarcks. Doing so would entail a very hazardous year's work for a still underequipped, understrength Marine amphibious force: a full-scale air war and three major assault landings.

Rabaul lay 560 air miles northwest of Guadalcanal. Since the island-studded seas posed a hazard to Halsey's two carriers, the air war against Rabaul would be waged predominantly by land-based aviation, which meant a significant role for the Marines. Thirty-three squadrons of Marine tactical aircraft would fight in the skies over Rabaul and its protective network. Their principal mission: defeat of the formidable Imperial Naval Air Force.

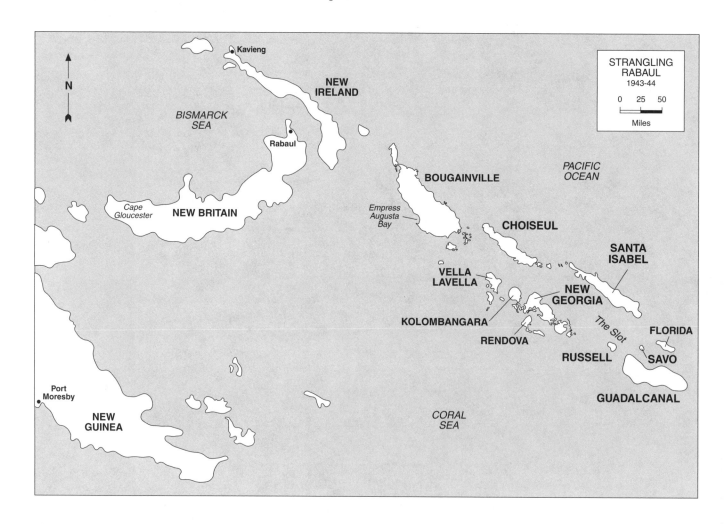

Marine Brigadier General Francis "Pat" Mulcahy, one of the few Leatherneck aviators to shoot down a German fighter in World War I, commanded the 2d Marine Aircraft Wing. Mulcahy's immediate concern became the new Japanese airfield built at Munda Point on New Georgia. The Munda fighter strip, only 175 miles from Guadalcanal, gave the Japanese Zeros much longer "legs" in the air battles over the Solomons. Mulcahy's pilots hit Munda often and viciously, but the enemy's air defenses and fighter cover exacted a high price. Munda would have to be seized by a landing force. The tedious joint planning process began.

Concurrently, the savage air war raged unabated. Marine pilots engaged in desperate air-to-air battles each day, making the most of the limited attributes of their F4F Wildcats with "hit and run" tactics against the superbly maneuverable Zeros. Then, on February 12, 1943, the first squadron of USMC F4U Corsair fighters arrived in the theater. The tables were about to be turned in the air war.

In the right hands, the Corsair became such an efficient flying and killing machine that a new generation of Marine fighter pilots emerged as legendary aces in the skies surrounding Rabaul. Lieutenant Kenneth Walsh became the first Corsair ace on May 13, 1943, shooting down his fourth, fifth, and sixth Zeros in a hectic morning. Walsh had earned his pilot's wings in 1937 as a Marine private and proved absolutely fearless in aerial combat. On August 30 he stormed single-handedly into a formation of fifty Zeros attacking USAAF B–24 bombers over Bougainville. In the wild melee that ensued, Walsh shot down four enemy fighters before being forced to crash at sea. Walsh survived, received the Medal of Honor, and returned to the air campaign, eventually claiming twenty-one authenticated kills.

Lieutenant Robert Hanson became the greatest Corsair ace of the war, achieving twenty-five kills from his F4U in the South Pacific. Hanson's performance was so meteoric that his squadron mates had barely started to call him "Butcher Bob" before he was done and gone. He shot down twenty Japanese planes in an incredibly brief six days. Hanson's luck ran out at the end. On the day before his twenty-fourth birthday, and just

THE BENT-WING WIDOW-MAKER

The gull-winged Vought F4U Corsair and the Marine Corps were made for each other. The big Corsairs proved ideal for the ground-based combat missions of the South Pacific (and later served well aboard carriers in the final amphibious assaults of the war). The Corsair was larger, more powerful, and much faster than the F4F Wildcat it replaced and the Imperial Navy Nakajima Zero it fought against. Propelled by its huge Pratt and Whitney 2,000-horsepower engine, the Corsair could climb 3,000 feet a minute, cover a thousand-mile range, and attain a scorching 417 mph of airspeed. Japanese Zeros greeted the newcomers in a bloody dogfight over Bougainville on February 14—"the St. Valentine's Day Massacre"—but the Corsair pilots soon established superiority over the older Zeros and the newer Franks and Jakes. Infantry Marines came to love the Corsairs for their superb close air support later in the war. Japanese troops in Okinawa and the Philippines described the Marine Corps F4U as "The Whistling Death." In the South Pacific, teamed with Navy carrier-based F6F Hellcats and USAAF Lockheed P–38 Lightnings, the Corsairs provided a nigh-invincible trinity of ascendant American airpower.

A Marine SBD Dauntless dive-bomber flying low over Bougainville to attack Rabaul farther to the northwest. (U.S. Marine Corps)

days before he was due to be rotated back to the States, Hanson lost a duel with antiaircraft batteries at Cape St. George on New Ireland. His Medal of Honor was a posthumous award.

Flamboyant and indomitable Major Gregory "Pappy" Boyington was the most widely known Corsair pilot to receive the Medal of Honor. "Pappy" accumulated his Corps-best twenty-eight kills in several different aircraft (he shot down his first six Japanese planes while a volunteer P–40 pilot for the "prewar" Flying Tigers in China), but he attained his greatest renown as skipper of VMF–214, an F4U squadron nicknamed "The Black Sheep."

Although his young lieutenants regarded their thirty-one-year-old commander as a living relic, "Pappy" led the way in every fight, downing the squadron's first kill, adding four more within a week. Leading his Corsairs in aggressive "fighter sweeps" over enemy airfields, Boyington tuned his radio to the Japanese frequency and challenged them to come up and fight. He became

THE BATTLE
HISTORY OF THE
US MARINES

a marked man to Japanese fighter pilots. They finally shot him down off New Ireland. A Japanese submarine surfaced alongside to take him prisoner. He survived brutal incarceration, returning at war's end to wide acclaim and his long-deferred Medal of Honor.

While colorful Corsair pilots like Walsh, Hanson, and Boyington captured the public's admiration, Marine dive-bomber and torpedo bomber pilots played equally critical roles in the sustained air battle for Rabaul. Indeed, Marines flying Grumman TBF Avengers executed some of the hairiest combat missions of the campaign: nighttime, low-altitude sweeps of enemy harbors to drop 1,500-pound aerial magnetic mines.

During one stormy night sixteen TBFs of Marine Torpedo Bomber Squadron 233 splashed their mines directly in Rabaul's Simpson Harbor, the epicenter of Japanese power. Heavy enemy fire downed six Avengers, killing each three-man crew. The surviving planes, badly shot up, barely made it back to their base.

Marine night fighters made their debut in the South Pacific in 1943, early pioneers of a tactic which would grow in value as technology improved. The essence of effective night fighter operations is the marriage between a ground control intercept (GCI) radar and an airborne interceptor. But the jungle canopy hindered GCI effectiveness, and the Marines' second-hand, twin-engined Vega PV–1 Venturas were marginal in locking-on distant targets in the tropical darkness.

The few night kills came at the hands of extremely brave pilots at outrageously short ranges. One Marine returned to base with his windshield smeared with Japanese blood and oil; another landed with pieces of his opponent's plane embedded in his engine cowling.

Later in the war, the Corps would employ modified F4U Corsairs and even F6F Hellcats as night fighters with deadly efficiency. In the Rabaul campaign, the Marines at least learned an invaluable lesson for amphibious warfare: Air defense of the newly captured beachhead was most critical the first night, when ships had to retreat over the horizon, leaving the assault force to its own devices against the inevitable waves of Japanese bombers. Getting the bulky GCI unit ashore and operational before dark on D-Day became an essential priority.

STRANGE TALES OF THE AIR WAR

Marine Sergeant Gilbert Henze, a rear-seat gunner in a TBD Avenger, uneasily took over the controls when AA fire killed his pilot. The wingman hovered nearby, giving Henze basic flight instruction and encouragement by radio. Sergeant Henze almost made it back to base on this, his "maiden flight," but the radios failed, the TBF ran out of gas, and he had to ditch. In his haste, Henze struck the stabilizer as he bailed out; the impact cut off his leg below the knee. He had the presence of mind to bind up the stump with an improvised tourniquet before he hit the water. Native Solomon Islanders rescued him off Tulagi.

In another incident, Marine Lieutenant Gilbert Percy bailed out of his crippled plane at 2,000 feet. His chute streamed but failed to open. Percy fell into the sea, striking the water feet first, and somehow survived falling a distance twice the height of the Empire State Building. He suffered a fractured pelvis, two sprained ankles, and 20mm shell wounds in his arms and legs. Barely alive and in excruciating pain, Percy swam three hours, finally finding a small reef. Native fishermen rescued him the next morning.

In April a handpicked section of USAAF P–38 pilots achieved the greatest coup of the year when they shot down the irreplaceable Admiral Yamamoto over Bougainville in a well-executed aerial ambush.

Marine Major John Condon bore a hand in the intercept. Condon, operations officer for the joint fighter command on Guadalcanal, plotted the course for the Lightnings to take from Henderson Field to Bougainville—directing them to fly outside The Slot, west of New Georgia, fifty feet off the deck. The plan worked to perfection. "Sounds as though one of the ducks in their bag was a peacock," signaled Bull Halsey at the news of Yamamoto's plane crashing in flames in the jungle.

In truth, flying any aircraft over the hostile skies of the Solomons and Bismarcks in 1943 placed a premium on skill and raw courage. Each week the aviators recounted great victories, stinging defeats, mysterious losses, miraculous survivals.

Such incidents became the stuff of legends, but in fact Marine aviators of all persuasions were earning their combat spurs in this protracted campaign. The infantry remained skeptical. In the Marine rifleman's somewhat provincial view, the ultimate measure of any pilot's effectiveness was his ability to support the guy on the ground.

Close air support in the jungles of the South Pacific was an imprecise art. Coordination, navigation, and basic communications suffered from poor equipment and inexperience. The sparkling performance of the Cactus Air Force in shooting up the Ichiki Detachment during the Battle of the Tenaru remained an exception.

To do the job right—and avoid killing friendly ground troops—required reliable communications between an experienced aviation ground party, hunkered at the side of the infantry commander. It was a hell of an investment, taking seasoned pilots out of their beloved cockpits and deploying them with "the grunts," but the value of having a seasoned dive-bomber pilot on the ground, assessing the target and talking his former cohorts into the attack, could not be beat. The 3d Marine Division at Bougainville experimented with ground-based air liaison teams with considerable success, an encouraging start.

The joint amphibious campaign to seize New Georgia and wipe out the nettlesome Japanese airfield at Munda Point bogged down because of inexperience, inadequate resources, and deadly enemy resistance. No Marine divisions were available for Operation Toenails. Thirty thousand Army troops would provide the bulk of the landing forces, beefed up by the Marines' 9th Defense Battalion. Marine raiders and parachutists would execute special operations missions behind Japanese lines.

Two companies of Marine Raiders jump-started the New Georgia operation on June 21, 1943, landing at Segi Point, rescuing an endangered Coast Watcher, then crossing the island in four brutal days to surprise and destroy the Japanese coast defense guns at Viru Harbor.

Admiral Kelly Turner landed the Army's 43d Divison and the 9th Defense Battalion on Rendova Island on June 30, scattering the handful of Japanese defenders. The veteran Marine defense battalion went right to work, registering their new 155mm "Long Tom" guns, digging in their AA guns, using their light tanks and LVTs to traverse the deep mud. Soon the Long Toms began pommeling Munda, eight miles away. So far so good.

Then came Japanese air raids from Rabaul. The first evening a Japanese pilot hit Turner's flagship, the *McCawley*, with a well-aimed torpedo. That was bad enough—Turner switched to a smaller ship, a tug took *McCawley* under tow—but the embarrassing conclusion came after dark when an American PT boat skipper mistook the huge transport for an enemy vessel and sank her with a spread of "friendly" torpedoes.

The disasters continued. On D+2 (the second full day after the D-Day landing) a flight of eighteen Mitsubishi "Betty" bombers and Zero escorts surprised the amphibious force and devastated the congested beachhead, bombing and strafing at will. By a combination of bad luck and human errors, every search radar on the island had become inoperational during that specific half hour, allowing the surprise attack. Marine 90mm gunners wheeled into action, eventually driving the raiders away, but the beach resembled a charnel house.

Among the 200 American casualties was a pugnacious and now incensed lieutenant colonel named David Shoup, an observer from the 2d Marine Division. Indelible memories of the helpless chaos of the Rendova beachhead that morning would steel Shoup to survive the even greater horrors to come on D-Day at Tarawa, four months later.

The star-crossed campaign struggled on. Army troops landed on northwestern New Georgia on July 2–3. Across the island, at Rice Anchorage on the Kula Gulf coast, Marine Colonel Harry Liversedge led a composite regiment of Raiders and Army infantry ashore. "Harry the Horse" Liversedge, an Olympic shot-putter and veteran of World War I, had too many missions for his light forces, but he exerted a magnificent effort.

Fighting through the jungle in a driving rainstorm, Liversedge's force crossed the Giza Giza River on improvised rafts of logs and ponchos, then drove the Japanese from the villages of Maranuso and Enogai on the east side of the Dragon's Peninsula. A futile roadblock in the middle of the jungle failed to restrict Japanese movements and tied up half the command. Liversedge led the rest of his men against the port of Bairoko.

Opposing Liversedge in the thickly jungled Dragon's Peninsula was Rear Admiral Minoru Ota, commanding one of the largest concentrations of *rikusentai* to fight the Americans in the war. For two weeks the Kure 6th Special Naval Landing Force slugged it out toe-to-toe with the Raiders and soldiers. Both sides suffered heavy casualties in vicious, point-blank jungle fighting. (The Marines would fight Admiral Ota again in 1945 on Okinawa's Oroku Peninsula.)

The *rikusentai* defending Bairoko had time to construct sturdy pillboxes of coconut logs and coral. The Raiders, light infantry in the truest sense, lacked artillery or bunker-busting weapons. At one point Lieutenant Colonel Samuel Griffith, a Guadalcanal veteran commanding the 1st Raider Battalion, notified Liversedge, "I have committed the works." It wasn't good enough. The Japanese stonewalled the Raiders' advance less than 300 yards from Bairoko.

Liversedge made the agonizing decision to call off the attack. Victory was close enough to taste, but Harry the Horse had already lost a third of his command; many were litter cases that would require man-handling back through the jungle for days to an evacuation point.

Munda Field eventually fell to three Army divisions and the 9th Defense Battalion after five weeks of steady fighting. The whole campaign—including the costly Bairoko "raid"—left a bad taste. Admiral Halsey helped restore morale by his commonsense decision to bypass heavily defended Kolombangara and strike Vella Lavella. There an Army regimental combat team and the Marine 4th Defense Battalion landed on August 15. As at Rendova, Marine antiaircraft gunners quickly dug in their 90mm guns around the beachhead. This time there were no lapses in the radar surveillance. The Marines withstood a dizzying succession of 121 Japanese air raids, knocking forty-two enemy planes out of the sky.

Seizing Vella Lavella abruptly rendered the Japanese fortress on Kolombangara irrelevant. In another masterpiece of nighttime deception, the Imperial Navy evacuated 12,400 troops from the island, their third amphibious extraction of the year (including Guadalcanal and Kiska).

The Allies were grinding inexorably north and west. New Georgia was under new management. The 9th Defense Battalion's big guns now defended Munda Point airfield, allowing Pappy Boyington's Black Sheep Corsairs to roar aloft in fighter sweeps against Rabaul, now 440 miles away.

Mountainous, wildly jungled Bougainville, northernmost island of the Solomons, was the next objective. The presence of five Japanese airfields on the island underscored the enemy's strategic appreciation for Bougainville. Ashore, Lieutenant General Haruyoshi Hyakutake, the wholesale loser of Guadalcanal, commanded 35,000 troops.

Attacking Bougainville would represent a giant step forward, but one fraught with risk for Bull Halsey. He lacked the combat power to seize and defend the entire island. At best Halsey hoped to use his Marines to catch Hyakutake by surprise, seize a foothold along the southern coast, then defend the enclave desperately while the SeaBees carved a pair of landing fields out of the jungle. The rewards would be great. The new airstrips would close the range to Rabaul to 210 miles, making it possible to hit the Japanese nerve center with dive-bombers and torpedo bombers as well as Corsairs.

Halsey assigned the Bougainville mission to the I Marine Amphibious Corps, commanded by General Vandegrift, the victor of Guadalcanal.

Vandegrift would use Major General Allen Turnage's highly trained 3d Marine Division to spearhead the assault landing, followed by the Army's 37th Division and fully supported by fifty-two squadrons of Allied land-based aircraft (including fourteen USMC squadrons).

But Vandegrift knew his landing would incur violent and immediate Japanese counterattacks from every point on the compass. Nor would the landing be as easy as that on Guadalcanal. The isolated landing site, Cape Torokina on Empress Augusta Bay, midway up Bougainville's southern coast, was subject to treacherous surf. Achieving even the modest mission of landing, building airfields, and holding on for dear life would require of Vandegrift uncommon luck, guile, and fortitude. Vandegrift opted to lead with guile.

Here was the ideal mission for Lieutenant Colonel "Brute" Krulak's 2d Parachute Battalion. Vandegrift ordered Krulak to execute a diversionary landing on nearby Choiseul Island and make the Japanese think he had a division on the rampage. The combative Krulak executed this to perfection. While the jungles of the South Pacific battlefields prohibited any employment of Marine parachutists as airborne forces, Brute Krulak's salty troops were fully capable of a noisy fracas.

The parachutists stormed ashore on Choiseul at midnight on October 28. Before the astonished Japanese could react, Krulak's well-trained warriors raided enemy installations along a twenty-five-mile sector. The 650 Marines raised holy hell throughout Choiseul for nine days. General Hyakutake took the bait, dispatching reinforcements from Bougainville even after the main landing there.

Against such numbers, the final firefights became desperate. Krulak, wounded himself, sought aid in evacuating his casualties. Two Navy PT boats, led by Lieutenant John Fitzgerald Kennedy, USNR, lent a hand. One of Krulak's corporals died on Kennedy's bunk. The raiding force withdrew intact, mission accomplished.

General Hyakutake began to curse the day he had ever encountered the United States Marines. Although originally an infantry officer, Hyakutake had become a communications specialist and spent the first two years of the war as a rear-echelon "Inspector General of Signal Training." His unexpected selection to command the Seventeenth Army seemed at first heaven-sent. Imperial General Headquarters told him his new army would conquer both Port Moresby, New Guinea, and the American outposts in Samoa and Fiji.

Then, for Hyakutake, came disaster at Guadalcanal. And now Choiseul. Krulak's diversion seemed to rattle Hyakutake. When the real American landing occurred at Bougainville, he withheld his counterattack orders a fatal week, worrying that these U.S. Marines were just another diversion. Hyakutake would survive the war on Bougainville but only as an increasingly toothless tiger.

Less than 300 Japanese troops opposed the November 1 landing at Cape

121

Torokino—Halsey had indeed "hit 'em where they ain't"—but the defenders and the hydrography combined to make the landing difficult.

Two reinforced regimental combat teams led the assault over twelve designated "beaches" along Torokina Bay on D-Day: the 3d Marines on the right, the 9th Marines on the left. Lieutenant Colonel Alan Shapley, blown off the *Arizona* by the Japanese air raid at Pearl Harbor, now commanded the 2d Raider Regiment and deployed his battalions in support of each infantry regiment.

Bougainville's heavy surf ruined the 9th Marines' combat debut, swamping eighty-six landing boats. The troops streamed ashore like drowned rats but quickly reorganized to overwhelm the limited Japanese opposition to their front. Enemy resistance proved deadlier on the right flank. There a single, well-served 75mm gun crew had open season against the 3d Marines' landing craft. The preliminary naval bombardment (four destroyers firing for a half hour) had been limited to preserve surprise; this strong point remained unscathed. In a matter of minutes the Imperial gunners sank a dozen boats at point-blank range.

As the assault waves faltered in the face of this fire, Marine Sergeant Robert Owens made his way ashore, recognized the crisis, and attacked the gun position single-handedly. Owen's self-sacrificing courage turned the tide. He silenced the deadly gun but died in the doing—and became the first member of the 3d Marine Division to receive the Medal of Honor.

As the landing force struggled to clear the near-shore jungle of Japanese defenders, the skies overhead erupted with screaming waves of Marine dive-bombers, taking advantage of the rare opportunity for both Leatherneck air and infantry to operate together. This one-two punch combination helped the assault units advance the beachhead line well into the swampy terrain behind the high-water mark, clearing the way for supporting waves.

Turnage kept pouring his troops ashore, despite the fearsome surf and spirited fire. By dark the 3d Marine Division had 14,000 troops ashore and dug-in, a significant achievement under decidedly adverse conditions. Losing 200 casualties on D-Day seemed an acceptable cost.

While General Hyakutake withheld his reserves to determine whether the Torokina landing was another American feint, the Japanese command at Rabaul mounted a furious and immediate series of counterattacks. Four waves of bombers and fighters attacked the vulnerable beachhead and the exposed amphibious task force on November 1 alone, but Halsey had plenty of Allied fighter squadrons aloft to give battle. Twenty-six of the raiders went down in flames, the others scattered.

With the night a Japanese surface force swept south from Rabaul seeking to achieve another Savo Island victory against the American invasion fleet. This time the U.S. Navy stood ready. The ensuing Battle of Empress Augusta Bay resulted in a stinging defeat for the Imperial Navy.

A follow-up counterlanding the night of November 6–7 caused greater

concern to the Marines ashore. Nearly 500 Japanese troops fought their way through the surf in the rear of the force beachhead line, took up firing positions along the Koromokina River, and raised hell with Turnage's support echelons. Killing them one by one took the Marines several anxious days.

Japanese air raids materialized each day and night. One flight of torpedo bombers from Rabaul intercepted a U.S. reinforcement convoy the night of November 17 and sank the destroyer-transport *McKean* with the loss of fifty-two Marines and sixty-four sailors. But by then Turnage had his 21st Marines ashore and was fighting shoulder-to-shoulder with the Army's 37th Division.

General Vandegrift, selected to become the next Commandant of the Marine Corps, turned over command of IMAC to Major General Roy Geiger and departed for Washington. Few Marines even batted an eye that an aviator now commanded the amphibious corps. Geiger was widely known for his enlightened leadership and blazing courage. The battle for the Bougainville beachhead continued in his capable hands.

Torokina Island, Bougainville. A Marine brings his sub-machine gun to bear on Japanese snipers in the heavy jungle just ahead. This occurred on November 1, 1943, D-Day for the 3d Marine Division landing at Empress Augusta Bay, Bougainville, in the Upper Solomons.
(U.S. Marine Corps)

123

The SeaBees inspected the swampy interior and determined that the only suitable sites for the airfields lay 1,500 yards inland from the beach. Hyakutake finally released his main combatant units, the 2d Infantry Division and a very good force of *rikusentai*, the Kure 7th, and these troops engaged the Leathernecks and GIs in a series of sharp brawls under hellacious conditions of terrain and foul weather. In six grueling days the 3d Marines fought as many skirmishes, collectively called the Battle of Piva Forks, losing a hundred men but killing a thousand Japanese.

Not every Marine action enjoyed such success. An ambitious raid down the coast at Koirari by parachutists and raiders on November 29 ran into an unexpectedly large and lethal Japanese battalion. The elite Marine units, long on valor but always short on firepower, suffered grievous losses and had to be withdrawn under heavy fire. This took considerable doing. At the end, protected by close-in destroyers and long-range artillery, the raiding force made it back through the surf to their ships, minus one man in every five.

Bougainville would mark the final chapter of Marine Corps special units like rangers and parachutists. They had fought with ferocious courage, but the Pacific War had outgrown their narrow services. Commando forces had proven useful to this point—Edson at Tulagi, Krulak at Choiseul—but henceforth the Marines would need integrated ("homogenized") *divisions*, whose basic maneuver element would be the infantry battalion. Many of the existing raiders and parachutists provided the nucleus of the 4th Marines, reestablished in honor of the regiment lost in the Philippines and commanded by Alan Shapley. Others would provide the cadre of combat leadership for the 5th Marine Division for its single cataclysmic fight at Iwo Jima.

The battle for the American beachhead at Cape Torokina continued unabated into December. The 21st Marines took the lead, fighting savagely to control the high ground known as "Hellzapoppin Ridge."

Marine dive-bomber squadrons lent a hand. The learning curve for close air support in a jungle battle ascended sharply after an inauspicious beginning. The standard white smoke grenades of the infantry proved unreliable; the Japanese would pop their own smoke to confuse the pilots, and on one occasion friendly troops died by errant bombing. Colored smoke grenades provided the solution. The Japanese could never match the variety of colors—green, blue, even *violet*—soon available to the Marines' forward liaison party.

When bomb fuses set to delay a tenth of a second upon impact failed to detonate in the mushy jungle, the bombardiers switched to four fifths of a second delay setting. These small improvements made a world of difference at Hellzapoppin Ridge. Given this support, the 21st Marines took and held the high ground.

The "short-legged" Marine dive-bombers that supported the 21st Marines so valiantly had launched from the nearby and newly constructed fighter strip at Torokina, which became operational on December 10, thanks to five weeks of backbreaking work by the SeaBees. On the twenty-eighth,

General Turnage turned over his positions ashore to the Americal Division; overall command of the campaign ashore passed from General Geiger's IMAC to the Army's XIV Corps. The Marines left steaming Bougainville with pleasure.

Marine casualties in the bruising campaign totaled 423 killed and 1,418 wounded. The operation completed the conquest of the Solomons, neutralized the five Japanese airfields on the island, and placed Rabaul within range of every tactical Allied aircraft in the South Pacific.

It became time for the 1st Marine Division, the Old Breed, to reenter the fray. Now they were "MacArthur's Marines," and their mission in the Southwest Pacific Area was to complete the isolation of Rabaul by executing a flanking amphibious assault on the western end of New Britain Island, the opposite end from Rabaul itself. The Marines' objective: the Japanese airfield at Cape Gloucester. Their principal opponent: Major General Iwao Matsuda, commanding the 65th Brigade, Imperial Japanese Army.

Of all the miserable battlefields where Marines fought the Japanese in the South Pacific, none could compare with Cape Gloucester in the winter monsoons. Unbelievably dense rains arrived on D-Day and remained. The mud became impassable. The dripping jungle swarmed with poisonous vipers and stinging insects ("even the damned caterpillars bite," complained one Leatherneck). At one point early in the campaign the Marines had suffered more casualties from falling trees than deaths by gunshot wounds. The Marines would fight in Gloucester's "Green Inferno" for four months.

Major General William Rupertus (Vandegrift's assistant at Guadalcanal) now commanded the Old Breed, assisted by Brigadier General Lemuel Shepherd. The division had taken nearly a year to recover from Guadalcanal, including the persistent strains of malaria that still haunted the veterans. Rupertus, twice a national champion with the Springfield ".03" rifle and former director of marksmanship for the Corps, used the interlude to supervise his division's transition to the M–1 Garand. The Old Breed Marines gave up their Springfields reluctantly, but under Rupertus's no-nonsense intendance, they became proficient with their new rifles.

The division staged in eastern New Guinea embarked their small flotilla of transports and landing craft on Christmas morning, and set sail with confidence for New Britain.

The amphibious landing on Cape Gloucester on December 26, 1943, was nearly flawless. While one battalion thundered ashore at Tauli on the west side of the cape to establish a blocking position, the bulk of the 7th Marines and 1st Marines invested Yellow Beach, closer to the objective airfields.

This would be the last of the Marines' major, unopposed ("hit 'em where they ain't") landings of the war. The surprise thrust caught the Japanese command in Rabaul off guard. The few defenders in the beachhead delivered a sharp fire, then melted into the jungle. Assault troops slung their rifles and wielded machetes to cut through the dense vegetation. Despite their prox-

The Old Breed, the troops of the 1st Marine Division, stream ashore at Cape Gloucester, New Britain, on the day after Christmas 1943. The division, by now fully recovered from the ravages of the Guadalcanal campaign, continued the fight up the Solomons chain to the very island occupied by Fortress Rabaul. (U.S. Marine Corps)

imity to Rabaul, the division's D-Day casualties were incredibly light: twenty-one killed, twenty-three wounded.

Then came the rains. Ironically, the Marines' field maps described the area just inland from Yellow Beach as a "damp flat." Troops cutting their way through the swamp had reason to bitch: "Yeah, I'm damp up to my neck!" Suddenly, well-armed Japanese troops began to appear, and the Marines got down to the serious business at hand.

The Old Breed readjusted to close combat quickly. The key leadership billets of the division included such legendary jungle fighters as Chesty Puller, Herman Hanneken, Bill Whaling, and a big, cold-eyed former football and wrestling star named Lewis Walt. Two battalions cleared the airstrips of the disorganized defenders on the fourth day. Rupertus borrowed a page from General Sherman's March Through Georgia in the Civil War by signaling the commanding general of the Sixth Army: "First Marine Division presents to you

Marines on Cape Gloucester advance warily through a shell-wrecked clearing before reentering the dense jungle. By now it was raining heavily, and the steaming island held special horrors. "Even the damned caterpillars bite," complained one Leatherneck.
(U.S. Marine Corps)

Bringing a wounded
Marine out of Cape
Gloucester's rugged
jungles made for
back-breaking work
by stretcher crews,
often comprised of
members of the
division band.
(U.S. Marine Corps)

as an early New Year gift the complete airdrome of Cape Gloucester. Situation well in hand due to fighting spirit of troops, the usual Marine luck, and the Grace of God."

Things got tougher after that. On New Year's Day, 1944, Rupertus unleashed General Shepherd with a composite task force of 5th and 7th Marines on a southeastern axis toward Borgen Bay. The next day Shepherd's force encountered the enemy well emplaced on the far side of a swollen jungle creek. Several days of hard fighting failed to dislodge the Japanese defenders. Casualties on both sides were so heavy that the place became known as Suicide Creek.

Shepherd needed more firepower and shock action to break the impasse, but his tanks had been unable to advance in the thick, sucking mud. Shepherd, like Rupertus, an avid Civil War student, saw the parallels of this battle with Grant's difficulties in the Wilderness, and he directed his combat engineers to lay down a "corduroy road" of thick logs through the swamp to support the weight of the tanks. This worked nicely, but the steep banks of the creek still held up the tanks.

Shepherd called for a bulldozer to cut a ramp. Japanese snipers knocked out one operator after another. Private First Class Randall Johnson figured out

the solution. Using an ax handle and a shovel as extensions for the dozer's controls, Johnson positioned himself *outside the cab* along the defilade side of the vehicle and coolly cut the embankment. The tanks and half-tracks rumbled across, closely followed by cheering Marines. When Japanese sappers leapt up to slap magnetic mines against the passing tanks, the riflemen promptly cut them down.

The Japanese pulled back sullenly toward Aogiri Ridge, an elevation not even shown on Marine maps. The fighting became savage and point-blank as the jungle grew thicker on higher ground. Chesty Puller fought magnificently in this advance, at one point taking command of two infantry battalions, and garnering his fourth Navy Cross. But the breakthrough at Aogiri Ridge would result from the inspired leadership of a new legendary warrior.

The Battle of Walt's Ridge

General Shepherd sent Lieutenant Colonel "Lew" Walt to the front on January 8 to take command of the 3d Battalion, 5th Marines, which had lost two commanding officers in the previous day's fighting. The battalion had stumbled upon Aogiri Ridge, the heavily defended terrain feature that dominated the sector, and had received the brunt of the fire. When Walt arrived late in the afternoon, ⅓ had been beaten to its knees. In the words of the combat report: "The undergrowth was so thick that the men could not see 10 yards in

The critical difference between life or death for a desperately wounded Marine on Cape Gloucester (and everywhere else) was the up-front presence of the rifle company's Navy corpsman.
(U.S. Marine Corps)

131

The Old Breed Marines dubbed the interior of Cape Gloucester "the Green Inferno." Here vigilant riflemen follow a Sherman M–4 medium tank across a contested jungle stream. (U.S. Marine Corps)

front of them. The Jap machine guns were cleverly concealed among the roots of trees, well protected by snipers." The troops had neither tanks nor artillery available, only a single 37mm gun. This weapon had been promising earlier, but now half the crew lay dead. Walt asked for volunteers to push the weapon up the steep ridge. No one moved. Walt was new; they were exhausted; manhandling the gun would be certain death. Walt's blue eyes flashed angrily, then he dashed for the gun, putting his shoulder to the muddy wheel, legs churning. The surviving crew members joined. They humped the weapon upward a dozen yards, fired a canister round, reloaded, pushed upward again. Machine gun fire rattled against the gun shields, striking down more crewmen. Walt kept pushing. His riflemen sprang to life; some opened a hot fire and others scuttled uphill to put their own shoulders next to Walt's. In this way, pushing upward, firing canister, advancing again, Walt got them to the top of the ridge. But now it was dark. The Japanese, only yards away, would surely counterattack. Walt hustled to get every available man up on the crest, dug-in and tied in. He rushed an artillery forward observer team up the ridge, just in time. The Japanese launched five major attacks throughout the night, each masked by the pouring rain. The fighting for the crest was as desperate and savage as any Marines ever experienced in the war. They literally held by their teeth. As they had done so well at Edson's Ridge the previous year, the 105mm gunners of the 11th Marines plastered the reverse slope of Aogiri Ridge all night long. With the dawn the high ground became "Walt's Ridge." The Third Battalion was in exceptionally good hands.

Seizing and holding Aogiri Ridge allowed Shepherd's task force to surge forward toward Borgen Bay. One last obstacle remained, the Japanese fortified positions on Hill 660. This became the objective of Lieutenant Colonel Henry Buse's battalion of the 7th Marines. Buse's first assault failed, but his enterprising riflemen slid to the flank, assaulted the hill's steepest face, pulling themselves up hand-over-hand among the roots, and drove the surprised defenders down the slope—squarely into the killing zone of Captain Joseph Buckley's concealed tanks and half-tracks. It was a textbook assault of a fortified position, smartly adapted, ruthlessly executed.

This defeat broke the back of General Matsuda's brigade. Starving and scattered, his remnants began a long retreat eastward toward Rabaul. Colonel Oliver Smith's 5th Marines leapfrogged down the coast, conducting a fifty-seven-mile shore-to-shore landing on the Willaumez Peninsula. Smith improvised his own amphibious fire support by stacking lumber under his tanks so they could fire over the ramps of their landing boats. An intrepid Piper Cub pilot flew overhead, dropping hand grenades on Japanese positions. The unorthodox assault worked. The 5th Marines seized yet another key airfield at the cost of 130 casualties.

The encirclement of Fortress Rabaul was now nearly complete. New Zealanders seized the Green Islands; an Army cavalry division seized Los

Negros and the Admiralties; Alan Shapley's 4th Marines took Emirau. In April 1944, General MacArthur finally released the 1st Marine Division from "The Green Inferno." By then, New Britain had cost the Old Breed 1,400 casualties.

The Allied strategy of encircling, pounding, and then bypassing Rabaul (and Kavieng, its outlying base on New Ireland) saved many lives and made the most of the modest amphibious assault resources available in the South Pacific. The aviators had delivered the most telling blows—and sustained some of the most grievous losses. One hundred Marine airmen died over Rabaul itself, and hundreds more over the long watery stretches of the Solomons and Bismarcks. The exchange rate was still favorable: Marine pilots shot down 1,520 Japanese planes in the long campaign.

With Rabaul finally defanged, both Chester Nimitz and Douglas MacArthur were free to pursue their separate roads to Tokyo. Nimitz would strike first. The Pacific War would change abruptly. The first of the great "Storm Landings" was about to explode in the remote Gilbert Islands. The eye of the storm would come ashore at Tarawa Atoll.

The unmistakable scowl and erect posture of Lieutenant Colonel Lewis B. "Chesty" Puller, here executive officer of the 7th Marines during the Cape Gloucester campaign. The veteran of guerrilla fighting in Nicaragua would lead his Marines in the toughest battles of Guadalcanal, "the Cape," Peleliu—and later Inchon, Seoul, and the Chosin Reservoir during the Korean War. No other Marine would match his five separate citations of the Navy Cross. (U.S. Marine Corps)

8: ACROSS THE REEF AT TARAWA

THE MARINES HAVE A WAY OF MAKING YOU AFRAID— NOT OF DYING, BUT OF NOT DOING YOUR JOB.

*First Lieutenant Bonnie Little, USMCR, 2d Amphibian Tractor Battalion,
posthumous Navy Cross, D-Day, Tarawa*

Time combat correspondent Robert Sherrod may have been the first to sense Tarawa's significance:

"Last week some 2,000 or 3,000 United States Marines, most of them now dead or wounded, gave the nation a name to stand beside those of Concord Bridge, the *Bonhomme Richard*, the Alamo, the Little Big Horn, and Belleau Wood. The name was *Tarawa*."

The American public's perception of Marines and war was broken into two eras: Before Tarawa and After Tarawa. The *Saturday Evening Post* illustrator's version—grinning, hell-for-leather surf-striders in neatly pressed utilities, bedecked with a glamorous bandage here and there—was replaced by the shocking truth. A sun-baked beach littered with bloated, blackened corpses that had once been strong young Marines. It would have been too much to expect the mourners to see the sad flotsam along Red Beach as something other than what it was: startling evidence of a heroism that, having stormed in life the very Gates of Hell, might have evoked in death the salute of heaven itself.

For its duration, the short, savage Battle of Tarawa was the bloodiest amphibious assault of the war. When it shuddered to a halt, seventy-six hours after the initial landing,

Dead Marines and wrecked amphibian vehicles bear mute testimony to the savage fighting to wrest Red Beach One at Betio Island, Tarawa Atoll, from the defending Japanese. Both assault vehicles, the primitive LVT–1 Alligator (right) and the newer LVT–2 Water Buffalo (left), were logistics craft field-modified with scrap iron to lead the 2d Marine Division's attack across the reef. A half century after the battle, the rusting tracks of these same two vehicles were still visible at low tide. (U.S. Marine Corps)

nearly 6,000 men lay dead in an area smaller than the space occupied by the Pentagon and its parking lots. Eleven hundred were United States Marines. "Victory was inevitable," observed Colonel David Shoup, the sole surviving Medal of Honor recipient. "The only question was the price we would have to pay for it."

In such a violent, near-run battle, the prize of victory dangled precariously on a thin web of small incidents, oversights, and earlier decisions.

Across the reef at
Tarawa, 1943
(Charles Waterhouse)

The sudden appearance in the Gilbert Islands in late November of a major American invasion force astonished the Japanese.

Imperial General Headquarters figured the U.S. assault on southern Bougainville on November 1 would be the principal enemy offensive of the winter, perhaps to be followed by a modest campaign against Rabaul the following spring. The Central Pacific, quiet since the summer of 1942, seemed to pose no threat.

But at Pearl Harbor, Admiral Chester Nimitz had devoted most of the time since his victory at Midway to steadily building up his forces and studying new concepts of naval warfare. As the once-devastated docks and anchorages of Pearl Harbor filled with new, more powerful, highly specialized warships, Nimitz quietly picked the most qualified officers in the sea services to lead a great new juggernaut westward. The Marines would be blessed by his choices.

His top three selections would rock the Imperial Japanese Navy to its barnacles: Admiral Raymond Spruance to command the Central Pacific Force; Admiral Kelly Turner to command Spruance's amphibious forces; General Holland Smith to command the amphibious corps—the tens of thousands of Marines and soldiers who would provide the cutting edge of the greatest sustained amphibious campaign in history.

Spruance's Central Pacific Force (soon to become the Fifth Fleet) would feature Marines as a centerpiece of the revolution in naval warfare in the Pacific.

No more would U.S. offensives be cautious, half-step, threadbare expeditions, limited to the protective range of land-based air. Nimitz would cast loose on the high seas a semi-independent legion of new *Essex*-class fleet carriers, ranging far and wide with their own task forces of new battleships, cruisers, and destroyers.

On their heels would come the first large-scale, self-sustaining, amphibious task forces, loaded for bear with assault troops and accompanied by the reborn battleships of the Pearl Harbor fiasco—too slow for the fast carriers, but ideal in their big guns to support the amphibs. Sustaining both forces would be high-speed logistics ships, fully capable of replenishing and repairing the fleet at sea for extended periods.

Yet many senior officers (including General Douglas MacArthur) still questioned whether any naval force would be strong enough to overcome and

occupy the strategic islands of the new theater—small atolls, fortified to the teeth, surrounded by barrier coral reefs. The war was nearly two years old, and there had yet been no acid test, no real trial by fire of the doctrine of amphibious assault. The time had come. Ahead lay crucial landings at Normandy and Iwo Jima. Could *any* group of Marines or soldiers really land against heavy fire?

The Joint Chiefs at first wanted the initial blow of the Central Pacific campaign to strike the Marshalls. Nimitz demurred. No amphibious commander could hope to succeed without first obtaining advance aerial photos of the target. In 1943 in the Pacific, this could be achieved only by USAAF medium bombers. The Marshalls were out of range. Defer the Marshalls, Nimitz recommended, and attack the closer, smaller Gilberts first, following photo missions by the Seventh Air Force in the Ellice Islands.

We would convert the Japanese airfield at Betio Island, Tarawa Atoll, into the advance base needed to begin the campaign against the Marshalls. Makin and Apamama, in the same chain, would also be taken.

The Joint Chiefs accepted Nimitz's suggestion for hitting the Gilberts first, but rejected his time schedule: D-Day for the Marshalls had to follow in just six weeks.

Nimitz thus advised Spruance: "Get the hell in, then get the hell out."

Fast footwork would contribute to strategic surprise, preserve the Marshalls' countdown, and reduce the risk of a major Combined Fleet counterattack as well. Unfortunately, the Marines would pay a price for these strategic restraints on their tactical flexibility.

Few amphibious battles in the Pacific would levy such terrific demands on Marine leadership. Every man would be tested in this fiery crucible, but none more so than those at the front of the shock troops.

Commandant Thomas Holcomb had selected Major General Julian Smith to command the 2d Marine Division. Some considered Smith too soft-spoken and inexperienced to lead a 20,000-man division into brutal combat. But Holcomb, who had seen war at its worst in France, knew Smith to be fearless under fire and a superb trainer of men.

Smith, in turn, picked Colonel Merritt "Red Mike" Edson, hero of Tulagi and Guadalcanal, for his chief of staff, and—acting on a shrewdly perceptive hunch—kept the unknown, unproved Lieutenant Colonel David Shoup as his amphibious planner. Later, just before the battle, Smith would follow another hunch and give Shoup command of the assault regiment (promoting him to colonel in the process), wisely making his talented subordinate both the architect and executioner of the forcible seizure of Tarawa.

Sobered by Betio's elaborate fortifications, Julian Smith, Edson, and Shoup requested a preliminary seizure of an offshore island as an artillery fire support base, three days of combined naval, air, and artillery pounding, a diver-

Tarawa's Formidable Defenders

The Americans never really appreciated how rapidly a force of Japanese troops could convert an island into a defensive fortress. At Peleliu, Iwo Jima, and Okinawa, common riflemen would dig elaborate cave, bunker, and tunnel systems with hand tools in six months or less. The garrison on Betio had *fifteen months* after Carlson's Raid to prepare their defenses—and in this instance they didn't have to dig. Imperial General Headquarters provided the nation's best fortifications experts, a talented naval construction battalion, plenty of raw material, and major weapons galore. In July 1943 they dispatched Rear Admiral Keiji Shibasaki, a veteran *rikusentai* officer, to take command of Tarawa's defenses. Shibasaki would mirror many of Julian Smith's attributes: steadfast leader, superb trainer, innovative tactician. With 2,600 hard-boiled *rikusentai* from Yokosuka and Sasebo, plus 2,000 well-armed construction troops, Shibasaki proclaimed "a million Americans could not take Tarawa in a hundred years." In private, Shibasaki accepted a more realistic goal: Hold any American landing force at bay for three days—the time required for the Combined Fleet to steam 1,300 miles from Truk Lagoon and destroy the enemy invasion force in the long-sought "decisive sea battle."

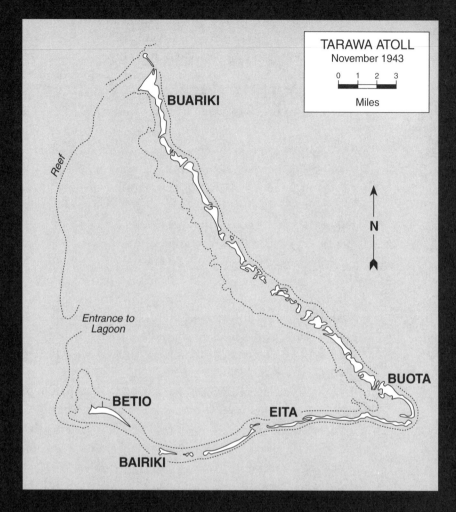

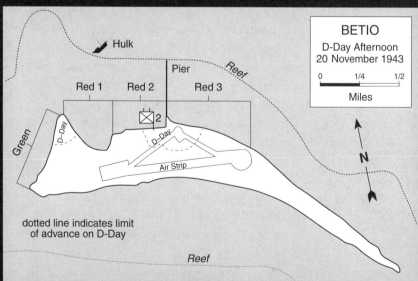

sionary landing, and full use of the 2d Marine Division's three regimental combat teams. Nimitz and Spruance had to reject all of this. Speed of execution would prevail.

Then Holland Smith announced his intention of withholding the 6th Marines as corps reserve in case the green Army division attacking Makin Atoll ran into trouble. The 2d Marine Division would have to execute a frontal assault on Betio with only three hours of preliminary bombardment and without one of its three maneuver elements. Succeeding under these handicaps would demand nigh-perfect intelligence and execution.

Few Marines in late 1943 knew anything about the remote Gilbert Islands, a scattering of small Micronesian atolls lying just above the Equator, roughly 1,300 miles east of Rabaul and 2,400 miles southwest of Pearl Harbor. The Japanese had seized the longtime British possessions the day after Pearl Harbor, landing unopposed on Makin and Tarawa.

The Gilberts had remained an operational backwater until August 1942 when Lieutenant Colonel Evans Carlson led his 2d Raider Battalion ashore at Makin in a submarine-launched raid.

The costly Makin operation, intended to divert Japanese attention from Guadalcanal, proved strategically shortsighted. Imperial Japanese Headquarters immediately began an urgent militarization of the Gilberts and accorded highest priority to fortifying Betio, key to Tarawa Atoll and the entire island chain.

The strength of the Japanese garrison on Betio came as no surprise to Julian Smith, Red Mike Edson, or David Shoup. The quality of aerial photographs provided by the Seventh Air Force was matched by the shrewd analysis of division intelligence officer Lieutenant Colonel Thomas ("Jack") Colley. The landing force knew a month in advance the location and field of fire of 95 percent of Betio's 500 pillboxes and gun emplacements.

No one had to remind Red Mike Edson or the veterans of Tulagi and Gavutu-Tanambogo about the fighting spirit of the *rikusentai*.

Shoup wanted to land on the north shore, through the lagoon, a dangerously long ship-to-shore movement, yet rewarded by approaching Betio through the one sector Shibasaki had not strewn with mines.

But the reef and the tides remained worrisome unknowns.

The concept of converting the thin-skinned, unarmored, logistical amphibian tractors (LVTs) into reef-crossing, assault landing craft to carry storm troops ashore over a fringing reef originated with Lieutenant Colonel Brute Krulak in an earlier "crash test" elsewhere in the South Pacific, but the 2d Marine Division troops at Tarawa were the pioneers who gambled with the idea when all the stakes were on the line.

Shoup favored using LVTs to assault Betio from the git-go. Major Henry Drewes, commanding the 2d Amphibian Tractor Battalion, organized an enter-

prising crew of tinkerers and scroungers to convert the best seventy-five of his beat-up Guadalcanal vehicles for tactical use. They applied lightweight, bolt-on armor to the cabs, festooned the topsides with machine guns, and made field-fixes to the exhaust and bilge pump systems to better survive the extended ship-to-shore movement.

But seventy-five old LVTs were too few to do the job. That's when Julian Smith energized Howlin' Mad Smith to "howl" at "Terrible" Turner to ensure delivery of at least fifty of the new LVT–2 Water Buffaloes. "No LVTs, no landing," Smith barked.

Major Drewes dispatched a provisional company of "amtrackers" (LVT crewmen) to Samoa. There, very late in the preliminary stage, they received delivery of the new vehicles, quickly mastered them, and just as quickly took off in three LSTs (tank landing ships) to join the Tarawa task force off Betio on the early morning of D-Day, in the very nick of time.

David Shoup, unsure till the last whether the new LVTs would arrive at all, developed two landing plans—one with just the basic seventy-five Alligators, one with the augmented Water Buffaloes—but both involved dangerous gunwale-to-gunwale troop transfers from boats into tractors at night. That would be bad enough; the greater concern was whether the reinforcing elements could traverse the reef at a rising neap (low) tide in their Higgins boats. Julian Smith flatly warned his Marines to be prepared to wade ashore from the reef. Maybe it wouldn't be such a big deal. The Navy promised to "obliterate" Betio in its allotted three hours of preliminary bombardment.

The red dawn on D-Day brought swift, deadly reality.

One thing went right. Spruance's Central Pacific Force indeed achieved strategic surprise in the Gilberts. Admiral Shibasaki was astounded to scan the waters offshore at the beginning of morning nautical twilight on November 20 and find himself surrounded by U.S. warships of all descriptions—including transports.

Shibasaki opened the battle with his four turret-mounted eight-inch naval rifles (bought from the British during the Russo-Japanese War of 1904–1905). Three U.S. battleships—two resurrected from the muddy bottom of Pearl Harbor—answered instantly with their mammoth fourteen-inch batteries. Vengeance came swiftly for the Pearl veterans. In ten minutes Shibasaki lost the teeth of his coast defenses.

Abruptly Shibasaki's "back door" was open. Through the smoke he could see enemy minesweepers and destroyers leading a double column of landing craft through the channel, into the atoll, forming to assault his northern shoreline—the one sector still lacking the complete network of mines and concrete obstacles. Greatly alarmed, Shibasaki sent emergency messages to the Combined Fleet commander, burned his papers, and began the desperate shifting of forces from south shore to north under a galling fire from the bombardment force.

But now the Americans' inexperience in conducting large-scale amphibious assaults under fire began to show. Cracks appeared, plans unraveled.

The command ship's principal radio net became the first casualty. Each time the battleship *Maryland* fired her main guns, the concussion knocked more landing force radio nets out of commission. Julian Smith would suffer from marginal to nonexistent communications with Shoup, his tactical commander ashore, for the next thirty critical hours.

The vaunted prelanding bombardment never came close to "obliterating" Betio. Inexperience led to ill-advised selections of shells, fuses, angles of fire, and firing rates. Many shells fired from close range at zero elevation simply glanced off Shibasaki's well-built bunkers and created dangerous ricochets among the ships off the far side of the island. Thick smoke obscured adjustments.

Nor were the carrier pilots effective in their two strafing and bombing missions. One arrived late, the other early; neither did any real damage. The eagerly expected mission of USAAF medium bombers with 2,000-pound "daisy-cutter" bombs failed to materialize. It turned out they never got the request submitted by the Marines weeks in advance. This error would cost scores of lives.

Shibasaki may have been poorly served by his coast defense guns, but his dual-purpose (antiair, antiboat) gun mounts had a field day shooting horizontally at point-blank ranges against the U.S. landing craft. These deadly guns, ranging from 75mm to 127mm, sat in open emplacements, fully vulnerable to air-burst munitions that had not been used. Now the Marines would have to overrun each position by direct assault with rifles.

Rear Admiral Harry Hill, commanding the amphibious task force, ordered "Cease-fire!" for the shore bombardment at 08:55. He could no longer see the wallowing LVTs through the smoke and worried he might hit the assault waves with friendly fire.

Smith and Edson raged at Hill—the assault waves, barely across the Line of Departure, were still twenty minutes north of the beach and at their most vulnerable. Hill refused to budge.

Admiral Shibasaki had executed amphibious landings of his own and knew how often things could go awry. The premature cease-fire was the break he had been looking for. In the sudden quiet he saw to the final redeployment of his forces and replenished their ammo. He also looked appraisingly at the reef, expecting it to derail the approaching assault waves.

But Shibasaki had never seen Marine Corps LVTs ("little boats on wheels" his survivors would call them). He stared in concern as the long line of sixteen-ton amphibians struck the reef, slowed, then crawled over the top, slithering across like so many mechanical spiders. Now they lumbered shoreward, their hundreds of machine guns raking the seawall. "The god of death has come!" exclaimed one terrified Japanese sailor. But the officers lashed their men, the big 13mm machine guns opened fire, and the battle was joined.

Just as the first waves of LVTs struck the reef, a pair of accompanying Higgins boats raced forward to the seaward end of the long commercial pier which ran from Betio's north beach to the edge of the reef. Out swarmed Lieutenant Deane Hawkins and his handpicked storming party of scout-snipers and combat engineers.

Wielding automatic rifles and flamethrowers, Hawkins's men worked through the maze of improvised emplacements which Shibasaki's redeploying machine gunners had rigged during the cease-fire. This was desperate work. The pier marked the dividing line between Red Beach Two and Three, and Japanese gunners in the pilings would have flanking fire against the LVTs.

Hawkins's stalwarts distracted most of these gunners, but they were too enthusiastic with their flamethrowers. The mid-portion of the pier became engulfed in flames, preventing Hawkins from sweeping the entire 500-yard structure. Japanese gunners on the shoreward side of this conflagration would shoot the hell out of the advancing Marines for the rest of D-Day.

Incredibly, despite the interminable ship-to-shore movement and the hot reception provided by Shibasaki's gunners, the first three assault waves of Marines in their LVTs made it ashore in wholesale numbers. Japanese gunners, perhaps flustered by the LVTs, knocked out only eight of the eighty-seven assault vehicles. David Shoup's great gamble had paid off in spades. In ten minutes he had 1,500 Marines hugging the seawall along Betio's north shore.

Then the wheels came off the assault. The Marines hoped by mid-morning to have enough water over the reef for their Higgins boats to cross with ease. But something was terribly wrong. When Admiral Hill radioed his observation plane, "Is reef covered with water?" the reply was a chilling "Negative!" The fourth and fifth waves, mounted in Higgins boats, crashed to a halt all along the partially exposed reef. The troops were still 500 to 600 yards from the beach, and the water was already dotted with crisscrossing machine gun bullets, the air rent by terrifying near-misses from the antiaircraft guns.

Shoup's "Plan B" called for the empty LVTs to return to the reef, transfer troops from the boats, and recycle to the beach. This worked only momentarily. Then the big, untouched, dual-purpose guns began to spout their deadly fire at the thin-skinned LVTs, blowing them up, setting them ablaze.

Shibasaki's heavy machine guns, the heart of his defense, stitched the amtracs unmercifully. Those vehicles recrossing the reef, trying to carry the first loads of wounded Marines back to sea, were shot so full of holes that they sank immediately in deep water. Brave Major Drewes died violently during his third cycle from reef to beach when a Japanese 75mm gun pinwheeled the cab of his LVT–2. His battalion bled and died with him, losing in short order 90 of their 125 vehicles and 300 men.

The Marines in the follow-on waves could only curse, scramble out of their grounded boats, climb across the razor-sharp coral, and begin the agonizingly slow wade ashore. Here was the first day of Belleau Wood reincarnated. The blue-green waters of the lagoon turned a milky crimson.

Each of the assault battalion commanders had chosen to land in the fourth wave; each now dealt with the reef and the unrelenting fire in his own fashion.

On the left flank, Red Beach Three, where the volume of enemy fire was slower to build, the veteran Major Henry "Jim" Crowe strode furiously ashore on the heels of the assault elements of his 2d Battalion, 8th Marines. Crowe's men enjoyed limited success on D-Day, actually penetrating the seawall and seizing positions halfway across the skinny island. But there they faced increasing fire from three sides, plus strafing by their own Navy planes, and had to pull back to the beach.

The Japanese would shortly amass most of their combat power against that flank, and Crowe would spend three days trying to advance 200 yards to the southeast.

In the center, Lieutenant Colonel Herbert Amey leapt out of his grounded landing craft and rushed through the shallows, seeking to rally the scattered elements of his 2d Battalion, 2d Marines. Japanese machine gunners killed him before he could even reach dry sand. When his executive officer could not get ashore, Lieutenant Colonel Walter Jordan, an observer from the 4th Marine Division, stepped in and assumed command. But 2/2 was hard hit and badly fragmented. Their enclaves were barely dozens of yards inland.

Japanese fire was particularly vicious on the right flank, where Red Beach One included a dangerous concave reentrant, soon called "The Pocket." Here a battery of four Japanese 75mm dual-purpose guns butchered the approaching landing craft.

So ghastly was the slaughter that Major John Schoettel honestly believed he had witnessed the loss of his entire 3d Battalion, 2d Marines. When Shoup radioed him to slide left, land near the pier, then work his way back west, Schoettel replied bitterly, "We have nothing left to land."

Unknown to Schoettel, one of his company commanders, Major Michael "Mike" Ryan, had survived the bloodbath with at least half of his force intact by staying low and shifting westward, beyond the killing zone.

Ryan scrambled ashore on a piece of real estate to be immortalized as Green Beach, looking back over his shoulder as the rest of his men attempted to follow. "They looked like turtles," he said. "All I could see were helmets with rifles held over them." Ryan's modest beachhead soon resembled a shipwreck. Dozens of soaked stragglers, the human debris of four different landing teams, many weaponless, gravitated to Ryan.

These would become "Ryan's Orphans"; collectively they would win this dreadful battle.

Colonel Shoup's personal ship-to-shore odyssey took four hours, during which he lost two thirds of his regimental staff and suffered minor wounds and a badly wrenched knee. The profane, barrel-chested Indianan reached Betio's Red Beach Two at high noon on his hands and knees.

Here Shoup's recent experience under fire at chaotic Rendova served him

well. In spite of the absolute hell that was Betio—and in spite of the total collapse of his intricate assault plan—Shoup kept his head and his blazing will to win.

With a handful of aides he established a command post on the lee side of a still-occupied Japanese bunker near the base of the pier. He would not budge from this spot—nor even sit down—for the duration. The Rock of Tarawa was ashore and in command.

Shoup had expected big things from the company of medium tanks attached to the division at the last moment (everything was "at the last moment" in this operation). He ordered the fourteen brand-new M–4 Shermans ashore early. This went well at first.

Each tank was preloaded in its own medium landing craft in the well deck of a strange-looking amphibious ship, the *Ashland*, the Navy's first dock landing ship (LSD). *Ashland* entered the fire-swept lagoon, ballasted down ("squatted and flooded her well deck"), then lowered her enormous stern gate and dispatched the landing craft directly to the reef. The Shermans clambered out over the reef without difficulty, then began approaching the beach, eight on the left flank, six on the right.

The sturdy tanks proved impervious to Japanese machine gun fire, but the buttoned-up drivers were virtually blind and the vehicles had arrived without their deep-water fording kits.

One Sherman foundered in an unseen shell hole, drowning its crew. Seeing this, the tanks on the right deployed scouts ahead on foot, who literally felt their way around the shell holes while the tanks slowly followed. Japanese marksmen downed scout after scout. The last of the scouts, Sergeant James Atkins, was the bravest of all, leading the invaluable column safely to Red Beach One before dying in the shallows.

Combat engineers had blasted a hole through the seawall for the tanks, but the gap was now clogged with dead and wounded Marines, and the commander refused to crunch across their bodies. Instead he turned the column around and looped westward.

Without the slain Sergeant Atkins as a guide, four of the six tanks sank in shell holes. Two finally rumbled ashore, and Mike Ryan scarfed them up.

Seven of the eight Shermans reached Red Beach Three safely, but Jim Crowe had no experience in operating with tanks (nor did any other battalion commander in the division) and simply waved them inland. There, unsupported by infantry, all but one of them came to grief against Japanese antitank guns or clueless Navy dive-bombers.

The sole remaining tank, *Colorado*, raced back to the beach on fire. The driver quenched the blaze by driving her into the lagoon. *Colorado* would survive to provide heroic support to Jim Crowe, but Shoup's secret weapon—the Pacific combat debut of the heralded Sherman tank—had come a cropper at Betio.

Four hours after his assault waves stormed ashore on Betio Island, Julian Smith realized his division was in the fight of its life. The "heaviest preliminary bombardment of the war to date" had failed to diminish the firepower and

fighting spirit of the Japanese *rikusentai* who infested the little spit of an island like a hive of deadly bees.

And Smith sensed that something was freakishly wrong with the tide. Each of Smith's reinforcing infantry units was hung up along the exposed reef in their boats—forced to wade ashore against that murderous machine gun fire. He had just committed his last reserves.

Smith sent a terse message to his superior officer, Major General Howlin' Mad Smith, commanding V Amphibious Corps, ninety-five miles away at Makin: "Request release of Combat Team 6. Issue in doubt."

"Issue in Doubt!" Senior Marine commanders used this expression twice in World War II: at Wake Island on December 23, 1941, and again on November 20, 1943, D-Day at Tarawa. The message got the immediate attention of Holland Smith and Admiral Kelly Turner. Tarawa, not lightly defended Makin, would require the 6th Marines, held in Corps reserve.

Julian Smith did not exaggerate. The Battle of Tarawa would truly hang in the balance for its first thirty hours. The stakes were enormous. Failure to storm Tarawa from the sea would ruin the Gilberts campaign, cripple the vaunted Central Pacific Drive, and fatally jeopardize the still-unproved doctrine of offensive amphibious warfare.

Several survivors of the Battle of Tarawa freely admitted their belief at the time that "this was one battle we could well have lost; one amphibious landing that could have been thrown back into the sea."

Shoup's ceaseless efforts to land reserves proved only marginally effective. Using a handful of the remaining LVTs, Major "Woody" Kyle's 1st Battalion, 2d Marines, got half their numbers ashore in the center to bolster Jordan's hard-pressed survivors, but the rest were driven westward by heavy fire (most straggled ashore to join Ryan's band).

THE TIDE THAT FAILED

Even a neap tide varies over a range of several feet, twice each day. The Marines at Tarawa had every expectation that the rising tide on D-Day morning would provide the necessary five-foot increase needed to float their Higgins boats over the coral reef. When instead the tide fluctuated no more than a foot for the first thirty hours they were confounded. The "laggard" tide at Tarawa remained a mystery for forty-four years until physicist Donald Olson discovered that D-Day's neap tide had coincided with the moon's furthermost orbit from the earth. The resulting "apogean neap tide," we now know, produces an uncommonly low tidal range. The coincidence is rare, and it occurred only twice in 1943, according to Dr. Olson. One was November 20—squarely on D-Day. Surviving Marine veterans, glad to have the chronic riddle solved, quickly pointed out that the "laggard" tide was not without benefits. Hundreds of Marines fell trying to wade ashore, about one fourth the battle's casualties, but once on the beach hundreds more were saved when the persistent low tide preserved the seawall as a bulwark against grazing enemy fire.

There were no LVTs left by the time Shoup ordered Major Robert Ruud's 3d Battalion, 8th Marines, to land on the left flank. Ruud's entire 880-man force, embarked in Higgins boats, smashed to a halt against the reef. Hundreds were shot down while wading in, despite Crowe's frantic efforts to provide covering fire. The majority would get ashore, somehow, but the process took a

day and a night and cost Ruud his unit integrity and most heavy weapons. *That goddamned tide.*

The grim situation ashore was brightened only by the exceptional courage of a few individual Marines.

On Red Beach Two, fiery Staff Sergeant Bill Bordelon, a combat engineer whose webbed toes had prevented his enlistment in the Navy (the Marines figured webbed feet were ideal for amphibians), launched a single-handed battle against four particularly lethal pillboxes. Bordelon boldly approached each one, sprayed the opening with rifle fire, then tossed in home-made dynamite bombs. Each time he applied the *coup de grâce* a doomed Japanese shot him. Bordelon would not go down, somehow retaining the strength to rescue one of his fallen engineers in the water.

He died in a final shoot-out, firing a rifle grenade through the slit in the fourth bunker just as its occupants shot him in the chest. Bordelon's spectacular sacrifice cleared a wedge of safety for scores of wounded men in the very epicenter of the cross fire sweeping northern Betio.

His would be the only enlisted man's Medal of Honor.

Shoup's artillery officer also had steel in his backbone that afternoon.

Lieutenant Colonel Presley Rixey knew the battle could well depend on whether he could bring ashore the 75mm pack howitzers of his 1st Battalion, 10th Marines. His firing batteries occupied several dozen Higgins boats, blocked by the reef, now circling aimlessly at the Line of Departure. Rixey and Shoup could see that the only reasonably sheltered route from the reef to the beach was to hug the western side of the pier. Rixey set out to make this work.

For the next fifteen hours his cannoneers maintained a near-suicidal human chain along that shallow channel, humping the dismantled components of the howitzers (some weighing more than 200 pounds) out of the boats, over the reef, and into the beach. As one man fell to enemy fire—or exhaustion—another picked up his load and kept it moving shoreward. By such superhuman efforts,

With insufficient tracked landing vehicles (LVTs) and a baffling low tide, most Marines assaulting Betio on D-Day had to wade ashore under heavy fire. Marines straggling ashore re-formed behind this seawall, then screwed up their courage to scramble inland to attack the Japanese in their well-built pillboxes. As costly as the wade ashore was, three fourths of Marine casualties in this violent battle occurred once they crossed the seawall.
(U.S. Marine Corps)

148

Rixey had the first two batteries ashore, dug in, and registered by daybreak, the crews using direct fire over open sights against the surrounding bunkers.

Shoup was never more vulnerable than that first night at Betio.

Five thousand of his Marines had crossed the Line of Departure. At least 1,500 lay dead or wounded. Many of the others were badly disorganized. Very few crew-served weapons had survived the disorderly wade from the reef.

Night came early, and the isolated pockets of Marines went to ground on full alert—Crowe and Ruud on the left, Kyle and Jordan in the center, and "Ryan's Orphans" cut off by 800 yards of heavily armed Japanese, hanging on to their northwestern corner of the island. Ryan had learned long ago at Gavutu that, "Enemy bunkers secured by grenades alone have a tendency to come back to life after dark," and applied the lesson to staying alive.

Each Marine unit expected a major counterattack during the darkness. A gut-wrenching anxiety hovered over the riflemen in their shallow holes.

Julian Smith, stalking the *Maryland*'s flag bridge, felt helpless. Crippled by the failure of his water-soaked or shock-blasted radio circuits, he could only wait for the worst and pray that his training would stiffen his men along that thin, ragged beachhead ashore.

"The night of D-Day was the greatest danger to our landing forces, the crisis of the battle," he would later admit.

Shoup was particularly vulnerable to a concerted counterattack from the east. Jim Crowe was a combat giant, but he had less than 400 effectives guarding that threatened sector. The *rikusentai* had a thousand men available on the eastern end of the island, virtually untouched by the battle, well equipped with automatic weapons, light tanks, and flamethrowers.

All this force had to do was to advance about 500 yards westward along the beach, overrun Crowe, cut off the base of the pier, and annihilate Shoup's small command group. The great assault on Tarawa was that close to disaster.

Admiral Shibasaki had every intention of counterattacking in force that first night—he had specified this initiative in his contingency plans, and his men had rehearsed their movements often. But Fate had already intervened—although the Marines would not learn what happened for the next fifty years.

Where the Americans long believed that their D-Day bombardment had left Shibasaki too disorganized to attack, the impassioned admiral was in fact dead before dark.

At mid-afternoon, willing to forgo the shelter of his huge concrete bunker so that his hundreds of wounded men could find protection, Shibasaki ordered his command group outside, hailed a pair of light tanks, and began to shift to the alternate site. The luck of the Marines prevailed: One of their few working radios happened to be in the capable hands of a shore fire control party engaged in calling in shells from two destroyers in the lagoon against the same target grid square.

Suddenly the Marine spotter noticed a crowd of Japanese outside the bunker, yelled "Troops in the open!"—and called for a salvo of five-inch shells fused for air bursts.

Both destroyers responded unerringly. Sharp explosions at treetop height rained steel shards on the unprotected party of Japanese below. They died to the man. Shibasaki, his chief of staff, his gunnery officer, his adjutant, a dozen communicators and runners—all killed.

The abrupt loss of the garrison's entire command group prevented any serious counterattack that critical first night.

Not until the third night would several junior officers organize an attack of their own against the American invaders. The delayed assault had plenty of fire and fury, but it lacked Shibasaki's masterful hand, and by that time the Marines had quadrupled their numbers and firepower ashore.

Unaware of Shibasaki's death, Shoup and Julian Smith were extremely glad to greet sunrise of the second day. Yet the issue remained in doubt.

The Marines could still not get an organized unit ashore.

The 1st Battalion, 8th Marines, tired and seasick from spending the night in their Higgins boats, tried to land on line in the center (another communications failure: Shoup wanted them to come ashore in column along the pier as Rixey had done). They hit the reef hard, discovering in shock that the tide had not varied a foot in the last twenty-four hours, and proceeded to catch hell from every Japanese gunner on the island.

The sight of this slaughter caused Lieutenant Deane Hawkins to run amok along the pillboxes still dominating Red Beach Two.

Hawkins was an unlikely hero. Badly burned in a childhood accident, he had been rejected by Army recruiters who regarded his multiple scars as "disfiguring." The Marines accepted him unequivocally, and Hawkins fought at Guadalcanal with such distinction that he earned a battlefield commission. A quiet, self-effacing leader who took superb care of his men, Hawkins quickly transformed the scout-snipers into a proud, lethal unit.

This hellish morning, armed only with a handful of grenades and supernatural courage, Deane Hawkins attacked bunker after bunker. Hit several times, Hawkins raged against one emplacement after another, stuffing grenades through the firing slits, down vent tubes, into rear entrances.

No man could survive the snapping cross fire that chased him across the open spaces. One Nambu machine-gunner put a 7.7mm round through Hawkins's armpit, into his chest. He died in ten minutes, surrounded by his brokenhearted scout-snipers. "Boys," he said at the last, "I sure hate to leave you like this."

But Hawkins's personal vendetta diverted a lot of fire from the troops struggling ashore and inspired Kyle's shorthanded battalion to leap up and race across the island, runway and all, cutting Betio in two.

Shoup credited Hawkins with winning the battle.

151

THE BATTLE HISTORY OF THE US MARINES

EDDIE ALBERT'S GREATEST ROLE

As much as they admire John Wayne's war movies, there's one Hollywood figure held in special reverence by the Marines. One of the tiny, thin-skinned salvage craft meant to keep the landing boats shuttling toward the reef in bullet-swept Tarawa lagoon was commanded by a handsome, "overage" Navy officer named Edward Heimberger. Broadway and movie fans would have recognized him as the star called Eddie Albert. Lieutenant Albert, who could have been cozy in a USO unit, preferred to fight. During the height of the battle he found himself rescuing and defending scores of wounded Marines clinging to the seaward side of the coral reef. Japanese machine gunners soon infiltrated a sunken merchant ship and began shooting at the wounded men and their erstwhile rescuer. Directing his own gunner to duel the heavy Japanese weapons with the craft's light machine gun, Albert steeled himself to hang fully exposed from the gunwale to lift the casualties aboard, one at a time. He made several trips between the reef and the hospital ship and back, stopping only to swap boats when his salvage craft became riddled with bullet holes. Unsettlingly, the replacement boat carried drums of high-octane gasoline. Japanese incendiary bullets cut through the craft, some spinning crazily around the cargo compartment, dangerously near the drums. Albert and his crew danced a deadly jig, stomping out the small fires while continuing to rescue Marines and return enemy fire. Albert survived this ordeal, although it would haunt him—recalling one group of weaponless Marines whose boat had been sunk from under them. Albert offered to take them to safety—they said, "Bring us some rifles so we can go in and fight!" Doing so took time. When Albert raced back to the reef with the weapons, he found most were dead, shot down by the nearby Japanese gunners. Albert wrenched the survivors forcibly aboard his boat, whether they wanted his help or not. Altogether he and his shipmates saved more than three dozen wounded or stranded Marines from certain death. Eddie Albert would return to Hollywood to resume a fine film career, specializing in comedy, sometimes taking the role of a cowardly military officer. But tell that to the Marines.

A posthumous Medal of Honor went to his family. Julian Smith insisted the Navy name the captured airstrip "Hawkins Field," the only infantryman to earn such a distinction.

Tarawa was the kind of battle that evoked a procession of unlikely, unexpected heroes, each man surpassing and surprising himself, each contributing at a crucial point in the seesaw fighting.

Unknown to Shoup and Smith at the time, the greatest breakthrough of the battle was taking place along the western coast. There, in one brilliant hour, Mike Ryan led his "Orphans" in a carefully executed drive from north to south.

Making the most of his precious two Sherman tanks, and blessed with a shore fire control team whose radio still worked, Ryan swept south behind a protective wall of supporting fire, exterminating an entire company of *rikusentai* and a daunting tangle of pillboxes.

Suddenly—finally—Smith had a covered beach over which to land the 6th Marines, the combat team he had beseeched Holland Smith and Kelly Turner to release the day before.

In those years the first battalion of each infantry regiment had the standing mission of conducting a landing from rubber boats. But within the 2d Marine Division, only Major William ("Willie K") Jones took the task to heart. So assiduously did he train his 1st Battalion, 6th Marines, in their rubber

boat mission that he earned the derisive nickname "The Admiral of the Condom Fleet."

Julian Smith, appreciative of Jones's zeal, ordered 1/6 to land immediately on Green Beach—Ryan's beach.

Doing so took time, but late on the second day Jones's "Condom Fleet" crossed the western reef in eighty-four rubber boats. His Marines paddled with considerable anxiety. The 1,000-yard transit took an hour, during which they were helpless targets, vividly backlit by the setting sun. But so thoroughly had "Ryan's Orphans" cleared the coastline that not a single Japanese could uncork even a rifle shot in their direction.

Shoup, buoyed by finally having a fully organized and equipped battalion in the fight, released a situation report which quickly became a classic: "Casualties many; percentage dead unknown; combat efficiency: *We are winning!*"

Julian Smith, with eight of his nine infantry battalions committed, sent Red Mike Edson ashore to take overall command from Shoup.

The Marines now had the momentum. The third day of the battle bore little resemblance to the chaos of the first day and a half.

Willie K. Jones led his powerful battalion east down the length of the airfield, covering 800 yards before noon and relieving Woody Kyle's encircled troops on the south coast. Shoup led a violent attack by his 2d Marines east-

The 2d Marine Division's bloody victory at Tarawa resulted from small teams like these. Here, elements of a machine gun crew clear a new position with carbines and hand grenades. From H-Hour on, the antagonists fought the entire battle of Tarawa within hand-grenade range of each other.

(U.S. Marine Corps)

153

ward against The Pocket. Jim Crowe and the 8th Marines continued to beat against the large sand-covered bunker to their left front.

Here the biggest battle of the day erupted.

The improbable hero of the battle on Red Beach Three turned out to be First Lieutenant Alexander ("Sandy") Bonnyman, a free-spirited, one-time aviation cadet rejected by the Army Air Corps in the 1930s for buzzing the control tower.

Ironically, Bonnyman did not have to be there on Betio—or even in the armed forces. He was thirty-three (older even than Pappy Boyington), had a wife and three daughters, and owned a couple of copper mines—critical defense industries. He was triply exempt from the draft.

But Bonnyman's patriotism burned with an intense heat. Inspired by the news of Pearl Harbor, he had enlisted in the Marines, fought with distinction at Guadalcanal, and earned a battlefield commission. Now he was a combat engineer assigned to the division shore party and out of work since D-Day because no supplies could yet land over the beaches.

Eager to lend a hand, Bonnyman drifted down the beach to join the 8th Marines' siege of the large bunker.

Bonnyman studied the bunker, assembled and rehearsed a vagabond team of flamethrower operators and demolitionists, then led them in a sudden charge up the slopes of the fortress.

Japanese gunners reacted frantically, shooting down half the storming party, but they were too late. Bonnyman's engineers scorched the topside machine gunners with flame, then dropped thermite grenades down the vent pipes. With that, the 8th Marines arose with a yell and streaked up the slope to join the fight. Hundreds of Japanese boiled out of the rear of the bunker like enraged scorpions. The Marines, finally given live targets in the open, shot them to pieces.

But Sandy Bonnyman paid the ultimate price for his boldness. Kneeling on the highest peak of the bunker, he turned to yell for more explosives. A Japanese rifleman nailed him through the head.

Betio Island was so flat, and the Japanese pillboxes so artfully designed, that Marines literally took their lives in their hands every time they stood up to advance. Here "ammo humpers" dash forward under fire to deliver boxes of linked bullets to the machine gun crew to the left front. (U.S. Marine Corps)

154

This sand-covered Japanese bunker stymied the advance of the 8th Marines east of Betio's Red Beach Three until the third day of the battle. Then First Lieutenant Alexander Bonnyman led a storming party up the slope, wiped out two enemy heavy machine gun nests, and dropped thermite grenades down the vent pipes to flush out more than 100 defenders. This photograph captures the climax of the storming assault. Bonnyman is clearly visible, kneeling at the top of the wooden stairs in the center. A moment later a Japanese soldier shot him in the head. Bonnyman's Medal of Honor would be posthumous. (U.S. Marine Corps)

Most of the 8th Marines didn't even know the name of the lieutenant with the shore party markings on his helmet. He had appeared, taken over the assault, and personally pulled the plug from the drain.

Bonnyman's family would receive his posthumous Navy Cross first; later, as the facts became known, it would be upgraded to the Medal of Honor.

By dark on D+2, the 8th Marines and Willie K. Jones's 1/6 occupied parallel positions along opposite sides of the runway, two-thirds down the island. Julian Smith had come ashore to take command of his division, though sick at heart on viewing his appalling losses.

That night the surviving *rikusentai* organized a series of sharp attacks against Jones's forward positions, culminating in an all-out charge by 600 to 700 riflemen.

Few battalion commanders in the Pacific proved to be as adept in marshaling combined arms as Major Jones. His meticulous advance coordination of naval gunfire, field artillery, and tanks slaughtered the attackers. Those Japanese who overran the Marine lines met their match in the slashing, stabbing, bashing close combat that followed. Overhead star shells cast a ghastly half-light on the struggle—two proud, well-trained amphibious units slugging it out to the death.

Jones lost 40 killed and 100 wounded, but his disciplined companies held the line. The Japanese lost close to 500 men in the cataclysmic night fighting. Edson and Shoup could only whistle and thank their lucky stars this attack had not materialized the first night.

The fighting on Betio ended quickly the next morning. The 6th Marines swept to the eastern tail; the 2d Marines finally overran The Pocket.

Smith then unshackled Lieutenant Colonel Raymond Murray's 2d Battalion, 6th Marines, in pursuit of a strong force of 200 *rikusentai* occupying the outer islands in Tarawa Atoll. Smith's choice was fortuitous. Murray's fresh battalion, deeply pissed at missing most of the action in reserve, was hungry for a fight. Nor was there a battalion in better physical shape than 2/6.

Murray took off on November 24 and maintained a hot chase of the fleeing Japanese around the atoll for the

157

A Marine sergeant points out enemy troops ahead to his scattered squad. At the time of Tarawa, the Marine Corps had not yet adopted the four-man fire team built around the Browning automatic rifleman. Here the twelve-man squad was the smallest maneuver element, an unwieldy span of control for a young NCO in close combat. A total of 217 sergeants became casualties at Tarawa. (U.S. Marine Corps)

next two days. By the twenty-seventh, Murray had run the enemy to ground on Buariki Island. The Marines attacked with the dawn, and the fighting soon resembled the worst of Guadalcanal—dense jungle; hand-to-hand brawling at such point-blank ranges that the supporting artillery battery could fire only one salvo before the lines intermingled. The last of Shibasaki's *rikusentai* fought hard, inflicting ninety casualties among Murray's veterans, before dying to the last man.

Bloody Tarawa now belonged to the 2d Marine Division. The concurrent success of the Army at Makin and the Force Marine Reconnaissance Company at Apamama ended the campaign. Spruance had recaptured the Gilberts in just two weeks: one week of bombing, one of violent combat.

Seizing heavily fortified Betio cost the 2d Marine Division 3,407 casualties. One man died for every three hit, reflecting the savagery of the fighting. Eighty-eight Marines were never found.

The Battle of Tarawa attracted the rapt attention of those men of all

services who now faced the larger amphibious assaults to follow. Tarawa provided a treasure trove of operational lessons. Under the lead of Holland Smith and Kelly Turner, the amphibians identified critical improvements needed in radio communications, naval gunfire, close air support, hydrographic intelligence, and assault weapons.

Encouragingly, many of these changes came about fast enough to be on hand for the Marshalls campaign six weeks later. The Marshalls would provide the debut of an amphibious force flagship, underwater scout and demolition teams, waterproof tactical radios, close-in fire-support craft equipped with barrage rockets, flame-throwing tanks, and armored LVTs.

More than anything, the sacrifices of Tarawa had proven conclusively the validity of the doctrine of offensive amphibious assault first proclaimed by the handful of Marine and Navy pioneers at Quantico ten years earlier.

Most critical observers concluded that if the doctrine could work at Tarawa—under the worst tactical and hydrographic conditions imaginable—it could work anywhere. An assault on Fortress Europe, or the once-formidable Marshalls, or even the distant Marianas and beyond, now seemed achievable. Such was the optimistic validation dearly bought by the troops and corpsmen of the 2d Marine Division, whose collective valor gave the nation and the Corps one of their most hallowed touchstones. . . .

After some hesitation, President Roosevelt authorized the release of the uncensored documentary film *With the Marines at Tarawa*, shot by Marine combat correspondents on the island. The graphic footage simultaneously shocked and galvanized the American public. The film won an Academy Award, although Marine recruiting took a nosedive. But not for long.

There would always be the ferocious few willing to risk death with this gallant breed.

A FITTING POSTSCRIPT

In November 1995, on the fifty-second anniversary of the battle, the citizens of San Antonio banded together to bring Marine Staff Sergeant William Bordelon's body back from the Pacific for reburial in his hometown. His simple casket, graced with his Tarawa Medal of Honor, lay in state for two days and nights at the Alamo, surrounded by a Marine Corps Honor Guard. Bill Bordelon had finally come home.

Action in the Marshalls. Marines attacking Roi stare in awe at the huge explosion on neighboring Namur Island. The blast occurred when Marine engineers threw a demolition charge into what they thought was a Japanese bunker—it was a torpedo magazine. (U.S. Marine Corps)

9: WESTWARD TO THE MARSHALLS AND MARIANAS

> SAIPAN WAS WAR SUCH AS NOBODY HAD FOUGHT
> BEFORE: A CAMPAIGN IN WHICH MEN CRAWLED,
> CLUBBED, SHOT, BURNED AND BAYONETED EACH
> OTHER TO DEATH.
>
> *Lieutenant General Holland Smith, USMC*

A strange equation of death began to balance itself in the Pacific War. Both sides learned miserably expensive lessons from each succeeding bloodbath. The Japanese would change tactics and defenses in ways that would undoubtedly have defeated the American Marines in previous assaults. But with equal intensity, the Marines improved the weaponry and tactics of their invasions. So each new island campaign varied markedly from the one before it in combat technique and technology, but not in the ultimate balance of terror. The only discernible change in the outcomes was in the casualty lists, which continued to grow exponentially as the Marines clawed their way ever closer to the Japanese home islands. What did not change in the least was the courage of the opposing forces, which seemed to grow only stronger in the merciless forge of Pacific battle. Each campaign became literally a duel to the death. . . .

Navajo Code Talker
(Charles Waterhouse)

The abrupt, violent loss of their outpost bastion at Tarawa caused consternation among Japanese strategic planners. Suddenly their long-protected staging bases in the Marshalls were in grave jeopardy. Imperial General Headquarters hastily released the fragments of lessons learned from Tarawa— the Americans had some kind of amphibious tanks which could land Marines over coral reefs regardless of tidal conditions; the U.S. Navy had the gall and the firepower to force a landing from *inside* atolls. This was awful news for garrison commanders in the Marshalls; their main fortifications faced the sea; their antiboat guns targeted the gaps between reefs.

The Japanese agitation was justified.

With the Gilberts in hand, Chester Nimitz had turned quickly to the Marshalls, a far-flung scattering of 1,000 islands and 32 atolls. Already the Marshalls were being pounded by a deadly combination of USAAF bombers from Tarawa and rampaging Navy fighters from Vice Admiral Marc Mitscher's fast carrier task forces.

His intelligence staff reported that while 30,000 Imperial troops defended the Marshalls, the Japanese had stacked their defenses along the easternmost rim.

He needed no reminder that not far away lay Truk, home port of the still-dangerous Combined Fleet. Nimitz weighed the risks against the evidence of Spruance's success in the Gilberts using powerful new carriers and large-scale amphibious forces.

Nimitz boldly decided to open the campaign with a knife-thrust into the heart of the Marshalls—leapfrogging the heavily defended perimeter atolls and striking Kwajalein, 620 miles west of Tarawa.

Nimitz ordered Spruance to seize Kwajalein Island in the south, a regional enemy headquarters, and the twin islands of Roi-Namur to the north, site of a valuable airfield.

In late January 1944 Admiral Kelly Turner steamed westward with the 380 ships of his V Amphibious Force, at his side the pugnacious Marine Holland Smith. The tempestuous pair made the original "Odd Couple," but as Smith later wrote, "between the two of us we spelled hell on earth in big red letters for the Japanese."

For the assault on Kwajalein, Smith's expeditionary troops consisted of the 7th Infantry Division, Army veterans of the seizure of Attu Island in the Aleutians the previous year, and—making their combat debut—the new 4th Marine Division, which had sailed from San Diego loaded for bear.

Major General Harry Schmidt commanded the Marines. His division, whose infantry regiments were the 23d, 24th, and 25th Marines, would achieve lasting renown for waging four violently successful amphibious campaigns in barely a year, suffering 17,000 casualties in the process.

The invasion group also included the reinforced 22d Marines, a separate regiment fresh from eighteen months of guard duty on Samoa, well led by Colonel John Walker and spoiling for a fight.

Nimitz agreed to let Spruance kick off Operation Flintlock with a preliminary, stealthy seizure of lightly held Majuro Atoll in the eastern Marshalls for an advance naval base. Then, without delay, the 7th Infantry Division would seize Kwajalein Island; the 4th Marine Division, Roi-Namur.

On the last day of January, Marine Captain James L. Jones stole ashore on Majuro at the head of his Force Reconnaissance Company. This was old hat for Jones, who two months earlier had captured Apamama Atoll in the Gilberts. The "recon" Marines found Majuro lightly defended.

Captain Jones had the privilege of raising the first American flag over territory owned by Japan prior to Pearl Harbor.

While Marc Mitscher's fast carriers throttled the vaunted Japanese air attacks, Turner's gunships began their preliminary bombardment of the main objectives in Kwajalein Atoll. Here the lessons of Tarawa shone like a bright lamp.

This bombardment—three times as long, twice the weight of shells, and infinitely better executed than Tarawa—flattened most Japanese positions ashore. Rear Admiral Richard. L. Conolly commanded Turner's gunfire support with such audacity that admiring Marines nicknamed him "Close-In" Conolly. The name would stick.

A massive bombardment by Schmidt's artillery and Conolly's gunships greeted the Japanese defenders of Roi-Namur at dawn on February 1.

Turner's new Underwater Demolition Teams (UDTs) had cleared the approach lanes of mines and major obstacles. The landing force, though wondrously equipped with 240 LVTs (plus seventy-five new LVT-A1s, armored amphibians mounting 37mm guns), suffered a frustrating series of delays.

A touch of Tarawa's complex choreography still hampered the ship-to-shore process. Assault troops had to execute a time-consuming transfer by boat from transports to LSTs before they could board the amphibian tractors—risky business in the objective area, immobilizing crowded troop ships while vulnerable to enemy air raids.

Turner and Howling Mad Smith, fulminating on the bridge of their new amphibious force flagship, had to postpone H-Hour several hours.

"HALF FISH, HALF CRAZY"

The Marines at Tarawa had spent the first thirty hours in costly, fruitless searching for a boat channel through the barrier reef. After Tarawa the Americans' earlier obsession with achieving tactical surprise for their threadbare landings gave way to the realization that comprehensive "advance force operations"—the time-consuming, surprise-forfeiting combination of extensive naval bombardment, minesweeping, and underwater reconnaissance by stealthy swimmers—would save more lives. The detection and destruction of natural and manmade obstacles ahead of the actual landing became standard practice, but doing so required extraordinary deeds from uncommon men, the new Underwater Demolition Teams. Volunteer Marines and sailors went into these hostile beaches time and again, brushing past the usual terrors of cold, darkness, and riptides to the greater ones of mines, barbed wire obstacles, and enemy beach patrols to bring back minute descriptions of the hazards they themselves had managed to escape. That is, if they, with no wetsuits or SCUBA breathers yet invented, did escape. There are no adequate words for their sort of courage.

THE BATTLE HISTORY OF THE US MARINES

Finally, Colonel Louis Jones, commanding the 23d Marines, ran out of patience and ordered his combat team to launch their assault on Roi independently. Colonel Franklin Hart's 24th Marines would have to unscramble their LVTs and assault Namur on their own.

In thirty hectic minutes the 23d Marines landed on Roi, penetrated 400 yards inland, and prevailed in a dozen small firefights with the groggy defenders. Tanks and LVT-A1s led the way to the critical airfield. Jones radioed General Schmidt: "This is a pip—no opposition." His was a slight exaggeration, but by dusk the Marines controlled the airstrip and had reached Roi's northern shore. General Schmidt declared Roi "secure" at 0800 on the second day.

At nearby Namur, Colonel Hart finally said to hell with sorting out his assigned LVTs and launched the assault of his 24th Marines in piecemeal formations. It wasn't a parade-ground landing, but it worked. The 24th Marines stormed ashore with vigor, encountered a series of well-hidden spider holes, and began learning the realities of fighting diehard Japanese.

One of the greatest mishaps of the Pacific War occurred at this point on Namur. Marine engineers tossed high-explosive satchel charges into what appeared to be a Japanese bunker, a fateful act. The "bunker" was a huge magazine full of torpedo warheads. The explosion rocked both islands. "Great God almighty, the whole damned island's blown up!" exclaimed an aerial observer. The detonation cost the 24th Marines 120 casualties, half from a single rifle company. All of the assault engineers died.

Slowed by this catastrophe, the 24th Marines made less rapid progress than their counterparts on neighboring Roi. Only half of Namur was in their hands by nightfall. On the following day, February 2, General Schmidt transferred a battalion of the 23d Marines with additional tanks from Roi to lend Hart a hand. Fighting, at times intense, continued throughout the day. Resistance on Namur ended only when the two Marine assault forces joined up on the northern shore.

Compared to Tarawa, the capture of Roi-Namur came at a bargain cost. The 4th Marine Division seized both islands and the northern arc of Kwajalein, dispatched 3,500 Japanese defenders, and suffered less than a thousand combat casualties.

Meanwhile, the Army's 7th Division secured Kwajalein Island in four days of difficult fighting. By February 6, the advance elements of a Marine aircraft wing had arrived at Roi's airfield, ready for business.

Nimitz, well pleased, decided to increase Flintlock's momentum. He ordered Spruance to strike next at the far western edge of the Marshalls, seizing isolated Eniwetok Atoll, 330 miles beyond Kwajalein.

Spruance accelerated D-Day from the planned date of May 1 to mid-February, a terrific compression of the original schedule. Holland Smith knew Schmidt's division needed a quick breather after Roi-Namur, so he deployed the V Amphibious Corps reserve force, the 22d Marines, and two Army battalions—ten thousand troops in all—under Marine Brigadier General Thomas Watson.

Watson's objectives were Engebi, in the north, site of a 4,000-foot airstrip, and Eniwetok and Parry islands in the south. He assigned Engebi to Colonel Walker's 22d Marines and the southern islands to the Army.

As at Kwajalein, Captain Jones's Force Recon Marines landed stealthily on neighboring islands the day preceding D-Day to seize advance fire support bases for Marine and Army artillery units. These batteries combined their steady fire with spectacular naval and air bombardment on Engebi on D-Day to pulverize the exposed Japanese positions.

Under an awesome umbrella of fire the 22d Marines stormed Engebi and advanced swiftly inland.

The heart of the Japanese defense centered in a thick palm grove. The 22d Marines methodically snuffed out the spider holes and swept across the remainder of the island. The next morning, they raised the Stars and Stripes over Engebi to the sound of "To the Colors" being played by a Marine field musician on a captured Japanese bugle.

Eniwetok Island presented a more difficult objective. Counter to intelligence reports, Japanese soldiers occupied the position in force, and the preliminary naval bombardment proved inadequate.

No one had an easy time on Eniwetok. When the GIs continued to wrestle with strong resistance, Watson committed his reserve, the 3d Battalion, 22d Marines. The Marines had their hands full. Securing the thickly wooded island took three gruesome days.

General Watson, an impatient man at best, despaired of the Army being able to tackle Parry Island, the final objective, on schedule. Aware that Parry contained even more Imperial Army defenders than Eniwetok, he gave the job to Walker's 22d Marines, augmented by an enthusiastic unit from the 10th Defense Battalion (the Marines destined to garrison the atoll).

This time Watson ensured the preliminary bombardment would prove sufficient. Marine artillery firing from nearby Japtan Islet blasted Parry in advance. Navy gunships steamed in as close as 850 yards to fire their broadsides. On Washington's Birthday the 22d Marines landed on Parry, three battalions abreast.

While one battalion pushed north, the others joined forces for a southern advance. Marine tanks outdueled Japanese light armor. Sharp fighting characterized the inland struggle, especially at night.

The first night in combat on Parry proved a tense one for Marine Second Lieutenant Cord Meyer, who "stayed awake all night with a knife in one hand and a grenade in the other." But dawn of the second day brought the inevitable outcome.

A desperate force of fifty *rikusentai* launched a final banzai attack from the island's tip, but Meyer's machine gun platoon "cut them down like overripe wheat." Parry Island and the invaluable atoll had changed ownership.

Thanks to Tarawa's priceless lessons, Operation Flintlock succeeded at a speed and overall economy almost beyond belief to strategic planners.

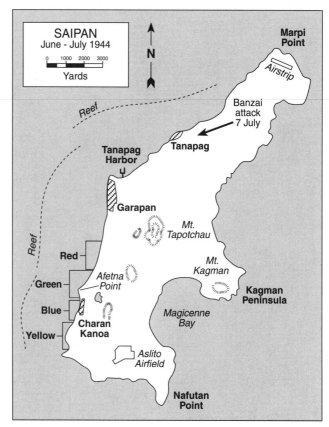

SAIPAN
June - July 1944

0 1000 2000 3000
Yards

N

Marpi
Point

Airstrip

Reef

Banzai
attack
7 July

Tanapag

Tanapag
Harbor

Garapan

Mt.
Tapotchau

Red

Green

Afetna
Point

Mt.
Kagman

Kagman
Peninsula

Blue

Charan
Kanoa

Magicenne
Bay

Yellow

Aslito
Airfield

Nafutan
Point

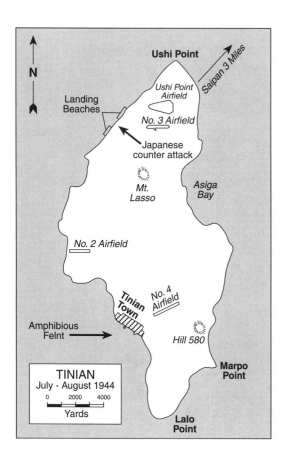

N

Ushi Point

Saipan 3 Miles

Landing
Beaches

Ushi Point
Airfield

No. 3 Airfield

Japanese
counter attack

Mt.
Lasso

Asiga
Bay

No. 2 Airfield

Tinian
Town

No. 4
Airfield

Amphibious
Feint

Hill 580

Marpo
Point

TINIAN
July - August 1944

0   2000   4000
Yards

Lalo
Point

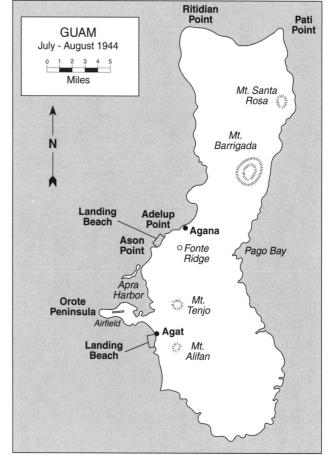

GUAM
July - August 1944

0 1 2 3 4 5
Miles

N

Ritidian
Point

Pati
Point

Mt. Santa
Rosa

Mt.
Barrigada

Landing
Beach

Adelup
Point

Agana

Ason
Point

Fonte
Ridge

Pago Bay

Apra
Harbor

Orote
Peninsula

Mt.
Tenjo

Airfield

Agat

Landing
Beach

Mt.
Alifan

Marines never appreciate their Navy or Coast Guard troop transports more than immediately following a battle. Here three exhausted Leathernecks of the 22d Marines savor the simple joys of survival and a hot cup of coffee after heavy fighting to secure Engebi and Eniwetok in the Marshalls.
(U.S. Coast Guard)

Amphibious prophet Pete Ellis had predicted a hell of a fight when the Americans came to the Japanese Marshalls. He would have been astounded at the one-sided victory. And he would have known that such luck could not go on.

Japan, like a wounded wild animal, coiled back toward its lair, more viciously dangerous than ever. Imperial General Headquarters established a fallback zone, the Absolute Defense Sphere, which included the Marianas and the Philippines.

In the Central Pacific, the Joint Chiefs ordered Nimitz to execute Operation Forager, a giant, thousand-mile leap westward to seize Saipan, Tinian, and Guam in the Marianas.

Bold in concept, enormous in scale, Forager would literally take the war to Japan's front yard, provide suitable airfields within range of the home islands for the USAAF's new B–29 Superfortress bombers, and—surely—lure the Combined Fleet out of hiding for a climactic sea fight.

Nimitz chose his "first team" of combat leaders for this difficult mission, pausing to promote each for their success in the Gilberts and Marshalls: four stars for Ray Spruance, three each for Holland Smith and Kelly Turner. The rank of lieutenant general was appropriate for Smith, now responsible for the 70,000 Marines and soldiers of the "Northern Troops and Landing Force" earmarked for Saipan and Tinian.

Three veteran outfits comprised this force: the 2d and 4th Marine Divisions and the Army's 27th Division. For Guam, Marine Major General Roy

Geiger commanded the 55,000-man "Southern Troops and Landing Force," built around the 3rd Marine Division, the 1st Provisional Marine Brigade, and the Army's new 77th Division.

Despite this muscular lineup, no American planners expected a cake-walk in the Marianas—especially at Saipan. Tarawa's tiny Betio Island—barely a half-square mile of sand and coral—had been bad enough. Saipan by comparison had seventy-two square miles of mountains, volcanic rock, cliffs, thick woods. All the potential for a nightmare.

Like Tarawa, Saipan had a fringing reef, but this time there would be no protective atoll; great Pacific rollers would plunge directly against the reef. Moreover, in the Saipan town of Garapan the Marines would encounter house-to-house fighting for the first time since Veracruz in 1914.

Holland Smith, ever the realist, called it right in advance. "We are through with flat atolls," he told reporters. "Now we are up against mountains and caves where the Japs can really dig in. A week from now there will be a lot of dead Marines."

Smith had done his level best to ensure his troops had the best possible weapons and equipment for the job.

Unlike the Solomons and Tarawa, the Marines would fight their way throughout the Marianas generously armed and equipped: plenty of flamethrowers, an experimental flame tank outfit, a full battalion of Sherman medium tanks per division, and an unprecedented number and variety of amphibian tractors, including the new, rear-ramped LVT–4s and upgunned LVT-A4s (mounting snub-nosed 75mm howitzers in their centerline turrets).

The landing force would need every one of these tracked amphibians to get ashore across Saipan's reef and surf zone.

Thirty-two thousand Imperial Army and Navy *rikusentai* awaited the V Amphibious Corps on Saipan, by far the largest concentration of forces the Central Pacific drive had yet encountered.

Command of the Saipan defenders devolved to Lieutenant General Yoshitsuga Saito, commanding the 43d Division. Saito's division had paid hell redeploying from Korea. American submarines sank half his transports; many of his troops arrived on the island half-drowned barely two weeks before the invasion. One submarine could be as effective as a Marine division.

Yet the Japanese garrison had one deadly surprise waiting for the enemy amphibians.

For the first time the U.S. Marines would be facing fully armed, well-sited field artillery regiments of the Imperial Army. These veteran cannoneers represented the professional best of the Japanese armed forces, and they knew their gunnery.

When the Americans outfoxed Saito by landing on the opposite coast from his primary defenses, the artillery commanders simply pivoted their guns and opened fire from reverse slope positions, using preregistered grids along the threatened shoreline. Saipan's steep terrain favored the extended

use of Japanese howitzers and heavy mortars—and these weapons would kill and maim many Marines in the ensuing twenty-four days.

Holland Smith's invasion plan called for the two Marine divisions to storm ashore along Saipan's southwest corner. The 2d Division, now commanded by Major General Thomas Watson, would land on the left, while Major General Harry Schmidt's 4th Marine Division would hit the beach on the right. Rocky, wooded Afetna Point separated the two invasion sites.

D-Day was June 15, 1944, following four days of heavy naval and air bombardment and extensive UDT preparations. Yet Navy assault wave control officers were puzzled to discover a number of small red flags that had appeared overnight along the reef. Then, as the LVTs churned toward the coral barrier just before H-Hour, the entire reef exploded. Astonished Naval officers thought the Japanese had mined the reef at the last minute. They had not. The red flags were range markers.

The Japanese field artillery had just executed a difficult—and massive—"time on target" concentrated salvo by every gun on the damned island. Some rounds scored direct hits on the approaching LVTs, blowing troops and crew to bits. Enormous geysers of water from near-misses caused other LVTs to swamp. The vicious plunging surf caught other LVTs with their sterns exposed as they struggled over the coral and flipped them end-over-end, spilling all heavily laden hands into the froth.

Surprisingly, the Marines lost but twenty LVTs to this deadly combination of artillery fire and brutal surf. Hundreds of others struggled through the gauntlet and rumbled safely out of the ocean onto Saipan's thick sand.

But here things took a turn for the worse.

Watson and Schmidt wanted their LVTs to keep the momentum, to break clear of the beach and pierce inland, supported on the run by the 75mm guns of the LVT-As. Neither vehicle proved equal to the role of light tank or armored personnel carrier. Shell-blasted terrain slowed their movement, often fatally, and Japanese gunners pummeled them relentlessly from unseen positions in the high ground. Most Marines were forced to abandon their LVTs near the beach and seek shelter.

Typically, among the first battalion commanders ashore was Tarawa's Lieutenant Colonel "Jim" Crowe, his trademark waxed red mustache bristling in the morning sun. Japanese fire had driven his landing waves off target. Now a dangerous gap existed between Crowe's outfit and the next.

Crowe, so calm under fire that one correspondent described him as "cool as ice-house lettuce," took off through the scrub bush accompanied only by his runner, seeking to find the adjoining battalion.

The Japanese had also seen the gap, and Imperial Army riflemen ambushed the two Marines at close quarters. Both men fell, badly hit, Crowe stuffing the butt of his carbine against the sucking hole in his chest. Other Marines lugged them to a nearby aid station, but the ordeal became more harrowing.

Japanese mortars sprayed the area with hot shrapnel, killing the corpsman and wounding the surgeon as they knelt over Crowe, and wounding him severely in five more places.

As stretcher bearers took him to the evacuation LVT, Crowe made them stop by Red Mike Edson, now assistant commander of the 2d Marine Division. The two warriors clasped hands. Crowe apologized for leaving Edson in the lurch so early in the fight. Crowe's indomitable spirit would keep him alive, but he would never again lead troops against the Japanese.

Despite such losses in leadership and nearly 2,000 casualties in their ranks, the assaulting Marines wrested a modest slice of shell-blasted Saipan from its defenders.

Holland Smith had 20,000 men ashore by nightfall, spread unevenly along a beachhead four miles long and maybe a mile deep.

Both divisions made herculean efforts to get their artillery regiments ashore to deliver counterbattery fires against their Japanese counterparts. But Japanese-held Afetna Point still separated the two divisions, General Saito's guns and mortars still dropped plunging fire along the crowded beach—and night was coming.

Veteran Marine combat correspondent Jim Lucas described the anxiety among the landing force that first nightfall: "There is something definitely terrifying about the first night on a hostile beach. No matter what superiority you may boast in men and material, on that first night you're the underdog, and the enemy is in a position to make you pay through the nose."

Japanese night counterattacks epitomized the opening weeks of the battle. The most dangerous attack occurred shortly after the landing and included the first armored night assault the Marines had faced.

Some forty Japanese medium tanks roared out of the darkness toward the beach. By coincidence, Lieutenant Colonel "Willie K." Jones and his 1st Battalion, 6th Marines, defended the threatened sector and bore the brunt of the attack. Yet even the tanks didn't rattle these veterans of the great counterattack on the third night at Tarawa.

Jones as usual had prepared his supporting arms like a maestro. His Marines hit the onrushing tanks with not just the kitchen sink, but the stove and the washing machine. Those dazed tanks that survived the torrent of naval gunfire, artillery, and mortar fire ran into a wall of direct fire from Jones's bazookas and rifle grenades.

The sunrise revealed a veritable junkyard of demolished and smoking Japanese tanks scattered throughout Jones's sector. There would be no "issue in doubt" messages from Saipan.

As the Marines expanded their beachhead, Admiral Spruance received electrifying news from an American submarine in the Philippines. The Imperial Navy was coming out to fight.

In the lead, Spruance learned, was Admiral Jisaburo Ozawa, commanding Japan's First Mobile Fleet—the carrier element of the Combined Fleet.

D-Day at Saipan, June 15, 1944. Saipan was a bitch, from start to finish. The drenched condition of the Marine in the foreground indicates his LVT was knocked out by Japanese fire en route to the beach. The LVT-A4 armored amphibian in the background appears out of action as well, but its snub-nosed 75mm howitzer may still be capable of direct fire support. (U.S. Marine Corps)

Marines on Saipan open fire with an M3 37mm antitank gun, a weapon virtually useless against the heavily armored German tanks of the European theater but ideal against the light tanks and pillboxes of the Japanese. The 2d and 4th Marine Divisions each employed thirty-six of these guns in the Marianas campaign. In addition to its antitank projectile, the M3 also featured a canister round—absolutely deadly against massed banzai charges. (U.S. Marine Corps)

An immense battle loomed in the vast Philippine Sea.

Spruance quickly turned to face the challenge, but first he looked to the protection of the Marines and all the amphibious forces clustered around Saipan, his primary mission.

Consulting with Holland Smith and Kelly Turner, he directed the immediate offload of the 27th Division, heretofore in floating reserve, postponed the Guam landing, and ordered the temporary pullback of the vulnerable amphibians, out of sight, but not—as at Guadalcanal—out of reach. Even so, the Marines looked nervously at that big, empty stretch of ocean offshore.

Now Spruance uncoiled Marc Mitscher's huge Task Force 58 to meet Ozawa.

The aerial battle quickly became known as "The Marianas Turkey Shoot." Mitscher's experienced pilots and antiaircraft crews shot down 476 of their adversaries with ease, "the biggest bag of the war."

Ozawa lost three carriers in the exchange and was lucky to escape with his life.

Spruance's red-hot aviators protested when he would not let them chase Ozawa's fleeing remnants all the way back to the Japanese home islands, but Spruance never lost sight of his amphibious mission in the Marianas, for which the Marines were profoundly grateful.

Smith's amphibious corps had hardly missed a beat on Saipan while Mitscher steamed off to win the titanic air-sea battle.

On D+1, the 8th Marines avenged Jim Crowe's severe wounding by sweeping the Japanese from Afetna Point, giving the Americans an unbroken line.

The 4th Division Marines and the 27th Division soldiers broke out of the beachhead and attacked east and south, the Leathernecks reaching Magicienne Bay on the far shore, the GIs capturing Aslito Airfield.

The first week of fighting had cost Saito half his numbers, mostly squan-

LEFT: Three Marines on Saipan take temporary shelter behind a knocked-out Japanese field gun. Tarawa, bad as it was, ended after seventy-six hours. The battle for Saipan was still an endless slugfest three weeks after D-Day. The strain of this round-the-clock assault shows here. (Note the omnipresent Ka-Bar, the Leathernecks' favored fighting knife for three wars, on the web belt of the near Marine.)
(U.S. Marine Corps)

OPPOSITE: Riflemen of the 2d Marine Division sprint through the burning streets of Garapan, the principal city of Saipan. This was the first house-to-house urban fighting for the Marines in the thirty years since Veracruz.
(U.S. Marine Corps)

dered in overambitious night attacks. Holland Smith's assaulting forces had sustained 6,000 casualties. Saipan was already proving to be one of the costlier amphibious battles.

The three divisions now swung northward abreast, the Army's 27th in the center, flanked by the Marines.

The battle up the island, including the heroic seizure of towering Mount Tapotchau, unfortunately became overshadowed by what has ever since been called "The Smith versus Smith Controversy."

Holland Smith, the Corps commander, became impatient with the less than fiery leadership of Major General Ralph Smith, commanding the Army division. The senior Smith had expressed unhappiness with Ralph Smith's leadership in the earlier campaigns in the Gilberts and Marshalls. Now the 27th Division was advancing so slowly that they had exposed the flanks of the more aggressive Marine divisions on either side. Holland Smith consulted with Spruance and Turner, then relieved Ralph Smith of command.

It was a tough but appropriate action. Ralph Smith's replacement, Army Major General Sanderford Jarmen, provided the fire and zip to lead the 27th Division forward.

The Marpi Horror

Even in the dreadful Pacific cauldron there grew a sense of how much was too much. At the culmination of the no-quarter battle for Saipan, even the case-hardened Marines were horrified at the sight of the mass suicides at towering Marpi Point, where trapped soldiers and civilians, including many women and children, sent themselves to eternity heedlessly. Great and often dangerous efforts were made by shouted appeals and loudspeaker teams to end the carnage. And when these were occasionally successful, the conquerors showed something perilously close to tenderness in the care of their ravaged enemies. But further in the background, there was the thought of this suicidally determined enemy defending their rocky homeland against United States Marines with the same fatal dedication. And that was a horror every bit as great in contemplation as the one witnessed at Marpi.

Regrettably, the thought of a Marine officer relieving an Army officer of his command in the midst of a battle proved too much for the Army brass to stomach. Charges were leveled against Holland Smith; Nimitz was besieged with visiting Army generals.

The whole case clouded the otherwise good relations between Leathernecks and GIs at Saipan and in fact led to poisonous senior-level relations between the two services for a generation.

The battle for Saipan continued, regardless of stratospheric tensions among American general and flag officers.

The fighting was particularly fierce in the town of Garapan, midway up the west coast, where the Japanese fought tenaciously from the rubble of destroyed buildings. The devastated city finally fell to the 2d Marine Division on July 3.

The American advance pushed inexorably northward, the Japanese doggedly resisting from caves and camouflaged bunkers. Marines used flamethrowers, tanks, artillery, air strikes, and naval gunfire to snuff out these strong points, one by one.

By July 5, D+20, all of Saipan's airfields and towns were in U.S. hands. On that evening, after ordering a final banzai attack, General Saito knelt outside his cave and committed suicide. His final order was carried out with bloody consequences early the next morning. Nearly 4,000 Japanese soldiers poured out of the highlands to fall upon surprised elements of the 27th Division in the greatest banzai attack of the war.

Hundreds of screaming, sword-waving Imperial troops found a gap in the Army lines and streamed through to assault Marine artillery positions well to the rear.

Desperate cannoneers leveled their 105mm howitzers to blast the attackers at point-blank range, but many died at their guns before reinforcing Marines could fight their way through to close the gap.

Savage fighting swirled in every ravine and cane field throughout the day. When the killing finally ended, the grisly battlefield revealed Japanese bodies lying everywhere, often three-deep.

The terrifying but futile banzai attack ended the battle for Saipan.

The Marines surged to Marpi Point, sickened by the sight of Japanese civilians leaping to their death from the cliffs in fear of the American conquerors.

The island was "secured" on the twenty-fourth day. The 2d and 4th Marine Divisions had fought with great élan but were exhausted. Sixteen thousand

Americans had been killed or wounded, three fourths of them Marines. Less than a thousand Japanese troops survived.

News of Saipan's fall devastated the Japanese high command. "Hell is upon us!" one official cried.

Tinian loomed next, too soon for the weary Marine riflemen.

This next objective for the 2d and 4th Marine Divisions lay only four miles away from Saipan's southern coast. Smaller, flatter, less heavily defended than Saipan, the island offered the potential of great rewards at a lower cost to the Americans.

The island already accommodated three military airfields. Engineers and SeaBees figured they could expand these, then carve three more extended airstrips out of the flat cane fields—all six laid out with the minimum 8,500-foot runways required by bomb-laden B–29 Superforts.

Nine thousand Japanese troops defended the fifty-square-mile island, loosely commanded by Colonel Keishi Ogata, Imperial Army. Many members of Ogata's regiment had seen combat in Manchuria, but overall the Tinian defenders lacked the heavy artillery of Saipan and suffered from the usual Army-Navy rivalries.

American intelligence proved superb. The Marines actually had copies of Ogata's tactical defensive plans in hand before advance force operations began.

THE MARIANAS COMMANDANT "GREENHOUSE"

The fierce battles for the Marianas were a magnificent showcase for the best Marine officers, and spawned a small battalion of future commandants. Six Marianas officers would make the jump to the highest Marine command: Clifton Cates, David Shoup, and Wallace Greene from Saipan and Tinian, and Lemuel Shepherd, Robert Cushman, and Louis Wilson from Guam. Not surprisingly, all were powerfully effective commandants.

Few photographs better portray the tight bonds between combat Marines and their accompanying Navy corpsmen. Here, on bloody Saipan, a rifle company "doc" administers plasma to one wounded Marine, while another waits his turn. The fact that all three men still wear their helmets in Saipan's suffocating heat indicates their proximity to bullets and shrapnel.
(U.S. Marine Corps)

177

"Fire in the Hole." A satchel charge full of explosives would usually take care of a Japanese bunker on Saipan. Effective but dangerous, the demolitions were sometimes lethal to the executioners. These Marines would have benefited from hitting the deck a second sooner—as their buddy on the right evidently did. (U.S. Marine Corps)

The Tinian campaign would represent the zenith of U.S. amphibious virtuosity, a masterpiece of intelligence gathering, innovative planning, audacious decision-making, efficient use of all supporting arms, and violent execution. It remains today a textbook example of "maneuver warfare from the sea," a classic amphibious *blitzkrieg*.

A new generation of amphibious leaders ran the Tinian show.

Kelly Turner gave way to Admiral Harry Hill; Holland Smith yielded command of V Amphibious Corps to Harry Schmidt; Major General Clifton Cates took command of the 4th Marine Division from Schmidt.

Tinian's lack of suitable landing beaches posed the main challenge in planning the assault. Steep escarpments protected much of the island. The only obvious invasion site was the broad, welcoming beach in the southwest, near Tinian Town, but the Japanese, recognizing this, had heavily fortified and mined the area.

But Schmidt discovered two narrow cracks in the escarpment near Tinian's *northwest* tip, more landing *points* than beaches, unlikely candidates to support division-level landings—yet intriguing.

Schmidt deployed Captain Jones's intrepid Force Recon Marines in a series of hair-raising, nighttime scouting missions along each possible beach.

Rifles have always
been high and holy
things to Marines.
Here the buddies of
this wounded Marine
on Tinian make sure
his weapon gets back
to the aid station
along with him.
(U.S. Marine Corps)

Jones's swimmers returned intact despite several narrow escapes from enemy
sentries and reported widespread mining at all points—but very light
defenses along the northwest coast.

Schmidt made his decision. He would wedge his divisions ashore
through these unlikely points, challenge his logisticians to revolutionize the
process of delivering sustainability ashore, and rely on deception, boldness,
and good weather.

The last factor was by no means the least. The monsoon season loomed.

Schmidt's invasion plan called for the 2d Marine Division to make a
large-scale feint at Tinian Town while the 4th Division knifed ashore directly
over the northwest sites. Cates would have to hold tight the first night; then
Watson's 2d Division would land behind him. Success would depend on heavy
naval and shore-based artillery support and a rapid buildup well inland.

The systematic pounding of Tinian began in July, and the troops found it

a joy to behold. Battleships, cruisers, and destroyers circled the island, lashing out violently against Japanese positions and facilities. Multi-service bombers and attack aircraft streaked over the length and breath of the island.

To cap it off, Army and Marine artillery on southern Saipan—136 guns, more than the Union Army had available to defend Cemetery Ridge at Gettysburg—rained 25,000 high-explosive shells on targets in northern Tinian. Never in the Pacific War had the table been so nicely set.

D-Day at Tinian came on July 24, 1944. The 2d Marine Division executed such a convincing amphibious feint against the Tinian Town beaches that Colonel Ogata was signaling Tokyo of his success in repelling the American landing attempt at the same time that the 4th Marine Division began streaming ashore through his unguarded "attic door."

Cates's main problem occurred with enemy mines, the Type 98 hemispherical antiboat mines ("steel basketballs with horns," the Marines called them), each filled with forty-six pounds of tri-nitro-anisol boosted by picric acid. LVTs stood little chance against these weapons, and when three amtracs in a row blew up approaching the landing point, the momentum slowed.

Fortunately for the Marines, the Japanese had allowed most of the mines in this area to deteriorate. No other LVTs detonated mines, and the assault resumed its accelerated passage through the shoreline bottleneck to the plateau beyond.

Cates, calling the shots from the weather deck of an offshore LST, had full view, good communications, and iron control. He pushed his division ashore with a calm intensity, ensuring that his artillery regiment would have plenty of time to land and register their guns before dark.

Incredibly, in view of the difficulties imposed by the tiny "beaches," Cates had 16,000 Marines ashore, tied in, and on full alert by sunset.

Everything Cates had learned at Guadalcanal indicated his toehold on Tinian would be challenged that night by Ogata's surprised but veteran troops. Ogata did not disappoint Cates.

Utilizing the one tactical skill with which Imperial troops always seemed to retain mastery over their American foes—the ability to organize large counterattacks of combined arms at night—Ogata deployed most of his forces north and into attack positions around the 4th Marine Division's perimeter. What followed would be no crazed banzai charge like Saito's last-gasp spasm on Saipan.

Here, as at Tarawa, the Japanese probed the American lines smartly, marking the automatic weapons, finding the seams between regiments.

A hail of mortar fire blanketed Cates's front lines; Japanese tanks clanked into action; and with a great yell Ogata's Manchurian veterans swept forward. A battle royal developed throughout the rest of the night. Cates would later state that, "This was the real battle of Tinian." He would also add, "Here we broke their backs."

Ogata's men may have fought the Russians along the Siberian border, but

The forcible seizure of Tinian by the 2d and 4th Marine Divisions was an absolute masterpiece. Here LVTs steam shoreward under the protective guns of a Navy cruiser. This scene may have been the successful amphibious feint off Tinian Town. The ruse diverted Japanese attention from the main landing along the northwest coast.

(U.S. Marine Corps)

in the 4th Marine Division they faced a large, lethal force of combined arms, ably led at all echelons, and thoroughly schooled in night-fighting from experiences in the Marshalls and at Saipan.

It was a deadly them-or-us showdown, in some corners as savage and desperate as any to be seen in the war, but dawn revealed the inevitable outcome. Nearly 2,000 of Ogata's best troops lay twisted and silent; the remnants fled south. Cates had indeed broken their backs.

The 2d Marine Division wasted no time pouring ashore the next day. Schmidt's logisticians worked absolute miracles in keeping the flow of combat support moving. Everything came in by LVTs or DUKWs—and never stopped.

The two divisions shouldered into line, swept across the first airfield, and wheeled south.

Marines then had the unique experience of chasing a fleeing enemy in open country, riding atop tanks and half-tracks as they raced along country roads through the cane fields.

Everything clicked. Fire support by field artillery, aircraft, and ships battered and confounded the disorganized Japanese. Enemy mines, booby traps, and snipers took their toll, but the Marine juggernaut proved unstoppable.

Ogata's survivors, their backs to the seaside cliffs along the island's southern coast, fought a final desperate battle, some heaving armed mines as crude hand grenades, but they fell one by one to the onslaught.

Lashed to its precarious perch on a cliff like an eighteenth-century ship's cannon, a Marine 75mm pack howitzer fires at a Japanese cave on southern Tinian. The Model 1923-E2 howitzer was perfect for Marine use. Originally designed for expeditionary service with pack mules, the weapon could be disassembled into a half-dozen components for delivery to the battlefield, then quickly reassembled for action—ideal for the early amphibious assaults, equally suitable for the cave warfare of the last years of the Pacific War. (U.S. Marine Corps)

When the fighting finally ended on August 1, Schmidt proclaimed the island "secure." His two divisions of Marines had destroyed Ogata's mixed forces and captured the invaluable island in nine days at a "steal": 2,355 casualties.

Holland Smith, usually sparing in his praise, congratulated Schmidt for executing "the perfect amphibious operation of the Pacific War."

The battles for Tinian and Guam overlapped each other. Spruance now had enough ships and Marines to conduct two major amphibious campaigns simultaneously. While General Schmidt's V Amphibious Corps ran roughshod over Tinian, General Roy Geiger's III Amphibious Corps engaged in bitter fighting to liberate Guam.

The Battle of the Philippine Sea had knocked Guam's invasion schedule off the boards for a month, much to the chagrin and discomfort of Geiger's Marines. The troops languished on their crowded transports in the tropical heat. The steel decks of the LSTs became so ungodly hot that Lieutenant Colonel Alan Shapley had to hospitalize the entire war dog platoon assigned to his 4th Marines—the paws of the Dobermans painfully burned.

News that Guam finally had "the green light" aroused hoarse cheers from the troops.

Guam lies 130 miles southwest of Saipan, and with an area of 225 square miles it is the largest of the Northern Marianas. Geiger had followed the difficult fight to seize Saipan with keen interest.

Compared to Saipan, Guam was three times the size, with bigger mountains, much more jungle, and fewer suitable landing beaches. The island's convoluted topography favored the defender, and Geiger knew Lieutenant General Takeshi Takashina's combined force of 13,000 soldiers and 5,000 sailors would provide stiff opposition.

Fortunately Roy Geiger and his Naval counterpart, Admiral "Close-in" Conolly, got along like sugar and spice. No other U.S. amphibious assault in the Central Pacific would be preceded by such thorough training and preliminary Naval bombardment.

Geiger also had full confidence in his major maneuver units.

Major General Allen Turnage's 3rd Marine Division had earned its spurs fighting in the jungles of Bougainville.

Major General Lemuel Shepherd's 1st Provisional Marine Brigade was a new outfit but comprised of two veteran regiments.

Shapley's 4th Marines, its ranks brimming with former raiders, and Colonel Merlin Schneider's 22d Marines, had been convincing victors at Engebi, Eniwetok, and Parry.

The Army's 77th Division was new but well led and thoroughly trained. Geiger was the most joint-minded of senior Marines.

Guam would reflect the experience, power, and leadership of this force.

General Takashina expected the Americans to land at Tumon Bay, site of the principal Japanese landing in 1941, and concentrated his defenses in that

area. But Geiger fooled him, divided the landing force to hit two smaller beaches, five miles apart.

Geiger realized the risk. Rough terrain and resolute enemies would slow the linkup inland, but Geiger had faith that both the 3d Marine Division in the north and the 1st Brigade in the south could fight independently for as long it took.

The amphibious assault on Guam exemplified the growing American capability of concentrating overwhelming combat power at the point of attack. Spruance allocated an armada of 274 ships to launch Geiger's 54,000-man "storm landing."

Close-in Conolly blasted western Guam for thirteen days, the best bombardment of the entire war. His UDT swimmers methodically cleared away Takashina's antiboat mines and offshore obstacles—pausing at the end to leave an impudent sign facing seaward along the reef: "Welcome Marines!"

On W-Day, July 21, 1944, Marc Mitscher's carrier pilots swarmed low along the coast, spitting fire and dropping bombs. Under this protective shield, the Marine LVTs swept over the barrier reef and onward toward the smoking beaches.

Despite this unprecedented pounding, enough Japanese survived to man their guns and contest the landing. One pair of 75mm gun crews, well protected in their hollowed-out coral cave, opened up a deadly fire against the

The amphibious assault on western Guam as it appeared from the air just before H-Hour on W-Day, July 21, 1944. Preceded by howitzer-firing LVT-As, the waves of troop-laden LVTs chug toward the target beach. Fires burning up and down the coast reflect the intensity of Admiral "Close-in" Conolly's marvelous preliminary Naval bombardment.
(U.S. Navy)

187

Riflemen of the 3d
Marine Division
establish a base of
fire on the high
ground beyond Asan
in early stages of the
Guam campaign.
(U.S. Marine Corps)

oncoming LVTs at a can't-miss range of 100 yards. For twenty minutes these two guns dominated the beach, knocking out a dozen amtracs and spilling the embarked infantry into the shallows. It took that long before adjacent Marines could work their way down the beach and snuff out the strong point from the rear.

Once ashore both veteran Marine forces continued the advance, methodically eradicating pockets of resistance. Soon the problems became logistical more than tactical.

General Shepherd came ashore early, assessed the budding bottleneck in getting supplies across the reef, and signaled Geiger: "Our casualties about 350. Critical shortages fuel and ammunition." Before long Geiger would have to commit one fifth of his corps to the unglamorous work of humping supplies along the tenuous route from ship to reef to LVTs to inland dumps.

The fighting on Guam would be characterized by foolish mistakes by senior Japanese officers, offset by spirited and often improvisational tactics on the part of their troops.

Takashina squandered most of his forces in a fierce but ultimately futile counterattack the night of July 25. This was a hell of an attack, one of the largest of the war, and it caught the Marines with their lines badly extended, "like a sieve." Hardest hit was Lieutenant Colonel Robert Cushman's 2d Battalion, 9th Marines, on Fonte Hill. Cushman barely fought off seven vicious attacks before dawn, losing half his men in desperate fighting.

Takashina's all-or-nothing night counterattack inflicted 600 casualties on the American landing force but achieved no lasting penetrations and cost him 3,200 of his best fighters.

The Marines resumed the offensive the next morning.

The 1st Brigade attacked Orote Peninsula in a series of frontal and flanking hammer blows. The 22d Marines had the distinction of recapturing the charred ruins of the old Marine Barracks, sacred ground. On July 29, a Marine bugler sounded "To the Colors," and Old Glory again flew over the parade ground.

By August 4 Marine Aircraft Group 21 began flight operations from Orote Field, reuniting Leatherneck aviators and riflemen in combat for the first time in many months.

Bitter fighting continued as Geiger's Marines and soldiers drove resolutely northward, but the end was in sight.

A Marine tanker killed General Takashina with his turret-mounted machine gun. Eleven thousand other Japanese lay dead along the ridges and ravines.

On August 10, the twentieth day, Geiger declared Guam secure.

The forcible recapture of Guam cost the III Amphibious Corps 8,000 casualties among Geiger's Marines and soldiers. But Guam provided two more B–29 fields to the budding springboard for the strategic air war against homeland Japan, and Admiral Nimitz would soon move his forward headquarters to the island to direct the closing chapters of the war.

Nimitz had already accelerated the pace of the Pacific War dramatically.

In eight weeks, his principal lieutenant, Admiral Ray Spruance, had conquered the three powerful Japanese bastions in the Marianas and won the Battle of the Philippine Sea.

Theater-wide, Admiral Nimitz's high-rolling offensive thrust had marched 2,500 miles across the Central Pacific in seven months, beginning with the Gilberts. His increasingly potent Fleet Marine Forces had led the way—and suffered the heaviest casualties. Nearly 7,000 Marines died and more than 19,000 fell wounded in forcibly wresting the Gilberts, Marshalls, and Marianas from Imperial Japan. Yet the worst was yet to come.

CAPTAIN LOU WILSON'S ORDEAL

One of Cushman's company commanders, twenty-four-year-old Captain Louis Wilson, earned a niche in the Marines' Valhalla that endless night on Guam. Wounded three times the day before, Wilson leapt up from his stretcher in the aid station at the outbreak of the Japanese night attack and limped back to the front to rejoin his company. Japanese troops swarmed over the position, and Wilson and his men, sometimes fighting back-to-back, cut them down with bayonets, rifle butts, and fighting knives. Spotting one of his wounded men surrounded by Japanese fifty yards away, Wilson painfully dashed out, swept up the Marine, and fought his way back. Late in the battle, the Japanese seized a prominent hill nearby and raked Wilson's position with automatic fire. The captain quickly chose seventeen men to follow him in a storming mission up the slope. Their charge was near-suicidal—fourteen Marines fell—but Wilson and the survivors reached the crest and killed the machine gunners. Dawn found him still on his feet on the high ground. His Medal of Honor would mirror the blazing spirit of Marine leadership and training that will simply not accept defeat. Thirty-one years later Wilson would lead his Corps out of the post–Vietnam War doldrums as twenty-sixth Commandant.

189

The Browning .30 caliber, air-cooled light machine gun became the crew-served weapon of choice for Marines in the assault waves. Portable and faithfully reliable, the "Light 30" also featured a low-lying tripod that enabled the crew to assume a nigh-prone firing position (which these Marines will surely do as soon as someone starts shooting back!). Adopted in 1919, the "Light 30" served Leathernecks well for the next half century, including Marine armored units in Vietnam.

(Lou Reda Productions)

OPPOSITE: **Cave Warfare** (Charles Waterhouse)

PHILIPPINES

EVERY DAMNED AMTRAC IN OUR
WAVE HAS BEEN DESTROYED IN THE
WATER OR SHOT TO PIECES THE
MINUTE IT LANDED!

Colonel Lewis "Chesty" Puller, USMC, D-Day, Peleliu

Just when it seemed the Navy and Marines had perfected the difficult art of amphibious assault against fortified islands, the Japanese abruptly junked their doctrine of perimeter defense and adopted a deadlier strategy. Alarmed at their precipitous loss of the Marianas, the Imperial Army formed an "anti-amphibious" research team to figure out how their seemingly unassailable islands had fallen so swiftly to the American juggernaut.

The team's recommendation: Disrupt rather than oppose the landing; develop "honeycomb" protective positions well inland; avoid the wasteful banzai attacks in favor of small, stinging counterattacks; "bleed" the Americans in a costly, time-consuming battle of attrition. "Disrupt, honeycomb, and bleed" became the blueprint for Japanese tactics at Peleliu, Iwo Jima, and Okinawa—the three costliest battles of the war for the U.S. Marines.

The Marines stormed Peleliu because of an earlier promise Admiral Nimitz made to General MacArthur in the presence of President Roosevelt. It was a questionable military commitment from the onset, and changing events would render the seizure of Peleliu bloodily superfluous.

MacArthur, obsessed with returning to the Philippines to avenge his disastrous defeat, asked Nimitz to capture the Japanese bomber strip on Peleliu to protect the Army's right flank as they invaded Mindanao. Operation Stalemate, suitably named and star-crossed throughout, would be executed.

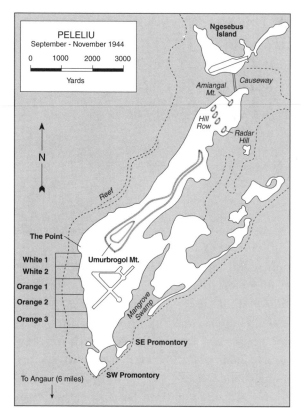

PELELIU
September - November 1944

0   1000   2000   3000
Yards

N

Ngesebus
Island

Causeway

Amiangal
Mt.

Hill
Row

Radar
Hill

Reef

The Point

White 1
White 2
Orange 1
Orange 2
Orange 3

Umurbrogol Mt.

Mangrove
Swamp

SE Promontory

To Angaur (6 miles)

SW Promontory

"Everything about Peleliu left a bad taste in your mouth," commented one Marine survivor of Stalemate.

The small, wretched island, the drooping tail of the Palaus, the westernmost appendage of the far-flung Carolines, had no redeeming graces. Peleliu's oven-hot climate was matched only by its convoluted terrain, the most ungodly scramble of coral cliffs and reeking mangrove swamps a defensive force could pray for. Defending it were some of the most proficient Japanese soldiers the Americans would face in the war.

Colonel Kunio Nakagawa commanded 10,000 Japanese troops on Peleliu, including his own infantry regiment, proud veterans of Manchurian border-fighting. Nakagawa had a supreme eye for the land. He saw immediately how suitable Peleliu would be for the new Japanese doctrine of attrition warfare.

The looming, trackless Umurbrogol, a jumbled spine of steep hills running north and south, contained more than five hundred limestone caves. Some were old mining caverns as much as five stories tall; many were connected by tunnels. Given several months reprieve while the Americans attacked the Marianas, Nakagawa imported mining engineers from Japan to help "militarize" the existing caves and construct elaborate new "honeycombs." The engineers equipped some caves with rolling steel doors and multiple openings for field artillery and heavy machine guns. The largest of Peleliu's caves could accommodate a thousand men.

Major General Roy Geiger and his III Amphibious Corps, recent victors of Guam, would tackle Peleliu. But Geiger got a late start on Stalemate when the fighting on Guam ran beyond schedule. Nor would he have his dynamic naval counterpart "Close-in" Conolly on this operation.

When Geiger finally arrived at the Stalemate planning site, his naval gunfire commander announced brusquely: "You're not going to get the preliminary bombardment you got at Guam; we don't have the time and I don't have the ammo."

Geiger tried but failed to reverse this critical shortfall. He knew any abbreviation of naval gunfire would cost Marine lives.

The 1st Marine Division drew the assignment to tackle Peleliu. The "Old Breed" had prevailed under awful conditions at Guadalcanal and Cape Gloucester. Peleliu would provide their supreme test.

Major General Rupertus, dour but experienced, still commanded. Three veteran colonels led his infantry regiments: Chesty Puller had the 1st Marines,

Harold "Bucky" Harris had the 5th, and Herman "Hard Head" Hanneken (the ice-blooded assassin of Charlemagne Peralte), the 7th.

General Rupertus exuded confidence as the division sailed toward Peleliu, saying, "We'll have some casualties, but this is going to be a quickie. We'll be through in three days, maybe two." Others were less optimistic. Said Admiral Halsey, "I smell another Tarawa."

While the Navy's UDT teams worked wonders clearing away antiboat mines and obstacles from the beach approaches, the naval gunfire effort proved not only insufficient in quantity but inexpertly delivered.

Most of Nakagawa's defenders, hunkered down in their caves in the Umurbrogol, had no fear of the bombardment, but even the one battalion Nakagawa left deployed to disrupt the landing suffered little from the light-weight pounding.

Geiger's corps included the Army's untested but superbly led 81st Division, yet Rupertus insisted his Marines could handle Peleliu without Army help. He planned to throw all three regiments abreast across a two-mile stretch of beach on Peleliu's southwest coast, leaving but a single battalion in division reserve.

Rupertus directed Puller to land on the left flank and seize the high ground to the north, the still-undefined Umurbrogol; Harris to land in the center and seize the vital bomber field; and Hanneken to land on the right and clear the southern bulge of the island.

D-Day was September 15, 1944.

As preplanned naval gunfire petered out "for lack of suitable targets," the steel doors of the Umurbrogol rolled open and Nakagawa's heavy artillery began raining hellish fire on the approaching waves of LVTs. Well-concealed 47mm antiboat guns opened up with enfilade fire from coral promontories on either flank. Heavy machine guns stitched the laboring craft without mercy. It was as deadly and ferocious an opposed landing as the Marines would ever face.

Peleliu was Private First Class Eugene B. Sledge's first battle. His experience in landing with the assault waves of the 5th Marines evoked this memorable account:

> The beach was a sheet of flame backed by a huge wall of black smoke, as though the island was on fire. Every Marine in that amtrac was sickly white with terror. Heavy Jap artillery and mortars were pounding the beach, and Marines were getting hit constantly. We piled out of our amtrac amid blue-white Japanese machine gun tracers and raced inland.

The slaughter in the shallows and along the beach was horrific.

An aerial observer reported cryptically: "There are amtracs burning on the reef." In the first hour Japanese gunners knocked out sixty LVTs and DUKWs.

Chesty Puller lost his entire regimental communications section when the 47mm antiboat gun on the left flank promontory (ever after known as "The Point") blew their LVT out of the water. Puller himself, slowed by his Guadalcanal wounds, barely dismounted from his beached LVT in time before

it erupted in flames from a direct hit by a high-velocity round from The Point.

Puller, fearless under fire, unscrambled the chaos and got his men moving inland, but General Rupertus's "quickie" had become a nightmare.

Knocking out The Point had been the mission of Captain George Hunt's King Company, 3/1, from the beginning. Puller and Hunt had figured the Japanese would likely occupy the stubby finger of coral to command the beach approaches. They had no way of knowing that The Point would be their introduction to the enemy's new "honeycomb" tactics.

The Japanese blasted holes in the coral with dynamite, emplaced a 47mm gun and a half-dozen 20mm machine cannons, then sealed the face of each opening with concrete except for a narrow firing slit. The Point was in effect a small fortress whose fire dominated all three landing beaches. Hunt's mission was suddenly urgent, pivotal.

Colonel Hanneken's 7th Marines had their own hands full overrunning the Japanese gun emplacements on the opposite flank. Those guns knocked out so many LVTs that hundreds of his Marines had to wade ashore from the reef, recalling chilling scenes of Tarawa.

In the center, Bucky Harris's 5th Marines scrambled ashore under heavy fire, the troops keeping a fearful eye out for the tips of huge mines protruding from the sand. The 5th, relatively clear of the enfilade fire raking both flank regiments, made the most progress of the day.

Against this center salient Nakagawa expended his tank company in an armored counterattack across the airfield. The 5th Marines poleaxed the late afternoon assault—assisted by every tank, howitzer, ship's gun, and dive-bomber in the neighborhood, a real shooting gallery. The thin-skinned Japanese tanks (technically, *tankettes*, mounting 37mm guns) were riddled and shredded; the accompanying infantry fell in ragged clumps.

D-Day ended with the 1st Marine Division occupying an irregular beachhead two miles long and ranging in depth from a mile in the south to a few feet along The Point on the north. Some of the lines were badly tangled, requiring an all-night effort by steel-nerved Lieutenant Colonel Lew Walt to restore tactical integrity.

The day had been rife with nasty surprises for General Rupertus, and the cost had been much greater than expected: 1,100 casualties, including 200 dead. Still, there was room for optimism. Total losses were less than D-Day at either Tarawa or Saipan, and Rupertus figured the Japanese were sure to crack now that their perimeter had been so forcibly penetrated.

For all his combat experience General Rupertus could

SEMPER CHESTY

Stumpy, pigeon-breasted, unsmiling, gruff, and remarkably homely, Lewis "Chesty" Puller was the last man on earth you would have chosen for a Marine recruiting poster. Yet if you asked the last million Marines to name the one Leatherneck who personified the dash and reckless, assault-the-center courage of the Corps, they would reply, Chesty, to the last man. Well versed in military history, he never missed an opportunity to enlighten his men about tactics or strategy or geopolitics. Of course, Chesty's pronounced indifference to his own personal safety, disdain for the static defensive, and penchant for closing with the enemy made him a controversial commander. And the most relentless enemy the Japanese would ever know.

THE TERRIBLE AND GLORIOUS POINT

King Company's battle for The Point became an epic of Marine Corps small-unit action.

One of Hunt's three platoons was pinned down for twenty hours in the killing zone of an adjoining coral fortification, most of his machine guns were lost in the water, he had no communications with his 60mm mortar section, and his right flank dangled in the air when the Japanese forced a wedge in the 1st Marines' lines. No one would have begrudged a well-called-for postponement of his mission.

Yet, in less than an hour, a single rifle platoon erased each of the fortified gun positions, one by one.

The 47mm gun cave was the hardest nut to crack, but Lieutenant William Willis crawled close enough to blind the Japanese with a smoke grenade, then Corporal Robert Anderson coolly lobbed a rifle grenade through the aperture. The explosion detonated the gun's high-explosive shells, forcing the gunners out in the open, coughing and burning, where they died in a hail of bullets.

Captain Hunt soon found that taking The Point was one thing—*holding* it was quite another. Colonel Nakagawa wanted the key terrain back, and was willing to expend three of his own companies in the endeavor.

For the next thirty hours, isolated and nearly maddened by thirst, King Company fended off four major counterattacks. Two nights of hand-to-hand fighting took a heavy toll, but there were Marines in this company who had crossed bayonets with the Kuma Battalion at Guadalcanal exactly two years earlier and they more than held their own against the Manchurian veterans.

Although reduced in ranks at one point to a dangerously low eighteen men, Hunt's company held The Point. The cost: 157 Marine casualties.

Later, at Quantico, the Corps would construct an exact duplicate of The Point and its weaponry as the *ne plus ultra* of an enemy position, thereby to teach new Marine lieutenants the difficult art of assault on doomsday defenses.

---

never accept the reality that the Japanese had changed their tactics, that this Colonel Nakagawa intended to lay low and fight smart for the next ten weeks.

Rupertus would keep butting his head against the Umurbrogol in the misbegotten belief that the Japanese defenders would soon degenerate into their traditional self-sacrificing banzai charge, leading to the routine mop-up. His three fine regiments would sequentially come to grief in the highlands the Marines quickly dubbed "Bloody Nose Ridge."

D-Day had been bloody enough, but unlike Tarawa, most of the Marine casualties on Peleliu would come well after the assault landing.

The 5th Marines on the second day raced across the exposed airfield under a shattering artillery fire from the high ground, an experience that Private First Class Sledge later stated was the most terrifying of anything he saw throughout Peleliu or Okinawa.

The contested airstrip, already dotted with wrecked Japanese tanks, became further garnished with dead and wounded Marines. But once across, the 5th Marines kept the momentum and pushed rapidly through the trees to the eastern shoreline.

The 7th Marines, meanwhile, engaged in a furious battle with Japanese troops holding a series of pillboxes and spider holes throughout the southern sector of Peleliu.

195

THE BATTLE HISTORY OF THE US MARINES

As temperatures soared to 115 degrees, the Marines suffered almost as many casualties from heat prostration as from wounds. To exacerbate the situation, the first expeditionary cans of water to be offloaded and delivered to the dehydrated troops turned out to be contaminated with fuel oil.

Nothing came easy on Peleliu, but no sector was rougher than the Umurbrogol.

The landscape was daunting enough—described by one survivor as "a series of submerged reefs suddenly thrust violently upward, with jagged, sharp cliffs, and ridges as steep as the roof of a house."

Here Chesty Puller led his 1st Marines in a gallant but fruitless series of frontal assaults. Even as proven a tactician as Puller could not prevail in the absence of maneuver room and in the teeth of Nakagawa's artfully concealed, mutually supporting cross fires. The 1st Marines clawed forward, ridge by ridge, cave by cave, but sustained terrible casualties every day.

Brigadier General Oliver Smith, assistant division commander, took it upon himself to visit Puller's position on Bloody Nose Ridge. Smith found he had to take his life in his hands just to reach Chesty's regimental command post, typically as far forward as his leading battalion. Smith followed the thin comm wires leading up the steep, exposed coral heights, and found Puller shirtless, barking commands over the radio handset and simultaneously ordering his aides to "knock out that goddamned sniper over there."

This would be Puller's final battle of the war. He grieved over the loss of his younger brother Sam, killed by a Japanese sniper on Guam a few weeks earlier. His festering Guadalcanal wounds still hobbled him.

Yet Chesty's fighting spirit blazed furiously.

When one battalion commander protested the latest attack order because he was down to a handful of men, Puller cut him short: "What do you mean you don't have enough men—*you're* still on your feet, aren't you? Attack, dammit!"

The attack succeeded. Smith, observing the desperate maneuvers, commented, "I don't see how any human beings captured it."

Major Raymond Davis commanded the 1st Battalion, 1st Marines, at Peleliu, a well-trained, experienced outfit. His Basic School tactics instructor had been then-Captain Lewis Puller of Nicaragua fame, and Davis had learned well from the master.

Davis, whose Marine Corps service would span three wars and include the Medal of Honor for the Chosin Reservoir campaign, always regarded Peleliu as his most difficult battle. "We never found a way to get the enemy out of his defenses—the deep caves with their small holes for fixed machine gun firing." Six days of endless fighting in the Umurbrogol would cost Davis the loss of a staggering 71 percent of his battalion.

One of Davis's company commanders, Captain Everett Pope, made the deepest penetration of the highlands that bloody first week, leading ninety men forward to seize what appeared on the imperfect maps to be Hill 100.

Peleliu's terrain favored the Japanese defenders. Marines wait tensely for some counterattacking force to materialize out of the mangrove swamps. Waiting was always the worst part.
(U.S. Marine Corps)

Getting to the crest of this feature took a full day of heavy fighting, but Pope then discovered that his objective was not a hill at all, simply the nose of a higher ridge—and the Japanese held the high ground all around.

Pinned down at day's end, Pope's few dozen survivors set up a hasty defense in an area smaller than a tennis court. Pope's message was grim: "The line is flimsy as hell, and it is getting dark. We need grenades badly."

The Japanese came at the outpost all night. Pope's survivors ran out of bullets, then beat back the attackers with knives and bare fists, throwing chunks of coral and empty ammo boxes in the faces of the advancing enemy.

Miraculously, they held till dawn, held long enough for Pope to lead his nine wounded survivors back down the hill to safety. Puller nominated Pope for the Medal of Honor, but it would be weeks before other Marines could recover the bodies of Pope's slain troops from the ghastly crest of "Hill 100."

General Geiger endeavored to let Rupertus fight his own battle, but after six days he ordered in the first regiment of the Army's 81st Division and directed Rupertus to relieve Puller's 1st Marines.

Puller raged to stay and fight, but by now Bloody Nose Ridge had cost his regiment nearly 60 percent of its landing strength. In small groups, carrying their wounded, the survivors came down from the Umurbrogol's blood-soaked ridges.

"Hey, you guys the First Marines?" a correspondent shouted. "Mister, there *ain't* no more First Marines," one answered.

The 7th and the 5th Marines, as well as the Army regiments, would have their own crack at the Umurbrogol, and in time they would encircle and overwhelm Nakagawa's disciplined cave-dwellers one by one.

When Private First Class Sledge's company of the 5th Marines took their turn in this unforgiving arena, he noted that "particularly at night by the light

A battery of the 11th Marines' 75mm pack howitzers opens fire in direct support of the infantry on Peleliu. The nearly horizontal angle of the muzzles indicates an enemy dangerously close at hand.
(U.S. Marine Corps)

of flares it was like no other battlefield on earth. It was an alien, unearthly, surrealistic nightmare like the surface of another planet." Sledge would survive the ordeal, but Peleliu would inflict 150 casualties on his 235-man company. Sledge regarded the Umurbrogol balefully: "It soaked up the blood of our division like a sponge."

One benefit of Nakagawa's "honeycomb" defense in the highlands: It left the beaches and airfield relatively clear for U.S. operations. Logistic support for the Marines flowed smoothly ashore, despite the need for transfer line operations along the reef. The 1st Marine Division had gotten good at this business, and with the early exception of the contaminated water, front-line troops did not suffer for want of ammo, rations, or medical support.

Meanwhile, the industrious SeaBees had the airstrip ready for advance operations as early as D+3. Captain Wallace Slappey promptly flew in with the tiny "Grasshoppers" of his VMO–1 and quickly commenced aerial spotting missions for both artillery and naval gunfire.

Marine infantrymen loved to see the Piper Cubs overhead, admiring their fearless pilots and observers, and dubbing them "Piperschmidts" or "Messercubs."

The morale of the embattled infantrymen took another boost on September 26 when the gull-winged Corsairs of Major Robert ("Cowboy") Stout's VMF–114 swooped out of the sky to land on the airfield.

Cowboy Stout and his Corsair pilots brought three welcome elements to the battle: rockets, napalm, and ferocious bravado.

The rockets proved better than dive-bombing against the steep cave fronts.

Napalm, first used experimentally at Tinian, served better at Peleliu, first to burn away the vegetation hiding cave entrances and spider holes, then to roast the occupants. In cases where the lines were too intermingled for the

tumbling canisters of napalm to be delivered safely, the pilots simply dropped inert tanks, then wiggled their wings as they pulled clear, the signal for the riflemen to detonate the bombs with white phosphorous tracers.

Delivering all of this close support required the pilots to risk everything on low-level attacks subject to heavy enemy ground fire.

Their targets were so close to the airfield that the pilots never bothered to crank up their landing wheels—fifteen seconds after takeoff they would be scorching into their assault runs—then they would circle back to reload and take off again.

The 1st Marine Division, despite its dreadful losses, was learning valuable lessons about coordinating supporting fires to pulverize enemy strong points.

No regimental commander was more proficient at this than Colonel Bucky Harris of the 5th Marines, whose stated policy was "I prefer to be lavish with ordnance but stingy with my men's lives." And no action in the Battle for Peleliu better illustrated Harris's mastery of fire support coordination than his assault on Ngesebus Island on September 28.

Ngesebus was connected to northern Peleliu by a narrow causeway, well covered by fire from the defenders. The island contained an unfinished fighter strip, an appealing target to Geiger. Bucky Harris recognized the causeway as a likely death trap and decided to use LVTs to force his lead battalion across in a shore-to-shore landing.

Harris and his executive officer, Lieutenant Colonel Lew Walt, developed an integrated fire support plan using naval gunfire, heavy artillery from Army 155mm guns, howitzer fire from the 11th Marines, 75mm fire from leading LVT–As, and last-second strafing runs by VMF–114. The results were awesome.

Cowboy Stout's Corsairs screeched in a mere thirty feet off the deck just as the lead LVTs rumbled ashore.

Ngesebus fell to the 5th Marines like a rotten apple. A dazed Japanese officer, captured alive, admitted to Lew Walt that the attack had surpassed in savagery and coordination anything he'd experienced in his career.

But Nakagawa continued to rule the high country, and the meat-grinding assaults continued to exact a heavy toll. By October 15 the Old Breed had been shot up to the point that Geiger replaced them with the 81st Division.

The Army resorted to siege tactics in the Umurbrogol, but the costly battle raged on another six weeks.

At the end, Nakagawa signaled his superior: "Our sword is broken and we have run out of spears." With that, he burned his regimental colors and committed suicide. Tokyo promoted him to lieutenant general posthumously in recognition of his valor. Few Marines or soldiers who fought him would have denied him that accolade.

The long-drawn-out victory at Peleliu cost 9,600 American casualties— 6,500 Marines, 3,100 soldiers. For all their bravery and sacrifice, the spoils of victory proved sparse.

None of the airfields in and around Peleliu provided any significant support for MacArthur's return to the Philippines. Nor was Peleliu ever useful as a major staging base for further campaigns in the Pacific.

Ironically, the biggest plum came at the least cost. Ulithi Atoll, at the northern tip of the Palaus, fell to a regiment of the 81st Division without the loss of a man. Within that enormous lagoon the warships of the Fifth Fleet would assemble for the subsequent invasions of Iwo Jima and Okinawa—a definite strategic boon.

Peleliu provided only a single, undeniable benefit for the Old Breed. The experience they gained at such cost in utilizing all supporting arms to assault heavily fortified positions would prove invaluable in the longer, even bloodier island campaign to come at Okinawa a half-year later.

Peleliu is often described as "The Forgotten Battle." The fact that it occurred in such an obscure corner at the same time as MacArthur's celebrated return to the Philippines and the Allies' piercing of the Siegfried Line in Europe meant minimum media coverage. But it would remain the headline event of the lives of every survivor and the grieving families of the dead.

The effectiveness of Marine close air support of ground troops at Peleliu shone brightly, but that luxury had been an exception in the war thus far. Too often, Marine fighter and dive-bomber squadrons could not participate in these bloody island-hopping campaigns because of the sheer vastness of the Central Pacific. The smaller planes simply lacked "the legs" to get to the fight.

Having a relatively protected airfield directly next to the battlefield at Peleliu was a fluke. In most cases—Guam for example—the contested island's airfield was still too hot to use until the very end of the assault campaign.

Marine infantry units continued to be serviced by Navy carrier pilots, strong-hearted aviators all, but necessarily preoccupied with competing missions. How to get Marine tactical air to the island assaults?

General Holland Smith had tried for years to convince the Navy to embark Marine squadrons on carriers, especially the CVEs ("Jeep Carriers") whose main mission became support of amphibious assaults. After all, the Marine Corps had plenty of combat aviation assets to offer. By mid–1944 the Corps had 126 squadrons—and with more coming every month. Getting the Navy to agree took a long time.

Finally Commandant Vandegrift flew from Washington to

Peleliu exacted a frightful cost among the assault troops of the 1st Marine Division. The island also baked in temperatures that reached 115 degrees. Here a Marine shares his canteen with a badly wounded buddy after a firefight.
(U.S. Marine Corps)

By the time of Saipan and Peleliu in 1944, the Marines had adopted heavier artillery for island assault. As the Japanese reverted more and more to caves, including some protected by heavy steel doors, the need grew for the assault forces to pack a heavier punch. This 155mm howitzer combined long range with high-velocity impact.

Pearl Harbor to make his case before Chester Nimitz.

The sensible admiral agreed to accept eight Marine carrier groups (each with an eighteen-plane fighter squadron and a twelve-plane torpedo-bomber squadron) for duty on board the CVEs. In the interim, Nimitz suggested, the Marines might look for employment in the larger islands southwest of the Central Pacific theater—with MacArthur in the Philippines.

MacArthur returned to the Philippines on October 20, 1944, wading ashore in eastern Leyte behind his assault waves.

Fifteen hundred Marines accompanied the enormous Army forces, principally the V Amphibious Corps artillery, lending their 155mm guns and expertise to this campaign in between commitments in the Marianas and Iwo Jima. Marine Major General Ralph Mitchell accompanied MacArthur and suggested opportunities for employment of his 1st Marine Aircraft Wing. MacArthur accepted.

Among the first to arrive for combat duty were the F6F Hellcats of

FLYING LEATHERNECKS AND THEIR SEA JEEPS

Sometimes great weapons are simplifications of complicated ones. Such were CVE, or escort aircraft carriers. Usually laid down on tanker or merchant ship hulls in Kaiser shipyards and dead slow, they were to the big fast carriers as lightning bugs were to lightning. But they could be spat out in machine-line quantities by middling shipbuilding equipment, and the handfuls of planes they carried packed an outsized sting and took the strain when the fast carriers had to be elsewhere. To be sure, cocky Marine pilots often made scornful comments, insisting that CVE stood for "Combustible, Vulnerable, and Expendable." But Jeep carriers got sizable quantities of flying Marines untethered from backwatered island bases and onto flight decks. Never mind that the Marine Corsairs had earlier been found too ornery for sea duty by the Navy, and that those tiny flight decks and lack of intensive carrier training made for a grim accident record. Landing the speedy, high-rise Corsairs on the pitching, truncated deck of a CVE demanded exceptional teamwork. The Leathernecks learned to love their lumbering, dangerous, fragile little "Kaiser Coffins."

Marine Night-Fighter Squadron 541. General Mitchell put them to work flying out of muddy Tacloban Field. Then came four squadrons of Corsairs of MAG–12, up from the Solomons and looking for a fight.

When the Army's 77th Division conducted its end-run amphibious assault on Ormoc, the Corsair pilots had a field day, shooting down enemy fighters and thwarting the counter-landing operation by sinking Japanese destroyers and transports.

On Luzon, seven squadrons of Marine dive-bombers lent their close air support skills to the 1st Cavalry Division's drive on Manila. As the fighting intensified, Marine aviators supported all ten Army divisions, as well as Philippine guerrilla units in the bush.

The Marines demonstrated the key ingredients of successful close air: the dive-bomber pilot circling overhead, and his aviator counterpart on the ground in a radio jeep—the Air Liaison Party (ALP).

Army officers began to demand Marine air support.

Lieutenant Colonel Keith McCutcheon, MAG–24's veteran operations officer, would often take doubting Army officers up in his plane to let them see firsthand what Marine air could do for them on the battlefield. He invited Army infantry commanders and operations officers to brief his pilots on their plans and needs.

"The more you know about the other fellow's problems, the better you can work with him," McCutcheon insisted.

When the Army's 41st Division landed on Zamboanga on March 10, McCutcheon ensured his Marine ALPs accompanied the assault forces—"probably the first time Marine aviation ever made an assault landing," he claimed.

Following one particularly effective mission in support of the Sixth Army near Mount Mataba, an appreciative Army general exclaimed: "These Marine pilots dive-bombed a pinpointed target located between two friendly forces with accuracy comparable to field artillery."

Although not in the close-support business and well removed from media acclaim, other Marine aviators fought their own deadly battles against the Japanese in the Pacific.

Marine medium bomber squadrons equipped with Army-surplus North American B–25 Mitchells (designated "PBJs" by the Marines) pounded still-dangerous Rabaul by night and day, month after month. The big planes with their six-man crews could cover extended ranges and absorb a beating, but no aircraft proved invincible against Japanese antiaircraft fire or fighter interceptors. The Marine PBJs suffered a stiff twenty-six combat losses.

Now, at last, the war's focus swung northward toward the Imperial homeland itself. For Marine pilots everywhere, their long and frustrating restriction to the backwaters and short hops of the Pacific war had come to an end.

LEFT: A Marine dive-bomber begins its strike against Japanese positions on Luzon, Philippine Islands, in late 1944. The Marines were among the first military forces to experiment with dive-bombing techniques in their primitive biplanes against guerrilla strongholds in Central America during the 1920s. In the Philippines, Marine aviators perfected the tactics of close air support of ground units—in this case, the U.S. Army. (U.S. Marine Corps)

BELOW: The Marines fielded several medium bomber squadrons during the Pacific War, most equipped with the PBJ, the Marine version of the North American B–25 Mitchell bomber. Many of them flew day and night missions to pound still-dangerous Rabaul. Thankless work, now in the backwaters of the war, but ever deadly. The Marines lost twenty-six PBJs in combat. (U.S. Marine Corps)

11: SULFUR ISLAND

(Iwo Jima, 1945)

D-Day at Iwo Jima, February 19, 1945. The 4th and 5th Marine Divisions land abreast in an assault so powerful that one Japanese defender described it as "an enormous tidal wave." Note how the extinct volcanic crater Mount Suribachi dominated the landing beaches.

(U.S. Navy)

VICTORY WAS NEVER IN DOUBT. ITS COST WAS. WHAT WAS
IN DOUBT WAS WHETHER THERE WOULD BE ANY OF US
LEFT TO DEDICATE OUR CEMETERY AT THE END, OR
WHETHER THE LAST MARINE WOULD DIE KNOCKING OUT
THE LAST JAPANESE GUNNER.

Major General Graves Erskine, dedicating his 3d Marine Division cemetery
at Iwo Jima just after the battle

Iwo Jima was the largest Marine amphibious battle of all time. It was also the costliest.
The all-Leatherneck landing force sustained more than 26,000 casualties—the equivalent
of losing a division and a half of Marines. More than 6,000 died. So did 21,000 Japanese.

Iwo Jima represented an ironic twist on an old mission for the Marines. For decades
they had trained to seize advance naval bases in support of a seaborne campaign. Yet by
1944–1945 the Marines were engaging in their bloodiest battles—Saipan, Guam, Tinian,
and now Iwo—to seize bomber strips in support of the strategic air war against the
Japanese homeland.

The unholy marriage between the assault Marine and the long-range B–29 Superfortress spelled death and ruin to the Japanese empire.

Seventy-two thousand U.S. Marines assaulted heavily fortified Iwo Jima island in February 1945 as the spearhead of a veteran amphibious force at the peak of its lethality. No surprise, no subtlety here. Simply massive, unremitting force, battering ashore on a godforsaken sulfuric rock to seize a pair of invaluable airfields on the very doorstep of Japan.

The Marines expected a tough fight. Tokyo was 650 miles to the north, less than three hours' flight time. The island itself was a defender's dream—few beaches; broken, convoluted ground; a lunar landscape of cliffs, crags, and caves. With its pork chop–shaped area less than seven square miles, Iwo was bigger than Tarawa and Peleliu, but much smaller than the Marianas.

The volcanic island reeked of sulfur, leaked steam, and looked evil—"like hell with the fire out, but still smoking," said one unimpressed Marine.

The Japanese spared no expense in fortifying the island, using the Empire's most gifted mining engineers. Soon miles of tunnels linked fighting positions carved out of the soft rock. Pounded daily by Seventh Air Force bombers, the garrison simply moved underground, living and dying as moles. They had plenty of big guns, heavy mortars, enormous rockets—and scores of the wickedly effective 25mm automatic machine cannons, emplaced to fire horizontally at troops and landing craft.

The Browning Automatic Rifleman
(Charles Waterhouse)

Lieutenant General Tadamichi Kuribayashi commanded the Iwo garrison with an iron will and was well served by a brilliant artillery chief and several veteran infantry officers.

American intelligence knew little about Kuribayashi, fifty-three, a cavalry officer with an unremarkable record. The Marines would quickly discover their chief adversary had the soul of a samurai, the lethal caginess of a wounded tiger. Soon they would describe Kuribayashi as "the most redoubtable commander we faced in the entire war."

For the Marines, Iwo Jima would be the last battle for the old amphibious warhorse, Lieutenant General Howlin' Mad Smith. One final time he would rage against the Navy's parsimonious allocation of preliminary naval bom-

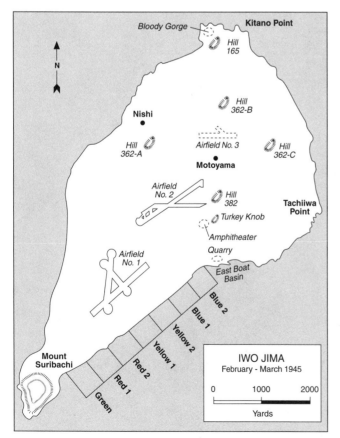

IWO JIMA
February – March 1945

0   1000   2000

Yards

bardment. One last time he would scoff vehemently at some "staff puke's" prediction of an easy victory. When Smith darkly suggested the island would cost 15,000 Marine casualties, his Navy counterparts thought he was out of his mind.

While Holland Smith battled the Navy's top brass, real leadership of the Marines storming Iwo Jima devolved to Major General Harry Schmidt, commanding the V Amphibious Corps. Schmidt's stirring victory at Tinian in that capacity made him well qualified to lead the largest contingent of Marines ever to fight a battle. The 3d, 4th, and 5th Marine Divisions would provide the landing force, each unit as well led, trained, and equipped as any outfit that ever crossed the Line of Departure in the Pacific War.

As always, the Marines' first challenge was getting this large a landing force ashore with full tactical integrity.

Schmidt planned to assault Iwo Jima's southeast coast with two divisions abreast, Rockey's 5th on the left, Cates's 4th on the right. The high ground on both flanks was worrisome.

On the left flank the 28th Marines of Colonel Harry "the Horse" Liversedge would have to cut directly across the island before assaulting 556-foot Mount Suribachi.

On the right, Lieutenant Colonel Justice "Jumping Joe" Chambers's battalion of the 25th Marines would have to storm the near-vertical walls of the "Rock Quarry" from the water's edge.

Although Iwo Jima's steep beach approaches and violent surf prevented the Japanese from planting antiboat mines, the garrison made good use of the soft sand along the inland terraces to sow hundreds of antitank mines, some improvised from naval torpedoes planted vertically. The D-Day mine wreckage shown here includes two LVTs knocked ass-over-teakettle and a Sherman tank with its starboard track blown off.

(U.S. Marine Corps)

*THE BATTLE
HISTORY OF THE
US MARINES*

Said a worried General Cates, "If I knew the name of the man on the extreme right of the right-hand squad I'd recommend him for a medal before we even go in."

Schmidt would hold Erskine's 3d Marine Division initially in reserve. And Holland Smith, looking ahead to the titanic battles to come against the Japanese homeland, would piss off all hands by holding one regiment of Erskine's division, the 3d Marines, in strategic reserve throughout Iwo Jima.

On D-Day, February 19, 1945, the weather held good. Admiral Kelly Turner ordered, "Land the landing force," and the intricate choreography began, this time clicking like a fine Swiss watch.

Everyone there, from Kuribayashi's wary gunners to the Marines waiting to debark, had a spectacular view. "Iwo Jima was a rude, ugly sight," said one observer. "Only a geologist could look at it and not be repelled."

As the pounding of Iwo Jima by naval guns reached a crescendo, the Marines grinned appreciatively when the old battleship *Nevada*, so valiant yet seemingly doomed at Pearl Harbor, churned daringly close to the island to deliver her smoking broadsides against Suribachi's caves and pillboxes.

Another cheer went up from the troops when two squadrons of Marine Corsairs swept in low, splattering rockets and machine gun bullets against the Rock Quarry. These were Lieutenant Colonel William "Tex" Millington's carrier pilots from Task Force 58, hitting Iwo as an interlude between raiding the Japanese home islands, but on this day of days they were magnificent.

"Drag your bellies on the beach," Tex Millington ordered his pilots.

This they literally did, shrieking barely fifty feet above the terraced beaches just as the assault waves of troop-laden LVTs churned ashore.

The assault landing was an awesome spectacle, the pinnacle of the amphibious war, flawlessly executed by the veteran Navy-Marine team. As a

THE SPIRIT OF BELLEAU WOOD

The personal awards of each division commander at Iwo Jima reflected hard campaigning with the Marine Brigade in France in WWI: Major General Graves Erskine (3d Division), Silver Star and two Purple Hearts; Major General Clifton Cates (4th Division), Navy Cross, two Silver Stars, two Purple Hearts; Major General Keller Rockey (5th Division), Navy Cross. Their collective combat experience would yield dividends in the battle for Iwo Jima—attrition warfare at its worst, units jammed shoulder-to-shoulder, shredded by heavy mortars and artillery—the kind of fighting described as "throwing human flesh against concrete."

The critical point on D-Day at Iwo Jima came when the Japanese commander opened fire on the crowded beachhead with his heavy guns from the highlands. The hunched shoulders of these Marines hugging Iwo's black sand beach indicate heavy shrapnel whickering just over their heads. Note the broached landing boats and mired vehicles along the water's edge. The presence of a beached medium landing ship (LSM) reflects the bravery of the Navy's amphibious force in direct delivery of Marine tanks even during this awful shelling. (National Archives)

ABOVE: Marines cross the first sand terrace on Iwo Jima under fire on D-Day. The loose black sand made running difficult , but the men were terribly exposed to withering Japanese fire from Mount Suribachi (background) and other highlands to the north and west. (U.S. Marine Corps)

OPPOSITE: Assaulting a defended beachhead on D-Day often became lonely work. This Marine knows to get off the exposed beach, keep low, keep advancing toward the enemy. There was no alternative. (U.S. Marine Corps)

Japanese officer observed from his Suribachi cave: "At nine o'clock in the morning, several hundred landing craft with amphibious tanks in the lead rushed ashore like an enormous tidal wave."

Within minutes General Schmidt had 8,000 Marines ashore, struggling through the soft, black sand of Sulfur Island.

So far, so good. No cakewalk, but plenty of momentum. Within ninety minutes the 1st Battalion, 28th Marines, reached the opposite coast, 700 yards away. Steaming, hulking Suribachi had been severed from the rest of the island, like cutting off the head of a dragon.

Kuribayashi watched these developments intently, waiting for the beaches and inland terraces to become clogged with troops and equipment. The time had come.

At his signal there was a barely perceptible stirring throughout the highlands—doors and hatches opening, enormous muzzles emerging. Another signal from the island commander, then all hell broke loose. Every gun, howitzer, and mortar on the island began pounding the exposed American Marines.

This was the bloodiest bombardment the Marines ever suffered in the war. The enormous 320mm spigot mortar rounds, visibly tumbling through the air like demonic fifty-five-gallon oil drums, blew groups of Marines to smithereens.

The 25mm machine cannons swept across the open spaces like giant scythes, leaving wide swaths of bloody bodies. There was no shelter, the vol-

canic sand too loose for digging, the terraces heavily mined. The Marines cursed and kept moving ahead, thousands of men lurching forward, nearly blinded by the fire.

Jumping Joe Chambers had landed early with his battalion on the right flank under punishing fire from Japanese in the Rock Quarry. Kuribayashi's heavy bombardment greatly complicated Chambers's task of leading his exposed troops up the rocks.

"You could've held up a cigarette and lit it on the stuff going by," Chambers said. "I knew we were in for one hell of a time."

Guadalcanal hero Gunnery Sergeant Manila John Basilone had forsaken the comfortable stateside routine of Victory Bond speeches by Medal of Honor awardees and volunteered to return to action. Suddenly he was in the fight of his life. His machine gun platoon lay pinned down along the beach as great fireballs of high explosives stalked them relentlessly.

Steeling himself, John Basilone leapt upright and yelled, "Come on, you bastards, we've gotta get these guns off the beach!"

His men swallowed hard, struggled to their feet, and swept forward behind their bandy-legged sergeant. But Basilone lacked the luck of Sergeant Dan Daly at Belleau Wood. A mortar round cut him down, killed him. His men

Three combat photographers recorded the dramatic flag-raisings atop wind-swept Mount Suribachi on the fourth day of the battle. Marine Staff Sergeant Louis Lowery of *Leatherneck* magazine accompanied Lieutenant Harold Schrier's combat patrol that seized the summit and raised a 54-by-28-inch American flag. Lowrey's photograph was historic but unexceptional. Several hours later a senior officer ordered a larger flag erected, one that could be seen by "every sonofabitch on the island." A beached LST donated the flag, a different group of combat Marines raised it, and Associated Press photographer Joe Rosenthal took the heralded still picture that would win the Pulitzer Prize. Marine Staff Sergeant William Genaust took the stirring motion picture footage. Watching the flag go up from the beach caused Navy Secretary James Forrestal to proclaim to Holland Smith: "The raising of that flag means a Marine Corps for another 500 years!"

The exultant Forrestal would have been astounded had someone advised him that capturing Suribachi and raising the flag represented only "the end of the beginning," that the bloody battle would rage on without respite for another full month.

The first flag-raising on Mount Suribachi was captured in this photograph by Staff Sergeant Lou Lowery of *Leatherneck* magazine, who minutes later had to dive for cover when Japanese gunners cut loose from a nearby cave. The desire for a larger flag (one that can be seen by "every sonofabitch on this island") led to a second flag-raising later in the day, the scene immortalized by AP photographer Joe Rosenthal and movie cameraman William Genaust, a Marine staff sergeant. (U.S. Marine Corps)

stared in disbelief at an immortal fallen—until some young corporal broke the spell, snarling, "All right, you sons of bitches, move it! *Move it!*"

The Fifth Fleet did not take kindly to this unwelcome ambush of their landing force by Japanese gunners in the highlands. Ships and planes reacted quickly, giving Kuribayashi a taste of his own medicine, stinging his exposed gun positions with shrapnel and napalm. The little island seemed to rock and quake, literally hell on earth.

The Marines suffered and bled but did not panic. The veterans in the ranks steadied the rookies, junior men took over from fallen leaders, and shot-up units merged quickly to maintain the attack.

Communications never failed in this battle. Schmidt kept pouring men ashore, despite the steep beach, savage surf, and ungodly enemy fire.

Dr. Michael "Irish Mike" Keleher, a tough-as-nails field surgeon making

his fourth combat landing with the 25th Marines, stared in horror as he dashed ashore at noon: "Such a sight on that beach! Wrecked boats, bogged-down jeeps, tanks burning, casualties scattered all over."

Reported one veteran Marine combat correspondent: "At Tarawa, Saipan, and Tinian, I saw Marines killed and wounded in a shocking manner, but I saw nothing like the ghastliness that hung over the Iwo beachhead."

Field radios crackled with urgent pleas to the fleet for plasma, stretchers, mortar shells—and sandbags.

The loose sand would allow no foxholes ("like digging a hole in a barrel of wheat!").

Schmidt and his marvelous staff filled each demand with an urgency of their own. The stuff flowed ashore—and somehow kept moving inland. So did the reserve battalions and regiments of the assault divisions. By dark Schmidt had an incredible 30,000 Marines ashore, well supported by tanks, half-tracks, and field artillery. Already the Marines outnumbered the Japanese on the island.

As for the price—2,400 casualties, comparable to American losses at Omaha Beach on Normandy's D-Day—steep, sobering, but affordable. Proportionately better than the first days at Tarawa or Saipan.

Howling Mad Smith, who always had a better way with words than the efficient but tongue-tied Harry Schmidt, would describe Iwo Jima as "the most savage and the most costly battle in the history of the Marine Corps." No exaggeration there.

Just getting ashore was a bitch. Crossing the terrace minefields was a bitch. The Rock Quarry was a bitch (Jumping Joe Chambers lost 22 officers and 500 men from his 3d Battalion, 25th Marines, scaling those heights on D-Day alone!). And seizing Mount Suribachi was beyond a bitch.

But Suribachi had to fall. From its cave-dotted heights Japanese gunners continued to shoot Marines in their backs as they wheeled north to wrest the first airfield from Kuribayashi's disciplined defenders.

Three of the six flag-raisers in the historic Rosenthal photograph would die in the fighting to come; two others would fall wounded. Photographer Genaust would die in a cave shoot-out.

And the battle for Iwo Jima had only just been joined.

Dead ahead lay Kuribayashi's main defensive belt and the island's increasingly broken terrain, all uphill from the landing beaches. The island was too constrained for major flank attacks; towering cliffs along the northern shoreline ruled out any end-run amphibious landings.

Schmidt had no option other than attacking frontally into the teeth of the Japanese strength.

Ashore came Erskine's veteran 3d Marine Division. Schmidt ordered them to occupy the center of a three-division line as the huge force surged forward, uphill, always manacled by the loose sand.

"Here everything is beach and you can't get off it," complained one sergeant.

General Kuribayashi kept iron controls on his subordinate commanders. With one exception there were no sacrificial banzai attacks.

But every night Kuribayashi sent out his "prowling wolves," small patrols that attacked Marine sentries and listening posts with bayonets and grenades.

The Japanese were also good at reverse-slope defenses. The Marines might finally capture a long-contested ridge, only to face swarms of the enemy boiling out of nowhere, an innocuous hole in the rocks, and the fighting would be desperate, hand-to-hand.

One battalion of the 21st Marines seized a crucial knob only to discover their high explosives had kicked up so much wet volcanic dust their weapons were fouled. True to form, here came the Japanese counterattack from just beyond the crest, forcing the Marines to resort to bayonets, entrenching tools, rocks—anything at hand—to drive them off. The knob quickly resembled a cattle-yard slaughter pen.

The fighting took a heavy toll of proven Marine leaders. Five of the twenty-four infantry battalion commanders who landed on Iwo Jima were killed in action; twelve others fell wounded.

Jumping Joe Chambers had qualified for the Medal of Honor on D-Day for leading his survivors over the crest of the Rock Quarry, but three days later his luck wore out. A Japanese Nambu gunner shot him in the chest late in the day.

Dr. Irish Mike Keleher got to him quickly, but the wound was critical, the position terribly exposed. Scrambling on knees and elbows, Keleher and his corpsmen snaked their stricken commander out of the line of fire—but now the beach was closed.

A passing DUKW driver refused to make a twilight run out to the hospital ship. Keleher, acutely aware that Chambers was dying fast, drew his pistol and took dead aim at the driver's head. There was an abrupt change of view.

The driver accepted his precious cargo, lumbered out to sea, and made it to the ship at the absolute last minute.

Twenty-six Marines and Navy corpsmen would receive the Medal of Honor for this cataclysmic battle. Exactly half would be posthumous awards. Jumping Joe Chambers would live to receive his.

Iwo Jima took such a toll on leaders that junior officers and enlisted men assumed roles of responsibility unimaginable in garrison.

Captain James Headley took command of Chambers's battalion after the fourth day and led it effectively through the heart of eastern Iwo's "Meat Grinder" for the next three weeks.

Sergeant Hubert Faltyn, a former Raider, became the sixth commanding officer of Dog Company, 2/26, in the fourth week of the fighting. Private First Class Dale Cassell commanded a rifle platoon in Baker Company, 1/28, until he was killed in action three days later.

Lieutenant Colonel Robert Cushman, future commandant, commanded the 2d Battalion, 9th Marines, throughout the battle and suffered egregious

losses. "By the time Iwo Jima was over, I had gone through two complete sets of platoon commanders," he said. "We had such things as artillery forward observers commanding a company and sergeants commanding the platoons."

Likewise, Lieutenant Colonel Lowell English commanded 2/21 until a Japanese machine gunner shot him through the knee on the twelfth day. "I lost every company commander," he said. "It was pretty goddamned rough."

Sunday, March 4, the end of the second week of the battle, seemed at first to be simply another day of the extended bad dream, another cold and drizzly day, another day of slaughter. The V Amphibious Corps had already sustained the loss of 13,000 Marines, including 3,000 dead. The thrilling sight of the flag being raised on Suribachi ten days earlier seemed like a lifetime ago.

But now two events occurred to turn the tide of battle—one unseen and only later realized, the other visible to every man on the island.

Without knowing it, the Marines had finally cracked Kuribayashi's main defensive belt across the central highlands and killed Colonel Chosaku Kaido, the gifted artillery chieftain. Kuribayashi would this day abandon his well-sited command post and take refuge for the remaining three weeks in a cave in an ungodly gorge on the northwestern tip of the island, still in command, but considerably less in control.

The second key event of March 4 occurred unexpectedly that afternoon when the B–29 Superfortress *Dinah Might,* crippled in a raid over Tokyo, made an emergency landing on the fire-swept and still unconverted bomber strip on Iwo. The gigantic silver bomber, the biggest plane anyone on the island had ever seen in their lives, shuddered to a halt barely thirty feet from the edge of the field.

Marines in every foxhole let out a resounding cheer. "That's why we are here!" said one.

Mechanics swarmed over the plane. Thirty minutes later she struggled aloft, surviving a fusillade of fire from Japanese gunners, and wheeled southeast toward Saipan and safety.

The high drama of this emergency landing by a crippled B–29 repeated itself thirty-six times during the battle alone. Each time the sight boosted the sagging morale of the raggedy-assed Marines. "We felt good to see them land," said one squad leader in the 25th Marines. "We knew they'd just come from blasting Tokyo."

The Marines renewed the battle with multiplied fury, led by their tanks.

Iwo Jima marked the largest deployment of Marine Corps tanks in the war, 150 Shermans, and they were invaluable. The tank battalions combined forces to lead the Marines' assault across the hotly disputed second airfield against galling fire from Japanese 47mm and 57mm antitank guns, a spectacular, high-explosive firefight.

Eight of these tanks had been field-modified to mount an experimental flamethrower that could spout napalm-thickened fuel at a range of 150 yards through a look-alike tube in place of its main turret gun. These "Zippo Tanks"

Both the Japanese and the Americans used flamethrowers against each other in the Pacific War. For the Marines, from Tarawa on, the tactical use of flame proved the ultimate arbiter against diehard Japanese defending "gun-port caves." Slowed by their eighty-pound loads, you can bet that these two flamethrower operators did not get this close to the Japanese bunker on their own. Not shown is the rifle squad, whose covering fire kept the enemy buttoned up until the moment of truth. (U.S. Marine Corps)

became the weapon of choice of the landing force—and the target of most urgent priority for the Japanese 109th Division.

The flame tanks proved ideal against Iwo's rugged caves and concrete fortifications. The Sherman's legendary ruggedness helped them withstand near-constant hits from desperate Japanese gunners. Marine maintenance crews worked around the clock to keep them repaired and operational. Marine riflemen protected their Zippo Tanks like worker bees protecting their queen—shooting down every sudden rush by Japanese suicide demolitionists.

The Marines had good friends in high places as well.

In addition to the Navy carrier pilots (the Marine squadrons departed with Task Force 58 on the third day) and a brutally effective squadron of Army P–51 Mustangs, the riflemen were faithfully served by their Marine "Grasshopper" observation crews in their fragile Piper Cubs.

"Out of the frying pan, into the fire," seemed an appropriate motto for the Grasshoppers, many of them launched at sea by means of the crudely experimental Brodie catapults on a lowly LST. "Like a peanut fired from a slingshot," remarked one unamused commander after watching two of his planes go spinning into the sea from the bizarre rig.

But once ashore, the Grasshoppers flew a thousand combat missions, calling in a rain of death and destruction on any Japanese gun crew that exposed itself.

General Kuribayashi had exhorted each of his troops to kill at least ten Americans in exchange for their own lives. While few achieved this distinction, the ratio of 1.25 Marine casualties (killed, wounded, missing) for every Japanese killed was the highest in the war. It was the first and only time a Marine landing force suffered greater casualties than they inflicted on the defending garrison.

Fortunately, casualty handling at Iwo was the best of the war.

A wounded Marine had a good chance of survival if he could just endure those awful first minutes until his intrepid corpsmen could crawl up to him, bind his wounds, give him a shot or two of morphine, and dispatch him to the rear with some strong-backed, nimble-footed litter bearers.

MARINES AND THE MEDIA

Marines in WWII got along famously with their accompanying combat correspondents, most of whom endured the same conditions of hell and high water. This affinity did not extend to certain stateside editors, especially William Randolph Hearst, an unabashed MacArthur advocate. Hearst's front-page editorial in the *San Francisco Examiner* on February 27 (the ninth day of the Battle for Iwo Jima) was downright blatant. Hearst cited "awesome evidence" that ill-advised Navy and Marine tactics were causing "enormous and excessive casualties" at Iwo Jima. "We need MacArthur," Hearst concluded. *"He saves the lives of his own men."* So incensed were the Marines at Camp Pendleton upon reading this, they drove 500 miles north to San Francisco to storm the *Examiner*'s office to demand an apology. But the damage was done. For the first time in this war Marines in battle received mail from home with news clippings criticizing their conduct of the fight. Bitterness was widespread. In the view of many Marines, MacArthur had dodged his only dangerous battle. Who the hell was he—*and who the hell was Hearst?*—to criticize anyone about the desperate struggle for Iwo Jima? It rankled.

Field surgeons like Irish Mike Keleher would be waiting at nearby battalion aid stations, backed up by a series of field hospitals of amazing sophistication.

Iwo was the first battle where *whole blood*, not plasma, was widely used—fresh blood donated stateside one day, flown into the theater the next, delivered ashore the third, and injected into the waiting arm of some desperately wounded Leatherneck that night.

Fully equipped hospital ships loitered offshore to receive serious cases—although the worst aspect for the evacuee was enduring the rocking, rolling ride in an LVT or DUKW while strapped in a stretcher!

And 2,500 badly wounded Marines benefited from perhaps the most felicitous treatment of all—direct evacuation from Iwo to Guam by transport aircraft, each passage lovingly administered by a Navy flight nurse, truly an angel of mercy, tenderly grasping one grimy hand after another, whispering, "Hold on, son, just hold on. . . ."

One "veteran" flight nurse, just twenty-three years old herself, wept as she saw shattered eighteen-year-olds cling to her as though she were their mother. . . .

Yet the savage fighting on Iwo Jima worked counter to all these blessed amenities. An abnormally high ratio of men died of their wounds, reflecting the point-blank exchanges of gunfire as well as the proliferation of high explosions, with their quadruple lethality of shrapnel, blast effect, shock, and burns.

The Battle of Iwo Jima also featured the largest concentration of Navajo Code Talkers in the war to date. The Navajos spoke one of the most unique dialects in the world. They drove Japanese cryptologists crazy in their repeated attempts to break or translate U.S. tactical communications.

Each division at Iwo employed about two dozen trained Navajos—all United States Marines—to transmit operation orders and situation reports, the critical information so earnestly sought by the Japanese. But not once—not at Iwo, or anywhere—were the Japanese able to "break the code." And like every other Marine ashore at Iwo, the Navajos

THE GLORIOUS UNSUNG

It was no accident that one of the six troops immortalized by Joe Rosenthal's photo of the Suribachi flag-raising was not a Marine but a U.S. Navy hospital corpsman—Pharmacist's Mate Second Class John Bradley. In the photo, as with the gigantic bronze statue in Arlington National Cemetery, Bradley is indistinguishable from the Marines in the group. All six are working together toward the common goal of raising the flag. This perfectly illustrates the tight bond between Marines and the Navy Medical Corps, forged in battle as early as the Spanish-American War. Each of the three divisions engaged in the Battle of Iwo Jima included a hundred Navy surgeons and a thousand hospital corpsmen in its ranks ashore. All of them performed their lifesaving missions under constant risk—and paid an exorbitant price. Twenty-three surgeons and 827 corpsmen were killed or wounded in action, a casualty rate twice that even of bloody Saipan. The wounded corpsmen included John Bradley of Suribachi fame. Four corpsmen received the Medal of Honor: Francis Pierce, George Wahlen, Jack Williams, and John Willis, the last two posthumously. Combat Marines, then and now, hold their corpsmen as dear to their hearts as their rifles, Ka-Bar knives, and dogtags.

were also trained to drop their handsets and pick up their bayoneted Garands whenever Kuribayashi's "Prowling Wolves" came calling at night.

African-American Marines made their mark at Iwo Jima as well.

The small Marine Corps, with its prevalence of Southern-born officers and NCOs, had been slow to accept these newly integrated troops, but their battlefield performance at Saipan and Peleliu had paved the way.

THE BUCK ROGERS MEN

Marine riflemen at Iwo Jima had a love-hate relationship with the forward-deploying, futuristic little rocket trucks and their plucky crews—the "Buck Rogers Men." The combat vehicles were International one-ton four-by-fours modified to carry 4.5-inch rockets. A good crew could launch a "ripple" of thirty-six rockets within a matter of seconds, smothering a target with high explosives. This the infantry loved— but each launching always drew heavy return fire from the Japanese, who hated the "automatic artillery." The little trucks could cut and run, but the troops had to stay and suffer the pounding. Despite this handicap, the rocket launchers' short range, steep angle of fire, and saturation effect kept them in high demand, especially in defilade-to-defilade preassault bombardments in northern Iwo's broken country. The Buck Rogers Men fired 30,000 rockets in the battle—but never more than two salvos at a time. "Speedy displacement" was the key to their survival.

Black Marines at Iwo served as ammo humpers and stevedores by day—keeping the vital flow of combat cargo moving north into the lines—and fought the Prowling Wolves at night. Privates James Whitlock and James Davis received Bronze Stars for their valor in derailing a violent Japanese counterattack with unerring carbine fire at great personal risk.

Once the Marines forced General Kuribayashi to evacuate his headquarters in the central highlands for the northwest coast, the discipline of his principal subordinates began to crumble.

A brigade commander who had successfully withstood the assaults of the 4th Marine Division in the "Meat Grinder" for weeks gave in to despair one night and launched a traditional banzai attack.

This was welcome news for General Cates and his veterans, who had faced a more critical attack the night of D-Day at Tinian.

The 4th Division, glad to have live targets in the open for a change, reacted calmly, set the stage with illuminating rounds from the ships offshore, laced the approaches with artillery and mortars, shredded the attacking columns with well-sited machine guns, then rose up with a vengeance to greet the survivors at bayonet point.

The Japanese brigade commander and 700 of his troops lay lifeless among the rocks at daybreak.

Given this windfall, the 4th Marine Division accelerated its advance to clear the east coast, finishing the job with a flourish two days later.

Then they began backloading their ships. Their battle was over. Next stop, they grimly realized, would be Japan itself.

The Marines long believed that the ultimate anticave weapon would be a long-range, high-capacity flamethrower mounted in the turret of a Sherman medium tank. When factory production of such a system lagged behind embarkation for Iwo, Marine tankers (with good help from Army Chemical Corps engineers and an inventive Navy SeaBee) field-modified eight of their Shermans for the battle. These proved invaluable. (U.S. Marine Corps)

Captain William Ketcham commanded Item Company in the division's 24th Marines throughout the battle. His company landed on D-Day with 133 riflemen in its three rifle platoons. Only nine of these Marines were still on their feet when Ketcham led them back aboard ship six weeks later.

"All I ever wanted to get out of Iwo Jima was my fanny and my dogtags," said Corporal Edward Hartman of 2/24.

The 3d Marine Division reached the north coast on March 16, the advance patrol leader sending a canteen of seawater back to General Schmidt marked "For inspection—not consumption."

On that date the top brass declared the island secured, a communiqué received with snorts and hoots by the 5th Marine Division, still fighting desperately against a well-armed, intractable enemy near Kuribayashi's final cave in what was now being called "The Bloody Gorge."

Using time-proven but costly "blowtorch and corkscrew" tactics to clear the final gorge took the division another ten days of bitter fighting. Erskine's 3d Division took over part of the sector for the final knockout blows.

The end at Iwo Jima came with a bang.

Kuribayashi had put up a whale of a fight. For a long time the Japanese nation held breathlessly on every word of his nightly reports from the embattled island. The Emperor honored the defenders by imperial decrees.

But Kuribayashi, a seventh-generation samurai, grudgingly recognized the warrior qualities of his opponents. Granted, their supporting arms from the Fifth Fleet were awesome. But these American Marines had displayed their own special courage, attacking valorously, skillfully. The fact that these Americans had maintained the offensive so relentlessly, with such a cold fury, in the face of such terrible casualties, did not bode well for the Japanese defense of their homeland.

Kuribayashi burned his colors and prepared to die. Spurning the ceremonial hari-kari, the commander led his emaciated survivors—some 500 of them—out of the cave at nightfall, clear of the sulfuric gorge, and halfway down the island where they fell upon the tents of a freshly arrived and unwary fighter squadron.

A ferocious brawl developed. Those Army pilots who survived being stabbed in their bunks joined a patchwork team of Marines and SeaBees who counterattacked. Wild fighting went on for hours. Sunrise highlighted the macabre scene. Several hundred American bodies lay intermingled with 500 Japanese corpses.

One of the dead—no one ever knew which—was Kuribayashi, who at least died on the offensive.

Abruptly the great battle was over. An Army division took over the cleanup of isolated diehards. The SeaBees finished repairing and extending both fields. Soon USAAF P–51 Mustangs were roaring aloft to escort Marianas-based B–29s on their raids over Tokyo.

And the flow of emergency landings by crippled B–29s on Iwo Jima never diminished. By war's end some 2,251 Superforts had been saved by American ownership of Iwo Jima—the equivalent of 24,000 crewmen who did not have to risk ditching their sixty-five-ton warbirds in the cruel sea. Said one of these redeemed airmen whose shot-to-pieces B–29 made it safely to Iwo: "Thank God for the Marines!"

Hanson Baldwin, military editor of the *New York Times*, had a fitting riposte for William Randolph Hearst's slam against the Iwo Jima Marines: "In the last analysis, when our men face a fortress like Iwo, it is spirit, guts, the willingness to die that pulls them through. The Marines have it to the full. That is why the American flag is flying on Iwo today."

But it would be Admiral Chester Nimitz's accolade that would endure longest, now chiseled into the granite base of the enormous bronze statue of the Suribachi Marines and their faithful corpsman at Arlington Cemetery: "Uncommon valor was a common virtue. . . . "

12: AMPHIBIOUS CAPSTONES

(Okinawa to V-J Day)

YOU NEVER KNEW WHEN YOU WERE DRAWING YOUR
LAST BREATH. YOU LIVED IN TOTAL UNCERTAINTY, ON
THE BRINK OF THE ABYSS, DAY AFTER DAY. THE ONLY
THING THAT KEPT YOU GOING WAS YOU JUST FELT YOU
HAD TO LIVE UP TO THE DEMANDS OF YOUR BUDDIES
WHO WERE DEPENDING ON YOU.

Private First Class Eugene Sledge, USMC, 1st Marine Division, Okinawa

Marines hit the beach on Okinawa loaded for bear. Unexpectedly, the Japanese decided not to oppose the landings, waiting instead in their subterranean Shuri defenses several miles inland. Note the LVT–4, the first assault amphibian with a debark ramp. (U.S. Marine Corps)

As the massive American invasion armada descended on Okinawa, most Marines commented on the irony of the chosen landing date: April 1, 1945. It was both Easter Sunday and April Fool's Day—which would prevail?

The U.S. Fifth Fleet was an awesome sight as it sortied from Ulithi Atoll and a dozen other forward anchorages to advance on Okinawa. Those Marines who had returned to the Pacific from the original amphibious offensive at Guadalcanal thirty-one months earlier whistled at the profusion of assault ships and landing craft. The new vessels covered the horizon, boggling the mind. "We've come a long way since Operation Shoe String," said one Solomons veteran.

Troops of the 2d Marine Division were miffed to have only a bridesmaid's assignment for this, the biggest landing of the Pacific War. They were to conduct an amphibious feint against Okinawa's southeast coast, distracting the Japanese defenders from the real landing against the opposite shore. The "Second to None" Division had done a masterful job of deceiving the enemy at Tinian. Today, this Easter Sunday, they churned shoreward in seven long waves under a hearty bombardment.

The Marine commander ensured his fourth wave crossed the Line of Departure at exactly 0830, H-Hour for the real landing, then recalled all waves to their ships, expecting an outburst of fire from Japanese shore batteries. But the beaches were ominously quiet.

The Japanese were about to unveil their newest—and deadliest—weapon against Marine landings: massed kamikaze air attacks.

The counterstrike waited until the Marines of the demonstration force had all returned to their ships—then hit the ships.

There was no air cover.

All combat air patrols were protecting the main fleet across the island. Ship's antiaircraft crews, pale substitutes for Corsairs or Hellcats, began plugging away furiously, desperately. Some kamikazes exploded spectacularly over the task force; others veered aside in the face of the stream of fire and crashed into the sea. But both the troop transport *Hinsdale* and *LST 844* suffered multiple hits.

The 2d Marines and the 2d Amphibian Tractor Battalion, two units which had lost so heavily at Tarawa, quickly suffered fifty casualties.

Ironically, the one division assigned a virtual noncombatant role on the first day at Okinawa would lose more men by far than any assault division in the U.S. Tenth Army. April Fool's Day, indeed.

Okinawa was the biggest and costliest single operation of the Pacific. The battle was enormous in scale, desperately contested, fought under unimaginable conditions of mud and rain and heavy ordnance. For each of its eighty-two days of combat, the battle would claim an average of 3,000 lives among the antagonists and the unfortunate noncombatants.

Army Lieutenant General Simon Buckner's 182,000-man Tenth Army included the veteran, all-Marine III Amphibious Corps, still commanded by

Okinawa's
"Plum Rains"
(Charles Waterhouse)

Major General Roy Geiger, who had proven himself at Guadalcanal, Guam, and Peleliu.

The affable aviator still preferred to see the situation firsthand. More than once during the battle of Okinawa he would disappear from his headquarters, commandeer an aircraft, and conduct a leisurely reconnaissance of the battlefield. As a result, Geiger usually knew more than his own staff—and more than Buckner and *his* staff—about what the Japanese had waiting for the Americans up ahead.

Geiger's command included the 1st and 6th Marine Divisions, the oldest and the newest. Major General Pedro del Valle, the imaginative artillery honcho at Guadalcanal and Guam, now commanded the Old Breed. And Major General Lemuel Shepherd commanded the brand-new 6th Marine Division, the only division formed overseas, made up of the 4th, 22d, and 29th Marines—veterans all. Geiger's fellow aviation pioneer from World War I, Major General Francis ("Pat") Mulcahy, commanded the Tenth Army's Tactical Air Force (TAF).

The Marines had seized Iwo Jima to enhance the strategic air campaign against Japan. But Okinawa would provide the essential springboard for the final invasion of the Home Islands. The skinny, 60-mile-long island, only 350 miles below Kyushu, had plenty of ports, anchorages, airfields, and training areas to support the massive staging necessary for this last leap. Some smooth-tongued staff dandies talked about Okinawa as "the England of the Pacific," comparing the way the Allies staged for the Normandy invasion.

Except for the kamikazes, Okinawa would be the only major "unopposed" landing of the war for the Marines—but it was a dubious distinction. Lieutenant General Mitsuru Ushijima, commanding the 100,000-man Thirty-Second Army, intended to wage the bloodiest possible defensive battle to buy time for the massed kamikazes to savage the American fleet.

Given seven months to prepare his defenses, Ushijima wisely forfeited the upper two thirds of the island, the obvious landing beaches at Hagushi, and the nearby airfields at Kadena and Yontan.

These tactics would have been heresy a year earlier. But the Japanese had learned from Peleliu and Iwo Jima. Here they would go to ground along the

WITCHES ON BROOMSTICKS

The Japanese high command had actually set the table for Okinawa six months in advance when Admiral Takijiro Onishi reported to Tokyo from the Philippines: "The enemy can be stopped and our country saved only by crash-dive attacks on his ships." Indeed, individual white-scarfed kamikaze pilots took a toll of U.S. Navy ships off Leyte and Luzon. Now, for Okinawa, the Japanese decided to *mass* their ultimate weapon, launching huge clouds of suiciders—up to 350 planes at a time—in *kikusui* attacks ("floating chrysanthemums"). Every pilot would die in the attempt; most would never even come close to an American ship. But those that penetrated the concentric screens and combat air patrols and heavy AA fire wreaked hideous damage on the Fifth Fleet, so vulnerably tied to supporting the Marines and soldiers in their protracted battle ashore. By the end of the campaign, the fleet would suffer 34 ships sunk, 368 damaged, and more than 9,000 casualties—the greatest losses ever sustained by the U.S. Navy in a single battle.

concentric ridges extending from Shuri Castle, the ancient Ryukyuan fortress whose guns commanded the port of Naha on one coast, and the highly coveted protected anchorage of Nakagusuka Bay on the other.

The American landing would be unopposed only temporarily.

Once again Imperial soldiers armed with nothing more than spades, picks, and buckets of wet cement began toiling like ants—digging "fire-port caves," observation posts, connecting tunnels, and reverse slope exits along the steep ridges. Southern Okinawa began to bristle like a porcupine. The subterranean headquarters of the Thirty-Second Army eventually measured 1,287 feet long by 160 feet deep.

Ushijima had an unusually large concentration of artillery and heavy weapons units in his patchwork field army. The Marines and GIs might walk ashore unopposed, but as soon as they stumbled into the Shuri defensive gridwork they would be hit by 150mm howitzers, 120mm mortars, ubiquitous 47mm antitank guns, and the always-frightful 320mm spigot mortars.

The size of the armada had an intimidating effect on the Japanese. As one Imperial soldier recorded in his diary after observing the fleet concentrating off Okinawa's southwest coast: "It's like a frog meeting a snake and waiting for the snake to eat him!"

Like Tarawa and so many other Central Pacific islands, Okinawa enjoyed the protection of a barrier coral reef. Unlike Tarawa, the reef made no difference to the Marines. Fourteen hundred new-model LVTs were on hand to land the assault elements of the Tenth Army— four divisions landing abreast, Marines to the north, Army to the south—covering eight miles of the Hagushi beaches.

Leading the way were hundreds of LVT-As, armored amphibians, the developmental grand-progeny of the long-ago Christie tank, firing on the move from their snub-nosed 75mm turrets.

And behind all the LVTAs and LVTs could be seen waves of 700 DUKWs bearing the first of the direct support artillery battalions. The amphibious assault plan was clicking on all cylinders.

Naval guns and attack aircraft delivered a final crescendo along the beaches as the lead waves plugged shoreward. The Marines were having a glorious Easter. Hardly a round was being fired their way. Private First Class Eugene Sledge, veteran of Peleliu's difficult landing, joined his

OKINAWA
April - June 1945

0   5   10

Miles

mortar section in singing "Little Brown Jug" at the tops of their lungs as they sped to the beach unmolested. A cakewalk at last!

So great was the momentum of this invasion force, so well-oiled the mechanics of launching a massive assault from the sea, that the Tenth Army rammed 16,000 combat troops ashore in the first hour.

Corporal James Day, a rifle squad leader in the 22nd Marines, could hardly believe his good fortune: "I didn't hear a single shot all morning—unbelievable!" Said another man: "I've already lived longer than I thought I would!"

The ship-to-shore movement never stopped. Sherman tanks swam in with experimental flotation gear, rumbled up to dry land, then blew away the awkward kits with light explosives as nonchalantly as a dog shaking himself after a bath.

More artillery poured ashore; big stuff—Marine 155mm guns ("The Long Toms") and the Army's awesome eight-inch self-propelled howitzers.

The 6th Marine Division, operating on the extreme left flank of the Tenth Army, seized priceless Yontan Airfield by 1300. The Army seized nearby Kadena. By dusk that Easter Sunday, General Buckner had 60,000 troops ashore, occupying a beachhead eight miles long and two miles deep.

For a few eerie weeks, times were good for the Okinawa Marines.

The 1st Marine Division seized the Katchin Peninsula on the third day, effectively cutting the island in two. Meanwhile, General Shepherd's 6th Marine Division swung north and engaged in a campaign of high mobility against what seemed to be a fleeing enemy. Troops rode tanks and self-propelled guns at breakneck speeds along country roads, having the time of their lives.

By April 7, the division had seized Nago, the largest town in northern Okinawa, and the Navy obliged by opening the port with minesweepers and UDT swimmers to bring in rations and ammo. "Hell," said Corporal Day. "Here we were in Nago. It was not tough at all. Up to that time my squad had not lost a man."

The 22d Marines continued up the spine of the island, reaching the northernmost point, Hedo Misaki, on April 13, having covered fifty-five miles through largely broken country since landing over the Hagushi beaches.

Abruptly, the honeymoon ended for the 6th Marine Division.

Their elusive foe, Colonel Takesiko Udo and his Kunigami regiment, finally went to ground in prepared positions in a six-square-mile area around 1,200-foot Mount Yae Take on the Motobu Peninsula, a few miles beyond Nago.

Said division operations officer Lieutenant Colonel Victor "Brute" Krulak, "They weren't going anywhere—they were going to fight to the death."

Udo had prepared his ground well, mining the approaches, covering the minefields with well-hidden, grazing machine gun fire, making the most of several major-caliber naval guns mounted deep within caves.

The five-day battle for Mount Yae Take was a demanding crucible for the 4th and 29th Marines.

Shepherd and Krulak supported them well, calling in naval gunfire from

the nearby South China Sea and Marine Corsairs, already flying combat missions out of newly rebuilt Yontan. But the infantrymen still had a hell of a fight rooting out the Kunigami Detachment—violent fighting in steep terrain at point-blank range.

Colonel Udo and his troops indeed fought to the death, and in doing so they bloodied the new division with nearly 1,000 casualties, including over 200 killed.

For the price, Shepherd's Marines learned a great deal about fighting as a team against Japanese fortified positions. In the heavy combat that lay ahead against the Shuri defenses no other outfit would be as adept in orchestrating close air support and naval gunfire as the 6th Division.

General Shepherd, who had learned his profession under equally stressful conditions in France in 1918, always sought good relations with the guys with the big guns. During the height of the struggle for Mount Yae Take he penned a message to the commander of the Northern Attack Force offshore: "The effectiveness of your gunfire support today was measured by the large number of Japanese encountered. Dead ones."

The 1st Marine Division for a while had time on its hands, operating a small-scale counterguerrilla campaign and processing refugees in the middle of the island. The Old Breed welcomed the break in the action, and this part of Okinawa was cool, dry, and clean—in sharp contrast to both Peleliu and "Pitiful Pavuvu," their dubious interim home in the Russell Islands.

But General del Valle's Marines could recognize the ominous signs of trouble brewing in the south.

The Army troops had rather quickly discovered the main lines of Japanese resistance and were now engaged in hard fighting. The Marine veterans behind them could distinguish the sounds of Japanese heavy artillery and knew their time would come.

Sure enough, the Tenth Army staff began requesting pieces of the 1st Marine Division: first their ammo stocks, then their artillery regiment, then their tank battalion.

Del Valle hotly resisted the splintering of his command, and Geiger backed him up. With that, Buckner detached the entire 1st Marine Division from Geiger and ordered them into the right flank of the Shuri lines.

The Old Breed began relieving the shot-up 27th Division on April 30, exuding a certain amount of disdain for the exhausted soldiers in the process. "It's hell in there, Marine," said one passing soldier to Private First Class Sledge, who replied saltily, "I know—I fought at Peleliu!"

Yet in the next instant Sledge was running for his life. "We raced across an open field as Japanese shells of all types whizzed, screamed, and roared around us. . . . The crash and thunder of explosions was a nightmare. . . . It was an appalling chaos. I was terribly afraid."

Such was the Old Breed's introduction to the Shuri defensive network, against which they would pound and scratch, one bloody yard at a time, for the longest month these veterans would ever experience.

General Ushijima's hidden network of caves, bunkers, and tunnels extended across the island, but the battlefield was extremely compressed. From Yonabaru on the east coast to the bridge over the Asa River above Naha is a linear distance of barely 9,000 yards. Yet Buckner would soon deploy four U.S. divisions shoulder-to-shoulder, attacking southward within this narrow corridor.

For now, it was the Old Breed on the right, or west coast, with two Army divisions to their left. Their first objective: the deadly Awacha Pocket, a broken country of rocky hills dotted with enemy caves and reeking with the bodies of the U.S. soldiers who had died in the first two weeks' attempt to punch through.

General del Valle had plenty of Peleliu veterans in his ranks who had fought the Japanese in their caves on Bloody Nose Ridge, and these men set to their grim work.

Where the 6th Marine Division was proficient with naval gunfire, the 1st Division ruled supreme in its integration of infantry with tanks and artillery. The Old Breed took fierce care of their tanks, often assigning rifle squads the responsibility for individual Shermans. This personalized vigilance won a special distinction. The First would be the only division on Okinawa—Marine or Army—not to lose a tank to Japanese suicide squads.

But no riflemen on earth could protect the Marine Shermans from hidden Japanese antitank guns. The broken terrain of the Awacha Pocket hid hundreds of 47mm and 57mm guns, carefully arrayed in mutually supporting fire fans.

The 11th Marines, the division's artillery regiment under Colonel Wilbur "Big Foot" Brown, were adept at showering their most exposed tanks with airburst shrapnel to decapitate enemy troops in the vicinity, but their howitzers did not have the wallop and the angle to take out the cave-port guns.

Increasingly the infantry commanders called up the regimental M–7 self-propelled 105mm guns.

More siege guns than half-tracks, the new M–7s became the weapon of choice in firing high-velocity, high-explosive shells into the very throat of each cave. They lacked the Sherman's mobility and durability, but they packed a bigger punch. The troops loved them.

The 5th Marines paid dearly for every cave and bunker they conquered in the Pocket. As at Peleliu, the Japanese proved masters of reverse slope defenses, and some of the wildest battles occurred late in the day, when the remnant of a rifle company, having finally wrested some godforsaken ridge spur, sat down to have a smoke—then had to leap up and fight for their lives as a nest of Imperial troops suddenly popped out of the very rocks under their feet. "Like sitting down on a goddamn hornets nest," observed one survivor.

And every night without fail came fresh Japanese infiltrators, looking for throats to cut, foxholes to grenade. Few Marines slept, despite their proven buddy systems.

These Leathernecks of the 1st Marine Division attack the Wana Ridge complex on Okinawa with two of the Marines' favorite weapons, the Thompson submachine gun and the Browning automatic rifle. (U.S. Marine Corps)

At this point General Ushijima foolishly made things easier for the Americans.

Yielding to his hotheaded subordinates, he agreed to launch a massive counterattack, even agreed to expose much of his field artillery from its subterranean positions to provide mass preassault fires.

The Japanese high command in Tokyo cooperated by directing a huge *kikusui* attack against the fleet. It made for a hell of a night.

But the U.S. Army veterans of the fighting at Leyte and the Old Breed veterans of Cape Gloucester and Peleliu simply leaned into their weapons, called for illumination, directed the firing of preregistered naval gunfire, artillery, and mortar barrages, and calmly shot the attacking Japanese to pieces.

On the coast along the right flank of the 1st Marine Division's sector, the 1st Marines and the 3d Armored Amphibian Battalion intercepted an enemy amphibious envelopment attempt, shooting down 700 men before they even touched dry land.

The Army, receiving the brunt of the attacks, had more prolonged fighting to do, but the Marines made short work of their attackers, then turned loose their war dog platoons to track down the survivors.

Ushijima's blunder cost him 6,000 first-line troops and fifty-nine invaluable artillery pieces. He also lost real estate. The opportunistic General del Valle advanced his Marines several hundred yards across no-man's-land as soon as the attackers faltered. Said Colonel Hiromichi Yahara, operations officer (and senior surviving officer) of the Thirty-Second Army: "This disaster was the decisive action of the campaign."

Yet the Battle of Okinawa would drag on another seven bloody weeks, in part because General Buckner's unimaginative, frontal-assault campaign played right into the hands of the attri-

An F4U Corsair of Marine Air Group–33 attacks Japanese targets on Okinawa with rockets. The Corsair earned its spurs in multiple roles (air-to-air, close air support to troops) in the Pacific War and the first years of the Korean War. Leathernecks dubbed the Corsair the "Bent-Wing Widow Maker." The Japanese called it "The Whistling Death."

(U.S. Marine Corps)

tion warfare Ushijima sought. Buckner stubbornly resisted the beseeching requests of the Marines—and several Army division commanders—that he open a "second front" by executing a left hook amphibious landing.

Chester Nimitz saw *time* as the biggest problem with Buckner's frontal approach. The kamikazes hit the Fifth Fleet each day in small groups, supported by conventional bombers, and the hordes of *kikusui* planes struck once or twice a week. "I'm losing a ship and a half a day out here," he told Buckner, adding bluntly, "If you can't get this thing moving, I'll put in someone who can." But Buckner couldn't, and Nimitz didn't, and the battle dragged on.

Marine air was in this fight big time.

General Pat Mulcahy had moved his Tactical Air Force headquarters ashore as early as the second day. Under his experienced eye, the SeaBees and engineers quickly completed repairs to the bomb-damaged Yontan and Kadena airfields. Typically, the first American aircraft to test the field was a tiny Marine Piper Cub, one of the Bird Dog observation planes, touching down on April 2.

Two days later, the fields were ready to accept fighters. Mulcahy's fighter arm, the Air Defense Command, became fully operational under Marine Brigadier General William Wallace. Shortly, Marine Corsairs began swooping in from the escort carriers offshore.

Yet, as much as Roy Geiger needed those Marine fighter squadrons to fly in support of his embattled divisions, Admiral Ray Spruance deemed the Japanese air arm to be the greatest threat to the campaign and deployed them as combat air patrols over the Fifth Fleet.

A strange flip-flop ensued. Each dawn Marine Corsairs would take off from Okinawa to go fight Japanese pilots over the East China Sea, while a horde of Navy Hellcat pilots arrived from the carriers to provide close air support to the ground troops.

Marine pilots engaged daily in ferocious dog-fights well out at sea, sometimes against inexperienced kamikaze pilots, but as often as not against late-model Jacks and Franks flown by veteran Imperial Navy pilots.

Colonel Ward Dickey's MAG–33 led the way with 214 confirmed kills. More than half of these came at the cool hands of Major George Axtell and his VMF–323 "Death Rattlers." Axtell himself became an instant ace, downing five Japanese raiders in one whirlwind thirty-minute melee.

His exultant ground crew wondered why Axtell insisted on inspecting his aircraft upon landing instead of celebrating with them. "I was waiting for my damned knees to stop knocking!" he confided later.

The Japanese Imperial General Headquarters expected each service and command to contribute "special suicide" units to the crucial battle for Okinawa.

Nor was the surface Navy spared. This led to the bizarre "death run of the *Yamato*," the mammoth super-battleship, last of the breed, with its intimidating 18.1-inch guns. Her sister ships had gone down fighting the previous year. Now came *Yamato*'s moment of glory.

The Japanese dispatched *Yamato* to Okinawa with no air cover and only enough precious fuel for a one-way trip. Her main mission: Distract Spruance's fleet to the north so another mass *kikusui* could sweep in and savage the anchored amphibians. If she could survive the suicide run, *Yamato* was ordered to beach herself and level her giant guns on the American ground troops within range. Only a handful of ships provided escort—more honorary pallbearers than a protective screen.

Admiral Spruance did not overreact. Marc Mitscher was in the area with Task Force 58. Spruance gave Mitscher the nod. Soon, Mitscher's carrier pilots found the forlorn convoy.

Within minutes it was over. The Hellcats, Corsairs, and Avengers sank the mighty *Yamato* with bombs and aerial torpedoes almost as easily as the U.S. battleships had been slaughtered at Pearl Harbor.

THE AMPHIBIOUS CARD NOT PLAYED

The 2d Marine Division, the Tenth Army's floating reserve, had gone back to Saipan in disgust after days of inactivity following their costly demonstration landing. But their ships were still at hand and combat-loaded, and no other division could top their cumulative combat experience at Guadalcanal, Tarawa, Saipan, and Tinian. Yet General Buckner ignored the suggestions of Generals Geiger and Shepherd to order an amphibious landing at Minetoga on Okinawa's southeast coast. He likewise turned a deaf ear to the imprecations of visiting Admiral Chester Nimitz and the Marine Commandant, General Alexander Vandegrift. The Tenth Army would continue its meat-grinder frontal tactics. This even baffled the Japanese. Said Colonel Yahara after the battle: "The absence of a landing puzzled my staff, particularly after May when it became impossible to put up more than a token resistance in the south." Colonel Samuel Taxis, operations officer for the 2d Marine Division, was bitter: "The Tenth Army should have thrown a left hook down there in the southern beaches the instant they bogged down. . . . They had a hell of a powerful reinforced division trained to a gnat's whiskers."

Marine Lieutenant Kenneth Huntington swept in through blinding AA fire to drop his bomb squarely on the battleship's forward turret—a pinwheel bull's-eye. In the admiring words of war correspondent Robert Sherrod: "One Marine, one bomb, one Navy Cross."

Back on the ground, the 1st Marine Division took a week to hammer through the Awacha Pocket, losing 1,400 men in the process. But ahead lay even tougher concentrations of Japanese defenses: Dakeshi Ridge, Wana Ridge, and the hell-to-pay Wana Draw.

A LEAP OF FAITH

Marine Lieutenant John Leaper of VMF–314 was returning to base in a good mood, having shot down two Japanese bombers near Okinawa at the cost of only a shattered windshield. Suddenly a Zero strafed him and wheeled to attack his wingman. Leaper gave chase, fired his last ten rounds, then climbed until he was just under the Zero and tried to saw off its tail with his propeller. It didn't work. Leaper, unfazed, pulled above the terrified enemy pilot and dug his prop into the nose of the Zero, chewing up large parts of cowling. The explosion knocked both planes out of the sky. Leaper managed to stream enough air into his torn chute to slow his descent. He landed in the drink, dog-paddled for ninety minutes, and got picked up by the USS *Cheyenne*. Another day, another dollar of flight pay.

Geiger saw that the Old Breed was spread too thin. He offered to deploy Shepherd's 6th Marine Division into the lines if Buckner would reassign the 1st Division back to his III Amphibious Corps. Buckner agreed.

Shepherd asked for the extreme right flank, seaward of del Valle's division, wanting to retain direct access to his supporting naval gunfire. Del Valle squeezed in his lines to accommodate Shepherd, glad to have Marines on at least one flank. Both commanders picked up the pace.

Then the "plum rains" began to fall.

Okinawa has a semitropical climate with distinct rainy seasons. In 1945, these rainy seasons more closely resembled monsoons. The unpaved roads became quagmires. Mud ruled the battlefields.

As one unit reported its day's activities: "Those on forward slope slid down; those on reverse slope slid back; otherwise no change." Private First Class Sledge of the 5th Marines simply recorded: "Misery beyond description."

Shepherd's 6th Division had their collective eye on the prize port of Naha but found themselves abruptly yanked to a halt by a complex of three unimposing hills under observed fire from not-too-distant Shuri Castle. The hills formed a triangle with its apex, Sugar Loaf, facing north toward the approaching Marines, while the flanks were superbly covered by fire from the two outlying hills, Half Moon and Horse Shoe.

Colonel Seiko Mita and his 15th Independent Mixed Regiment defended the complex. An assault on one hill would subject the attackers to shredding bands of cross fire from the other two. Heavy mortars blanketed all approaches from well-sited reverse slope positions. The 6th Marine Division's own week of hell was about to begin.

Lumpy Sugar Loaf, rising steeply but only fifty feet above the plain, was no Mount Suribachi, but it effectively blocked the advance on Naha. Too small a target for big naval guns, the hump-shouldered hill also precluded an assault

by anything larger than a rifle company. A half-dozen companies from the 22d and 29th Marines would be mangled in desperate fighting.

Corporal James Day, the squad leader from the 22d Marines who had marveled at the lack of opposition upon landing, saw enough close combat on Sugar Loaf to last a lifetime.

Day led his squad up the steep rise on the second day's assault. By night-fall he had just two men left. They hunkered in a shell hole on the enemy side of the crest, near Sugar Loaf's right shoulder. Incredibly, they would cling to that exposed position for four days and nights— reluctant occupants of front-row seats at that classic battle.

During the first night of the ordeal, Day heard the sounds of Major Henry Courtney's improvised relief force scrambling up the rocks on the opposite shoulder to rescue the Marines wounded in the earlier fighting. The Japanese, aware of the Marines' inevitable return to retrieve their casualties, opened a hot fire. Day and his men did their part, picking off Japanese as they scuttled across the ridge trying to get behind Courtney. But the rescue party lost nearly all hands.

Brave Henry Courtney died, later to receive the Medal of Honor. As the night grew quiet, Corporal Day heard the sounds of another relief team dragging out the bodies of the slain.

The Japanese knew of Day's presence and tried to overrun him every night. They killed one of the three Marines, wounded the other two. Day held on. "We could hear them climbing up the rocks. We had plenty of grenades and the darkness behind us. Those who survived the grenades would be silhouetted as they climbed over the ledge and we'd shoot 'em."

General Ushijima funneled fresh troops and more ammo into the Sugar Loaf complex each night. The Japanese gunners always seemed primed to unload on the next Marine assault. Corporal Day watched each new Marine assault with high hopes. "The sixteenth was the day I thought Sugar Loaf would fall," he said. But this assault, too, came to grief.

"The real danger at Sugar Loaf was not the hill itself where we were," Day said, "but in a 300-yard-by-300-yard killing zone which the Marines had to cross. . . . It was a dismal sight, men falling, tanks getting knocked out. . . . The division probably suffered 600 casualties that day."

Day and his one surviving squad mate were pulled off Sugar Loaf the fourth morning so the supporting arms could pulverize the sorry mound. This

THE MAGNIFICENT SLEDGEHAMMER

If the best Marine histories are all well weighted with the pithy comments of Private First Class Eugene "Sledgehammer" Sledge, it's because he brought to the party three attributes almost impossible to find together in WWII combat Marines: He endured the bloody battles of Peleliu and Okinawa as a 60mm mortarman in a front-line infantry company; he was an indefati-gable diarist, concealing his notes within his New Testament (the keeping of diaries being forbidden); and, most important of all, he stayed breathing to eventually print those diaries in his magnificent memoir, *With the Old Breed*. Many analysts have stated that Sledge's book was the definitive enlisted-man's account of combat in World War II, the twentieth-century equivalent of Stephen Crane's *Red Badge of Courage*.

Elements of the 5th Marines in a spirited firefight for a ridge near the Okinawan capital of Naha. Among their weapons are Garand M–1 carbines and rifles, and the M–9A1 2.36-inch rocket launcher or "bazooka." (U.S. Marine Corps)

was awesome but ineffective, the Japanese too deeply dug-in to be much fazed by bombs or shells.

Sugar Loaf would not fall until the eighteenth of May. By then, both the 22d and 29th Marines were badly shot up. Shepherd brought in Colonel Alan Shapley's fresher 4th Marines to seize and defend the outlying hills, enduring a vicious 700-man counterattack on Horseshoe in the process.

The Battle for Sugar Loaf, then and now, gets the most attention from military historians, but the simultaneous Battle for Wana Draw by the 1st Marine Division was its equal in desperate fighting and high drama.

Wana Draw resembled the prototypical "Apache Pass" of B-grade movies: steep cliffs pocked with cave openings towering over a twisted, brushy streambed. The Japanese 62d Infantry Division had strewn every possible approach with mines. From hidden observation posts in the cliffs they directed deadly cross fires from a hundred machine guns.

Marine Brigadier General Oliver Smith (here a staff officer, but a superb field Marine who would five years later command the Old Breed in their historical breakout from Korea's Chosin Reservoir) reported "Wana Draw proved to be the toughest assignment the 1st Division was ever to encounter."

The division's operational summary for May 18 reflects the agonizing pace of the struggle for Wana Draw: "Gains were measured by yards won, lost, then won again."

The 7th Marines, which lost 700 men taking Dakeshi Ridge, lost 500 more the first five days at Wana. In one three-day stretch Lieutenant Colonel Hunter Hurst lost twelve officers among the rifle companies of his battalion.

In a single day during this battle the 1st Tank Battalion fired 5,000 75mm cannon shells, 173,000 .30 caliber machine gun bullets, and 600 gallons of napalm.

By such measures the Old Breed finally wiped out the Japanese defending Wana Draw and struggled southward in the heavy rains.

So severe had been the opposition and the terrain that the 1st Division gained an average of only fifty-five yards per day over the preceding eighteen days.

Then came a lucky break.

General Ushijima this time listened to Colonel Yahara, and instead of defending the subterranean complex under Shuri Castle to the death, the Thirty-Second Army took advantage of the awful weather to execute a pull-back to a final line of ridges along the southern coast. Only a sacrificial handful of rearguard troops remained.

On May 29, sensing this suddenly light opposition, the 5th Marines asked General del Valle for permission to cross the division border into the U.S. Army zone to seize the seemingly deserted castle. This was too rich a prize to pass up. Del Valle knew his bordering Army unit would be deeply pissed at this intrusion, but they were a day behind, and the opportunity could well be lost by waiting.

Del Valle gave the go-ahead. Able Company of the 5th Marines darted

across the ridge, entered the ruined citadel, and raised a certain red flag criss-crossed by starry blue stripes.

The company commander, a South Carolinian with a sense of humor, had just raised the battle flag of the Confederacy.

General del Valle, already on the phone apologizing to every Army commander on the island for his coup in seizing Shuri, now had to do a rug dance when Buckner called, irate about the rebel flag. Del Valle figured Buckner of all people should have been sympathetic—after all, his father had been a Confederate general at Fort Donaldson.

Because the flagstaff was within the sights of a hundred Japanese gunners, it took two more days before the Old Breed could pull down the Stars and Bars and hoist the Stars and Stripes.

The rain and mud slowed the pursuit by the Tenth Army of the retreating Japanese. General Buckner's propensity for preceding each movement with massive artillery prep fires further slowed the advance. By the time the Marines approached the Kiyamu Peninsula, the southernmost five miles of the island, they found the Japanese as well dug in as ever along "a series of cross ridges that stick out like bones from the spines of a fish."

Colonel Big Foot Brown, commanding the Old Breed's artillery regiment, decried Buckner's daily overuse of heavy artillery and his reliance on illumination shells from dusk to dawn. "I felt like we were the children of Israel in the wilderness—living under a pillar of fire by night and a cloud of smoke by day."

On the right flank, General Shepherd examined the looming Oroku Peninsula that blocked his final approach to Naha airfield. Doing the expected thing—cutting across its base, forcing a crossing of the Kokuba River, attacking seaward east to west—would be a bloody, protracted affair. The Fifth Fleet stood ready to help.

FLAME WAS THE NAME OF THE GAME

The backpack portable flamethrower, so much in demand at Tarawa, was no longer the weapon of choice at Okinawa. A man trying to cross the open spaces within Wana Draw while carrying an eighty-pound flame pack was a distinct liability. A much safer and more effective weapon was the Zippo Tank, the converted Sherman with its long-range, turret-mounted flame rig. These proved ideal against caves. But in Wana Draw, many of the caves were halfway up some steep cliff, out of range. Against these the Marines resorted to the ancient use of fire in medieval siege tactics. Troops of Lieutenant Colonel Stephen Sabol's battalion of the 1st Marines wrestled heavy fifty-five-gallon drums of napalm up the reverse side of one of the cave-dotted cliffs—five hours of backbreaking labor—then split them open and tumbled them down the gorge. A couple of well-placed white phosphorous hand grenades then set the whole damned cliff ablaze. So much for hi-tech weaponry.

Maybe Shepherd could skin the cat by executing a division-sized amphibious landing across the estuary, catching the defenders by surprise in the flank. Maybe.

Roy Geiger liked the idea; Buckner waffled. Abruptly he consented, but gave Shepherd only thirty-six hours to plan and launch this complex maneuver. Shepherd put Brute Krulak to work immediately.

Krulak needed firsthand information. He sent Major Anthony "Cold

Steel" Walker and his 6th Reconnaissance Company on a stealthy scout across the estuary by dark of night.

Walker's Marines found the beaches unmined, the bulk of the defenders facing the Kokuba. Intelligence analysts had already reported the peninsula was guarded by an old adversary, Rear Admiral Minoru Ota, the former *rikusentai* who had fought the Marines at Bairoko in New Georgia.

Ota had no special naval landing forces, only a ragtag group of naval gunners, mechanics, and laborers. But Ota could breathe fire into any group of sailors.

WHAT GOES AROUND . . .

By the time of the Oroku Peninsula invasion, each of the infantry regiments of the 6th Marine Division was commanded by officers who had endured the shock and shame of the Pearl Harbor air raid. Colonel William Whaling (29th Marines) and Colonel Harold Roberts (22d Marines) had directed the fire of antiaircraft machine gunners that endless morning. And Colonel Alan Shapley (4th Marines), blown off the battleship *Arizona* by an explosion, had stalked naked across Ford Island at the height of the second raid, looking for a weapon. Now each man commanded a "weapon" of great lethality against the Japanese in this titanic battle—the Marine regimental combat team.

This time he armed them with an inordinate number of heavy machine guns and automatic cannons taken from wrecked aircraft, brought in some very heavy weapons from abandoned ships, sewed the hinterland of the peninsula with thousands of mines. This was not going to be easy—even with surprise.

K-Day for the Oroku Peninsula assault came on June 4 and produced a little jewel of an amphibious assault.

Everything clicked. Naval guns and aircraft provided magnificent support in spite of a looming typhoon. The thrust against his exposed flank surprised the hell out of Admiral Ota. As he reacted like a wounded tiger to confront the 4th and 29th Marines to his rear, Ota experienced another spearpoint when General Shepherd unbridled the 22d Marines to attack across the Kokuba. The three regiments converged.

Admiral Ota's sailors took a particularly heavy toll of General Shepherd's tanks, obliterating at least two with point-blank fire from a hidden eight-inch naval cannon. But the 6th Marine Division was now a well-oiled killing machine in its own right. Ably supported by naval gunfire from both flanks, Shepherd advanced ruthlessly against Ota on three fronts.

The old *rikusentai* sent one final message to Ushijima: "Enemy tank forces are now attacking our cave headquarters; the Naval Guard Brigade is dying gloriously." With that, he donned his dress uniform and committed suicide.

The 6th Division now had the peninsula and soon Naha itself.

The ten-day operation had cost 1,608 Marine casualties and thirty tanks, but Shepherd's men had killed 5,000 of Ota's men and captured another 200. Nobody knew it at the time, but this would be the final opposed amphibious landing of the war.

For their part, the 1st Marine Division now faced the 32d Infantry Regiment defending Kunishi Ridge, a steep escarpment of coral and rock,

which dominated the low-lying rice paddies. The ridge, much higher and longer than Sugar Loaf, was honeycombed with Japanese bunkers. Taking it by storm would be exorbitantly costly. General del Valle's commanders sought alternatives.

Colonel Edward Snedeker, commanding the 7th Marines, hitched a ride in an observation Bird Dog and formulated a different scheme.

"I saw we would never capture Kunishi in daytime. But a night attack might be successful," Snedeker said.

Marines and soldiers fought the entire Pacific War by dominating the days and conceding the nights to the Japanese. The number of large-

Bazookas became available to Marines too late for Tarawa (they would've been terrific against Betio's log-and-coral bunkers), but were used for every subsequent landing. This 2.26-inch bazooka proved handy against lightly armored Japanese tanks, yet after this war the Marines would face formidable Soviet-built tanks and require increasingly larger rocket launchers and (eventually) antitank guided missiles.

(U.S. Marine Corps)

sized night attacks launched by Americans in the Pacific Theater could be counted on two hands. But Snedeker sent a pair of battalions against Kunishi Ridge at 0330 the next morning. It worked. The lead companies swarmed over the crest 90 minutes later, surprising the Japanese at their breakfast.

Now came the hard part. The Marines still lacked the numbers to ferret out the Japanese from their subterranean bunkers. All they could do was set up a 360-degree circle and wait for the next counterattack to come bubbling out of the rocks.

Meanwhile, mortar fire from nearby Mezado Ridge spiked the casualty count. Both battalions needed to get their wounded out, their reinforcements and water in.

This rescue and supply became the mission of the 1st Tank Battalion, who for the next several days made run after run under very heavy fire, ferrying small bands of riflemen up to the crest of the ridge, unloading them via the bottom-mounted escape hatch, then trundling over top the wounded Marines to be pulled to safety through the scuttle.

This took a leap of faith for the casualties, lying there nervously as this 32-ton monster centered itself directly over them. But it was the only way they would get off Kunishi alive.

Another innovation during the battle for Kunishi Ridge saved more lives.

Getting the wounded back from the ridgeline was one thing; but the casualties still had to endure a painful six-hour ride by jeep-ambulance back to the main hospital at Kadena after that. Enter the beloved Bird Dogs. Engineers cleared a grass strip near Itoman for the Piper Cubs to land, receive a wounded Marine on a stretcher in the rear (observer's) seat, and take off for Kadena, eight minutes away.

In this, the dawn of aerial medevacs for the Marines, the dauntless observation squadrons successfully evacuated 641 critically wounded troops in 11 days.

The fight for Kunishi chewed up all three regiments of the 1st Marine Division (PFC Sledge lost half his company in 22 hours on the ridge). General Geiger, worried about the awful costs of this prolonged battle, managed to get General Buckner's permission to pry loose one regiment, the 8th Marines, from the 2d Marine Division back at Saipan.

The fresh troops first seized two offshore islands for use as early warning radar sites and fighter direction centers to help the Fifth Fleet in their never-ceasing battle against the kamikazes.

The 8th Marines then landed on Okinawa and reinforced the Old Breed.

General Buckner came out to see the 8th Marines in action. He had been very impressed with Colonel Clarence Wallace's regiment during a pre-invasion inspection visit, and was anxious to watch them perform against the last of Ushijima's veterans in the south. It was a tragic visit.

General Buckner's official party attracted the attention of an enemy gunner across the valley who uncorked four rounds of cannon fire. One struck

a coral outcrop and drove a splinter into General Buckner's chest. He died in minutes, the senior U.S. officer to be killed in the Pacific War.

General Roy Geiger took command of the Tenth Army, to the delight of the Marines and soldiers on the island—but to the consternation of the Army brass out of the line of fire.

A senior Army general received emergency orders to hasten to Okinawa to take command. He arrived too late.

Geiger had presided over the final defeat of the Thirty-Second Army, the death by suicide of General Ushijima, and the day of victory. Fittingly, Roy Geiger, the laid-back, highly competent, unconventional battle leader, became the only Marine, and the only aviator of any service, to command a field army.

The Battle of Okinawa officially ended on June 22, leaving the island a virtual charnel house. While exact numbers may never be known, estimates of Japanese deaths have ranged as high as 100,000 and of Okinawans as many as 150,000. Marine Corps casualties overall—ground, air, ships detachments—exceeded 19,500. An additional 560 members of the Navy Medical Corps attached to Marine units became casualties.

Ten Marines and three Navy corpsmen received the Medal of Honor. Eleven of the thirteen awards were posthumous.

The Secretary of the Navy awarded the Presidential Unit Citation to the 1st and 6th Marine Divisions, the 2d Marine Aircraft Wing, and Marine Observation Squadron Three (VMO–3) for extraordinary heroism. (VMO–6 received the award as a specific attached unit to the 6th Division).

Corporal James Day, now the sole survivor of his squad, suffered painful injuries from a Japanese satchel charge the last week of the battle but survived. Forty years later he would return to Okinawa as Major General Day, commanding all the island's Marine bases.

For several worrisome weeks the Marines prepared for Operation Downfall, the invasion of the Japanese home islands. The reward for the thinly spread Marine and Army infantry divisions in the Pacific seemed funereal:

A GOOD MAN GONE

Marines are in a position to think a lot about how much luck "The Gunny in the Sky" allows even the best Marine. Take Colonel Harold Roberts, commanding the 22d Marines. He had received the Navy Cross as a corpsman with the Marines in World War I. He had sparkled at Pearl Harbor. During the battle of Tarawa he had landed on D-Day as an observer from the 4th Marine Division. When sniper fire threatened his small party wading ashore east of the pier, Roberts borrowed an M–1 Garand, squared his shoulders, and fired a round from a rock-steady offhand position. Missed. He spat in the water, fiddled with the windage and elevation knobs, brought the piece back to his cheek, squeezed off two careful shots. Two Japanese snipers tumbled out of the pier pilings into the water. Roberts grinned, returned the M–1 to its wide-eyed owner, and continued to the beach. At Okinawa, however, his boldness bothered General Lemuel Shepherd. "For God's sake," Shepherd told Roberts the night before he was killed, "don't expose yourself unnecessarily." But on June 18, the same day that General Buckner died, Roberts thought it necessary to lead from the front. His third Navy Cross would be awarded posthumously.

Those who survived Leyte and Iwo Jima would get to assault Kyushu; the invasion of the Tokyo plain awaited the Luzon and Okinawa survivors.

Already Major General Harry Schmidt and his battle-tested V Amphibious Corps were hard at work on plans for their portion of the Kyushu assault, scheduled for November 1, 1945. On that date, the 2d, 3d, and 5th Marine Divisions would storm ashore below Kushikino in southwestern Kyushu.

The target beaches were narrow, dominated by dunes, and fully exposed to fire from a line of 600-foot hills less than a mile away. The Marines would also have to force a crossing of the Ozato River, which flowed parallel to the beach about 500 yards inland. The Japanese 40th Division defended that sector.

Colonel Samuel Taxis of the 2d Marine Division visited the assigned landing sites shortly after V-J Day and whistled at what he saw. "We would've faced a very difficult landing against vicious opposition," he reported.

News of the atomic bombs and the unconditional surrender of Japan brought all planning to a standstill and the Marines to their knees in prayerful gratitude. The three divisions scheduled to assault Kyushu had already suffered the combined loss of 32,759 battle casualties in the Pacific, including 7,580 dead. For the survivors, suddenly—they were going to live to adulthood. It was over!

The Marine Corps had reached an undreamed-of peak strength of 476,709 in mid–1945—a seventeen-fold increase over the prewar Corps of July 1940. The figure included 116,000 aviation Marines. Nineteen thousand women Marines served in billets ranging from stenographers to motor mechanics, cryptologists to parachute riggers.

The Marine Corps sustained nearly 92,000 combat casualties in World War II. Those who paid the ultimate sacrifice (killed in action, died of wounds, missing presumed dead) numbered 19,215. In addition, 518 of the 2,220 Marine Corps POWs in the Pacific did not survive captivity—about one in every four. The Marines, who comprised less than 5 percent of all Americans who served in the armed forces in World War II, suffered 10 percent of all the nation's casualties.

Déjà Vu

Mercifully, the Marine landing in Japan in late August 1945 resembled nothing of the massive storming assaults of the past four years—it looked more like the small landing conducted by Brevet Major Jacob Zeilin with Commodore Perry in 1853. A provisional brigade of U.S. Marines and sailors and Royal Marines and sailors landed after the cease-fire to seize Yokosuka.

The historic surrender ceremony on board USS *Missouri* in Tokyo Bay included Lieutenant General Roy Geiger but precious few other Marines. Conspicuously absent in a small tragedy: Lieutenant General Holland Smith. Chester Nimitz never forgave Howlin' Mad for upsetting the applecart of jointness by summarily relieving the Army general at Saipan. Yet Holland Smith had contributed a lion's share to the Pacific victory, developing the amphibious assault techniques which would bring the Japanese Empire to its knees. His absence from the *Missouri*'s quarterdeck during that triumphant moment pleased no Marines.

An average of 73 percent of all members of the armed forces served overseas in the war. *Ninety* percent of all Marines did so. A quarter of a million Marines were serving in the Pacific Theater at the war's end.

Eighty Marines received the Congressional Medal of Honor in the war–forty-eight posthumously. The eighty-first award went to Guadalcanal machine gunner Anthony Casamento in 1980.

The war in the Pacific was girt with a special horror, but the Marines who fought there brought home a distinctive sense of achievement, an 8,000-mile, four-year campaign against a savage and relentless foe under some of the worst conditions imaginable.

The Marines' well-earned homecoming was felicitous. And, it would turn out, rather short.

The atomic bombs would make Okinawa the final battle of the Pacific War, but at the campaign's end these survivors of the 4th Marines fully expected to lead the next assault against Japan. Taking pleasure in small things, they celebrate their current victory by bathing in a shell crater near the captured airfield on Oroku Peninsula.

(U.S. Marine Corps)

13: THE FIRE BRIGADE

(Korea, Summer 1950)

I AM HEARTENED THAT THE MARINE BRIGADE WILL MOVE
AGAINST THE NAKTONG SALIENT TOMORROW. THEY ARE
FACED WITH IMPOSSIBLE ODDS . . . BUT THESE MARINES
HAVE THE SWAGGER, CONFIDENCE, AND HARDNESS THAT
MUST HAVE BEEN IN STONEWALL JACKSON'S ARMY OF
THE SHENANDOAH. I CLING TO THE HOPE OF VICTORY.

Report of the British Liaison Officer to the U.S. Eighth Army, August 15, 1950

The first armed force to sail from the United States to reinforce South Korea was the 1st Provisional Marine Brigade, a combined-arms force, which included these Corsairs of Marine Fighting Squadron 323 being loaded with rockets on the flight deck of the escort carrier Badoeng Strait.
(U.S. Marine Corps)

The gratitude of princes. Machiavelli might have written the last mocking word on it, but the Washington, D.C., of post–WWII could have given him another chapter. For suddenly the bloody masterpieces that the Marines had wrought in the Pacific were thought so trifling that the princes whose bacon the Marines had done so much to save thought there should be no Corps at all. Several things saved them, narrowly. And none greater than readiness.

"First to Fight" is nice. Getting quickly to the newest battlefield is good. But getting there trained, armed, organized, and motivated enough to fight outnumbered and win is everything. Combat readiness in spades.

Five years of demobilization, disengagement, and an overdependence on the promise of technology had left America woefully unprepared to fight a limited, unconventional war—the kind that would set the deadly tone and pattern for the rest of the century.

This was the dawn of the Cold War, and the vacuum created in the Pacific by the end of World War II left the new superpowers, America and the Soviet Union, grinding and clashing like tectonic plates.

This was also the dawn of the Nuclear Age. In its early blush the U.S. Marines seemed abruptly antiquated, irrelevant, maybe even quaint. And ripe for massive "downsizing," or worse.

While the manpower levels of all armed forces shrank sharply from wartime peaks, the Marines were going down the tubes. Less than 75,000 Marines remained on active duty in mid–1950.

Secretary of Defense Louis Johnson made no bones of his dislike for the Corps (he abruptly banned the traditional celebrations of the Corps' November 10 birthday), and he vowed to cut another 10,000 Leathernecks by year's end. Secretary Johnson wasn't alone in his hostility to the Corps.

President Truman, the former Army artillery officer, professed no love for his Marines.

Popular Army wartime commanders like Omar Bradley and Dwight Eisenhower led the charge to downsize the Corps to a ceremonial naval guard force. Bradley announced that the atomic bomb had rendered amphibious landings obsolete. Eisenhower admitted to Commandant Vandegrift he had resented the Marines ever since their publicity coup at Belleau Wood in far-off 1918.

There were other motives at work. The Army wanted the Marines' weapons and manpower billets; the new Air Force wanted Marine aircraft. Number-crunching Washington bureaucrats eyed the Corps as a fire sale.

The Marines fought back. General Vandegrift appeared before Congress to take the case to the American people. Tall, dignified, his well-fitted uniform graced by the Medal of Honor awarded for his crucial victory at Guadalcanal, the Commandant pulled no punches:

"The First Firefight"
(Charles Waterhouse)

We have pride in ourselves and in our past, but we do not rest our case on any presumed ground of gratitude owing us from the nation. The bended knee is not a tradition of our Corps. If the Marine as a fighting man has not made a case

*for himself after 170 years of service, he must go. But he has earned the right
to depart with dignity and honor, not by subjugation to the status of useless-
ness and servility planned for him by the War Department.*

The Marines also took a hard look for themselves at the effect of atomic
weapons on the future of amphibious assault.

The great amphibious battles of Saipan, Iwo Jima, and Okinawa had involved
massive concentrations of amphibious and fire support ships close to the target
islands—dead meat in the nuclear game.

Fittingly, General Roy Geiger rendered one final service to the Corps before
his death in 1947. Sobered by the A-bomb's awesome effect on the ships moored at
the Bikini Lagoon test site, Geiger warned the Commandant: "Time for drastic
surgery on our battle-tested amphibious doctrine."

Vandegrift convened the best and brightest combat commanders in the Corps,
including Generals Lemuel Shepherd and Oliver Smith, and Colonels Victor "Brute"
Krulak and Merrill Twining.

Was Omar Bradley right? Did atomic weapons spell the end for the Marines'
propensity for up-close-and-personal, kick-down-the-front-door, direct assault
from the sea?

No, the ad hoc committee concluded, no more than Gallipoli had been the
death knell of amphibious assaults after 1915. *Dispersion* of the assault force was the
obvious solution, and the critical limiting factor was the short-range, slow-moving,
surface ship-to-shore movement. *Transport heli-
copters*, ferrying troops ashore from distant
small-deck carriers, were the answer.

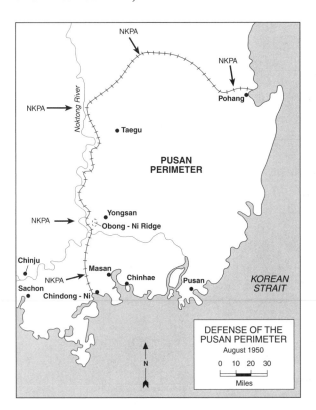

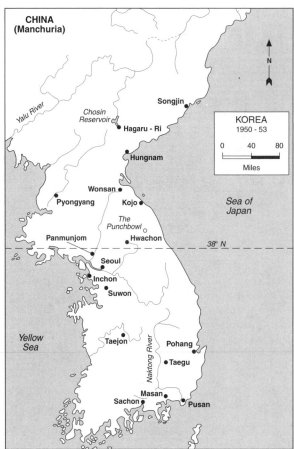

Krulak and Twining had a "how-to" field manual on heli-bore assaults on the streets by 1948—in fact months before the primitive two-passenger Sikorsky helicopters made their historic first amphibious assault from the escort carrier *Palau* into a Camp Lejeune landing zone.

"Vertical assault" had become a reality in two years. Could the Marines hold on long enough to prove it out?

Before the end of 1948 the Marines acquired their first true transport helicopters, the Piaseki "Flying Bananas." The Corps' detractors remained underwhelmed. Nobody wanted a war. But the one that was coming would arrive as timely as the old U.S. Cavalry for the Marines.

In the predawn darkness of Sunday, June 25, 1950, armored units of the North Korean People's Army (NKPA) breached the 38th Parallel and roared into South Korea. Followed closely by 90,000 infantry troops, veterans of the Chinese civil war, the Communist tank forces raced for the capital of Seoul.

Despite its beguiling name as "The Land of the Morning Calm," Korea's 500-mile peninsula, jutting southward from Manchuria, had long known war at the hands of its more aggressive neighbors. When World War II ended a half-century of repressive Japanese rule, Korea was occupied by the United States in the south, Russia in the north, divided arbitrarily by the 38th Parallel.

After the United States and Russia departed the country in the late 1940s, relations between the Communist industrial north and the democratic agrarian south gradually worsened.

Officials in Washington were in an uproar throughout the first week of the North Korean invasion. One who kept a cool head was General Clifton Cates, USMC, of Tiptonville, Tennessee, now the nineteenth Commandant.

Cates respected the NKPA but did not hold them in any great awe. His Marines had already squared off in live combat against Communist troops in north China during 1946–1948. They were good fighters, but hardly supermen.

What did concern Cates most was the systematic dismantling of his Fleet Marine Force by the Truman administration.

So enthralled was Secretary Johnson with the Atomic Age that the total ground forces of the country had shriveled to ten divisions, two of them Marines. But Cates knew both the 1st and 2d Marine Divisions had been skeletonized by subsequent budget cuts. Rifle companies dropped from three platoons to two; rifle battalions from three companies to two—fatal tinkering with fire and maneuver units.

Moreover, the Marines were far removed from the action. In such austerity, the Navy-Marine team could afford only one forward-deployed amphibious unit, a battalion serving with the Sixth Fleet in the Mediterranean. All other Fleet Marine Forces were back in the continental United States, the 1st Division at Camp Pendleton, California, the 2d at Camp Lejeune.

Cates remained one of the few unflappables during all the hue and cry then rampant at the Pentagon and White House. He knew the Marines' moment would come, and they would be ready.

In Washington, President Harry Truman worked feverishly through the United Nations to build an allied coalition to defend the long-neglected nation. Geared for a potential nuclear war, the U.S. defense establishment had precious little in the cupboard for a sustained conventional war erupting literally at the ends of the earth.

The NKPA overran Seoul in three days, then crossed the Han River and swarmed south toward Taejon, the fallback center for the disorganized Republic of Korea (ROK) forces. General Douglas MacArthur, Supreme Allied Commander in the Far East, left Tokyo for Taejon to see the situation firsthand. He came back greatly alarmed.

The ROK Army commander could not account for two thirds of his forces. The Soviet-trained NKPA veterans used Russian weapons and tactics to perfection, leading each assault with seemingly invincible T–34 tanks, well covered by artillery and mortars, and with a heavy emphasis on night action.

MacArthur sought Truman's permission for immediate deployment of American ground troops to help stem the tide. The President readily agreed. But the first U.S. Army troops to arrive were occupation troops, stale and softened by years of garrison duty in Japan, fed piecemeal into chaos.

The NKPA columns collided with the U.S. 24th Division at Taejon, shattered the green forces like an overripe melon, captured the division commander and the key city, and swept on toward Pusan, the last major port available for reinforcing U.S. and Allied forces. As American as apple pie was the old tradition of unreadiness at the beginning of a war. And here Marine Commandant Cates held an ace.

A well-trained, provisional air-ground brigade, the core of the 1st Marine Division, was fully armed and ready at Pendleton.

Like former commandants Archibald Henderson and George Barnett, Cates's difficulty lay in getting Washington to recognize this available asset.

First he quietly alerted the 1st Marine Division to make all preparations for going to war. Then he got the message to MacArthur that a Marine brigade was ready to go—his for the asking. MacArthur responded immediately, requesting the Joint Chiefs of Staff to assign the Marine brigade to his beleaguered forces in Korea.

Even in 1950 the Commandant of the Marine Corps was not a member of the Joint Chiefs, not even when Marine matters were on the agenda. Cates could care less. On July 3, knowing MacArthur's request for the Marines was on the table, Cates "crashed" the JCS meeting, answered the thinly veiled barbs about the readiness of his forces, and received the green light.

The next day General Lemuel Shepherd and Colonel Brute Krulak, the commander and the operations officer, respectively, of the Pacific Fleet Marines, flew from Hawaii to Tokyo to confer with MacArthur.

Where the Marines and MacArthur had often been at loggerheads during the Pacific War, they were now very much in synch.

MacArthur promised not to mess with the Marines' air-ground team— he would not give away the Marines' "flying artillery" to the Air Force.

MacArthur then pointed to a large map of Korea's west coast, to Inchon. "If I had a Marine division, I'd land them here and trap the NKPA between a hammer and an anvil." Shepherd grinned and promised him a full division by the first of September—brave words for the threadbare Corps.

First things first.

Three days after the JCS approved MacArthur's request for the Marines, Brigadier General Edward Craig assumed command of the 1st Provisional Marine Brigade, an expeditionary force made up out of whole cloth from 1st Division/1st Marine Aircraft Wing assets.

Proven veterans of the Pacific War led the provisional outfit. Craig had fought at Bougainville, Guam (Navy Cross), and Iwo Jima. Lieutenant Colonel Raymond Murray, commanding the 5th Marines, was a veteran of Guadalcanal, Tarawa, and Saipan (Navy Cross). And Brigadier General Thomas Cushman, commanding MAG–33, had learned close air support in Haiti and Nicaragua and had commanded an air wing in the Pacific.

Cushman's air group consisted of three fighter-bomber squadrons of late-model F4U Corsairs and an observation squadron that included four Sikorsky helicopters hastily forwarded from experimental tests at Quantico.

Murray's 5th Marines were reinforced with tank and amphibian tractor companies and an artillery battalion. Altogether, the force numbered 6,534 Marines, not a hell of a lot larger than a standard infantry regiment of the previous war.

But like Archibald Henderson's improvised expeditionary force in the Seminole War, Cates had quickly produced for the nation a credible force of regulars, fully armed and equipped, ready for combat.

The invasion of South Korea by the well-trained North Korean People's Army had just passed the sixteen-day mark.

In the dark of night, the American heavy cruiser *Juneau* and the destroyer *Mansfield* knifed through the waters off North Korea's northeast coast, slowing only long enough to launch a whaleboat embarked with five Marines, heavily armed, faces grease-painted.

The Corps was off and running.

The Navy coxswain eased them into the surf as planned south of Songjin. The Marines scrambled ashore, made directly for a railroad tunnel, planted two large demolition charges, then withdrew. Shortly afterward an NKPA supply train chugged into the tunnel—and was blown to kingdom come.

It was one small stroke in what would be a bitter, three-year, undeclared war, but the fact that U.S. Marines were already on the scene, stinging the new enemy far behind the lines, was a rare source of comfort in those dark days.

By coincidence, perhaps, with dawn of the next day sailed the 1st Provisional Marine Brigade for Korea, the first armed force to deploy from the United States in the widening crisis. Ahead, for the Marines, lay five months of

incredible challenge and sublime glory—followed by years of grinding, form-less, thankless hammering.

This was not the first time the U.S. Marines splashed ashore in Korea with fixed bayonets. Captain McLane Tilton's seagoing detachments had stormed the Salee River forts in bloody fighting back in 1871. His description of the country would not improve over eighty years. "Appalling mudflats, surrounded by a chopped sea of immense hills and deep ravines lying in every conceivable direction."

The brigade sailed on July 12, only five days after being organized.

MacArthur had to change their destination en route.

While he wanted the brigade to serve as the nucleus of his strategic envelopment at Inchon, things got so bad in the Pusan Perimeter he had to order them to land in support of the U.S. Eighth Army.

The Marines debarked at Pusan on August 2, a month to the day after MacArthur's initial request to the Joint Chiefs.

Army Lieutenant General Walton Walker commanded the Eighth Army, a thankless job. His force was in dire straits, having been hammered by the NKPA back into a 100-mile semicircle around the port of Pusan.

By the end of July, Walker had suffered 6,000 U.S. casualties; the ROK Army had lost 70,000. His only hope was to hold the perimeter to permit rein-forcements to land at Pusan.

On July 29 Walker addressed his harried troops: "A Marine unit and two regiments are expected in the next few days to reinforce us. . . . There is no line behind us to which we can retreat. . . . There will be no Dunkirk, no Bataan. We must fight until the end."

As the Marines debarked at the bustling Pusan docks, stiff-jointed and rubber-legged from their three-week sea cruise, word quickly spread that the enemy advance, now less than fifty miles away near Masan, was about to renew in greater strength. Walker told Craig his Marines would be going into the line immediately and could expect nigh-continuous commitment as the Eighth Army's "fire brigade."

The brigade's aviators drew first blood. Corsair pilots of VMF–214, the fabled Black Sheep Squadron of Pappy Boyington fame, fired the first Marine rounds of the new war in anger, launching strikes from the carrier *Sicily*.

Within two days, one of the Black Sheep pilots, Major Kenneth Reusser, racked up the first Navy Cross of the Korean War for the Marines, making repeated low-level strafing runs against NKPA troops and vehicles despite heavy machine gun fire.

More Corsairs, these of VMF–323 flying off the *Badoeng Strait*, joined the fray. The third squadron, the night-fighters of VMF(N)–513, set up shop in Japan and commenced nightly raids across the Korean Strait, finding plentiful targets among the nocturnal resupply efforts of the NKPA.

Marine Corsairs, the familiar old "Bent-Wing Widow Makers," were back in business, growing long in the tooth and more vulnerable in this, the advent of the Jet Age, but still lethal.

The Marine Brigade rushed to the Chinju/Masan corridor to face the North Korean 6th Division and an unusual outfit, a motorcycle regiment, kind of an Asian "Desert Patrol" of jeeps and motorcycles with sidecars—vulnerable as hell, but highly mobile and festooned with machine guns.

Symbolically, the ground war for the Marines kicked off on August 7, eight years to the day since the 5th Marines' historic landing at Guadalcanal. Now the 5th Marines and North Korean soldiers began to take each other's measure for the first time.

As the left flank unit of an Army task force, Craig's Marines began attacking westward, toward Sachon. The attack coincided with one launched by the North Koreans, and the first day's fighting featured all the confusion of a high-speed train wreck. The battles were localized but intensely violent.

The 5th Marines' initial objective was to relieve an Army unit surrounded on steep-sloped Hill 342. Here the first enemy became the body-sapping heat.

Here, in the south, in the height of summer, the temperature surpassed 112 degrees. This was Peleliu heat. *Vietnam rice-paddy heat.* Unconditioned troops dropped like flies to heat exhaustion. (None could know that four months later these same Marines would be fighting and losing fingers and toes to unbearably frigid arctic conditions.)

The Marines prevailed in these initial battles along the Chinju-Masan corridor, blunting the NKPA attacks, driving them back a good distance, but it wasn't pretty.

THE DOWNSIZING BLUES

Austere peacetime budgets forced the Marines to place into cadre status the third rifle company of each infantry battalion. Fighting short-handed until trained replacements could arrive led to a desperate month of combat by the 5th Marines. The Marines, the only unit in the Eighth Army to maintain the tactical offensive throughout the defensive perimeter, paid a cost in unwarranted casualties because of this artificial downsizing. It vitiated the proven adage of "two up and one back," the basic tactical doctrine of using two elements to advance by maneuver while the third provides a hot base of covering fire against the objective. This meant the Marines' heralded Sunday punch lacked some of its wallop—and certainly all of its counterpunching threat. As casualties mounted and the NKPA adopted reverse-slope defenses, this became critical. A rifle company might force its way to the summit of a contested ridge, at cost, but—unsupported—would have a hell of a time consolidating its prize in order to defend against the counterattacks which inevitably arose from the far side of the ridge after dark.

The many greenhorns in the ranks committed the usual first-battle blunders—bunching up by day, waxing trigger-happy by night. The veteran NCOs maintained a steady stream of profane guidance, punctuated by an occasional well-placed boondocker.

Nor were their NKPA opponents forgiving of tactical errors. The Marines found the North Koreans to be good fighters, adept marksmen, camouflage-disciplined, unafraid of close hand-to-hand combat, and well supported by

Five years after the Japanese surrender the Marines were once again fighting in the Western Pacific, this time against the North Korean People's Army (NKPA). Here a grim-faced veteran corporal of the 5th Marines leads his rookie BAR-man past a dead NKPA soldier and into close combat along the Pusan Peninsula. (David Douglas Duncan)

damnably accurate machine guns, mortars, and artillery. Night attacks were particularly unpleasant events.

That the Marines fought consistently as a combined-arms team made the difference between victory and defeat.

Their small tank and artillery components surpassed themselves in supporting the infantry. But what really saved the Marine Brigade's bacon at Pusan was the bravura performance of their Corsair pilots.

General Cushman's aviators included a higher ratio of veterans of Pacific War combat than their counterparts among the ground-pounders. Both the North Koreans and the adjacent U.S. Army troops were left agog at the precision with which the Marine pilots could deliver rockets, napalm, or 500-pound bombs a scant football field ahead of the advancing Leatherneck riflemen.

Captain Vivian Moses of VMF–323 was shot down on August 10 behind NKPA lines but was hauled out by that superb new rescue device, the helicopter. On the very next day NKPA gunners shot him down again as he roared through Taedabok Pass in support of the 5th Marines. He crashed and drowned in a rice paddy, the first Marine aviator to die in Korea. Luck comes and goes quickly in the Marine low-level air support business.

After driving the North Koreans back almost twenty-two miles in the first significant UN offensive action of the war, the Marine Brigade's advance on Sachon was interrupted by word of an emergency in another sector of the perimeter. Twenty-five miles away, in the area of Chindong-ni, two Army artillery battalions had been overrun by NKPA forces. A major breakthrough seemed imminent.

General Walker called for his "fire brigade," ordering General Craig to assist the beleaguered Army units. The promising Chinju-Masan counteroffensive had to be abandoned.

Craig rushed Lieutenant Colonel Robert Taplett's battalion of the 5th Marines to Chindong-ni. Taplett arrived in good order, stanched the rupture, restored the lines. Craig, now operating on two fronts, shuttled back and forth effectively by helicopter.

But Walker now faced a far greater emergency. Near Miryang, seventy-five miles farther north, the NKPA 4th Division had forced a crossing of the Naktong River at several points, its troops now consolidating their strength among a nest of steep ridges before snaking eastward toward Miryang. Walker feared the consequences.

If Miryang fell, the provisional ROK capital of Taegu would almost certainly follow. Loss of Taegu would prompt the loss of Pusan and cause the withdrawal of UN forces from Korea altogether.

On August 15, with the hole at Chindong-ni plugged, General Craig consolidated his brigade and quickly packed them aboard troop trains for the haul up to Miryang.

General Walker put Marines under the control of the Army's hard-

pressed 24th Division, although not before warning its commander, "I am going to give you the Marine Brigade. I want this situation cleaned up and quick." Black Jack Pershing had used similar words in 1918.

On the morning of August 17, the Leathernecks went into action against "the Naktong Bulge," fighting alongside the 9th Infantry, their old comrades-in-arms from Samar and the Boxer Rebellion.

The Marines would tackle Obong-ni Ridge, a sprawling, mile-and-a-half-long complex dubbed "No-Name Ridge." It would be the Marines' bloodiest battle of the peninsula war.

The Marines' hasty rail deployment to Miryang led to piecemeal tactical commitment, the infantry plunging ahead before its supporting artillery could arrive and roll into firing positions. Compounding the shortfall, miscommunications led to late arrival of the Corsairs. The first day's attack on No-Name was snake-bit before it started.

The North Koreans, virtually untouched by the reduced preliminary bombardment, waited until the 2d Battalion, 5th Marines, advanced halfway up the exposed slopes before shredding them with cross fire from both flanks.

Commanding an understrength rifle company in the bloody battle for No-Name Ridge in the Naktong Bulge placed a terrible strain on Captain Ike Fenton, as reflected in this memorable photograph.
(David Douglas Duncan)

The Marines were ripped and torn, smashed and hammered. Scores of casualties soon littered the hillsides. Marines and corpsmen going to their rescue fell in droves. It was as awful a morning as the battalion ever experienced in Okinawa, Peleliu, or Belleau Wood. Sixty percent of the assault force went down before noon. The attack failed. As Colonel Murray would later report, "2/5 took a terrible beating."

Murray replaced the shot-up remnants with the 1st Battalion, but the going remained extremely rough.

As dark fell and a steady rain started, Captain Francis "Ike" Fenton led his rifle company to the crests of the two northernmost hills of the Obong-ni complex. To Fenton's left, Captain John Stevens's company could scratch their way only to the saddle below Hill 117, a precarious position, before dark. Here, especially, the absence of the third rifle company was keenly felt.

Just before dark Marine outposts heard an ominous sound growing from the east—*North Korean tanks!* Army troops on the next ridge watched in horrified fascination as four sturdy T–34s rumbled directly for the Marine lines, followed by howling infantrymen. The T–34s had bowled over Army antitank defenses in the retreat south.

Fortunately, the Marines now had all elements of their combined arms team back in place, including Corsairs on station.

Craig's own M–26 Pershing tanks lurched forward to give battle—each loader hastily removing the 90mm high-explosive shells and ramming home armor-piercing (AP) rounds.

The Corsairs came screeching down through the gathering twilight. The Marine pilots pounced on the fourth tank in the enemy column, quickly set it ablaze, then strafed the infantry into ragged clumps.

Marines clinging to the slopes of Obong-ni weren't up there empty-handed. Soon spiteful streaks from 75mm recoilless rifles and 3.5-inch rocket launchers battered the Soviet-made armor. The tanks slowed and stopped, turrets swinging wildly, seeking their tormentors. That's when the Pershings lit into them with close-range 90mm AP fire.

In five minutes the uneven battle ended, all four "invincible" T–34s burning furiously. *"Son-of-a-BITCH!"* exclaimed an admiring Army general.

But a very long night lay ahead for the two decimated rifle companies of the 5th Marines.

On the heels of a punishing mortar attack, NKPA infantry blew bugles, fired flares, and swarmed against the Marine positions. Hand-to-hand fighting erupted in a dozen places. Marine positions were overrun, recaptured, lost again. Sergeants succeeded fallen lieutenants, patched together makeshift platoons, counterattacked again. And again.

The artillery battalion of the 11th Marines provided sensational support with illumination flares and time-fused, high-explosive airbursts over the reverse-slope assembly areas of the NKPA.

With the dawn, the surviving Marines, thoroughly enraged, coalesced quickly into fighting units, and attacked Hill 117.

First light meant Marine Corsairs back on station, and the North Koreans began to lose heart. When Captain John Kelley dropped a 500-pound bomb precisely in the middle of four NKPA machine gun nests—and less than fifty yards from the advancing Marines—the enemy knew this day was going to be different.

Now the Marines had the momentum. With the 3d Battalion sweeping the hills to the west, the Marines by mid-afternoon stood masters of all they could survey from every crest along No-Name Ridge.

Forcibly squeezing the 4th NKPA Division out of the Naktong Bulge had cost the Marine Brigade 350 casualties, but the tide had decidedly turned.

Disorganized North Korean units attempting to retreat back across the Naktong now had to run a fearsome gauntlet of fire from Marine artillery and diving Corsairs. Darkness brought little respite, as Marine night fighters took over the strafing. The river became a gently flowing pallbearer, carrying hundreds of bodies downstream to the sea.

The Marine Brigade inflicted 4,000 casualties on the 4th NKPA Division and captured thirty-four major artillery pieces. The threat to Pusan, for now, eased.

Back in Washington, General Cates struggled to fulfill Lemuel Shepherd's optimistic promise of a full Marine division to MacArthur by September.

President Truman, a fast learner, helped all the services in their struggles to expand for the crisis by calling up the reserves. The President called up 33,528 members of the Organized Marine Corps Reserve on July 19 and 50,000 Volunteer Reserves on August 7, the day the 5th Marines first went into action.

Now Cates had the numbers, but the administrative details of the call-up took forever. Unit integrity and cohesion would all have to be sorted out in combat.

Cates gutted Camp Lejeune to get the last of the current Fleet Marine Force into the 1st Marine Division.

BLACK MARINES IN THE FOXHOLES

African-Americans served in the Continental Marines but not again in the U.S. Marines until World War II. In that conflict they were still segregated by units under white officers, serving overseas in defense battalions, and as ammo handlers and stevedores. Reforms in the late 1940s led the way to truer integration, but the Korean War accelerated the process. Finally given the chance to fight for their country and their Corps, they did so bravely. White acceptance away from the battlefield came grudgingly, but it came. Nearly 15,000 blacks served in all units of the Corps in that conflict. Said General Oliver Smith, commanding the 1st Marine Division: "I had a thousand black Marines in Korea. Two won the Navy Cross; many, the Silver and Bronze Star Medals. They did everything, and they did a good job because they were integrated and they were with good people." Integration was hardly seamless, or painless, but it worked especially well in combat in Korea. Not all great Marine battles made their way onto the battle streamers.

In Hawaii, the venerable warhorse Colonel Lewis "Chesty" Puller voluntarily gave up his plum assignment as CO of the Pearl Harbor Marine Barracks to return to the FMF and command his old Peleliu/Cape Gloucester regiment, the freshly reactivated 1st Marines.

In Camp Lejeune, Colonel Homer Litzenberg attempted to patch together the 7th Marines. One of his three battalions would come from the unit afloat with the Sixth Fleet; they would transit the Suez Canal and meet the new regiment somewhere in Korea. Whatever.

The raw and rambunctious 1st Marines sailed under Chesty Puller on August 15, the same day the Marine Brigade began its hasty redeployment north to the Naktong Bulge.

But the 1st Marines were bound for Kobe, Japan, not the Pusan Perimeter. They would in fact become the nucleus of MacArthur's new force to strike a strategic amphibious blow at Inchon.

The Marines adopted the sturdy, dependable Garand M–1 rifle in late 1942 but never gave up their long love affair with the old Springfield bolt-action "03." Here a Marine sniper takes aim with his match-conditioned, scope-mounted "03" against distant North Korean positions. (U.S. Marine Corps)

In the first week of September, the NKPA launched a 98,000-man offensive against the Pusan Perimeter in a final effort to close the port to Allied reinforcements. Once again the Naktong Bulge swarmed with North Koreans. The 1st Provisional Marine Brigade could not yet be released for MacArthur's rapidly approaching end run.

Back to the Bulge came the "Fire Brigade," this time operating under the 2d Infantry Division, their old World War I outfit.

The fighting reprised the intensity of the first "Bulge" Battle, and for a while it looked as if the 5th Marines would have to take Obong-ni Ridge all over again, one bloody hill after another. But these North Koreans came down from the hills to fight, well supported by T–34 tanks.

Operating in a driving rain to zero the American air power, the T–34s took the measure of a couple of Marine Pershings before the combination of antitank infantry weapons and tank guns blew them apart. The burned-out hulks resembled a demolition yard.

The Marines suffered 250 casualties in the fighting of September 3–5, but the NKPA offensive sputtered to a halt. Pusan enjoyed a final reprieve.

MacArthur now demanded the Marines back from Walker. The Eighth Army had certainly gotten their money's worth from this doughty Fire Brigade. In exactly one month of fighting, the Marine Brigade had launched four major counterattacks, sustained 900 casualties, and inflicted more than 10,000 casualties on the enemy. Not a single Marine had been captured. Marine aviators had flown nearly a thousand close air support missions, mostly controlled by Tactical Air Control Parties deployed with the infantry.

Nobody was talking about eliminating the Marine Corps.

The 1st Provisional Marine Brigade got a week's rest, replaced its combat losses—and finally received enough new troops to form the missing third companies in each infantry battalion. Then the brigade went out of existence, its job done.

MAG–33 rejoined the 1st Marine Aircraft Wing, just arriving from the States.

Colonel Ray Murray's 5th Marines caught up with Puller's regiment to form the nucleus of the bare-bones 1st Marine Division just in time for MacArthur's master stroke at Inchon. The Marines were going back into the amphibious assault business.

14: THE GREAT END RUN

(Inchon, 1950)

A Marine wounded in the Seoul fighting gets rushed to an aid station by four stretcher bearers, the entire crew vulnerable to sniper fire from the tall buildings to the right. (National Archives)

IT IS MY CONVICTION THAT THE SUCCESSFUL ASSAULT ON INCHON COULD HAVE BEEN ACCOMPLISHED ONLY BY UNITED STATES MARINES.

Rear Admiral James Doyle, Commander, Amphibious Group One, Inchon

How do you figure? At the end of 1945 the United States Marine Corps is the juggernaut that swept one of the toughest adversaries in the history of war out of the Pacific. And then, hardly five years later, they are a ragtag, undermanned, underequipped underdog fighting a killer retreat from a war machine whose reserve of fanatical fighting men is effectively without limit. The old Marine story. An undersupply of everything that has to be bloodily papered over with an oversupply of guts.

"Make up a list of amphibious don'ts," said one crusty admiral, "and you have an exact description of the Inchon operation."

Oddly, the landing at Inchon was so risky that only General Douglas MacArthur and the Marines believed it would work—mere voices in the wilderness against the institutional wisdom of the Joint Chiefs of Staff and other naysayers.

The sheer audacity of MacArthur's amphibious seizure of Inchon by United States Marines in September 1950 still echoes through the years. No other major assault from the sea in the twentieth century—not even Normandy or Iwo Jima—had such an immediate strategic effect on a war. Regrettably, America then escalated its war aims and squandered the advantage.

Inchon in 1950 was a port city of 250,000, about the size of Omaha. But it was a port that imposed severe restrictions on shipping—and one that seemed almost impregnable to a seaborne assault.

The approach to Inchon from the Yellow Sea was bad enough, requiring a dozen miles of precision navigation through the narrow Flying Fish Channel. Vast mudflats ruled the shoals and shallows of the port itself. But it was Inchon's *tides* that proved so daunting to the U.S. Marine landing force.

Marine sniper
(Charles Waterhouse)

Both port and channel were wildly affected by spectacular tidal ranges, up to thirty-two feet in height, among the highest in the world. Indeed, deep-draft warships could expect to attempt that passage only during three days in any month.

A less visionary commander would have rejected Inchon out of hand and merely landed on the coast to establish a static blocking force, the stationary anvil for the Eighth Army's hammer. But MacArthur had the intuition of an assassin. And he knew his Marines.

MacArthur never doubted the Old Breed would overrun Inchon and Seoul.

He knew the 1st Marine Division had cracked the extremely tough nut of Peleliu on his behalf six years earlier. He also knew a dagger thrust deep into Inchon and Seoul would cause irreparable psychological damage to the NKPA.

Major General Oliver Smith was now commanding the 1st Marine Division. Smith had served the Old Breed at Peleliu as assistant division commander. He knew they could fight like tigers. He only worried that the pell-mell pace of deploying the patched-together division to the Korean War would prove too costly before his Marines could fuse together into a force resembling the lethal fighting machine of 1942–1945.

Because of the narrow tidal window, D-Day at Inchon had to go on September 15. MacArthur would not wait another month, and Smith fully agreed. But this meant that one of Smith's three regimental combat teams, the brand-new 7th Marines, would not arrive in time.

It also meant that Colonel Chesty Puller's newly formed and freshly arrived 1st Marines would have no time to train and rehearse for the complicated landing. And it meant that the 5th Marines, fully engaged in urgent combat in the Pusan Perimeter, would have precious little time to catch their breath before leaping into even more desperate fighting.

"We'll be ready," Smith promised MacArthur.

268

THE BATTLE
HISTORY OF THE
US MARINES

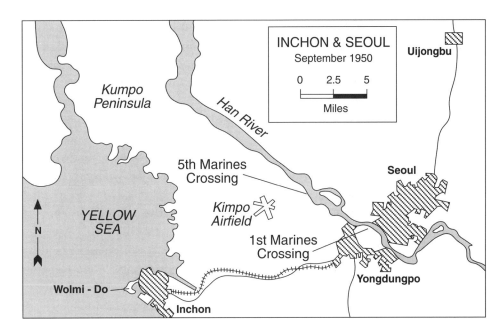

As Smith studied the Inchon operation maps he recognized two major challenges for his Marines.

First was the island of Wolmi-do, jutting out into the harbor of Inchon as an ideal combat outpost for NKPA defenders. No landing could be undertaken against Inchon without first overwhelming Wolmi-do, and because of the drastic tides, this meant a unique and risky division of forces.

To hell with surprise—a Marine battalion would have to seize Wolmi-do on the morning tide, then hang on for dear life for the next dozen hours until the tide returned and brought with it the remainder of the landing force. And that force would itself be strapped to execute its assaults on Inchon proper in the two hours of daylight remaining.

General Smith chose the veteran 5th Marines to provide the lonely "Lost Battalion" for Wolmi-do.

Smith also recognized that Inchon had no beaches *per se*, just miles of seawalls along an industrial waterfront. Scaling ladders would help get the troops ashore from their assault craft, but Smith knew the bigger problem would be the convergence of two of the most difficult military operations in the book—an opposed amphibious assault, immediately followed by heavy street fighting in a major city.

The Old Breed knew amphibious warfare to a gnat's ass, but there had been no cities on Guadalcanal, Cape Gloucester, or Peleliu, and only a handful of ruined towns in their sector of Okinawa.

Moreover, the division would need to acquire their street-fighting skills fast. Ten days after the landing the Old Breed was slated to be engaged in the fight of their life in the capital of Seoul. Truly on-the-job training.

The invasion force of 260 ships that deployed from Japan paled in comparison to the mighty armadas of World War II. The narrow channel and mudflats of Inchon would place a premium on the ugly duckling of warships, the lowly tank landing ship, or LST. But America had allowed her amphibious fleet to atrophy in the postwar years. Among the forty-seven LSTs wending their way through Flying Fish Channel were thirty "borrowed back" from our erstwhile enemies, the Japanese.

The Marines along with soldiers of the 7th Infantry Division made up the newly formed U.S. X Corps, under command of Major General Edward Almond, confidant and chief of staff to MacArthur. Included with the 1st Marine Division were the enthusiastic members of the 1st Korean Marine Corps Regiment, already developing a fighting *esprit* of their own.

General Smith had good use for the Korean Marines. Just before the landing the Secretary of the Navy decreed that no U.S. Marines younger than eighteen would be authorized to participate in amphibious assaults. This political whimsy knocked 500 trained troops out of action as quickly as a malaria epidemic.

Preliminary bombardment of Inchon began a healthy five days before the landing. The Marines did what they should have done at first on Peleliu's deadly Umurbrogol Mountain: They employed Marine Corsairs to drop napalm on Wolmi-do's hills to burn off the underbrush to reveal cave openings and gun positions.

And the Navy borrowed a page from Iwo Jima, sending four iron-hearted destroyers through the channel to pound Wolmi-do up close and entice NKPA gunners to return fire and reveal their positions. Both strategies worked. The napalm denuded the hills and spoiled the day for many defenders. The ships suckered the surviving gunners into opening up. Two destroyers took hits, but all four blasted back with telling accuracy. So far, so good.

On D-Day morning, the advance elements of the naval assault force maneuvered through Flying Fish Channel without major opposition.

At 0633 Lieutenant Colonel Robert Taplett's 3d Battalion, 5th Marines, hit the Wolmi shore, shrugged off intermittent enemy fire, and streamed inland. Within twenty-two minutes, Sergeant Alvin Smith raised the American flag over Radio Hill, Wolmi's highest point. MacArthur smiled, put down his glasses, and said, "That's it, let's get some coffee."

Over that hot mug, MacArthur penned one of his artful communiqués: "The Marines and Navy have never shone more brightly than this morning."

Ashore, the Marines fought across the humpbacked island, forcing the North Koreans from their fortified positions with demolitions and flamethrowers.

A company of Marine tanks crunched over obstacles, leveled strong points. Diehard defenders who refused to surrender were entombed in their bunkers by armored bulldozers.

Taplett quickly mined and guarded the 600-yard causeway leading to Inchon City to hinder enemy reinforcements from the mainland.

By 0800, most of Wolmi-do was in Marine hands. The assault troops watched as the receding tide drove the amphibious task force back up the channel to the sea, as expected. Taplett and his thousand Marines completed their seizure of North Korean gun emplacements, aware they were on their own until the rising afternoon tide.

Seizing Wolmi-do cost fourteen Marine casualties, all wounded.

Maintaining absolute mastery of the air helped immensely. Marine Corsairs and Navy Skyraiders circled close over Taplett's head, on call. Other aircraft fanned out during the long day, probing beyond the Inchon landing sites for approaching enemy reinforcements. They found none. The Americans had of necessity telegraphed their punch, but they had caught the NKPA flat-footed.

The U.S. naval bombardment resumed at 1430, setting the Inchon waterfront ablaze. Low-flying planes swept over the city, streaming fire into NKPA emplacements. Close-in fire support craft poured 6,000 rockets into the objective area as the Marines debarked into their landing boats and amphibian tractors. The late afternoon light began to fade. As the assault craft neared shore, Inchon City was barely visible through the smoky haze.

The invasion plan called for the remaining two battalions of Lieutenant Colonel Ray Murray's 5th Marines to land in Higgins boats with scaling ladders at Red "Beach," a stretch of stone seawall in the heart of the city. At the same time, Puller's 1st Marines would land by LVTs over Blue "Beach," three miles to the southeast, a suburban industrial area with few egress ramps from the shallow water. After landing, the 5th Marines would collect Taplett's Battalion from Wolmi-do and attack through the city while Puller's regiment cut the highway to Seoul in the rear.

Surprise or not, the veteran 5th Marines had a fight on their hands in the opening rounds of the main event.

Their 5:30 P.M. landing occurred in good order, but the troops lost time and momentum having to rely on scaling ladders to debark. The first men over the crest of the seawalls experienced the same sense of vulnerability to direct

"TRUMAN'S POLICE FORCE"

As the 1st Marine Division took dead aim at the difficult objectives of Inchon and Seoul, their hometown newspapers erupted with a negative slam against the Corps by the Commander-in-Chief. In response to a congressman who had written suggesting the Marine Commandant be accorded a voice among the Joint Chiefs, President Harry S. Truman vented his spleen. "For your information," he replied, "the Marine Corps is the Navy's police force and as long as I am President that is what it will remain. They have a propaganda machine that is almost equal to Stalin's."

A firestorm of outraged public opinion appeared when this letter was published in the papers on September 5 (a mere ten days before D-Day at Inchon). Truman seemed amazed at the extent to which the Marines' unofficial "subway alumni" took offense at his remarks. He apologized to Commandant Cates. The Marines in Korea took the news in stride. But more than a few crews of Pershing tanks and amphibian tractors emblazoned the sides of their vehicles with "TRUMAN'S POLICE FORCE" before they rolled ashore at Inchon.

D-Day at Inchon, September 15, 1950. A rifle platoon of the 5th Marines scrambles ashore over the seawall on Red "Beach" via scaling ladders from their LCVP. North Korean resistance, initially deadly at this landing point, soon crumbled. (U.S. Marine Corps)

enemy fire as their ancestors in the same regiment felt in "going over the top" in the trench warfare of 1918.

Lieutenant Baldomero Lopez led his platoon up the ladders and into the open just as NKPA gunners opened up from nearby bunkers. Lopez pulled the pin from a grenade, but enemy fire raked him just as he cocked his arm to throw it. He sank to his knees, the armed grenade spinning on the ground, his platoon members rushing up behind him. Lopez did the only thing he could—he dove forward, smothering the grenade with his body, saving his men by absorbing the blast. His would be a posthumous Medal of Honor.

The 5th Marines pressed on. Another platoon in Lieutenant Lopez's company seized Cemetery Hill on the left flank, their only casualties coming from wild firing by U.S. Navy gunners as the LSTs chugged in to beach themselves in the shallows.

NKPA defenders on twin-peaked Observatory Hill on the right held out longer, but by 8 P.M. the rifle companies of Captain Sam Jaskilka and Captain Ike Fenton had captured both knobs.

The 1st Marines met less opposition but encountered more snafus in the smoke and growing darkness.

The final shelling had blocked several egress ramps from the harbor with debris; engineers had to rig cargo nets over the rubble for troops to debark. Some troops had to wade ashore several hundred yards (nervously recalling the scenes of Tarawa) when their LVTs grounded in mudbanks. Some units landed on the wrong sites, intermingled with other units, creating classic scenes of chaos. Inexperience and the absence of a rehearsal landing temporarily slowed the advance.

Chesty Puller came ashore barely thirty minutes behind the first assault wave and stomped up and down the waterfront in a cold fury until things became unscrewed.

Lieutenant Colonel Henry Crowe, a Tarawa stalwart fully accustomed to beachhead chaos, came ashore with his 1st Shore Party Battalion and—his characteristic red mustache bristling—quickly sorted things out as well. Neither Puller nor Crowe suffered fools. Order replaced disorder, the troops moved inland, and combat cargo flowed in on their heels.

MacArthur and the Marines had made their case. By midnight, Smith had 13,000 Leathernecks ashore, rampaging through town. The cost of this great gamble: no ships lost; 22 Marines killed, 174 wounded. Of all the major Marine landings in the Pacific War, only Guadalcanal and Okinawa had been less costly on D-Day.

As the second day dawned, General Smith assigned his 3,000 South Korean Marines to mop up the bypassed centers of resistance in Inchon while his assault regiments advanced eastward toward Seoul. Three miles outside of the port city, the 1st and 5th Marines linked up along the Inchon/Seoul Highway.

Ray Murray's 5th Marines then moved out along the northern side of the road before veering left in the direction of Ascom City and Kimpo Airfield.

South of the highway, Chesty Puller's 1st Marines struck out for Yongdong-po, an industrial suburb on the west bank of the Han River, directly across from downtown Seoul.

Major General Almond pressed O. P. Smith to keep the 1st Marine Division moving aggressively forward. He said MacArthur had promised that Seoul would be in UN hands by September 26, the three-month anniversary of its seizure by the invading North Koreans. Almond made it clear that he had every intention of seeing that MacArthur was not disappointed. Smith refused to be hurried. "I can't guarantee anything," he said. "That's up to the enemy." Smith's reply angered Almond, who would take a long time learning that Marines practiced caution usually for a damned good reason.

Smith was discovering that the quality of enemy resistance was increasing proportionately as the Americans advanced closer to Seoul.

The NKPA troops defending Inchon had been spirited but disorganized, second-echelon troops seeing their first real combat. These were hardly a match for Murray's 5th Marines, who had spent the previous month locked in combat with the first-line NKPA troops threatening the Pusan Peninsula. But now the North Korean high command in Pyongyang reacted to the surprise Allied thrust at Inchon by redeploying experienced brigades and regiments to reinforce Seoul.

The Marines' first encounters with the heavier NKPA forces came as meeting engagements.

At daybreak on the second day, an advanced outpost of the 5th Marines heard the unmistakable rumble and squeal of T–34 tanks approaching from the direction of Seoul. The troops quickly hunkered down, reported the attack to the rifle company's main body on the hill to the immediate rear, bided their time—then cut loose with small arms fire against the lumbering tanks and their accompanying infantry.

The NKPA slowed to return fire, providing just enough of an opportune target for Corporal Okey Douglas to knock out the lead target with his seemingly toothless 2.36-inch bazooka. This lucky shot caused so much pandemonium among the NKPA armored column they hardly noticed all the activity gearing up on the hill just to the rear.

No ambush in the Old West ever worked to greater perfection. In a series of blinding flashes, Marine Pershing tanks, 75mm recoilless rifles, and 3.5-inch bazookas cut loose on the enemy tanks. While Corporal Douglas and his well-armed outpost shot down the NKPA infantry by the score, the big guns on the hill lashed out with terrible lethality. Within minutes the battlefield grew silent: the six T–34s burning furiously, the highway and right-of-ways littered with dead and dying NKPA riflemen.

As luck would have it, just as the Marines were poking cautiously through the ruins of the enemy tank column, a convoy of VIPs, reporters, and escorts came whizzing up the highway from Inchon. *General MacArthur was ashore!* Suddenly the skirmish scene became transferred into a giant "photo-op" for the general

and his entourage. All sought to be photographed against a backdrop of burning T–34s, the tanks so recently considered impervious to American weapons.

General O. P. Smith seemed embarrassed to be part of this royal bravado. When Army staff officers accused him of staging "another typical Marine publicity stunt," Smith began a slow burn. He hustled MacArthur rearward. There was a war to be fought.

Minutes after the official entourage turned and left, the Marines flushed seven armed North Korean soldiers out of a culvert under the road. General MacArthur's jeep had been parked directly over their heads.

That night, with the 5th Marines hanging on to one corner of the prized Kimpo Airfield, another North Korean tank attack erupted. These tanks proved harder to kill.

Fierce fighting raged throughout the remainder of the night, but the Marines held. With dawn they swept forward, and by mid-morning the entire 6,000-foot runway was back in American hands. Appropriately, the first U.S. aircraft to touch down that day was a Marine helicopter bearing General Lemuel Shepherd and his operations officer, Colonel Brute Krulak.

On the following day, Major General Field Harris deployed the first three squadrons of his 1st Marine Aircraft Wing ashore at Kimpo. With two more fighter squadrons flying from carriers just offshore and another night-fighter squadron providing the honors from Itazuke, Japan, Marine air was as closely committed to the campaign as their ground counterparts.

When Puller's 1st Marines first sailed from California in August, the troops had to gain their "sea legs," to reorient their bodies to the three-dimensional forces of gravity on board small amphibious ships. Now they were gaining their "combat legs," engaging in an increasingly deadly series of firefights against NKPA troops determined to sting their ranks for every mile advanced toward Yongdong-po.

The presence of Chesty Puller, naturally, offset much of the greenness of the new troops. Under his stern gaze, and in the capable hands of veteran company commanders and NCOs, the rookies among the 1st Marines learned the essential lessons of combat rapidly.

One new member of the 1st Marines who learned his lessons well was Private First Class Walter Monegan, a bazooka gunner with the 2d Battalion, 1st Marines. When a NKPA tank column attacked the battalion's positions at dawn just west of Yongdong-po, Monegan leaped into action.

Having knocked out two T–34s with his 3.5-inch rocket launcher in earlier fighting, Monegan knew to tackle the behemoths from the flank. He and his loader raced down the hill to take up a firing position less than a hundred yards abeam the lead tank. While his squadmates on the hillside covered him by fire and held their breaths, Monegan calmly knocked out two more tanks with two expertly placed shots. But the distinctive backblast of the 3.5-inch bazooka always pinpointed the gunner's exact position. Monegan could either play dead or cut and run. He did neither.

As Monegan knelt upright to attempt an unprecedented third kill, the

next tank cut him down with its coaxial machine gun. The nineteen-year-old from Melrose, Massachusetts, would receive the posthumous Medal of Honor.

Now came time to cross the Han River. The 5th Marines would do so first, forcing a crossing west of Seoul to attack the capital through the rugged country in that quadrant. The regiment would then take up positions to cover the crossing of the 1st Marines after they fought their way through the outpost city of Yongdong-po.

The Continental Marines had crossed the ice-clogged Delaware with George Washington, but their modern-day descendants had made few deep-water river crossings under fire—the Meuse River, the last night of World War I, being the principal exception.

The Han would prove a challenge. Army officers, past-masters of the art, watched intently as the Marines made their preparations.

The preliminary efforts came to grief.

An advance squad of stealth swimmers from the division Recon Company under Captain Kenneth Houghton set out the night of September 19–20 to pave the way. The recon Marines stripped to their skivvies and slipped into the river, towing two rubber boats with their weapons and radios behind them. Safely across, they checked the surrounding hills and ridges for enemy concentrations. Finding none—or believing they had found none—they signaled the main body of the company to cross in LVTs. Big mistake.

The noise of the tractor engines could wake the dead. And the hills came alive with NKPA gunners.

Captain Houghton, astounded by the outburst of heavy mortar fire, gathered his small force to meet the LVTs and turn them back. His was a mission of reconnaissance, not conquest. But a mortar round exploded in the river nearby, stunning the captain, wounding others.

Four LVTs became stuck in the mud and were abandoned. His men stuffed Houghton and the other wounded into one of these stranded vehicles, then scrambled on board the surviving LVTs as they recrossed the river in unceremonious haste.

Gunnery Sergeant Ernest DeFazio was made of stronger stuff. He swam back across the Han at the head of a few volunteers, unstuck the mired LVTs, and rescued his captain before the long night ended.

Ray Murray refused to be dismayed by the night's misadventures.

THE MAD MAN OF HILL 85

It's the unspoken nightmare of every officer that he would lead an assault and then turn around to find himself alone. That would be big trouble—unless you happened to be Second Lieutenant Henry Commiskey of the 1st Marines. He led his platoon in a headlong assault against stubborn NKPA defenders on Hill 85. In his zeal, Commiskey outran the rest of his platoon, scrambling up to the crest alone, armed only with his service .45 automatic pistol (best described as an "extreme short-range revenge weapon"). Without even time to cuss, much less be nervous, Commiskey leapt directly into an NKPA machine gun emplacement, snapped off four quick shots that slew four enemy soldiers, then killed a fifth opponent with his bare hands. His blood lust raging, Commiskey picked up an NKPA rifle, advanced on an adjoining machine gun nest, and coldly shot both occupants to death. The remaining North Koreans, unnerved by this crazed Marine running amok in their midst, abandoned the hill in haste. It would take Commiskey a long time to realize what he had done—and that he would be one Marine who would receive his Medal of Honor while breathing.

A THUMB IN THE DIKE

The 1st Marines' battle for Yongdong-po had become a real catfight on both flanks when a single Marine rifle company found the center unguarded and penetrated into the heart of town. Captain Robert Barrow led Able Company boldly through this unexpected breach. Barrow had fought behind Japanese lines with Chinese guerrillas in the past war and had pure ice water in his veins. He quickly seized the city's key "terrain," a 25-foot-high, 100-yard-long dirt dike that provided just enough elevation and cover for his men to interdict NKPA movements into and out of the city. From this position, Barrow's Marines blew up a major ammo dump and cut down counterattacking NKPA forces. With nightfall, Barrow made his men dig deep foxholes in the soft dirt—just in time. A column of five NKPA tanks roared down the parallel highway, thirty yards away, leveling their 85mm guns at the dike as they rumbled past. The tanks would make five firing passes like this in the next hour. The Marines' deep holes and the soft dirt saved their hides—incredibly, they lost only one man to this point-blank bludgeoning. Barrow's machine gunners dueled the T–34s on uneven terms but managed to pepper the tanks' vision ports often enough to blind the crews while the bazooka Marines popped out of their holes to fire quick shots. In time this worked. The intrepid 3.5-inch gunners damaged three enemy tanks and drove the survivors off. Then it became a matter of withstanding five separate infantry counterattacks in the darkness. Tiring of his static role, Barrow dispatched Corporal Billy Webb into the burning streets to nip the next assault in the bud. Webb spotted the NKPA officer exhorting his men to attack again and dropped him with one shot from his Garand M–1. Downtown Yongdong-po grew quiet. Daybreak revealed over 300 enemy bodies scattered around Barrow's Dike. The irritating little salient had become a major disaster for the NKPA, and the Old Breed was abruptly poised to cross the Han into Seoul. A nice night's work. . . .

The Marines may have been novices in crossing rivers, he figured, but all they had to do was apply the principles of amphibious assault. Murray arranged for a comprehensive plastering of the east bank of the Han by Corsairs, tanks, and artillery. Even the heavy cruiser *Rochester* pitched in—lobbing high-explosive eight-inch shells on the commanding high ground from fifteen miles away.

Under this protective umbrella, the 5th Marines, organized into boat teams assigned to LVTs, took off in assault formations, one wave after another. Within minutes the east bank was breached. Minutes later there were Marines signaling from the tops of the nearby ridge lines. The Army observers raised their eyebrows appreciatively.

Murray pressed on, phasing his entire 5th Marines across the Han before dark on September 20. The infantry battalions consolidated, then formed assault columns, and moved out into the eight miles of broken country between them and the capital.

But some of Pyongyang's best fighters now lay waiting for the Marine regiments on both sides of the river.

From his X Corps headquarters, General Almond kept hounding General O. P. Smith to accelerate the advance on Seoul to meet MacArthur's deadline.

Almond even bypassed Smith to issue attack orders directly to Chesty Puller and Ray Murray. Smith was livid with fury. "You give your orders to me, and I'll see they're carried out," he snapped. Almond apologized, but the strained relationship would worsen over the months ahead.

The truth was, the 5th Marines had a hell of a fight on their hands as they battled their way through the 25th NKPA Brigade to reach the capital. In one bloody day's engagement, Dog Company of the 2d Battalion lost 178 casualties among their 206 Marines. *These were Peleliu-like casualties.* Ray Murray mourned the loss of his front-line leaders. Of the original twenty-four company commanders and platoon leaders who had landed in Pusan, all but two had been killed or wounded.

Moreover, the North Koreans had rushed antiaircraft units into the outskirts of Seoul, and Marine pilots now faced a hellacious "Flak Alley" as they endeavored to support the 5th Marines' advance.

Murray's weary legions maintained the offensive, arriving on the high ground above the river in time to cover Chesty Puller's crossing.

On September 21 the orphan 7th Marines under Colonel Homer Litzenberg arrived in Inchon, completing their long collective odyssey from Camp Lejeune and the Mediterranean Sea. All the parts of the 1st Marine Division were finally in place.

"Litz the Blitz" asked O. P. Smith what he wanted first from the 7th Marines. "An infantry battalion," replied Smith instantly. And next after that? "Another damned infantry battalion!"

Meanwhile, far to the south, General Walker's Eighth Army broke out of the Pusan Peninsula and began chasing the fleeing NKPA forces northward.

The final assault on Seoul kicked off on the morning of September 25 with coordinated assaults by both the 1st Marine Division and the 7th Infantry Division, each augmented by their appropriate ROK regiments.

AND THE SAME TO YOU

Assault is so much a part of the Marine mystique that it is easy to forget that they have traditionally been the best marksmen in the services. The Marine sniper, exhibiting a low profile both figuratively and literally, has taken a startling toll of the enemy, and his counterparts among them. In Seoul, enemy snipers seemed to occupy every shot-out window, each pile of smoking rubble. Marine countersnipers proved invaluable assets in this kind of fighting. Working in teams, one Marine would use binoculars or a spotting telescope to detect and designate enemy targets for two shooters, both typically armed with special Garand M1C sniper rifles—superb match-conditioned weapons graced with 2.2x scopes, flash suppressors, cheek pads, and leather slings. Directions were cryptic: "Yellow building, fifth floor, third window from the left, lower right-hand corner." Most NKPA snipers were lucky to crank off more than one shot before the Marine teams nailed them. Snipers were the only Marines who didn't work diligently at sharpening their bayonets.

While many of the NKPA's best defenders now lay dead in windrows in the heavy preliminary fighting against the Marines' advances from the northwest and south, those that remained had merely to erect barricades and take to the rooftops to inflict heavy losses among the Americans in the narrow streets.

General Almond's exhortations for speed notwithstanding, the huge city had to be taken block by block in slow, methodical, deadly fighting. Enemy roadblocks blossomed at every corner.

THE BATTLE HISTORY OF THE US MARINES

Tanks sought to rule the city, but even they were subject to Molotov cocktails tossed from the high-rises, or to sudden bursts of rocket fire from the innards of a burned-out building.

When September 25 arrived, MacArthur's Tokyo headquarters issued a communiqué announcing the capture of Seoul. In the midst of the mayhem, a correspondent remarked, "If this city has been liberated, someone forgot to tell the North Koreans."

Now the North Koreans and Marines collided in midnight meeting engagements in the burning streets. Major Edwin Simmons's Marines, holding the front line astride Ma Po Boulevard, absorbed the brunt of one armored thrust but stood their ground throughout a very long night. His small band, ably supported by Marine artillery, knocked out 7 NKPA tanks and killed 475 enemy soldiers. Blood flowed through every gutter in the intersection.

In the 5th Marines' zone, Corporal Bert Johnson, a machine gunner, and Private First Class Eugene Obregon, his ammo humper, tried to set up their weapon in an advanced position. The North Koreans swarmed close, wounding Johnson with sub-machine gun fire.

Obregon emptied his pistol at the shadows closing in, then dragged Johnson to a defilade position to dress his wounds. The North Koreans followed like hungry wolves. Obregon picked up a carbine, emptied clip after clip at the enemy, always shielding Johnson with his body.

The NKPA soldiers finally shot him to rags. But he had delayed their attack long enough for other Marines to fill the gap. And he had saved his buddy's life. Obregon's family would receive his posthumous Medal of Honor.

The 1st Marines shouldered into Seoul's main thoroughfare, fighting furiously for the government buildings. Leathernecks raised the American flag over their United States Embassy with a great cheer. It felt so good they repeated the process at the French—and many other—embassies.

An envious Army officer from Almond's staff chided Chesty Puller: "Ever since that flag-raising picture on Iwo Jima got published, I'm convinced you Marines would rather carry a flag into battle than a weapon." Puller regarded the man icily. "Not a bad idea," he growled. "A man with a flag in his pack and the desire to run it up on an enemy position isn't likely to bug out!"

The battle for Seoul raged until September 28 when the collapse of the last enemy pockets ended the resistance. The charred and blackened South Korean city was at last in UN hands.

Fighting beyond Seoul sputtered on another week. The new 7th Marines got bloodied in the three-day fight for Uijong-bu, north of the capital, but began to jell as a combat team.

Abruptly, on October 5, the Old Breed was relieved by the U.S. 1st Cavalry Division and ordered back to Inchon to reembark on amphibious shipping for yet another end run.

The 1st Marine Division and 1st Marine Aircraft Wing had done themselves proud. They had deployed quickly to this unexpected war, armed and equipped for instant combat. They had fought fiercely against a tough, well-trained, well-armed opponent. And they had coalesced again as an amphibious, combined-arms force from all over the globe in time to execute—brilliantly—one of the most difficult combat landings in history.

The price had been steep but acceptable. Among the Old Breed, 421 died, another 2,029 suffered wounds—about half of the casualties being incurred in the street fighting for Seoul. Enemy ground fire downed eleven Marine aircraft.

"The Navy's Police Force" had rarely achieved a more difficult task with such high-spirited efficiency. And the nation knew this. President Truman thereafter kept his opinions about the Corps to himself.

The Marines' landing at Inchon and forcible recapture of Seoul within twelve days effectively ended the NKPA invasion of South Korea. Clear sailing now? Not bloody likely.

15: FROZEN CHOSIN
(North Korea, 1950)

Army and Air Force generals urged Major General Oliver P. Smith to abandon his combat equipment and allow the 1st Marine Division to be evacuated by air from Hagaru-ri in a massive aerial Dunkirk. Smith demurred. The 1st Marine Division would fight their way out "as Marines," with their wounded and their gear.

(U.S. Marine Corps)

"Home by Christmas!"

Prediction widely spread by MacArthur's Headquarters, October 1950

ONLY FOURTEEN MORE SHOOTING DAYS UNTIL CHRISTMAS!

Sign painted on side of Marine Corps tank during the breakout from the Chosin Reservoir, December 1950

Ironically, the Marines' greatest battle occurred during one of the nation's most bitter military defeats, the routing of American and Allied forces in upper North Korea by the People's Liberation Army (PLA) of Red China.

For the United States, top-level arrogance and an abysmal disregard of strategic intelligence very nearly led to the annihilation of the 1st Marine Division. China's abrupt entry into the war placed the Old Breed Marines in desperate straits—seventy-eight miles away from their sea base, surrounded by seven PLA divisions, and burdened with thousands of wounded and frost-bitten casualties at the onset of the coldest winter ever recorded along the Manchurian border. Many officials in Washington considered the Marines a lost cause—trapped, isolated, doomed.

Instead, there ensued a tactical masterpiece, an unlikely epic fighting withdrawal of the stuff of legends, two weeks of extraordinary hardship and valor. No Marines ever had to fight under worse sustained conditions.

Yet "the race to the Yalu" was an undeniable strategic defeat. And unlike previous defeats, there would be no great comeback victories in this war to offset the sting. There would be just a bittersweet, even transcendent glory. For all its death, pain, lost fingers and toes, Chosin was in a warrior's way . . . beautiful.

At first it seemed so easy. MacArthur, having succeeded famously with his celebrated "left-hook" landing at Inchon, decided to use his Marines again for a "right-hook" landing at Wonsan, on the east coast of North Korea, creating another hammer-and-anvil scenario against the still-retreating NKPA forces.

Major General Oliver Smith's 1st Marine Division, having prevailed at Inchon and Seoul, cheerfully reembarked on board their amphibious ships

Chosin breakout (Charles Waterhouse)

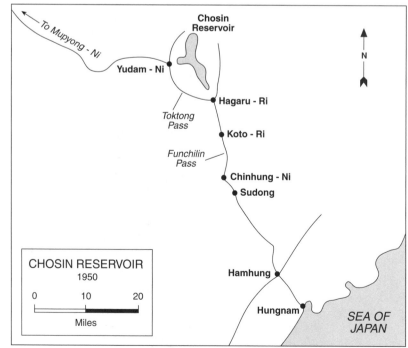

CHOSIN RESERVOIR
1950

To Mupyong - Ni

Chosin
Reservoir

Yudam - Ni

Hagaru - Ri

Toktong
Pass

Koto - Ri

Funchilin
Pass

Chinhung - Ni

Sudong

Hamhung

Hungnam

SEA OF
JAPAN

N

0   10   20

Miles

and sailed into the Korean Strait, bound for Wonsan. Then came an unpleasant shock.

Naval intelligence reported that the North Koreans had used their ancient fishing craft to lay thousands of surplus Soviet mines in the harbor. The mines were primitive but effective. Clearing safe channels for the Marines to land took sixteen tedious days and included the spectacular loss of three Allied minesweepers.

When the Marines finally came ashore at Wonsan on October 26, 1950, they were mortified that not only had the South Korean forces preceded them, but the Marine Corsair pilots of MAG–12 had already established an expeditionary airfield and were razzing them unmercifully.

Most ignominious of all: Bob Hope and his USO Show was already in Wonsan before the 1st Marine Division could execute their landing!

General Almond, still commanding X Corps and ever reflecting the notions of Douglas MacArthur, assigned Smith an enormous operating area, and urged him to press north toward the Chosin Reservoir, not far from the Manchurian border. These were heady days for the United Nations Command. Suggestive phrases like "the race to the Yalu" and "home by Christmas" captured the fancy of correspondents and raised false optimism among some of the troops.

Smith suffered none of these delusions. The eastern sector of the Taebaek Mountains was nothing less than forbidding. Winter was coming, there were undeniable signs that Red Chinese "volunteers" were crossing the Yalu in force, and there remained sizable NKPA units in the area to engage and defeat. While any red-blooded Marine would take pride in being the first to reach the Yalu River, Smith would not permit any unwise "race" north.

Chesty Puller's 1st Marines drew the division's initial combat missions in North Korea. One battalion outdueled a first-echelon NKPA regiment at Kojo, just south of Wonsan, in a nasty two-day battle. Another of Puller's battalions seized and held the vital crossroads town of Majon-ni against an aroused 15th NKPA Division. The battle for Majon-ni lasted two weeks.

When the North Koreans interdicted the only roads in and out of the town, the Marines hacked out a crude airstrip. Marine light helicopter pilots braved intense enemy fire to dart in and evacuate casualties.

On November 10, the one hundred and seventy-fifth anniversary of the founding of the Corps, the Marines paused to celebrate with an improvised "birthday cake" of composite B-ration materials, and to hell with the strictures against such celebrations by the Secretary of Defense.

While Chesty Puller kept the last NKPA fighting units at bay, General Smith sent the main body of the division north along the mountain track that twisted and turned for seventy-eight miles from the port of Hungnam to the western shoreline of the Chosin Reservoir, site of a valuable hydroelectric facility.

Chosin. That's what the Japanese called the big reservoir, and the Marines used Japanese maps of North Korea for this campaign. (Its Korean name is

Changjin, but "Chosin" rhymes with "Frozen" so the name remains uncorrected a half-century later.)

The one-lane gravel road that wound north among the towering Taebaeks led first through the villages of Sudong-ni and Chinhung-ni, then threaded through tortuous Funchilin Pass to Koto-ri and Hagaru-ri, the latter on the southern shore of the reservoir. Smith didn't like anything about this route. While his infantry could, with difficulty, cover the mountainous ridges on both sides, his tanks, artillery, and supply trucks were helplessly road-bound for most of the way.

Enemy destruction of any one of many bridges over otherwise impassable chasms would bottle up the Marine convoy dangerously. Evacuating casualties from that rugged country so far from the sea would be chancy at best.

Colonel Homer Litzenberg's 7th Marines led the way north and almost immediately engaged a Chinese Communist division in a five-day battle around Sudong-ni.

Here was the irony and the bankruptcy of the high command's myopic strategy. While MacArthur first denied the presence of organized PLA units in North Korea, then dismissed their tactical value, the Marines were already fighting for their lives against a very well-organized Chinese division, mostly veterans of years of guerrilla combat against the Japanese and Nationalist Chinese, and easily the most proficient night fighters the Marines ever faced.

Once again Marine Corsairs, these flown by the smart-mouth pilots of MAG–12 out of Wonsan, came slicing out of the clouds to chew up PLA formations with rockets, napalm, and machine guns. Napalm quickly got the enemy's attention.

Lieutenant Joseph Owen of the 7th Marines described one daylight "nape" strike: "a spectacle of awesome and terrible beauty. The pods slid from the planes, tumbled across the ground, then exploded. Black smoke billowed and red flame leapt against the white snow. . . . Chinese soldiers were aflame, running about in frenzied circles. They threw themselves, flailing, into the snow."

On November 7 the Chinese broke contact and simply disappeared.

The Marines would not encounter another organized PLA unit for nearly three weeks, when they would abruptly discover themselves surrounded by an entire PLA army group.

Almond continued to press Smith to get into gear, to truly "race for the Yalu." Smith demurred, more worried than ever. He brought Puller's 1st Marines up to guard the MSR (main supply route, a euphemism for the single-lane goat-track of a road), began staging extra supplies of ammo, rations, and fuel along the route, and directed his engineers to build emergency airstrips at the mountain villages of Koto-ri and Hagaru-ri. "What for?" asked Almond. "To evacuate my casualties," replied Smith. "What casualties?" the corps commander inquired, still not getting it.

Almond urged Smith to press on past Hagaru-ri to Yudam-ni in prepara-

tion for a major cross-country jaunt to link up with the Eighth Army, eighty mountainous miles away.

With a heavy heart, Smith dispatched the 7th and 5th Marines west of Chosin. An Army regimental combat team worked its way up the reservoir's east coast toward the Manchurian border, terribly exposed. Smith used helicopters to fly his forward command post into Hagaru-ri (the Marines were still the only outfit in Korea with their own choppers).

The freakish Siberian winter then hit with a fury.

Temperatures plummeted. Smith issued the division's cold weather clothing, but there were not enough of the heavy parkas and gloves to go around. Smith demanded that his infantry troops get first priority.

Private First Class Wayne Queen, serving as a rifleman and ambulance driver for the division's medical battalion, recalled the cold as excruciating. "The wind never stopped; the wind-chill factor was ungodly."

Nineteen-year-old machine-gunner Private First Class Win Scott described how hard it was to fight under those conditions: "Everything froze. Our carbines wouldn't work. Artillery rounds fell short, sometimes into our own positions. Morphine froze hard as a stone—the corpsmen carried the syrettes in their mouths to keep them thawed enough to help numb the wounded."

The 7th Marines crossed 4,000-foot Toktong Pass on November 24, leaving Fox Company behind to defend it, and descended into Yudam-ni.

The next day came terrible news that the Eighth Army on the west coast had been overrun and routed by Chinese forces. General Walton Walker's forces, which had fought all the way from Pusan to Pyongyang and beyond, reeled back in tragic disarray, abandoning most heavy weapons and many of their casualties.

General Smith nervously slowed the 7th Marines' advance, allowing the 5th Marines to link up with them in the hills around Yudam-ni.

The Chinese hiding in the eastern Taebaek Mountains waited until the night of November 27—twenty below zero, blinding snow—to spring their trap. General Sung Shih-lun, commanding 120,000 troops of the PLA Ninth Army Group, saw his mission as that of annihilating the crack Marine division, so temptingly strung out along forty miles of bad road. At his signal, tens of thousands of quilted soldiers came screaming out of the storm to the blare of bugles and glare of green pyrotechnics, firing their snub-nosed "Burp Guns" in disciplined bursts.

Red China had entered the Korean War big time.

Scattered Marine outposts in the high ground above Yudam-ni were engulfed by these inhuman waves, but the Chinese attacks were not totally unexpected, and the Marines rallied and held. Toktong Pass, the crucial link between the forward regiments and the advance base at Hagaru-ri, came under heavy attack. Captain William E. Barber's Fox Company settled in for a desperate defensive struggle to hold the pass. But no Fox Marines could then

Encircled by a Chinese
army group and pounded
by the onset of one of the
coldest winters ever
recorded along the North
Korean–Manchurian
border, the 1st Marine
Division begins its classic
breakout to the sea.
(U.S. Marine Corps)

The physical and mental strain of the Chosin campaign shows in this Marine's face. Fighting off the Chinese all night, marching toward the sea all day, enduring ungodly cold and high winds throughout—the 1st Marine Division somehow prevailed.

(David Douglas Duncan)

imagine they would have to man this post by themselves for the next five days.

The Chinese threatened Hagaru-ri, cut the MSR in a dozen critical places, and came close to destroying completely the isolated Army regiment northeast of Chosin. Several hundred soldiers managed to escape over the ice to join the Marine lines at Hagaru-ri. Gray dawn brought enough light for the fearless Corsairs, and slowly the odds began to even.

General Smith assessed the crisis. His own command post and advance base at Hagaru-ri was severely threatened by Chinese incursions into the surrounding highlands and he had precious few infantry troops at hand to spearhead the necessary counterattacks. He also had to reopen the MSR at least as far south as Puller's outpost at Koto-ri. But he worried most about his two regiments at Yudam-ni, fourteen miles west of Chosin, whose escape route was jeopardized by the Chinese attacks on Fox Company at Toktong Pass.

The 5th and 7th Marines would have to fight their way back to Hagaru-ri along the mountains on both sides of the narrow road.

Colonel Ray Murray began consolidating his 5th Marines into more defensible positions. The ungodly cold produced macabre sights. Many of the Chinese soldiers were from the southern provinces and suffered even more than the Marines. "We'd find some of them frozen stiff in firing positions," said Private First Class Scott. "Others were in the final stages of freezing to death—all they could move were their eyes."

After defending Hill 1282 in desperate fighting for two days, Scott's company of the 5th Marines received orders to bring out their dead and relinquish the high ground for a stronger position farther east. Scott brought up the rear, brandishing his machine gun. Suddenly an explosion sent him cartwheeling down the slope. "I woke up face down in frozen brush. It felt like my back was blown wide open. A corpsman gave me morphine, and the Marines placed me on a poncho and dragged me down the hill. I passed out."

Scott spent the next five days on a stretcher, lashed to a jeep trailer, in great pain, unbearably cold, sharing the ride with the dead.

Scott recalled: "Bodies strapped on the barrels of artillery, on the sides of

trucks, across hoods, anywhere there was space. They were rigid. A wounded guy next to me froze to death the second night."

Unlike many other embattled United Nations forces, the Marines were coming out with their wounded and their dead.

But no vehicles could go very far along the MSR with so many Chinese occupying the commanding heights. They would have to be rooted out, one snowy ridge after another, by a decreasing number of Marine riflemen.

Chesty Puller meanwhile tried to send a relief force north from Koto-ri to Hagaru-ri, despite the Chinese presence in strength at several critical stretches of the MSR. He formed "Task Force Drysdale," named after the commander of the Royal Marine Commando, reinforced with U.S. Marine tanks, trucks, and assorted troops, less than a thousand in all.

The enemy contested Drysdale's hodgepodge force at each passage and every narrow gorge, and the odyssey lasted all night. In the end, Drysdale, most of the tanks, many of the Royal Marines, and a company of United States Marines made it through to Smith's endangered base at Hagaru-ri. But a full half of Task Force Drysdale came to grief en route. The Chinese killed or captured hundreds of Americans and burned their trucks to cinders.

Smith's situation remained extremely critical.

BATTLEFIELD MATH

The endless night was not without its gallows humor. An adjoining ROK commander called Chesty Puller to report a major Chinese attack in his sector. "How many Chinese are attacking you?" asked Puller. "Many, many Chinese," replied the excited Korean. "Goddammit," swore Puller, "put my Marine liaison officer on the radio." In a moment, an American voice came over the air: "Yes, sir?" "Lieutenant," growled Chesty, "exactly how many Chinese you got up there?" "Colonel, we've got a whole *shitpot* of Chinese up here!" "Thank God," exclaimed Puller, "at least there's someone up there who knows how to *count!*"

The 5th and 7th Marines, bloodied but intact, were having a hell of a time blasting their way clear of the trap that surrounded them at Yudam-ni. And for all the importance of fighting for the immediate high ground to get their road-bound convoy moving, the whole force would be in deadly peril unless a relief column could be sent to the aid of Captain Barber's survivors, still holding Toktong Pass by sheer guts and world-class supporting arms.

Colonel Litzenberg tried four times to reach Fox Company; each failed. Finally he called for Lieutenant Colonel Raymond Davis, commanding the 1st Battalion, 7th Marines. "Nothing works. You've got to get to them. Come back in twenty minutes with a plan."

Ray Davis was never one to toot his own horn. It was months before the many reservists in his new battalion learned that their skipper had commanded a battalion and won the Navy Cross under Chesty Puller at Peleliu. He was a proven, rock-solid combat leader—but trying to rescue Fox Company at Toktong would be his greatest test.

Davis realized that any attempt to reach the pass by road would be doomed. So would any daytime maneuver. He proposed to Litzenberg that his

shot-up battalion strip to the essentials and take off cross-country, over the ridges, at night, approaching the encircled Fox Company lines from the north. "Go!" said Litzenberg.

Artillery units in the valley recorded the temperature at 24 degrees below zero at dusk, the time Davis began his ridgeline journey. Then the winds came. Davis figured the wind-chill factor was probably seventy-five below—mind-numbing, strength-sapping, bone-chilling cold. "We would freeze if we didn't move."

Davis and his 500 Marines lurched painfully through the snow, making noise in spite of every effort. But the shrieking wind masked their movements. And the Chinese never expected a Marine battalion to leave their foxholes at night and mush cross-country behind their lines.

The blowing snow made navigation difficult. Davis found a single star, providentially stationed over his intended compass bearing, but it slid in and out of sight with the scudding clouds, or as the Marines slipped and stumbled over the broken terrain.

Lieutenant Joseph Owen left a moving account of the journey. "The trail became icy, packed by the feet of those ahead. Men slipped to their knees, staggered up, and slipped again. . . . Exhaustion was telling on us. . . . Under the heavy parkas our bodies sweated with the strain, but our hands and feet were frozen numb. The wind-borne cold attacked with terrible fury. We shivered violently."

Ray Davis was shivering violently, too, but he moved ceaselessly up and down the long column, breaking his own trail, encouraging his men in his soft Georgian accent, keeping them focused.

Hours later the slogging column encountered the outer ring of Chinese attacking Fox Company at Toktong Pass. At first, the PLA forces thought the snow-covered troops were Chinese reinforcements and let them traverse unchallenged. Then the Marines unveiled bayoneted M–1 Garands and unmistakable BARs amid Chinese cries of surprise and delivered a point-blank volley. A vicious firefight ensued, but more Marines came up, now unmindful of the cold, ready to shoot. Very quickly the battalion cleared a wedge in the circle of attackers.

Ray Davis raised Captain Barber on the radio. Barber, badly wounded, offered to lead out a patrol of his survivors to guide Davis into the perimeter. This brought tears to Davis's eyes. "Thanks, but we know where you are, and we'll fight our way in at daybreak," he replied.

Both officers would receive the Medal of Honor for their respective roles at Toktong Pass.

Fox Company's five-day defense of Toktong Pass rates among the greatest holding actions in Marine Corps history, one of the same magnitude as Wake Island, Quilali, or Edson's Ridge. Captain Barber lost half his 240-man company in killed and wounded; another 40 could not walk due to severe frostbite. But Fox Company had dished out more pain than it received.

Lieutenant Owen stared in astonishment at the battered perimeter at first light after the ordeal of getting there. Hundreds of Chinese bodies lay in crumpled heaps, dangerously close to the Marine lines. The Fox Marines had fought on borrowed time, fewer and fewer responding to each new charge. "We stood in wonder," said Owen. "Men bowed their heads in prayer. . . . Tears came to the eyes of the raggedy Marines who had endured bitter cold and savage battle to reach this place of suffering and courage."

The 5th Marines had experienced their own series of brutal battles to clear the high ground in their sector. Finally, with Taplett's "Dark Horse" Battalion leading the way (and by now a very long way from sultry Wolmi-do Island), the two regiments linked up beyond Toktong Pass, the commanding heights now painstakingly cleared of PLA forces.

Marine aviation was never more effective under more desperate conditions than during their support of the 1st Marine Division's epic breakout from the Chosin Reservoir. Here Marine Corsairs of the 1st Marine Aircraft Wing drop napalm bombs on a Chinese Communist roadblock near Hagaru-ri.
(U.S. Marine Corps)

"RETREAT, HELL"

Marines at Belleau Wood had startled the dispirited French troops by proclaiming, "Retreat, hell, we just got here." Major General Oliver Smith, a commander not given to hyperbole, used a similar phrase to wide-eyed reporters who flew in to Hagaru-ri for a half-hour interview with the beleaguered Marine. Accounts vary, but Smith simply refused to accept the dire accounts of his situation there on the southern tip of Chosin Reservoir, so far from the sea. "We're not retreating," he said. "We're simply attacking in another direction." In a later, more cynical age, this would resonate as the words of a "spin doctor," but from the plain-speaking Smith in December 1950, this was his view of reality. His 1st Marine Division had fought all the way north from Sudong-ni to Yudam-ni the previous month; now they would simply fight their way out. As Marines. With all their gear, their wounded, and their dead—even with their thousands of Chinese POWs and tens of thousands of terrified North Korean civilian refugees. Nor would the retrograde be any pell-mell dash for the sea, with only the strongest or luckiest surviving. Smith would employ the same successful tactics that had brought the division this far north: Marine infantry leapfrogging along the parallel ridges overlooking the MSR; Marine engineers repairing the bridges; Marine fighters close overhead; Marine tanks and howitzers, road-bound but deadly, the guns unlimbering on the spot in the middle of the convoy to blast any Chinese incursions at point-blank range. The division's objective was to reach the port of Hungnam with its tactical integrity fully intact. An equal objective was to kill or maim as many Chinese Communist soldiers as possible along the route. Both objectives were handsomely attained.

Extricating themselves in orderly fashion from the Yudam-ni trap and withdrawing the fourteen miles back to Hagaru-ri took the two regiments seventy-nine hours, an eerie equivalent in time to the Battle of Tarawa.

Ray Davis, now at the head of the long, ragged column streaming toward Hagaru-ri, ordered his Leathernecks to "stand tall—look like Marines." What they looked like to the cheering garrison of Hagaru-ri was hell on earth—wild mountain men, against whom no enemy force in the world could hope to prevail.

Oliver Smith had to wipe his eyes at the sight of the 5th and 7th Marines striding into the perimeter. These men would never know defeat.

Just earlier General Almond had flown into Smith's improvised airstrip at Hagaru-ri, no longer questioning its military worth.

Almond, crestfallen and somber, ordered Smith to escape to the sea posthaste, leaving behind his heavy weapons and equipment. "No, sir," replied Smith quietly. "We'll fight our way out as Marines, bringing all our weapons and gear with us."

Smith delivered the same statement to an astonished Air Force general who flew in to Hagaru-ri to orchestrate a massive evacuation of the Marines, less their weapons and equipment, an "aerial Dunkirk," he called it, with relish. Smith thanked him and sent him on his way.

Then came Major General Field Harris, commanding the 1st Marine Aircraft Wing: "What do you need from us?" Smith and Harris quickly worked out the air cover plan for the breakout to Hungnam: Marine fighters directly overhead the Marine column every day; Navy fighters from Task Force 77 on either side of that envelope; Air Force fighters further out, intercepting Chinese reinforcements and supply columns; Air Force "Goonie Bird" transports to evacuate his 4,000 casualties from Hagaru-ri.

"We'll cover you all the way," promised Harris (whose son, a battalion commander in Smith's division, would die in the subsequent breakout).

Wounded machine gunner Win Scott was unconscious and in critical condition by the time the 5th Marines fought their way back to Hagaru-ri. Corpsmen in the crowded perimeter were told to prepare the dead for local burial—engineers would thaw the frozen earth with flame; bulldozers would scrape out suitable graves—because there would be sufficient airlift to evacuate only the most grievously wounded.

Believing Scott to be dead, the corpsmen consigned his stretcher to the long silent row of bodies awaiting burial. Some sixth sense roused Scott. He saw the bodies, the yawning graves, and screamed: "I'm not dead, dammit!"

The corpsmen nearly jumped out of their skivvies in fright, but quickly bundled the resurrected Marine on board an Air Force C–47 transport, bound for a warm hospital in Japan.

General Smith maintained strict standards for evacuating his thousands of frostbite cases. To qualify, his Leathernecks had to be worse off than Dr. Chester Lessenden, the Navy surgeon still serving the 5th Marines despite both feet being painfully frozen. Moving south, only drivers, gunners, and radio operators would ride—everyone else would walk.

The Marines spent much of the brief period between WWII and the Korean War developing tactical helicopters and the new doctrine of "vertical assault." They were the first armed force to deploy helicopters in Korea. Here a chopper from HMR–161 delivers a pallet of supplies despite the winter climate and mountainous terrain.

(U.S. Marine Corps)

On December 6, Ray Murray's 5th Marines cleared the Chinese off East Hill in fierce fighting that raged past midnight. The hill dominated the MSR between Hagaru-ri and Koto-ri. Both sides recognized its value. The Chinese counterattacked throughout the night, inflicting heavy casualties among Murray's veterans but dying by the hundreds in the cross fires. Daybreak, as usual, brought the Corsairs, and there were no more counterattacks.

Securing East Hill opened the back door out of Hagaru-ri, and the division moved out the next morning, its ranks now swollen by Royal Marines and U.S. soldiers.

The distance to Koto-ri was "only" eleven miles—General Smith flew there in ten minutes in his helicopter to begin preparing the next stage of the breakout—but fighting their way along that route would take the troops a day and a half and cost another 600 casualties.

The route twisted past a surreal landscape of snow-covered, burned-out vehicles—the wreckage of ill-fated Task Force Drysdale—and through a dozen Chinese strong points. When the PLA forces failed to turn back the 7th Marines, leading the long column, the Chinese laid low and waited for softer targets, the service troops farther along.

Tiny Koto-ri now bulged at the seams. Ten thousand troops and 1,000 vehicles poured in from Hagaru-ri, swamping Chesty Puller's meager facilities, providing crowded targets for Chinese heavy mortars. General Smith knew the column had to continue its momentum south immediately, but now there was a major problem at hand.

Well below Koto-ri, the Chinese had blown a bridge over a chasm with such precipitous drop-offs that there was simply no bypass available. Once again, the Old Breed seemed bottled up. Here's where the U.S. Air Force and Marine and Army engineers stepped in to execute an early Christmas miracle.

The engineers examined the chasm, made some swift calculations, then called for eight sections of what was called a Treadway Bridge. The Air Force artfully air-dropped these sections over the column the next morning. One was damaged, another drifted into enemy lines, but the engineers knew that six sections could do the job and went to work.

"EVERY MARINE A RIFLEMAN"

Every ground force has trained infantrymen, adept with small arms and imbued with aggressive spirit. But the Marines have traditionally taken this a step farther—training every Marine *first* as a rifleman, before the specialty training as cooks or bakers or candlestick-makers. In decades of Pacific combat, first the Japanese, then the North Koreans, Chinese, and North Vietnamese were always amazed to have executed a surprise raid on some Leatherneck logistics center, only to find the service troops battling back with disciplined, well-aimed fire, deftly lobbed grenades, and fixed bayonets jabbing straight and true. During the breakout from Hagaru-ri, motor transport mechanics and artillery ammo humpers teamed up to throw back concerted Chinese attacks on what in most armed services would be the "soft underbelly" of a convoy. Similarly, when the Chinese struck the division headquarters group, the Marine bandsmen swung into action with glee, manning machine guns and automatic rifles instead of trumpets and trombones. Other services may boast of better mechanics or trombone players; the Marines know all hands can fight and kill on demand.

No delicate engineering project could ever be conducted under worse conditions of bitter cold, enemy fire, and sheer desperation. And when an errant bulldozer damaged the provisional bridge—fatally some thought—the engineers again worked their field magic.

Tanks were left with an inch to spare on either side; jeeps for their part could not deviate an inch in either direction without falling through the missing center span. The whole thing was hairy, nerve-wracking, time-consuming. But one by one the Marines eased their combat vehicles across the chasm and continued southward.

Chesty Puller was the last senior officer to leave Koto-ri, striding defiantly afoot, his command jeep loaded with wounded and dead Marines.

The rear guard took compassion on the frightened Korean refugees, but they had already detected Chinese infiltrators in their midst. These had to be ferreted out with great care, one by one, and shot. The multitudes jogged along in trace of the main body of Marines, their protectors against the invading Chinese.

The last Marines included more engineers, methodically demolishing the bridges so carefully laid at the head of the long column.

Between Koto-ri and Chinhung-ni lay Funchilin Pass, now held in great strength by the Chinese.

General Field Harris pulled out all the stops, sending his Corsairs in at ridgetop level, strafing, bombing, and dropping napalm. But then the weather turned sour again. Smith ordered Puller to direct his southernmost battalion to attack north into the pass from Chinhung-ni to clear Hill 1081, yet another critical terrain mass dominating the road and several bridges.

The battle for the pass took place during a howling snowstorm; the temperature started at fourteen below zero, then dropped another ten degrees. Into this storm came Captain Robert Barrow's Able Company of the 1st Marines, the force that had almost single-handedly captured urban Yongdong-po three months earlier.

The storm was terrible to endure but worked in Barrow's favor, masking his movements up the sheer, reverse slope of Hill 1081. Able Company caught the Chinese peering through the snow at the road from Koto-ri and surprised them painfully.

The Chinese recognized the hill was their last best chance to stop and slaughter the 1st Marine Division, and they counterattacked furiously throughout a long, stormy, confusing night.

Desperate, deadly fighting continued to rage in the northern folds of Funchilin Pass. On one occasion Chinese troops rushed the column, swarmed over a Marine tank, and slaughtered its crew. The Old Breed Marines became incensed—their immediate "ancestors" had fought the entire Battle of Okinawa five years earlier with the distinction of being the only U.S. division not to lose a tank to direct infantry attack—now they literally tore the offending Chinese limb from limb.

The single-lane road leading through the Taebaek Mountains from the Chosin Reservoir to the sea at Hungnam could have been as much a death trap for the Marines as the equally torturous route used by the Eighth Army proved to be during their retreat south from the Yalu River. The key difference: Marine infantry covered the high ground overlooking the road below, leapfrogging ahead of the main column, driving off the Chinese divisions with artillery, close air support, and well-aimed rifle fire. The work was slow, painstaking, costly—and successful. (U.S. Marine Corps)

Marines fighting the
Chinese for control
of the towering
Taebaek range
needed the
legs, lungs, and
surefootedness of
mountain goats.
The wind, howling
out of Siberia,
never stopped.
(U.S. Marine Corps)

During one of the interminable firefights to clear the pass, Lieutenant Joe Owen went down with multiple gunshot wounds from close range. Owen would live, but his intrepid 60mm mortar platoon would be shattered, his company reduced to 27 effectives from more than 300 that fought in the Chosin campaign.

The storm cleared enough for the Corsairs to return to action.

Never had any Marines been better served by their "airdale" brothers. Even the most earthbound rifleman knew how great a risk these pilots ran every time they swirled in low to deliver their ordnance right on the nose. Chinese machine gunners were proficient against both two-legged and low-flying targets. In such extreme cold a parachute was little comfort to a stricken pilot. Hypothermic death would be swift, whether the chute came down in the mountains or drifted out to sea.

Nobody knew how much the Old Breed owed its collective ass to the aviators than Oliver Smith. In a heartfelt message to Field Harris, Smith spoke for each of his Marines: "During the long reaches of the night and in the snowstorms, many a Marine prayed for the coming of day or clearing weather when he knew he would again hear the welcome roar of your planes. . . . Never in its history has Marine aviation given more convincing proof of its indispensable value to ground Marines."

The Chinese could not hold Funchilin Pass. The 1st Marine Division poured through, pausing to swap good-natured insults with the 1st Marines

who had swept away the final Chinese strong point on Hill 1081. The division, reunited at last, seemed absolutely invincible.

The Chinese began to melt away, leaving the Marines a clear path back to the port at Hungnam. Their once-promising campaign against the single American division had become an unmitigated disaster. The PLA 9th Army Group sustained some 37,000 casualties, including 25,000 deaths to battle and extreme cold. Most of the seven divisions that attacked the Marines were so shot-up they simply disappeared from the rolls of the PLA.

The Marines suffered 4,400 casualties of their own in the Chosin campaign, including 730 killed, plus thousands and thousands of frostbite cases. But, God, what a sight the survivors made striding into Hungnam on December 12!

Said one admiring onlooker: "Look at those bastards. Look at those magnificent bastards!"

The Marines did not leave Hungnam without grateful company. Evacuated with them were 100,000 Korean refugees, escaping the totalitarian regime, one of history's greatest and least-recorded humanitarian transfers.

Not "home by Christmas," by any stretch, but the Marines had endured their greatest battle challenge with élan and grit and matchless discipline. A hot shower (or several), hot chow, a little sleep—and the 1st Marine Division was soon ready to reenter the war, now that the top-level foolishness about "racing to the Yalu" had proven its absurdity.

Army historian Brigadier General S. L. A. Marshall studied the disastrous UN campaigns in North Korea exhaustively and critically. He concluded: "No other operation in the American book of war quite compares with this show by the 1st Marine Division in the perfection of tactical concepts precisely executed, in accuracy of estimation of the situation, in leadership at all levels, and in promptness of utilization of all supporting forces."

COATS OF MANY COLORS

Marines fighting in such brutally cold weather for such a sustained period invariably wore their personal history smeared all over their filthy parkas and trousers. Every exposed foot of fabric, it seemed, contained its own telltale marks: streaks of syrup from half-frozen C-ration fruit cans; blotches of carbon and hair tonic from cleaning heavily used weapons in subzero temperatures; unmistakable evidence of rampant dysentery; mucous stains from chronic runny noses; and the universal black and scarlet patches of dried human blood—the Marine's, his buddy's, the enemy's. None of the survivors of Frozen Chosin would be fit for polite society for some time. But for everybody who had been rooting for them to battle out, each one of them seemed more beautiful than Marilyn Monroe.

16: THE SEESAW WAR

(Korea, 1951–1953)

The seesaw war in Korea that followed the Chinese intervention led to a war of outposts. Here a Marine light machine gun crew takes careful aim at a distant target (note the rear leaf sight extended).

(National Archives)

THE 1ST MARINE DIVISION BECAME THE WAR HORSE OF THE UNITED NATIONS FORCE IN KOREA, FROM THE CHOSIN RESERVOIR TO PANMUNJOM. BUT IT WAS NEVER TO PARTICIPATE AGAIN IN A GREAT STRATEGIC STROKE LIKE THAT AT INCHON. THE WINNING COMBINATION WHICH HAD TAKEN INCHON AND SEOUL HAD BEEN BROKEN UP. . . . THE 1ST MARINE AIR WING WAS SEPARATED FROM ITS TEAMMATE, THE 1ST DIVISION, THEREBY DESTROYING THE MOST EFFECTIVE AIR–GROUND TEAM THE WORLD HAD EVER SEEN.

Lieutenant General Merrill Twining, USMC

Korean Stalemate
(Charles Waterhouse)

The stirring records achieved by the Marines in Korea the first five months of that miserable war—the mobile "Fire Brigade" in the Pusan Perimeter, Inchon's bold landing, the forcible seizure of Seoul, the fighting breakout from the Reservoir—represented the Corps at its high-maneuver, unrestricted best. Then the war changed, grew conservative. Marine amphibious assault landings, by nature the most offensive and risky of all operations, went out the window. The Marines shouldered into line with the other land divisions, shackled and bound like Gulliver, engaging in pointless but deadly skirmishes against the North Koreans and Chinese. It was the kind of static standoff that Marines were not made to fight. Notwithstanding, they fought the rest of the war very goddamn well, thank you.

All wars are political. But those that America waged in the final half of the twentieth century were cost-conscious and media-savvy. The clock was always ticking toward the moment when public opinion would erode political resolve. In the Korean War, large-scale offensive actions gave way to grinding defensive struggle, hauntingly similar to the trench warfare of World War I.

Public opinion polls after the ignominious rout of most of the United Nations forces by the border-crossing Chinese revealed that Americans had turned sharply against the joint intervention. Two thirds of those polled said that the nation's military should get out of Korea. The Marines slowly realized this would be the nature of limited wars in the Nuclear Age—highly politicized, increasingly unpopular, a war waged more for propaganda points and opinion polls than for strategic objectives.

At the end there was little resemblance between the 1950 Marines who had stormed up and down the Korean Peninsula in Seven-League Boots and their politically fettered replacements of 1951–1953—except a certain pride and professionalism, which persisted even under the gloomiest circumstances.

The 1st Marine Division returned to Pusan following the Chosin breakout to recuperate, treat its collective frostbite, and absorb replacements.

The news continued to be all bad. So sweeping had been the rout of the U.S. Eighth Army by the PLA along the west coast of the Korean Peninsula that the enemy soon recaptured all the now-hallowed ground from Seoul to Inchon for which the Marines had fought and bled the previous September. To the Marines it seemed as if a giant eraser had swept across the contested landscape.

When President Truman subsequently sacked General Douglas MacArthur for blatant disobedience, the Marines also lost their strongest (if late-blooming) advocate in the Far East.

With MacArthur's departure went his unofficial, long-ago promise to General Lemuel Shepherd that he would never separate his Marines from the "flying artillery" of their vaunted close air support, provided in Korea by the 1st Marine Aircraft Wing.

Now the Fifth Air Force consolidated all air assets in Korea. All requests for air support had to go through the snooty Joint Operations Center. Response time for the Marine on the ground calling for help from his buddies in the Wing lapsed overnight from an average of fifteen minutes to eighty minutes—a virtual lifetime in close combat.

Many times there was no response at all. The "JOC" was after bigger, more strategic targets. They expressed little interest in sidetracking pilots from the big picture to pursue the phantom little men in quilted uniforms firing their murderous mortars into Marine outposts from reverse-slope positions.

This came as an unpleasant shock as the Marines returned to action.

The Old Breed, now the largest division in the war with its four infantry regiments (including the scrappy Korean Marines), was in high demand along the recently stabilized front lines. General Oliver Smith knew that the consolidation of aviation assets under the new JOC would vitiate his combat power and tried to position his men under the guns of their brothers in the Navy. He asked that his division be deployed along either coast, fully within range of the guns of the fleet and, by the way, instantly available for future amphibious end runs. This was the way the 6th Marine Division had fought the prolonged land campaign in the Battle of Okinawa, thoroughly linked with the fleet, lethally effective with such maritime synergy.

Instead, the Marines were plugged into central-eastern Korea and told to make ready for yet another great land offensive across the 38th Parallel.

On the brighter side, General Matthew Ridgway now commanded the Eighth Army. The Marines warmed to Ridgway's fighting heart—and his choice of operational code names ("Killer," "Ripper").

Operation Killer began on February 21, 1951.

The 1st Marine Division jumped off from Wonju. Advancing through rocky heights and narrow valleys, the Marines entered Hoengsong after three days of hard fighting. The many new replacements learned quickly the demands of mountain warfare against seasoned PLA and NKPA forces.

Ridgway kept the pressure on the Communist forces, and kept his Marines in the forefront.

Operation Ripper, aimed at the recapture of Seoul and restoring the 38th parallel, began on March 7.

The Marines, spared from another urban brawl in gutted Seoul, battled across broken country well east of the capital, their advance slowed as much by drenching spring rains as by enemy fire. After a week, UN forces captured Seoul for the second time in six months. Two weeks later the Eighth Army recrossed the 38th Parallel in force. Seesaw war. . . .

Another North Korean reservoir, the Hwachon, loomed ahead for the Marines. Beyond it, the Chinese were busily fortifying a mountain-flanked region that protected the heart of their supply and communications network. The Marines called it "The Iron Triangle."

THE MARINES ENTER THE JET AGE

The prop-driven F4U Corsairs had served the Corps admirably for close to a decade, but the faithful old war horses were wearing out in service just when Communist troops in Korea, equipped with sophisticated Soviet antiaircraft weaponry, were achieving new heights of lethality against low-flying U.S. aircraft. As recorded by one Marine infantryman, Corporal Martin Russ, "When a Corsair dives, the ground actually vibrates from the muzzle blasts of the concentrated fire power of the Chinese weapons. The noise is tremendous; a series of CRACKS . . . automatic, multi-barreled blasts." The Korean War–vintage Corsairs, equipped with more armor and no supercharger, could barely muster 450 knots of airspeed and were increasingly vulnerable. Time to enter the jet age.

The first Marine jet was a version of the Lockheed F–80 Shooting Star. Marine Fighter Squadron 311 began training with these newfangled aircraft in mid–1948. Said squadron commander Lieutenant Colonel John P. Condon (who five years earlier had engineered the intercept of Admiral Yamamoto): "The new pilots were thrilled to be in a propellerless aircraft—it was like changing from a bow to a rifle." By March 1950, VMF–311 had its first operational jet fighter on hand, the Grumman F9F–2 Panther. The Panther was a fighter pilot's jewel. It could fly at speeds exceeding 600 mph, attain a service ceiling of 50,000 feet, launch from carriers or dirt fields. The fighter sported four 20mm cannon in its nose and carried five-inch rockets, 500-pound bombs, and napalm pods.

Major John Bolt, a World War II ace, became the first Marine jet ace by downing six MiG–15s. Other legendary jet fighters surfaced. Future baseball Hall-of-Famer Marine Captain Theodore "Ted" Williams crash-landed his burning Panther jet after his first mission over North Korea. Williams, who had flown as a Marine in WWII, went on to execute thirty-seven combat missions in Korea. Future astronaut Marine Major John H. Glenn, while on exchange duty with the Air Force, shot down three MiGs in five days with his borrowed F–86 Sabre jet and received his fifth Distinguished Flying Cross.

Oliver Smith knew the Chinese would not abandon this territory. When he recognized signs that the Chinese were trying to lure him into another trap, he deliberately slowed the advance of his regiments, looked to his flanks, and called frequently for aerial reconnaissance of the high ground ahead. Increasingly, such missions, when approved by the omnipotent JOC, involved Marine Corps jet aircraft.

General Oliver Smith's sixth sense about the Chinese buildup proved eerily accurate. On April 22, a half-million Communist troops poured out of the Iron Triangle to begin a spring offensive aimed at the recapture of Seoul. Chinese POWs reported that their commissars had promised them a May Day celebration in the South Korean capital.

With their Hwachon Reservoir positions directly in line with the enemy attack, the 1st Marine Division weathered the brunt of the assaults. When an ROK division on the flank gave way to the Chinese onslaught, the Marines suddenly faced a ten-mile-by-ten-mile gap to their left. The Marines bent sharply back, their lines resembling a fishhook, but did not break.

Fighting became very intense, especially at night. Once again, the Marines experienced the telltale green flares and bugles, smothering mortar barrages, and hordes of Chinese troops swarming up the rocky draws leading into their positions. Marine artillery, mortars, and automatic weapons cut down the attackers by the hundreds, but invariably enough would survive to penetrate the lines in wild, hand-to-hand fighting. Counterattacks and fresh charges would occur throughout the night, the battle raging back and forth along the ridgetops.

The Marines fought stubbornly, gave up ground only grudgingly, and prevented any major breakthroughs. But elsewhere along the front the Chinese advanced once again toward Seoul, and the entire Eighth Army withdrew by stages, the Marines to Hongchon. This time the new lines held.

When the second phase of the Communist spring offensive began on May 16, the 1st Marine Division had a new commander. Major General Gerald Thomas, veteran of Belleau Wood and Guadalcanal, relieved Oliver Smith, whose thoughtful stewardship had given the Old Breed a new definition of the motto *"Semper Fidelis."*

This time 125,000 fresh Chinese troops welcomed General Thomas with a well-coordinated offensive which swept away several adjoining ROK divisions and opened a penetration thirty miles deep on the opposite flank. Once again, the Marines hunkered down, bent ("refused") their exposed flank, and used every bit of firepower they could muster to kill more Chinese.

This worked. The enemy offensive, weakened by heavy losses and lengthening supply lines, petered out. The weary Chinese withdrew into North Korea, leaving NKPA forces behind to fight a costly rearguard action.

The seesaw war of 1951 continued. The Eighth Army, now commanded by Lieutenant General James Van Fleet (another pugnacious Army officer admired by the Marines) assumed the offensive once again.

The 1st Marine Division pushed steadily northward, once more passing the Hwachon Reservoir. By late June, the Marines had successfully occupied a series of ridges overlooking a circular valley nicknamed "the Punchbowl."

Reaching the lower edge of the Punchbowl was one thing—forcibly evicting the enemy from the steep mountains along the northern perimeter was something else. Here the delays and ineptitudes of close air support provided offhandedly by the JOC began to cost Marine lives. The Air Force never seemed to appreciate the integrated combat power the Marines traditionally enjoyed from their distinctive air-ground team. Without their organic air component the Old Breed was dangerously undergunned to be attacking fortified enemy positions in these northern mountains.

With reliable close air support so hard to come by, General Thomas looked to the distant sea to enhance his division's combat power. On several occasions Thomas arranged for the battleship *New Jersey* to lob sixteen-inch shells ("about the size of a small sedan") into Communist positions in the surrounding mountains from twenty-five miles away. Marines on the ground cheered each great explosion, but this extreme-range plinking was no substitute for Marine-controlled, Marine-executed air strikes.

When General Thomas complained that the close air support provided his division was unsatisfactory—fully one third of requests never answered, others coming three to seven hours late—an Air Force staff officer replied, "The Marines want more than their share. The 1st Marine Division has to understand that it is just one more division in Korea."

The Fifth Air Force was preoccupied with Operation Strangle, the aerial interdiction of all Communist supply routes in the north, said with certainty to bring the enemy to his knees.

One Marine jet pilot, sent to blow up Chinese truck convoys, encountered

307

THE BATTLE
HISTORY OF THE
US MARINES

instead an enemy camel caravan delivering ammunition to the People's Liberation Army. A few well-aimed shots of 20mm cannon fire ignited the ammo and vaporized the camels, but the incident underscored the futility of applying twentieth-century technology against medieval Asian logistics systems. We would have to relearn this lesson in Vietnam fifteen years later.

Operation Strangle no doubt hurt Chinese and North Korean efforts to rearm their forces for another offensive, but General Thomas reported the North Koreans in the Punchbowl to be as generously supplied with weapons and ammo as any enemy the division ever faced.

The fighting in September 1951 to take those steep ridges by infantry was as costly and bloody as the great battles of the previous year. In four particularly bitter September days, the 1st and 7th Marines suffered 800 casualties in wresting Hill 749 on Kanmubong Ridge from dug-in NKPA forces.

The cost in dead and wounded Marines in the battles for the northern Punchbowl got the attention of Washington policy makers. With peace talks underway and the antiwar climate growing at home, General Van Fleet received orders to knock off the high-intensity battles in the north. Van Fleet had to admit "it was unprofitable to continue this bitter operation." On such a sour note, the war of movement in Korea ended.

The Marines were redeployed 180 miles westward to occupy an enormous stretch of the static Jamestown Line, protecting the historic invasion approach to Seoul and, not coincidentally, overlooking Panmunjom, site of the intermittent peace talks.

Within each Marine breast burns the spirit of the offensive, the hell-for-leather, action-oriented, freewheeling essence of maneuver warfare. They join the Corps *to fight*. Boot Camp focuses that aggressive spunk. Much of the Korean War to date had reinforced such collective élan.

But put a Marine too long in a static defensive position, shackle him with restrictive rules of engagement, fetter him with body counts as "measures of effectiveness," and that finely honed weapon starts to rust. Or grow barnacles.

Such was the case for the 1st Marine Division during their long months occupying static positions along the Jamestown Line. Scuttlebutt rumors of a cease-fire or armistice agreement flew up and down the line every week, yet the dangers, and the killing, continued.

The Marines defended their extended sector of the MLR (the Main Line of Resistance) by occupying a series of outposts on intermediate terrain features in no-man's land. The Leathernecks were stretched thin. Most positions were defended at night by infantry squads, at best a reinforced platoon. Risky business.

The "Outpost War" would prove inordinately costly. Fully 40 percent of Marine casualties occurred during the final fifteen months of the war, the so-called "stalemate" period of the conflict.

The Marines squared off against some 50,000 Chinese in their sector. These particular Chinese were formidable night fighters, diligent diggers, and not at all hesitant to go hand-to-hand against the Marines. The Old Breed had by now heard of Chinese Communist Mao Tse-tung's heralded principles of

guerrilla warfare: "Distract in the west, strike in the east." Marines defending outposts named Yoke, Bunker Hill, Berlin, or the Hook could add two proven Chinese corollaries: "Bombard from the north, ambush in the south."

A typical Chinese night attack involved a terrifyingly accurate cloud-burst of mortar or artillery fire—often as much as one round per second exploding on the outpost—followed by a feint against one sector, the main attack against the opposite side, and a cunning ambush to intercept Marine reinforcements rushing out from the MLR.

Small-unit night-fighting had become the nature of warfare along the Jamestown Line in 1952–1953. The Marines—indeed, most Occidental troops—had much to learn about fighting at night, but during the Outpost War they learned rapidly.

Patrols of some kind left the MLR every night—stealthy reconnaissance sweeps, larger "Cadillac" sorties looking to snatch a prisoner, the occasional big combat patrols, armed to the teeth and looking for a fight. Patrol leaders had no trouble filling their ranks with volunteers. Most Marines would rather go out and fight, even at night in the meandering minefields and stinking rice

As the Korean War became more conservative, Marines continued to refine the tactical use of helicopters to redeploy rein-forcements, resupply outposts, and retrieve casualties.
(National Archives)

MARINES AND HELICOPTERS

The Marines' major contribution to this vicious, unde-clared "Police Action" was the operational use of heli-copters to exercise command and control, transport assault troops and cargo, and evacuate the wounded. Developed to furnish an added dimension to amphibious assault, the choppers proved admirably well suited for tactical support in mountain warfare. While low-capacity choppers had accompanied the Marines to Korea from the git-go, the first true transport helicopters did not see service until September 2, 1951, when Marine Helicopter Squadron 161 arrived in Pusan. The squadron introduced the brand-new Sikorsky HRS–1, which could carry four to six troops, or 1,500 pounds of cargo, or three to four litters. The new choppers immediately proved their worth by fulfilling the

two greatest needs of Marines fighting in the mountains: ammo in, casualties out. Before September's end, HMR–161 made front-page headlines throughout America by conducting the first heliborne landing of a combat unit in history. Under the leadership of Colonel Keith McCutcheon, the chopper pilots quickly estab-lished a reputation as "an on-call tactical tool," responding readily to missions varying from search and rescue to external sling delivery of the faithful 75mm pack howitzers to yet another mountaintop. In between actions the crews refined amphibious "vertical envelopment" from the ships of Task Force 77, hoping in vain for another Inchon.

But to the Marine ground-pounder, the most wondrous benefit of these strange whirlybirds was their quick response to medevac their wounded buddies. Marine helicopters evacuated more than 10,000 casualties in the war, making the survival rate for combat wounds the highest in Marine Corps history. Conceived, developed, and deployed in an astonishingly short span, the Marine transport chopper readily became a cen-

paddies, than die of boredom standing watch along the MLR.

Corporal Martin Russ wrote this honest account of his first night action on patrol in the 1st Marines' sector:

> *I won't deny that I was excited as hell about taking part in the raid. When the bombardment and the shooting started, I was so god-damned fascinated by the idea that people were out there who were trying to kill each other that I wasn't afraid—a stupid ass. Not appalled, fascinated. During the withdrawal, when I saw that people were hurt and that one of them was dead, I became very much afraid.*

In late October, heavy fighting erupted for control of a critical Marine position known as the Hook, a salient at the western end of the division's sector that dominated the Imjin River. The heaviest Chinese attacks struck two outposts, Warsaw and Ronson, defended by Colonel Thomas Moore's 7th Marines.

Chinese artillery and mortars delivered a staggering 15,500 rounds on the semiexposed positions. Hills were lost, then regained. The fighting, much of it at night, was as brutal and costly as any seen at the Pusan Perimeter or Chosin Reservoir.

The threat to the integrity of the MLR was so critical that the JOC for once provided ample close air support during the day. Seventy-two aircraft (sixty-seven of them Marines) circled and swooped, shooting rockets and dropping napalm. It was almost like old times. In the end, the Marines repossessed the Hook, having taken 500 casualties.

An Army historian observed of this fighting, "The Chinese have become as tenacious and earth-seeking as ants." Indeed the PLA forces had dug advanced firing positions and approach trenches close to Warsaw and Ronson for weeks. It was a lesson in patient, covert spadework that the North Vietnamese would soon emulate at Dien Bien Phu and Khe Sanh.

Against such effective siege tactics the Marines' policy of defending undermanned outposts at dangerous distances from the MLR proved flawed. Marine valor and derring-do could not indefinitely withstand the ability of the Chinese to surprise an outpost with smothering fire and overwhelming numbers at the point of attack.

In March 1953, a Communist offensive exploded against the Eighth Army's outposts all along the MLR. Heavy concentrations of Chinese fell upon the right side of the line, in an area manned by the 5th Marines, ten miles northeast of Panmunjom. The attacks were centered on the "Nevada Cities" outposts—Reno, Vegas, and Carson. The PLA 358th Regiment attacked the outposts with great mass, firepower, and velocity, outnumbering the Marine defenders by as much as twenty to one.

Outpost Reno fell first, the Chinese sealing some Marines up in their caves with as much brutal efficiency as the Leathernecks had applied to the Japanese in the Central Pacific islands. The defenders of Vegas and Carson held

on for dear life. Colonel Lew Walt, led his 5th Marines out from the MLR. The Chinese bloodied the reinforcements with ambushes and hellacious mortar fire, but Walt kept the momentum, and the battle raged.

This was a hell of a brawl, four days and nights of desperate, ruthless fighting at extremely close range. Here, with all the chips on the line, the JOC again came through with four fighter squadrons (three USMC) that savaged the Chinese daytime positions in and around the disputed hilltops. Marine and nearby Army artillery units fired support missions around the clock. Yet Lew Walt had to ask for help from the 1st and 7th Marines.

In the end, Outpost Carson held, though only after a vicious round of close combat with knives and bayonets. Vegas, lost, regained, lost again, was finally and convincingly recaptured on the fourth day. But Reno, closest to the original Chinese and 1,600 yards from the MLR, was lost for good.

In the cold calculus of things, the Marines came out ahead, inflicting probably 2,200 casualties against the Chinese regiment at the cost of 1,015 Marines killed, wounded, or captured. A tattered American flag fluttered proudly over smoking, reeking Vegas, but Marines began to question the cost.

"This is the highest damned beachhead in Korea," said one.

Good point. The Marines, no dummies in tactical combat, then abolished their exorbitant system of fortified outposts. The Eighth Army allowed them to reduce the long lines of their sector, permitting a more effective defense in depth. Still, the need for Marines to prowl through no-man's-land at night never diminished.

MAINTAINING BURRS UNDER THE SADDLE

In a little-known adjunct to the main fighting on the Korean Peninsula, the Marines and Navy occupied and defended several strategic islands off both coasts of North Korea throughout 1951–1953. The islands proved ideal bases for commando raids, fire direction centers, and observation posts. U.S. Marines and Korean Marines manned the defenses. Their presence bothered the North Koreans immensely. Many of the islands endured heavy shelling from enemy positions on the mainland. In February 1952, a battalion of North Koreans tried to seize Yang-do, off the east coast, in a flotilla of thirty sampans. The subsequent battle for Yang-do, small in scale but ferocious in nature, stormed throughout the night. In the end, the American and Korean Leathernecks prevailed, driving the invaders back into the sea. It was the only failed amphibious assault experienced by either side in the war.

As the summer of 1953 bled on, the end of the damned war seemed almost palatably close at hand. Yet the Chinese unleashed a series of sharp attacks against the Jamestown Line in order to influence the final boundary.

One of the bloodiest of these occurred against the Marines at terrain features along the MLR known as Boulder City and Hill 119. These were not mere outposts. Loss of these key positions would make the Eighth Army forfeit a huge chunk of territory and part of the Imjin River to the Communists.

No Marine wanted to be the last man to die as the peace negotiators

Although the Marine Corps entered the jet age in 1950 when VMF–311 flew its first Grumman F9F–2 Panther, the Leathernecks retained several Corsair squadrons for close air support roles throughout the Korean War. Here a Marine ground crew loads rockets on an F4U for another air strike.

(U.S. Marine Corps)

waited for the ink to dry on the armistice agreement that hot July, but the Chinese were attacking in enormous waves and the fighting was abruptly as desperate as ever.

The PLA forces suffered 72,000 casualties in carving out substantial pieces along the MLR, but they failed to budge the 1st Marine Division from Boulder City or Hill 119. The successful defense of the positions cost the Marines 1,611 men killed, wounded, or captured.

The Korean War lasted three years, one month, two days. During that time fully 60 percent of the Marine Corps saw action, either with the division, the air wing, the offshore islands, or the ships of Task Force 77. Marine losses were substantial—4,267 killed, 23,744 wounded—more than double the losses of the Marine Brigade in World War I.

Forty-two Marines received the Medal of Honor; twenty-six posthumously. The Marines lost 436 aircraft in action.

The Korean War demonstrated several enduring strengths of the Marines: combat readiness, tactical vision, a certain hard-nosed valor, the ability to transmit their high-spirited élan to foreign marines.

THE RECORD OF MARINE POWs IN KOREA

In general, the performance of Americans of other services held captive by the Communists during the Korean War shocked and disillusioned the American public. Many seemed passive and leaderless, easy marks for sophisticated "brainwashing" tactics. A distressingly large number made propaganda statements, admitting to American use of biological weapons, or other absurdities. Some even opted to remain in North Korea or Red China after the armistice.

The Marine POWs fared much better. Of 221 Marines captured, 194 survived, a rate of 87 percent (the average rate for all U.S. POWs was 62 percent). Marines proved harder to capture than troops of other services. One soldier in every 150 who served with the Army in Korea was captured; for the Marines, it was one in every 570. Many of these were captured with the ill-fated Task Force Drysdale during the Chosin campaign; others from the bloody battles for the outposts in the later years of the war. Twenty Marines escaped from captivity; others tried and failed. Where some POWs behaved brutally toward their fellow Americans, the Marines maintained both their sense of discipline and their adherence to the chain of command. And their smart-ass spirit. Marines in Camp Two celebrated the birthday of the Corps on November 10, 1952, by serving all hands a special cake made from stolen ingredients and topped off with a purloined bottle of rice wine. While one Marine officer succumbed to tortuous interrogation and issued a false statement (for which he was subsequently tried by USMC court-martial), the other Leathernecks kept their honor clean. As a subsequent Senate report concluded: "The United States Marine Corps did not succumb to the pressures exerted upon them by the Communists and did not cooperate or collaborate with the enemy."

Their performance prompted President Truman to sign Public Law 416 in 1952, a landmark statute that defined the Corps as a separate service within the Department of the Navy, sized at a minimum three divisions and three air wings, and awarded primacy in amphibious warfare. The Marines, fully into jet aircraft, transport helicopters, and body armor, now had the legislative legitimacy they had lacked the first 177 years. It was a great Marine victory that does not appear on their battle flag.

The Korean armistice went into effect the night of July 27, 1953. As hundreds of star shells lit up the darkness, a group of Chinese began singing some political chant from their positions near Chogum-ni. In reply, a grizzled Marine NCO cut loose with "From the halls of Mon-te-zum-a . . ." at the top of his lungs, and gave the Corps the last word in Korea.

17: COLD WAR CRUSADES (1953–1967)

I BELIEVE THERE IS A LIGHT AT THE END OF WHAT HAS BEEN A LONG AND LONELY TUNNEL.

President Lyndon Johnson, October 1966

THIS IS FIRST A POLITICAL WAR, SECOND A PSYCHOLOGICAL WAR, AND THIRD A MILITARY WAR.

Lieutenant General Lewis Walt, USMC, February 1967

Vietnam, March 8, 1965. A section of Marine medium tanks rides a Navy LCU from USS *Vancouver* to Red Beach, Da Nang, as the first U.S. ground forces are committed to the defense of South Vietnam. (U.S. Navy)

At first glance, Vietnam might have seemed like a good old-fashioned U.S. Marine drop-in straight out of the Philippines or Nicaragua. A brisk landing into the jungles, chase some bandits, shoot a little, bleed a little, take a little political heat, and home for dinner. But instead of Aguinaldo and Sandino, the Cold War had cooked up the likes of Mao Tse-tung and Ho Chi Minh and Vo Nguyen Giap. Dinner would be late.

Sooner or later the U.S. Marines seemed destined to fight a protracted land war on the Indochinese Peninsula. Indeed, rumors circulated widely among the amphibious ships evacuating the battered 1st Marine Division from Hungnam in 1950 that the next mission for the Old Breed would be to bail out the French in their desperate fight against Viet Minh guerrillas in Vietnam. "At least it ain't cold in Vietnam," exclaimed one frostbitten veteran, repacking his duffel bag.

Not yet. While American foreign policy sought to contain Communist expansion in east Asia, the nation could not afford to fight two wars—even two "Police Actions"—at once. The Korean War would have to be played out first. Meanwhile, the United States bankrolled French efforts to battle Ho Chi Minh's guerrillas to the tune of billions of dollars. Money down a rat hole. The spectacular victory of the Viet Minh over French Legionnaires and paratroopers at Dien Bien Phu in 1954 terminated that policy. Marines could then see the handwriting on the bulkhead.

The first U.S. Marine arrived in Vietnam less than six months after the fall of Dien Bien Phu. Lieutenant Colonel Victor Croizat's main responsibility was to train and inspire the nucleus of a Vietnamese Marine regiment, which would grow in proficiency and lethality into a very good infantry division.

While the U.S. Army necessarily had to devote the post-Korea years to gearing up for a major war with the Soviet Union, the Marines figured they would be fighting Soviet surrogates—Syrians, Cubans, or more likely, a host of faceless, Communist-inspired insurgents trying to topple some Third World democratic regime. Little new here. The Leathernecks of the 1920s–1930s had performed similar missions (minus the Communists) in Haiti, the Dominican Republic, and Nicaragua.

Now the principal focus for the Marines became Southeast Asia—especially Vietnam, Laos, and Cambodia, each threatened by Soviet-supported insurgencies.

Counterinsurgency became in vogue as a political-military art form. Marines studied the recent counterguerrilla campaigns in Malaya and the Philippines, read Bernard Fall's *Street Without Joy*, conducted war games involving the landing of expeditionary forces at a place halfway down the Indochinese coast called Tourane (later: Da Nang), and vied for the coveted thirty-day "OJT" (On the Job Training) assignments as observers to the hard-pressed ARVN (Army of the Republic of Vietnam).

The inauguration of President John F. Kennedy in January 1961 ush-

Riverside village,
South Vietnam
(Charles Waterhouse)

ered in a period of more adventuresome foreign policy. The Marines, ever prideful of their "First to Fight" motto, found themselves whipsawed through a series of pulse-quickening deployments and frustrating recalls.

In 1961 the 1st Marine Brigade sailed from Hawaii for a landing exercise in California, only to find the sun rising in a different direction at daybreak—an overnight crisis instituted by Pathet Lao guerrillas in Laos caused urgent orders for the task force to reverse course. The brigade circled in the Western Pacific for weeks waiting for the command to land somewhere, anywhere, and do something, anything. Nothing. Not yet.

The following year, Brigadier General Ormond Simpson led the 3d Marine Expeditionary Brigade ashore in Thailand, where they deployed north near the Laotian border for four months. And sat on their arms. Again.

Such was the frustrating nature of the Cold War. Marines often landed, but the diplomats and politicians always seemed to be on the beach ahead of them. There would be no Iwo Jimas.

The Cold War was largely a conflict of alarms and alerts, posturing and brinkmanship. Marines would deploy like "storm petrels" to the ends of the earth at the first heightening of international tensions, but many times that was the end in itself. They were a "show of force," or a "forward presence." Lebanon was one of those.

In mid-July 1958, four battalions of Marines landed in Lebanon, uncertain whether they would be opposed by rebels, the Lebanese Army, the Syrians, the Soviets—or all of the above. With some trepidation the Leathernecks in their amphibian tractors chugged toward Red Beach, just below Beirut, their initial objective. Concern gave way to distraction.

Red Beach was "defended" by hundreds of sunbathers, including a goodly number of nubile young women in bikinis. *What the hell?*

The "liberators" pressed on to the capital by fits and starts as the diplomats negotiated every advance. The Marines exchanged light fire with snipers, but soon the situation stabilized, the Lebanese held elections, and the Marines went back to sea.

Helping Lebanon would never again be so inexpensive.

In the long, scratchy seismograph chart of the Cold War, the next major "spike" would stand out—the Cuban Missile Crisis of 1962. If police actions were dull for Marines, a full-scale war of nuclear annihilation wasn't so attractive either.

For an agonizingly tense week the Marines and the entire nation braced themselves for imminent war with the Soviet Union over the discovery of Russian missiles staged in Fidel Castro's Communist Cuba. All U.S. military forces went on full alert.

The Marines reinforced their vulnerable outpost at Guantanamo Bay, Cuba, with a full regiment, deployed the rest of the 2d Marine Division on

317

THE BATTLE
HISTORY OF THE
US MARINES

board amphibious shipping in the Caribbean, and sailed the 11,000-man 5th Marine Expeditionary Brigade through the Panama Canal from California. Tactical aircraft of the 2d Marine Aircraft Wing deployed to advance bases in Florida and Puerto Rico.

Every Marine knew in his heart that the real danger was not fighting Cubans and Soviets in the streets of Havana. The knee-knocking threat was nuclear war, the dark demon that had lurked on the edge of the world's consciousness since Hiroshima. "The pucker factor was intense," said one Marine.

Fortunately for the human race, Soviet Premier Nikita Khrushchev "blinked" and agreed to dismantle his Cuban missiles. The crisis passed.

Cuba's Castro, seemingly bent on exporting revolutionary Marxism in the region, continued to bother the United States. When civil war erupted in the Dominican Republic in 1965, Washington policy makers feared Cuban influence in the sudden vacuum. President Johnson ordered 6,000 Marines ashore to stabilize the situation.

The Marines' first order of business was to evacuate American noncombatants from strife-torn Santo Domingo. Fortunately, the Marine Expeditionary Unit standing by in amphibious ships off the coast included a helicopter squadron. In a scenario that would become almost commonplace for the remainder of the century, a Marine infantry force quietly secured a landing zone—in this case, a former polo field—and Marine helicopters evacuated thousands of civilians to ships offshore.

When the U.S. Embassy came under heavy fire from rebels, more Marines came ashore and began advancing into the capital city.

Snipers hidden in a housing project took their toll on the approaching Marines, who hesitated to return fire without a clear target because of the proximity of native civilians. It made for slow, frustrating going, but eventually those snipers who stayed to fight were discovered and nailed with careful shots by Marine countersniper teams.

When the Marines linked up with Army Airborne forces in the heart of town, the urban fighting petered out. Security troops from the Organization of American States arrived, and the Marines left about as quickly as they had landed, having suffered nine killed and thirty wounded in the sporadic fighting. Not sweet, but short.

While Marine expeditionary units would continue to deploy on board amphibious ships in the Caribbean and Mediterranean throughout the era, the main effort for America's foreign policy—and its Marines—would become South Vietnam. On the usual Cold War scale of conflicts, the Marines' quick deployment to Santo Domingo and efficient urban combat had been significant. But this was 1965. "Nam" would eclipse "DomRep" and every other Marine commitment for the next ten years.

Marines in Vietnam would fight with highest valor and innovation, but

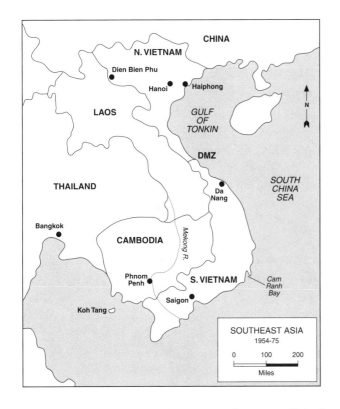

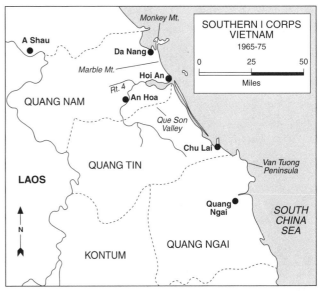

the nation's longest and most political war would yield few tangible benefits in exchange for the sacrifices of its troops. Never was the abiding philosophy of *Semper Fidelis* more severely tested.

Marines first deployed to Vietnam as organized units in 1962. A special radio detachment went to Pleiku, and Colonel Archie Clapp's medium helicopter squadron began "Shu-fly" operations in support of ARVN forces at Soc Trang. Here immediately was the face of the war-to-be: massive use of electronic intelligence combined with tactical mobility provided by transport helicopters.

The Shu-fly outfit soon moved north from Soc Trang to Da Nang. When things became hairier up there, the Marines flew an infantry platoon down from Okinawa to stiffen the ARVN defenders of the strategic airfield. And as conditions continued to degenerate, the Marines deployed a Hawk Missile battalion from Okinawa to 2,000-foot Monkey Mountain, overlooking the airfield and port. Escalation had arrived. Soon it became time to put up or shut up.

By now Congress, with its contrived "Gulf of Tonkin Resolution," had given President Johnson a virtual *carte blanche* to have his way in opposing the Communist campaign to overrun South Vietnam.

On March 8, 1965, Brigadier General Frederick Karch led ashore two battalions of his 9th Marine Expeditionary Brigade at Da Nang, one by air, one by sea. The landings were essentially unopposed—in fact, Karch was embarrassed to be greeted by Vietnamese "flower maidens" who adorned his sweaty neck with tropical garlands.

THE HELICOPTER WAR

No American weapons system—not B–52s and their carpet bombings, or "Puff the Magic Dragon" gunships, or Claymore mines, or the new M–16 rifles—would dominate the Marines' Vietnam War like the helicopter. The ubiquitous chopper proved ideal in providing rapid mobility to counterguerrilla forces, resupplying hard-pressed units "in contact," and evacuating casualties. The Marines began their "Shu-fly" operations in 1962 with the clunky old Sikorsky UH–34Ds. As the war progressed, newer choppers of greater capacity and longer range appeared, the CH–46s Sea Knight medium transports and the huge CH–53 Sea Stallions. The sleek and nimble "Slicks" and "Snakes" also appeared, the UH–1 command and control birds and Cobra gunships. The telltale *whop-whop-whop* of rotor blades became the dominant man-made sound in all of Nam. (No veteran today can hear the similar sound from a traffic helicopter overhead without an immediate and not altogether pleasant flashback.)

The low-flying, slow-speed birds were fair game to every Viet Cong or North Vietnamese foot soldier with a weapon. Marine helicopter crews who survived an entire tour unscathed led charmed lives. Enemy gunfire downed 1,777 helicopters during the first five years of the war; many others returned to base shot to splinters. Yet every Marine "grunt" in the bush knew full well that his fellow Marines flying those birds would risk hell on earth to evacuate him should he become seriously wounded.

(One vivid memory persists in the subconscious of this Marine: a damaged CH–46 laboring back toward An Hoa combat base, dangling a badly shot-up Force Recon team, freshly rescued through some jungle canopy by lowering a cargo net at the end of an impossibly long cable, the survivors holding two desperately wounded buddies onto the net by brute strength. The whole drama—would the bird make it to the airstrip? could the Marines keep their casualties from falling to their deaths?—was played out against a setting sun in front of thousands of breathless spectators, friend and foe, along both sides of that contested valley.

And as a general observation, I've yet to meet a Nam grunt who wouldn't leap to buy a Marine chopper vet a heartfelt drink.)

The Marines had landed—at last!—and true to form, they were the first ground combat forces to deploy to South Vietnam. The infantry battalions immediately deployed among the high ridges surrounding the Da Nang airfield, from which two squadrons of Marine helicopters were already operating around the clock.

The Leathernecks exchanged scattered gunfire with the Viet Cong. The first Marine casualties made headlines.

No one—*no one*—could have predicted that these few casualties were only the vanguard of over 100,000 Marines to be killed or wounded in action in the filthy war that ensued.

The Marine buildup went into high gear. The first Marine fixed-wing squadron, VMFA–531, flew its F4B Phantom II jets into Da Nang in April.

Later that month the 3d Battalion, 4th Marines, debarked into landing craft and proceeded eleven miles up the Perfume River to the ancient capital of Hue, loaded for bear—but relieved and delighted to find the riverbanks lined with cheering natives.

On May 6, 1965, Brigadier General Marion Carl, one of the Cactus Air Force aces from Guadalcanal days, led his 6,000-man 3d Amphibious Brigade ashore to

establish a Leatherneck enclave fifty-seven miles below Da Nang. The place was called Chu Lai, but no one could find it on their maps. Turns out Lieutenant General Victor "Brute" Krulak, now commanding the Fleet Marine Force Pacific, had picked the spot by his own reconnaissance, then named it using the Mandarin Chinese characters for his name.

Chu Lai was initially just a wide stretch in the sandy scrub, dangerously surrounded by high ground. Twenty-five days later the Marines had completed an 8,000-foot expeditionary airfield at Chu Lai, complete with carrier-like catapults and arresting cables, and graceful Marine A–4 Skyhawks were roaring aloft to provide close air support to Marine ground operations.

Other colorful WWII veterans arrived in Vietnam to assume leadership roles: Major General Lewis Walt commanded the newly created III Marine Amphibious Force (III MAF) its first two years of existence. Tarawa veteran Major General Wood Kyle took command of the 3d Marine Division. Brigadier General Keith McCutcheon, so innovative in the development of close air support in the Philippines and helicopter operations in Korea, took command of the 1st Marine Aircraft Wing.

With 16,500 Marines now ashore in Vietnam, General William Westmoreland assigned them the primary responsibility for what he called I Corps Tactical Zone (quickly shortened to "Eye Corps"), the country's five northernmost provinces, stretching from the increasingly contested demilitarized zone ("DMZ") along the 17th Parallel down the narrow waist some 265 miles. The Laotian border marked the west, the South China Sea the east.

Eye Corps was home to 2.6 million Vietnamese, many clustered in the major cities of Quang Tri, Hue, and Da Nang. The government controlled the major population centers, the Viet Cong the countryside, especially at night.

A Marine "Ontos," a thirteen-ton tracked assault vehicle mounting six 106mm recoilless rifles, trundles ashore at Da Nang as part of the second major delivery of U.S. Marine forces by Amphibious Squadron One. (U.S. Marine Corps)

THE BATTLE
HISTORY OF THE
US MARINES

Vietnam was foremost a helicopter war. Marine helicopter squadrons were among the first American armed forces to serve in the embattled country, and among the last to leave. Here a medium helicopter makes a hairy landing in a steep landing zone nine miles northwest of Da Nang in 1965. (U.S. Marine Corps)

Marine F8 Crusaders
pound Viet Cong
positions in Southern I
Corps. The Marines' first
objective was to secure
and defend the vital
airbase at Da Nang,
from which Marine
aircraft flew throughout
the war in support
of ground operations.
(U.S. Marine Corps)

Within weeks Marines were engaging in hot firefights with shadowy men in black pajamas who fired their AK–47 assault rifles and RPG–7 rocket launchers with authority. The Leathernecks invariably prevailed, but always at a cost. At the ninety-day mark after the first landings, the Marines had sustained 209 casualties, including 29 dead.

Then came Operation Starlite, and the war turned another corner.

Starlite began when Marine combat intelligence identified the presence of the 1st VC Regiment assembled in the Van Tuong Peninsula preparing to attack Chu Lai, nine miles north. Colonel Oscar Peatross led his reinforced 7th Marines in a surprise, multipronged assault on August 18.

This time the Viet Cong stayed and fought. The Van Tuong Peninsula constituted their regimental command post, their "home." Caves and spider holes laced the countryside. Many of the small villages were heavily fortified. A

Marine battalion commander described the hamlet of Van Tuong as "encircled with a trench line and double apron [barbed wire] fence. The streets had punji traps for personnel and vehicles, as well as spider traps. . . . There were numerous caves throughout."

Peatross endeavored to land west of the enemy positions and drive the enemy into the sea. This worked well in one sector, when a hundred VC poured out of the tree line onto the beach and attempted to escape by sampans. The destroyer *Orleck* opened up her five-inch guns with relish.

In other sectors the fighting broke down into localized brawls between small units, the VC maximizing their dug-in positions, the Marines grimly scratching them out by fire and maneuver as at Iwo Jima or Okinawa. Viet Cong recoilless rifles knocked out several Marine tanks and riddled the LVTs, but most damage came from mortars and machine guns.

The Marines fought back, calling in artillery, naval gunfire, and close air support in very tight quarters. Marine Phantoms and Skyhawks from Chu Lai flew direct assault missions so close to the end of their takeoff pattern the battle resembled Peleliu. Said one Marine aviator: "Air control was pretty racy. People were congested and the helicopters were being struck and burning. It was a pretty exciting two or three days."

The battle raged six days. General Walt gave Peatross all the support and reinforcements he could handle. In the end the Marines counted 641 dead VC, a huge bag, at the cost of 203 wounded and 45 killed of their own. Two Marines received the Medal of Honor during Operation Starlite: Corporal Robert O'Malley, a squad leader, and Lance Corporal Joe Paul (posthumously), a fire-team leader.

At the time Starlite seemed a significant tactical victory. The Marines had surprised and soundly whipped a main force Viet Cong regiment, inflicting disproportionate fatalities at the rate of fourteen-to-one. The media loved it. The United States, it seemed, could prevail over these Communist guerrillas where the Japanese and French had so badly failed. Dream on.

Never again would a Viet Cong force offer pitched battle against Marine regiments.

The VC would revert to their shadow war, stinging the Marines in a thousand small attacks and ambushes, leaving the bigger engagements for their better-armed brethren, the People's Army of North Vietnam (dubbed by the Americans the "NVA").

Two months after Starlite, a disciplined platoon of Viet Cong sappers in boats attacked the Marine helicopter field at Marble Mountain, south of Da Nang, under a smothering mortar barrage, a mini-amphib assault.

The Marines shook off the barrage to gun down all but six of the attackers, but the survivors caused spectacular destruction to an entire air group's worth of helicopters with Bangalore torpedoes and satchel charges. The fires of burning choppers and exploding ordnance could be seen all over Quang Nam Province.

Physical security for a Vietnamese village's leaders—its chief, teachers, priests, and militia hon-chos—was a powerful local concern in this war. True to Communist objectives, the Viet Cong made no bones about replacing the existing leadership hierarchy of a village with their own "ringers." The VC assassinated 6,000 village officials in this manner during the war. Marine commanders would always ask when moving into a new area: "Where does the village chief sleep at night?" If he retreated to the city at sunset, he in effect forfeited his village to marauding VC. But if he remained in the hamlet, he did so at great risk, often with a price on his head. (South of Da Nang in 1969, the Viet Cong offered big bucks to anyone who could knock off a brash Catholic priest who stayed his ground and protected his walled convent with a Thompson submachine gun.)

Beginning quietly in 1965, and spreading rapidly throughout Eye Corps in subsequent years, was a Marine Corps innovation known as the "Combined Action Platoon." The CAP concept was simple. A handpicked, carefully trained (language, customs, weaponry) Marine rifle squad, with a Navy medical corpsman attached, would be assigned to a village to be integrated with several dozen Popular Forces troops, the much-maligned, barely trained local militia. The Marines would move into the village to stay (sleep, eat, fight), patiently teaching military skills and virtues to the PFs, in exchange for their intelligence about local VC operations. Cultural misunderstandings abounded, but gradually—some said, *miraculously*—the PFs and other villagers accepted the Marine presence, gained confidence, and began producing villages and hamlets that were secure day *and night*. In nocturnal firefights against the VC, some PFs "skied" at first, but most stayed to fight shoulder-to-shoulder with the Leathernecks. In the words of General Brute Krulak: "The Vietnamese knew who the guerrillas were and where they hid; the Marines knew how to kill them." Before long the number of CAPs grew to the size of a full regiment, which made the top

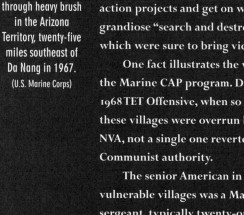

An M–60 machine gun squad from the 7th Marines patrols through heavy brush in the Arizona Territory, twenty-five miles southeast of Da Nang in 1967.
(U.S. Marine Corps)

brass in Saigon uncomfortable. They thought the Marines should stop frittering away their resources in civic action projects and get on with the grandiose "search and destroy" missions which were sure to bring victory.

One fact illustrates the viability of the Marine CAP program. During the 1968 TET Offensive, when so many of these villages were overrun by the VC or NVA, not a single one reverted to Communist authority.

The senior American in each of these vulnerable villages was a Marine sergeant, typically twenty-one years old. Few NCOs in any war, in any service, ever dealt so effectively with so much responsibility with so much on the line. Many voluntarily extended their tours.

Despite its unpopularity at the highest levels, the CAP Program was the major and most successful Marine Corps contribution to the Vietnam War.

A rifleman from the 9th
Marines warily checks a
Vietnamese "hootch" during
Operation Big Horn near
Dong Ha. The Corps had begun
its transition to the 5.56mm
M–16 rifle from the more
accurate but heavier
7.62mm M–14. (U.S. Marine Corps)

This disaster meant more Marines were needed to provide security to the high-tech war machines.

By now the entire 1st Marine Division had transplaced from Camp Pendleton to Vietnam, the Old Breed beginning their third Asian War in twenty years. On their heels arose the 5th Marine Division, reactivated for the first time since V-J Day, and Marines everywhere were stretched thin.

President Johnson didn't help matters when he refused to call up the Reserves. The Marines were infuriated. They had depended on their highly trained Reserves to provide such a wartime expansion, just as they had done so ably in Korea and WWII. Johnson's decision, intended to minimize the political impact of the rapidly growing war, rendered reserve duty meaningless, brought into the Corps reluctant draftees instead of proud, trained reservists, and required each regular Marine to serve multiple one-year tours in combat.

The dirty war was getting a lot dirtier. The Marines had already learned that running the VC to ground would require a massive effort—plus it was all doomed in advance unless they could first gain the trust, and provide for the security, of the people.

The war, the buildup, and the killing continued.

Marine pilots flew hair-raising attack missions over North Vietnam from carriers operating in "Yankee Station" in the South China Sea. Marine artillerists fired millions of rounds of heavy ordnance, sometimes at on-call

targets, others merely "harassing and interdiction fire" at night against enemy assembly areas and access routes. Marines patrolled everywhere, day and night, by foot, helo, LVT, or jeeps. Their engineers probed ceaselessly for mines or booby traps. But they couldn't find them all.

By the end of 1965, the Marines had suffered 454 killed and 2,093 wounded. A year later, with 67,000 Leathernecks deployed in South Vietnam, the casualty totals had quadrupled.

Gradually the focus of combat swung north, toward the DMZ. Increasingly, the enemy was the North Vietnamese Army, crossing the 17th Parallel in division strength, well trained, well armed, and easily supplied via the Ho Chi Minh Trail and its many tributaries.

Heavy NVA artillery sited just north of the border sent volleys of high explosives shrieking down the open corridors against Marine positions at Gio Linh, Con Thien, and "the Rock Pile."

Fighting along "the Z" took on the scale and nature of combat in the Korean War. Operation Hastings mushroomed from a modest probe into a full-scale slugfest involving eleven battalions and direct support from Guam-based B–52 bombers. NVA rockets and heavy mortars were well served and vicious.

Hastings gave way to a series of subsequent battles called Prairie, each with a higher Roman numeral and a higher body count on both sides.

Farther west along the DMZ there was heavy fighting around the godforsaken outpost at Khe Sanh. Nearby Hills 561 and 881 were bitterly contested, finally seized—then lightly outposted as the war shifted elsewhere. No one would deny the NVA were good fighters. By the end of 1967 Marine casualties totaled 5,479 dead and 37,784 wounded. A hell of a war. Only World War II had been costlier—and this one still had plenty of nasty surprises to come.

ABOVE: Thick jungle canopies frequently prevented Marine helicopters from landing to rescue wounded troops. If a man's wounds were not too severe—and enemy fire not too intense— he could be hoisted by cable and horse collar up through the trees to the chopper. Here members of the 4th Marines dispatch their wounded buddy to the unseen guardian angel hovering overhead during Operation Choctaw. (U.S. Marine Corps)

OPPOSITE: A patrol from the 9th Marines proceeds along a streambed in pursuit of North Vietnamese forces west of Cam Lo. Both the Viet Cong and the NVA were adept at planting booby traps and springing ambushes. The assistant patrol leader in the rear of this column is probably about to hiss, "Don't bunch up!" once again. (U.S. Marine Corps)

18: KHE SANH, TET, HUE CITY (1968)

Hue City, February 1968. An M–60 machine gunner from the 5th Marines opens up in close-quarters street fighting. The M–60, designed to be fired either freehand like this or braced with its folding tripod, was an effective assault weapon during the urban battle.

(U.S. Marine Corps)

THIS IS A DECISIVE TIME IN VIETNAM. THE EYES OF
THE NATION AND THE EYES OF THE ENTIRE WORLD—
THE EYES OF ALL HISTORY ITSELF—ARE ON THAT
BRAVE LITTLE BAND OF DEFENDERS WHO HOLD THE
PASS AT KHE SANH.

President Lyndon Johnson, February 19, 1968

The Marines were to decisively, rousingly win their greatest battles near the end in Vietnam. But such was the temper of the times that massive killing of the enemy had ceased to mean much, and the very flames of an immolated foe seemed to some like the pyre of a massively failed American adventure. While the Marines never flinched when the North Vietnamese Army laid siege to their frontier base at Khe Sanh, the perceived threat was enough to panic and rout certain politicians at home, the alternate front.

Few Marines ever held an exposed outpost longer, under more relentless pounding, than India Company of the 3d Battalion, 26th Marines, on Hill 881-South.

The wooded terrain feature, the most tactically critical of the hills overlooking the Marine Corps combat base at Khe Sanh, absorbed persistent North Vietnamese shelling and probing attacks throughout the grueling seventy-seven-day battle for the western DMZ.

Captain William Dabney's Marines would lose half their number defending 881-S but never their pride or willful humor. Each morning they would raise the American flag on a long antenna to the accompaniment of "To the Colors" on a bugle—and the not-too-distant *Chunk! Chunk!* of NVA heavy mortars being fired. By now the Marines knew they had just exactly enough time to finish the ceremony and dive back in their holes before the rounds impacted on the hilltop. Then, immediately after the barrage, the Marines would close their gritty ceremony by slowly waving another flag—a scarlet, tie-dyed T-shirt, the rifle-range symbol for "Maggie's Drawers," indicating the hapless shooter had not only missed the bull's-eye, he'd missed the whole damned target. So, rain or shine, began another day at Khe Sanh. . . .

Emergency medevac, Khe Sanh
(Charles Waterhouse)

Said one Marine officer: "When you're at Khe Sanh, you're not really anywhere. You could lose it, and you really haven't lost a damn thing." Tactically, he was correct; strategically, he was miles off target. In politically charged 1968, the defense of Khe Sanh became a national mania.

For several stomach-churning months the reinforced 26th Marines at Khe Sanh occupied the center ring in what became an international circus of politics and propaganda—an epic siege in the late winter–early spring of 1968 following the North Vietnamese Tet Offensive.

The media made much ado about the parallel between Khe Sanh and Dien Bien Phu. President Johnson became almost obsessed with fear that the Marines would not withstand the siege. "I don't want any damn Dinbinfoos," he repeatedly told General William Westmoreland.

The Marines had more confidence. The French post at Dien Bien Phu had been located in a valley surrounded by towering hills, the undermanned garrison totally isolated, resupply available only by parachute, always tricky.

Khe Sanh, by comparison, occupied a high plateau, and Marines like Captain Dabney's India Company defended even higher ground beyond.

Colonel David Lownds commanded more than 6,000 troops in his reinforced regiment and defended a hard-surface runway suitable for the largest multiengine supply planes. Khe Sanh was also well within range of the U.S. Army's big 175mm guns at Camp Carroll and the Rock Pile. Hundreds of U.S. and Allied attack aircraft and helicopters remained on call in direct support.

Westmoreland identified two compelling reasons to defend Khe Sanh: Provide a killing ground for NVA troops and prevent an NVA flank attack against Dong Ha and Quang Tri City.

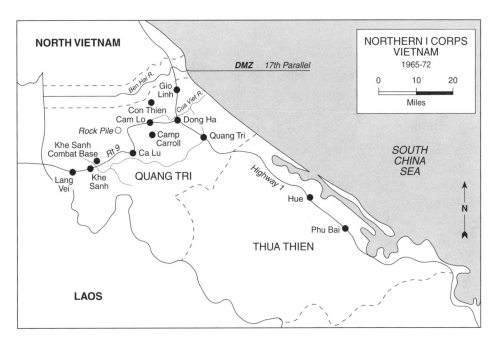

Colonel Lownds, forty-seven, whose two Purple Hearts reflected close combat at Saipan and Iwo Jima, exuded confidence. "Can we hold this place?" he responded to yet another reporter's question. "Hell, yes."

Yet unmistakable evidence of a North Vietnamese buildup near Khe Sanh in January 1968 proved worrisome. The NVA had little difficulty infiltrating down the Ho Chi Minh Trail along the Laotian-Vietnam border, then crossing laterally into the hills above Khe Sanh along what the Marines would call the Santa Fe Trail. NVA long-range artillery—heavy stuff, 130mm and 152mm in caliber—began plastering Khe Sanh from safe havens inside Laos.

When the NVA moved two very good divisions into the high ground above Khe Sanh, then cut the only overland supply road, Westmoreland became convinced that his counterpart in Hanoi, the now-legendary General Vo Nguyen Giap, intended to repeat his 1954 success against the French at Dien Bien Phu against the 26th Marines.

The "Hill Fights" of 1967 above Khe Sanh had been so bitterly contested that the ground still reeked with the sickly sweet smell of decomposing bodies every time a Marine dug a new foxhole. The very trees on Hills 881-South and 861 were so riddled with steel shrapnel that Marine engineers could not safely use their chain saws to cut lumber for bunkers.

Few Marines appreciated their assigned role. It went against their grain as an offensive striking force to sit tethered to a frontier outpost while an NVA force of seven times their number pounded them daily with heavy ordnance and dug siege trenches ever closer to the final protective wire.

On the other hand, in a shadowy war in which the enemy rarely stood and fought, the defense of Khe Sanh at least provided a "target-rich environment" for Marine gunners and their friends in other services. The bomb-scarred hills and valleys around the combat base became the ultimate "free fire zone" of the war. Marines would take maximum joy in its good use.

The 26th Marines inadvertently kicked off the "siege of Khe Sanh" on

RIGHT: The haunted eyes of a Marine exposed to pounding at Con Thien by NVA heavy artillery batteries sited well north of the DMZ. (David Douglas Duncan)

FAR RIGHT: Month after month, those Marines who occupied cantonments along the DMZ endured the most consistently hazardous duty in the Vietnam War. Often, the ubiquitous NVA mortars were deadlier than the more distant field guns or rocket launchers. The strain was tangible. (David Douglas Duncan)

January 20, 1968, when two companies patrolling the saddle between Hills 881-South and 881-North ran into a well-armed NVA battalion. Daylight battles against forces in this strength were uncommon, and the Marines pressed forward aggressively, suffering losses, but maintaining momentum. Captain Dabney was astounded when Colonel Lownds came up on the radio and ordered him to retire to his positions on Hill 881-South before dark.

Dabney did not know that the regiment had picked up an NVA defector, a lieutenant more than willing to reveal the NVA order of battle and attack plans. This was an intelligence gold mine, but there was no time to spare.

The NVA were in the neighborhood in great strength; the initial attacks were planned for that very night. Lownds could ill-afford to have Dabney's company strung out 1,000 yards north of its hill base.

The key features of the Khe Sanh battlefield were these. The combat base encircled the airstrip and overlooked the valley of the Rao Quan River to the north. Downhill from the base on the southern side ran Route 9—east (now closed by the NVA) to Ca Lu and Dong Ha, west to the village of Khe Sanh, the Special Forces Camp of Lang Vei, and the Laotian border.

Four miles northwest of the combat base sat two hills whose peculiar topography dominated the battlefield, 861 on the right, 881-South on the left. The NVA now occupied 881-North in force.

Dabney's patrol had derailed the planned enemy strike against 881-South, but shortly after midnight a battalion of NVA hit Hill 861 and soon a battle royal was underway.

On Hill 861, Marine machine gunners firing their "final protective fires"—interlocking bands of grazing fire along the perimeter—provided a baneful antidote to the sapper attacks. The disciplined gunners cut down swarms of NVA who suddenly emerged full-blown in the flickering light of

flares. But enough of the enemy survived to overrun an entire sector of Hill 861, and the fighting became hand-to-hand and merciless.

The NVA commander rushed reinforcements up the hill to exploit the breakthrough, but the steep slopes soon became bloodied by the Marines' mortar fire—light 60s fired by crews 100 yards away in the perimeter, the larger 81s fired from neighboring Hill 881-South, a thousand yards west.

The Marines on the hilltops, difficult to resupply, had to watch their ammo expenditure. The 81mm crews on 881-South nevertheless fired nearly 700 high-explosive shells that night to slaughter the NVA troops trying to ascend the next hill. At such firing rates, a mortar can glow red hot—dangerous to use. The Marines had to cool the tubes somehow—first by expending their scarce drinking water, then by emptying cans of C-Ration fruit juice, finally by lining up the troops and *urinating* on the tubes. It worked.

Encouraged by this rain of mortar fire which kept the odds even, the Marines of Kilo Company rallied and drove the NVA from their perimeter and back through the wire. Gray dawn revealed an unremarkable "body count" of forty-seven NVA sprawled throughout Hill 861. Two days later the stench of death emanating from the ten-foot-high elephant grass surrounding the base of the hill grew so bad the Marines had to don gas masks.

Victory for the Marines on Hill 861 was gratifying but costly and sobering. The hill outposts seemed more vulnerable than ever. Then, even before sunrise of that long night, the NVA uncorked a tremendous bombardment of Khe Sanh combat base itself, raking the compound with mortars, artillery, and rockets.

One of the first enemy rounds set off the main ammo dump, causing a chain reaction of fires and explosions that would create havoc for the next forty-eight hours and blow up 90 percent of the Marines' supplies. Pallets of artillery rounds detonated at once, creating powerful shock waves. Clouds of tear gas swept the compound, as did deadly bursts of flechettes, the tiny steel darts released from exploding Claymores and 106mm "Beehive" antipersonnel shells.

Throughout all this bedlam, the Marines on the perimeter manned their guns, repelled a good-sized NVA probe, and delivered fire missions in support of the natives defending Khe Sanh village against a heavy attack. By day's end,

NVA SAPPER ATTACKS

Most NVA veterans were good night-fighters, adept at camouflage and stealthy movement. The best of the lot were the *dac cong*, highly trained combat engineers, or sappers. In a typical night attack against the Marine defenses around Khe Sanh, the sappers would advance silently during a pounding mortar barrage, clearing passages through the barbed wire and minefields for the assault troops to follow. The work demanded terrific concentration. The Marines festooned their wire with pie-pan noisemakers, trip-flares, and deadly Claymore mines. The *dac cong* would advance as far as they could by sheer stealth, then blaze the final passage with a flurry of satchel charges and Bangalore torpedoes, hurling rolls of canvas over the final concertina wire—or using their own bodies as springboards for the infantry behind them. An experienced team of sappers could launch such an attack within minutes. The defenders, distracted by the heavy mortar fire, would be astonished to discover scores of NVA suddenly inside the perimeter, running amok. Always hell to pay.

Forward observers from the 26th Marines
endeavor to spot NVA mortar positions from the
Khe Sanh perimeter in 1968. (U.S. Marine Corps)

Colonel Lownds decided to evacuate the village, adding thousands of refugees to his crowded and now extremely hazardous compound.

These developments, widely reported in the media, gave concern to General Westmoreland. He directed Marine Lieutenant General Robert Cushman, now commanding III MAF, to beef up Lownds's garrison immediately.

Cushman deployed the 1st Battalion, 9th Marines, and a light battalion of ARVN Rangers to the combat base, the absolute most Lownds could keep supplied by air. Replacing his lost ammo during the monsoon season was going to be tough enough.

This was the situation in late January 1968 as the Allied forces drifted toward the annual Tet holiday and the usual cease-fire announcement by the Viet Cong: The 26th Marines, now 6,600-men strong, with plenty of shooters and a superabundance of supporting arms within reach, waited expectantly for the main attack to develop. Both Westmoreland and President Johnson were convinced that Khe Sanh would be Vo Nguyen Giap's main effort.

Westmoreland would later insist that the elaborate enemy Tet Offensive that materialized throughout South Vietnam had only been a smokescreen to distract Americans away from the real target, Khe Sanh.

Giap, of course, would forever insist that he had suckered the Americans north, away from the cities, with his thinly veiled threats to create "another Dien Bien Phu." The truth may have resided between both poles, but few could deny that Hanoi had pulled off a master stroke of surprise with their vast offensive of January 30, 1968.

The NVA/Viet Cong Tet Offensive struck simultaneously in the dead of the night and nowhere with such terrifying suddenness as downtown Saigon. Thousands of enemy troops seemed to pop out of thin air.

Some appeared with huge antiaircraft guns they had towed by hand for hundreds of miles, night after night, to place into action around Tan Son Nhut Airfield. A well-rehearsed team of VC sappers broke into the compound of the U.S. Embassy, killing several Americans, including two Marines, before falling to a vicious counterattack. The U.S. ambassador went into hiding.

Hundreds of towns and villages across South Vietnam—in thirty-six of the nation's forty-eight provinces—reported large-scale enemy attacks. Hue seemed to have fallen to a particularly heavy attack. The country was in an uproar.

At Da Nang, enemy forces that had infiltrated close to the air base launched an assault against Eye Corps headquarters. In the free-for-all battle, a combination of Marine MPs, Vietnamese Rangers, and a nearby Combined Action Platoon succeeded in blunting the attack.

The 1st Marine Division was more concerned by reports that the 2d NVA Division had infiltrated the area and was heading for Da Nang.

The division's recon Marines picked up movement in the foothills near An Hoa, investigated warily, and soon reported the entire NVA division streaming northeast toward Da Nang.

Circling south of the city in his helicopter, Lieutenant General Cushman was startled to see 200 NVA advancing in broad daylight. Cushman tracked them from a distance, all the while vectoring two infantry battalions toward an intercept point.

As III MAF honcho, Cushman at that point commanded more troops of more services and nations than any Marine in history. But for a brief moment he was a battalion commander back in Guam, where he had received the Navy Cross. His airborne coordination led to a series of sharp battles that staggered, then reversed, the NVA advance on Da Nang.

Along the coast to the south at Hoi An, ARVN troops under Cushman's command repulsed two vicious enemy attacks in prolonged fighting. Soon combined ground forces of Americans, South Vietnamese, South Koreans, and Australians overcame their shock and methodically threw the Communist troops out of the cities, villages, and hamlets.

Only at Hue did the situation remain in doubt.

Hue was the ancient imperial capital, the cultural center of South Vietnam, seat of a great university, and site of the Citadel, whose immense brick walls and moats had been built in 1802 by the Emperor Gia Long.

Now 3,000 North Vietnamese and Viet Cong troops occupied the city, fortified behind those same brick walls. An enormous Viet Cong flag fluttered from the King's Knight, the Citadel's highest parapet.

The first Marines to reach the scene in a truck convoy from Phu Bai played hell gaining tactical information. The Communists seem to hold the entire city except for two enclaves, the MACV compound south of the Perfume River, and the 1st ARVN Division's command post in the city itself. No one knew how many NVA or VC held the city.

The battle for Hue would run twenty-five bloody days.

A pair of infantry companies from the 1st and 5th Marines, accompanied by a platoon of tanks, tried bravely to retake control on the second day. The small force fought their way to the American compound, re-formed, then battled their way across the main bridge. The Marines were too few, too light to breach the Citadel, and fell back to the MACV compound to await reinforcements.

With American forces all across the land under attack during Tet, there weren't a hell of a lot of infantry units to spare for the recapture of Hue.

Once their force grew to two battalions, the Marines began a street-by-street, house-by-house sweep along the south side of the Perfume River. At the same time, ARVN forces under Lieutenant General Huang Lam began clearing the north side of Hue.

There was great reluctance to turn the full firepower of the Marines against the historic city and its civilian population. The Leathernecks relied principally on direct-fire weapons such as recoilless rifles and tank guns in the attack south of the river.

This was brutal, savage, heartbreaking fighting at point-blank range. Clearing the south bank and destroying two disciplined NVA battalions took a full week and proved costly.

The ARVN troops had it worse. When their attacks on the Citadel fell short, Lieutenant Colonel Robert Thompson's 1st Battalion, 5th Marines, entered Hue from the north by helicopter and landing craft. With U.S. Marines on the left flank, ARVN forces in the center, and South Vietnamese Marines on the right, the attack resumed.

RAPE OF A MAIDEN AUNT

This Leatherneck was one of the first Marines to reach Hue by landing craft up the Perfume River from its mouth on the South China Sea on April 14, 1965. I found the place absolutely charming—the cleanest, liveliest, most interesting city I ever saw in East Asia. I ordered dinner in a fine café, had a Tiger beer with the advisers in the MACV compound, slept under the stars on the riverbank. On Easter Sunday I attended Mass at the enormous old cathedral, self-conscious of my shoulder holster. The place was packed.

Four years later much of the city, including the cathedral, lay in ruins. More tragically, the NVA and Viet Cong had systematically rounded up teachers, students, physicians, and city officials, nearly 3,000 overall, and murdered them. The thriving city had been as violated and traumatized as a brutal rape. I could have done some murdering myself, right then.

NVA resistance was so fierce it still took ten days to close on the Citadel. Gradually, the restrictions on Allied firepower gave way to reality: Parts of Hue would have to be destroyed in order to save it.

There was little that was "surgical" about the ensuing bombardments by aircraft, artillery, and naval gunfire. It was as vicious an urban street fight as the Marines ever experienced—all the horrors of Seoul, Garapan, and Vera Cruz, and more.

On February 22, the southeast wall of the Citadel fell to the Marines. The Leathernecks then stepped aside to let ARVN troops make the final assault on the sacred Imperial Palace.

Before TET–68, Hue was a
pretty city of wide boulevards
and well-kept homes. The
Marines tried at first to
recapture the city using only
small arms, like this lone
rifleman from the 1st
Marines with his M–16,
or direct fire weapons.
The abundance of leaves on
the street in the foreground
reflects the storm of lead
sweeping the trees overhead.
(U.S. Marine Corps)

At dawn on February 24, the flag of South Vietnam flew over the scorched
and shattered Citadel. A week of mopping up followed before the Battle of Hue
was declared over. The protracted fighting had cost the Marines 1,000 casualties; 142 died. The war in the north had gone far past "counterinsurgency."

Tet stunned America.

Despite optimism so recently expressed by the Johnson administration
and top military commanders, the public now realized that the promised end of
the Vietnam War was nowhere in sight. It mattered little that the NVA regulars
and VC guerrillas has been soundly beaten everywhere during the Tet uprising.
What really mattered was how an "almost defeated" enemy had launched simultaneous attacks against 100 South Vietnamese cities, penetrated the U.S. Embassy,
fought the Marines to a virtual standstill in Hue—and still threatened to
overrun the forlorn Marine outpost at Khe Sanh. *What the hell was going on?*

General Westmoreland clung harder to the belief that Tet had been but a
distracting prelude to a major offensive against Khe Sanh and the other U.S.

enclaves along the DMZ. "I desperately need reinforcements," he wired the Chairman of the Joint Chiefs; "Time is of the essence." He got the 27th Marines and a brigade of Army paratroopers from the States.

But the nation's stockpile of conventional ground units was getting thin. And so was the patience of the American people. When Westmoreland asked for an additional 206,000 troops for duty in Vietnam it seemed to be the final straw.

His request came at a time when U.S. combat deaths exceeded 500 a week (in 1965 the weekly death toll had averaged 114) and the latest draft call reached 48,000, the highest since World War II.

Westmoreland also spoke darkly to the JCS about the possibility of using tactical nuclear weapons to help defend the Marines at Khe Sanh.

Within a month the administration began to crumble. Defense Secretary Robert McNamara quit his post. President Johnson replaced General Westmoreland with his deputy, General Creighton Abrams. Then Johnson announced the start of peace talks with Hanoi and removed himself from the 1968 presidential campaign. Tet had unhorsed the whole caboodle. . . .

Ironically, the only major American site not attacked during the Tet uprising was the Khe Sanh combat base.

Colonel Lownds and his Marines went to full alert as soon as the intelligence net lit up with so many attacks to the south and east, but—at Khe Sanh—Tet was conspicuously quiet.

The war came back to the 26th Marines before dawn on the fifth of February.

Electronic sensors strewn among the many approaches to the combat base gave the first warning that night. Lownds and his target intelligence officer blocked off a rectangle along the most likely approach route and tried to preempt the coming attack with a sudden concentration of 500 artillery and mortar shells.

For an hour they thought they had succeeded. Then came the familiar cough of NVA 82mm mortars. Hill 861 was under heavy attack.

Once again the *dac cong* sappers led a surprise assault through the wire, this time overrunning portions of Echo Company, 2/26, rampaging along the perimeter, knocking out Marine machine guns with their deadly rocket-propelled grenade launchers.

Captain Earle Breeding pulled his troops back to secondary positions, ordered them into gas masks, flooded the hilltop with CS tear gas, then counterattacked. The NVA attackers had stopped to scrounge through abandoned Marine foxholes for magazines or souvenirs. It was a fatal delay. Breeding's Marines burst upon them through the stinging gas clouds. Wielding bayonets, knives, rifle butts, and bare fists, the thoroughly enraged Marines left a trail of NVA soldiers lying motionless or writhing in the mud and drove the survivors back into the razor wire.

With daybreak, Captain Dabney's sharpshooting crews on Hill 881-South opened up with 106mm recoilless rifles, fearsome weapons that spoke with great authority on this particular battlefield.

Breeding lost 40 men but counted 109 dead NVA within the perimeter or in the wire. No telling what slaughter Dabney's 106s had wrought on the lower slope—nor what the distant 175s had done with their concentrations in the thick brush beyond.

Two nights later the NVA exacted revenge.

Shortly after midnight they struck the Special Forces camp at Lang Vei, five miles west, using nine Soviet-built PT–76 tanks and assault troops armed with flamethrowers and satchel charges. In thirteen minutes the NVA had overrun the camp; the survivors maintained an intermediate fire from scattered outposts, in dire danger.

Marine artillery at Khe Sanh opened up in support; an hour later the besieged commander called for fire missions directly overhead. The Marines responded with variable-time-fused ordnance, raining steel fragments over the camp. Said the Green Beret radio operator, "We don't know what you're doing, but for God's sake keep it up!"

Colonel Lownds faced an excruciating decision. A relief force hurrying west along Route 9 would slam into a certain ambush. Such was NVA tactical doctrine, and the steep terrain along both sides of the road was ideal ambush country. Avoid the road? In an earlier test, Lownds had dispatched a rifle company to Lang Vei by bushwhacking through the jungle. It had taken nineteen hours.

Lownds also knew his opponent wanted nothing better than to catch a force of Marines outside the wire.

And what to make of the tanks? The NVA had never employed armor before this night. Were these merely the vanguard of a new armored force poised to lunge at the combat base?

Given his primary mission to hold and defend Khe Sanh, Lownds could only set his face, ignore the radio calls for help, and wait for daylight.

His artillery fired throughout the night. At dawn, a helicopter task force of Marines and Special Forces took off from Quang Tri, escorted by attack aircraft, and extracted fifteen Green Berets and several dozen indigenous troops. Their losses had been severe. Everyone figured Khe Sanh would be hit next.

Lownds hated his static role, which forfeited so much initiative to the enemy gradually surrounding him.

A reinforced NVA battalion struck savagely against Hill 64, a low-lying outpost garrisoned by a platoon from the 1st Battalion, 9th Marines. No Soviet tanks, just the superb *dac cong* sappers working their stealthy magic through the wire, accompanied by a terrific pounding of Marine artillery positions within the combat base.

Fifty Marines defended the hillock. By daybreak all but one were killed, wounded, or captured.

Captain Henry Radcliffe, the company commander, led a relief force toward Hill 64 at sunrise.

The NVA remained on the captured ground to fight. Radcliffe orchestrated supporting fires from a dozen different sources during his advance, being wary of the inevitable ambush and extremely careful in pinpointing fire requests to avoid hitting his own casualties among the original garrison on the hill. A curtain of explosions ringed the hill, depriving the NVA commander of resupply or reinforcements.

Then Hank Ratcliffe led a frontal assault and settled the issue on the hilltop. His troops killed 150 NVA, a good morning's work, but Colonel Lownds could not even afford a casualty ratio of three to one. The Marines abandoned the outpost to the enemy, and the circle grew tighter around them.

The North Vietnamese occupied daunting defensive positions within Hue City, including some inside the mammoth walls of the old Citadel. Overcoming them took time, increasingly heavy firepower, and high casualties on the part of both the Americans and the South Vietnamese. Here members of the 5th Marines hustle a wounded buddy out of the line of fire.

(U.S. Marine Corps)

The overloaded chain of command weighed heavily on Colonel Lownds, second-guessing his decisions, micro-managing many of the external supporting arms. President Johnson called many of the shots, as did Generals Westmoreland and Cushman.

One senior officer who represented more of the solution than the problem was Lownds's immediate boss, Major General Rathvon Tompkins, commanding the 3d Marine Division.

Tompkins was no stranger to close combat. As a major at Tarawa, he had volunteered to deliver Red Mike Edson's attack order to the Marines on Green Beach in a six-hour odyssey through Japanese lines. At Saipan he commanded the 29th Marines in their capture of towering Mount Tapotchau.

Tompkins knew the load Lownds was carrying, both tactically and politically. He flew into Khe Sanh each day during the seventy-seven-day siege, under fire in both the coming and the leaving. Like a good blocking back, he gave his colonel a little buffer zone of time and space.

THAT GODDAMNED C–130

Early on in the siege of Khe Sanh, a big C–130 transport coming into the air strip took a hit and crumpled up. But, unfortunately, it didn't crumple up enough. To the delight of the media, it lay there, picturesquely crunched, just off the runway, an absolutely irresistible symbol of the shellacking the Marines were taking here at Khe Sanh. What a background for every inane shot they took of anything else. As the camera angles mounted, the casual evening news viewer at home could be excused for estimating that several hundred aircraft a day were being lost at Khe Sanh. The Marine brass hated that crippled bird.

For most of the 26th Marines hunkered down at Khe Sanh, the chief hazard was not the sudden sapper attack, scary as that might be, but the nigh-round-the-clock shelling of the compound by NVA gunners. The base was hit night and day by nine-foot-long rockets fired from Hill 881-North, heavy artillery shells fired from Laos, and medium mortar rounds fired from the ubiquitous 82mm tubes that closely surrounded the base.

The skinny forest of radio antennae atop Colonel Lownds's command post, an old French bunker, caught the attention of too many NVA forward observers. After his CP had been pinwheeled on two consecutive days, Lownds ordered dummy antennae erected on every structure in the compound, even those sheltering the four-holer toilets. The troops thought this overly generous.

But there was little humor to be found in being blasted with hundreds of incoming rounds day after day, night after night. Despite the protection of bunkers, helmets, and flak jackets, the clouds of whizzing shrapnel too often found human flesh. By the end of the first week of February, one Marine in ten at Khe Sanh had been hit.

Evacuating the critically wounded from Khe Sanh was never easy.

Each day Colonel Lownds had to orchestrate the evacuation of dozens of badly wounded or shell-shocked or acutely ill Marines, as well as the safe delivery of replacements and combat cargo—a staggering 185 tons per day. It

Medevac helicopters
always drew enemy
fire—especially
along the DMZ.
In this photograph,
a wounded Marine
forward observer
and his attending
Navy corpsmen brace
themselves while
NVA machine gun
fire rattles through
the thin sides of
the chopper.
(U.S. Marine Corps)

was a logistical nightmare, exacerbated by two complex factors, enemy fire and bad weather.

Monsoon weather conditions that persisted throughout February jeopardized the critical aerial lifeline between Khe Sanh and the outside world. "February made an old man out of me—it was 'zero/zero' every day," said General Tompkins, referring to the aviators' nemesis: zero ceiling, zero visibility.

Never in any previous campaign had Marine infantrymen been so lavishly supported by aviators of every stripe and service. On any given day, the skies immediately above Khe Sanh resembled a towering thunderhead of jet aircraft, often 35,000 feet high, the pilots patiently flying holding patterns, cycling ever lower in the queue, as Phantoms, Intruders, Sky Hawks, Crusaders, Thunderchiefs, and Super Sabers sequentially delivered their bombs and rockets.

Most overpowering of all were the B–52 Strato-fortresses flying from Thailand, Okinawa, or Guam. Anyone who ever witnessed a B–52 "Arc Light" mission in Nam knew this to be one of the most awesome conventional weapons in the nation's arsenal.

The ground for miles around would shake and quiver. Entire ridgelines would disappear.

Men caught in the killing zone became instant dogmeat. The B–52's knockout punch was so awesome—twenty-seven tons of bombs per plane—and the delivery so unexpected (dropped from above 30,000 feet, out of sight, no sound)—that a combined Arc Light could ruin the day for entire NVA battalions, the psychological shock being almost as deadly as the blast.

The B–52 missions in the highlands around Khe Sanh served to even the playing field for the Marines holding the line.

Not to be outdone, the Leathernecks at Khe Sanh developed what they called "Mini Arc Lights," utilizing their own artillery, the Army's 175mm guns at Camp Carroll, and flights of A–6A Intruders. The Intruders were no slouches in the payload business, packing twenty-eight 500-pound bombs per plane, all delivering a coordinated "time-on-target" concentration of high explosives within a 500-by-1,000-meter killing zone.

No one will ever know for certain how many NVA soldiers died under this rain of sudden doom from the skies. Friendly mountain tribesmen reported seeing huge improvised graveyards in the jungle, as well as stacks of bodies (or parts of bodies—courtesy of Arc Lights) awaiting burial. The stench of this violent death swept across the highlands, further fouling the macabre battlefield.

To their credit, the NVA fighters took all the Allies could dish out and still maintained the pressure on Khe Sanh. Rockets and artillery plastered the combat base relentlessly. On February 23 the base endured the worst shelling of the campaign—1,307 rounds in eight hours.

And now the NVA siege trenches were getting closer, advancing inexorably 200 to 300 meters each night, reaching like deadly fingers toward the prize airstrip. In one sector, a trench line materialized overnight no more than 300 meters away from the perimeter wire. Marines started listening for the unmistakable sounds of tunnels being dug underneath their lines, expecting anything, expecting the worst.

The Marines had been living like rats in a shooting gallery for too long. Correspondent Michael Herr caught the tense mood: "It was never easy to guess the ages of the Marines at Khe Sanh since nothing like youth ever lasted in their faces for very long. It was the eyes. They were always either strained or blazed out or simply blank."

The frustrated Marines yearned too hungrily for another chance to grapple with their nocturnal enemy. During a daylight patrol outside the wire on February 25, an infantry platoon ignored the warnings of its Kit Carson Scout (KCs were converted, jungle-smart, Viet Cong advisers) and allowed itself to be decoyed into a vicious ambush.

True to form, the NVA also ambushed the relief column, and it took Colonel Lownds all day to extract the survivors. The mood in the compound that night was vengeful. Most galling to the Marines, the bodies of twenty-five of their comrades were left on the field, the ultimate sacrilege.

The heaviest NVA thrust against the compound itself occurred on February 29. Believing this to be the long-awaited main attack, Lownds unleashed every weapon in the DMZ.

Even B–52s materialized, delivering a blockbuster series of Arc Lights along the NVA path of advance and retreat. Artillery and tactical airstrikes delivered "Mini Arc Lights" in close with stomach-turning effects. The

The Heartbeat of Khe Sanh

Keeping the Khe Sanh airstrip operational throughout the siege required exceptional teamwork. Marine engineers and Navy SeaBees filled and leveled craters after each heavy bombardment (never easy work: even a dud NVA 152mm shell would penetrate four feet into the ground). Each gunner stood ready to fire counterbattery missions against the array of NVA weapons teeing off against vulnerable U.S. aircraft streaking in and out of the contested corridor.

The most proficient resuppliers were the giant C–130 Hercules, capable of delivering fifteen to eighteen tons per sortie, but they attracted such a hellish fire that their use became problematical (the Grunts called them "mortar magnets"). Much faster on getting the hell in, unloading (a record two minutes in one case), and getting the hell out were the smaller C–123 Providers, though some of these also fell to NVA gunners.

In the end, the main workhorse of the resupply effort proved to be the Marine helicopters of MAG–16 and MAG–36. The choppers were also essential in resupplying the hill outposts. But the risks were grave. NVA gunners bagged at least five Marine helos trying to resupply Hill 881-South.

In response to this threat, Major General Norman Anderson, commanding the 1st Marine Aircraft Wing, brainstormed a means of rapid resupply of the hill redoubts coupled with a lethal escort service. This became the razzle-dazzle "Super Gaggle" tactic, which teamed a dozen A–4 Sky Hawks from Chu Lai with a dozen CH–46 Sea Knight helicopters from Quang Tri, each chopper carrying 4,000 pounds of cargo in external nets. The Sky Hawks would pave the way, first with bombs and napalm, then tear gas, finally smoke. On their heels would appear the laden Sea Knights, scurrying toward the hilltop zones. The Marines on the hills would then cut loose with every weapon on the line against NVA positions. Amid this cacophony the chopper would squat, release the heavy net, hustle the wounded aboard, then pull clear. It was still hazardous work, but the Leathernecks lost only two helicopters during a Super Gaggle. The hill outposts represented 20 percent of the Marines at Khe Sanh. Keeping them resupplied was key to the battle. Said Captain Bill Dabney on shell-torn Hill 881-South, "If it weren't for the Gaggle, most of us probably wouldn't be here today." High praise from probably the most shot-at man at Khe Sanh and its suburbs.

---

riflemen complained of not having any targets left to shoot after the big guns got through blasting the attackers. There was an abiding sense of having faced and crushed a major challenge.

The siege of Khe Sanh would run its bloody course for several more weeks. Enemy gunners would continue shelling the compound; Marines would die; helicopters would fall spinning from the sky; jets would cartwheel in flames into hillsides; but there would be no more large-scale ground attacks.

March brought an end to the monsoons, clearer observation of NVA movements (binoculars and spotting scopes by day, observation devices and "Starlite Scopes" by night), and even more responsive air support. Ground sensors and aerial observers indicated a sharp decline in enemy activity outside the Khe Sanh perimeter. Intelligence reports suggested that NVA strength had fallen below 6,000 men. In relative terms, the pressure on the base began to ease.

With General Tompkins's permission, Colonel Lownds began dispatching combat patrols well beyond the perimeter, looking for a fight.

In the most intense of these local battles, the Marines of Bravo Company exacted revenge for the earlier ambush and mauling of their platoon. Taking advantage of a

heavy fog bank, and under cover of a well-executed "rolling box" of supporting fires, the Marines surprised the NVA forces in their trenches, scorched them with flamethrowers, buried them alive with satchel charges, and shot down more than a hundred.

The North Vietnamese got another shock on March 17. A sudden barrage of artillery shells from the combat base released a strange green smoke upon the hills. *Poison gas?* Hardly. It was St. Patrick's Day. Lieutenant Colonel John Hennelly, commanding Khe Sanh's Marine artillery battalion, had decided to confound the enemy by expending his excess green smoke shells. "Top of the morning to ye, Mister Charles!"

Despite the easing of tensions by those most under the gun, the nation hung breathlessly throughout March on news that a relief expedition, Operation Pegasus, was being formed to save the besieged garrison.

The 26th Marines got a chuckle out of this. While it had been vexing to hunker and maintain a static defense at Khe Sanh, they believed two facts to be axiomatic. As long as aerial resupply operations worked they could hold the combat base and the hill outposts indefinitely. Conversely, should push ever come to shove, they had the muscle and the manpower to fight their own way out to the sea. The 1st Marine Division, after all, had faced greater odds and much more difficult weather in doing the same in the Chosin Reservoir campaign. Pegasus? Propaganda.

Although the relief force included Marines, the main element would be the Army's 1st Air Cavalry Division, and General Cushman insisted that the word "rescue" not be used in any context of Pegasus media briefings.

Operation Pegasus began on April 1 with a westward advance along Route 9 by the 1st Marines and 3 ARVN battalions. At the same time, the 1st Air Cavalry Division, joined by an ARVN airborne battalion, leapfrogged toward Khe Sanh. Lownds dispatched a battalion eastward toward Ca Lu.

By April 8 the 1st Air Cav troops had reached Khe Sanh. Reporters seeking a dramatic reunion between the siege-breakers and the recently besieged were disappointed. No bagpipes or bugles played. The Marines were mainly interested in what the soldiers had to eat. The GIs tried not to wrinkle their noses at the stench of the place and the raggedy-ass defenders.

There remained one piece of unfinished business at Khe Sanh. NVA rocket troops and machine gunners still occupied Hill 881-North, from which they had inflicted a great deal of pain and misery against the Marines within the combat base. Now came payback time.

On Easter Sunday, April 14, the seventy-seven-day siege of Khe Sanh ended exactly where it began—in the contested saddle between the two critical peaks.

The 3d Battalion, 26th Marines, swarmed up the steep slope under a stunning concentration of indirect and direct supporting fire. The NVA troops had been burrowing into this mountain for months; abruptly many were sealed up in their caves and bunkers for eternity. Those who struggled clear

Once again in this war, Marine ground units in contact with the enemy received premier close air support from their Leatherneck brethren in the air wings. Here a McDonnell F4B Phantom from Marine Fighter-Attack Squadron 323 (VMFA–323) roars aloft with a full ordnance load. (U.S. Marine Corps)

had no time to mount a coherent defense. Wild-eyed Marines were on them with thrusting bayonets. Cold steel wrapped up the fighting.

A Marine shinnied up a shell-shorn tree and tied on a huge American flag. Marines watching intently from every hill and bunker in the highlands cheered.

Subsequent news that the Khe Sanh combat base would be abandoned shocked the nation but surprised few Marines.

General Cushman wanted to graduate to a war of high mobility throughout Eye Corps, and he finally had enough forces to undertake this sea change. No more risking a regiment of Marines, restricted to a static defense while squarely in the crosshairs of a numerous and well-armed foe.

The Marines shipped out all material of value, destroyed the rest, and got ready to leave. Many paused to take a last look around the familiar landscape. The wooded highlands above Khe Sanh had once been breathtakingly beautiful. Now, as General Tompkins surveyed the scene, "the place was absolutely denuded. Everything was gone. Pockmarked and ruined and burnt . . . like the surface of the moon."

Defending Khe Sanh so resolutely cost the Marines 205 dead and 1,668 wounded. Losses among the ARVN, other Allies, and the air crews spiked the figures somewhat higher. But NVA deaths in this meat grinder easily totaled 10,000. They may have suffered 15,000 dead. The disproportionate figures beg the question, "Who was besieging whom?"

"Although the NVA attack was real enough," concluded historian Allan Millett, "Khe Sanh came no closer to being a Dien Bien Phu than Iwo Jima was to a Wake Island."

The enlisted Marines who fought and won at Khe Sanh left a special legacy. One anonymous Leatherneck scrawled this message on a cardboard C-Ration carton: "Life has a special flavor to those who fight for it that the sheltered never know." In a year of excruciating national despair, in the red-brown mud of this remote outpost, one small flame of duty, honor, and country flickered bravely in the spring rain.

19: LIMITED WAR, VIOLENT PEACE

(1969-1990)

WHEN WELL LED, THE AMERICAN MARINE
WILL MARCH DOWN THE BARREL OF AN ENEMY
RIFLE FOR YOU. IT CONTINUALLY HAS AMAZED
ME OVER THE YEARS JUST HOW GOOD THE
INDIVIDUAL MARINE COULD BE. AND THAT
IS SOMETHING THAT OUR COUNTRY CAN
CERTAINLY BE PROUD OF . . .

Captain Paul Goodwin, USMC (CO, K/3/3, 1969) in Otto Lehrack,
No Shining Armor: The Marines at War in Vietnam

For the Marines, Vietnam was one damned patrol after another. Few resulted in large-scale engagements with the enemy. Most encountered booby traps, mines, or snipers. These members of the 5th Marines return from a stressful sweep of Go Noi Island, twenty miles south of Da Nang, in 1970.
(U.S. Marine Corps)

Tactical successes against the United States Marines have come only to enemy commanders who figured out that the Leathernecks were at their best when you were coming at them toe-to-toe, presenting a clear-cut, kill-or-be-killed target. And that you did only a little better digging in, because they'd never stop coming at you with their hallowed blind, blast, and burn tactics. It was only when you appeared, ambushed, melted, sniped, mined, shelled, bushwhacked, moved, and appeared again—over a protracted period—that you could hope to hold them off long enough to win a political war.

The Marines wound up fighting two wars in Vietnam. One was the virtually unrestricted slugging match against heavily armed NVA divisions in the north along the DMZ. The other remained principally a counterinsurgency operation against Viet Cong and other NVA forces in the villages and rice paddies of Southern I Corps, an area best described as "the Rocket Belt of Da Nang."

A Marine could get himself killed just as quickly in either region.

The DMZ war featured heavy pounding by NVA artillery, rocket, and mortar crews against the 3d Marine Division. Around Da Nang, the 1st Marine Division experienced less shelling, but a much higher dosage of mines, booby traps, and ambushes. Throughout the war, half of all Marine combat casualties south of Da Nang came from these "silent" weapons and tactics.

350

Marines returning to Da Nang and Quang Nam Province for their second combat tours were appalled to see the wreckage of their earlier campaigns still scattered over the pockmarked landscape. Demolished bunkers, burned-out LVTs, and wrecked trucks marked long-ago ambushes and firefights.

Walking wounded, Vietnam, 1969.
(Charles Waterhouse)

Route 4 west of Hill 165 and Charlie Ridge remained a virtual "Trail of Tears." Blown-up tanks, LVTs, and dump trucks—even the crashed remains of spotter planes—marked the right-of-way like some grotesque chamber of horrors. And damned if there weren't refugee families now living in some of the hulks. "Home is where you dig it," applied to the refugees as much as to the Grunts.

Booby traps abounded in Quang Nam Province. Some were simple: an almost-invisible trip-wire leading to an unpinned grenade stuffed in a discarded soft-drink can alongside a trail. Others were more complex and deadlier, often using rearmed American ordnance.

Marine Lieutenant Lewis B. Puller, Jr., stepped on a booby-trapped 155mm artillery shell during a firefight near Viem Dong village in mid–1968. News that the legendary Chesty Puller's son had been blown up crackled through every tactical radio in the bush that night.

The first report said he had died. Next came word that he was still alive but had lost both legs, his left hand, and the thumb and finger of his right hand. "My God, which was worse?"

Marines wept openly, as much for the luckless lieutenant as for Chesty, their universal patron saint.

General Lew Walt, a consummate combat veteran in his own right, had grimly observed as early as 1966 that, "Fighting the guerrilla is not the easy part of the war. Half my casualties were from guerrillas, and these were the nasty kind of casualties—the dirty war." Now assistant commandant of the Corps, Walt undertook the painful duty of notifying his friend and former commander Chesty Puller that his son had been most grievously wounded.

Booby traps were bad; mines were worse. Bigger, more ubiquitous. Some detonated on contact. Others were "command detonated" by some watchful VC with a world of patience and an actuator.

The Marines hungered for combat action against real, flesh-and-blood enemies. The finely honed battle ax needed something to hew and hack. Pacification, the CAP Program, "Golden Fleece" rice-harvest protection duties, "County Fair" cordon-and-search operations—all essential counterinsurgency stuff—lacked the viscerally rewarding, old-fashioned firefight. One key to finding combat, it seemed, was to find the Viet Cong base camps and staging areas.

One major site was Go Noi Island, below Hoi An, east of Dodge City. Formerly the center of Vietnam's silkworm and mulberry industries, the scrubby island was honeycombed with tunnels and caves of the Viet Cong. Tired of cat and mouse games, the 1st Marine Division launched Operation

INCIDENT AT LIBERTY BRIDGE

Finding Viet Cong soldiers to fight required exhaustive patrolling. Quang Nam's many rivers and rice paddies limited the routes available to long-range combat patrols to heavily traveled roads and bridges.

Vietnam was a foot soldier's war. And a helicopter war. But it was also a war of ground tactical mobility, which for the Marines meant LVTs (amtracs), now in their fifth generation from the Tarawa prototypes. The LVTP–5 was superb in high surf—but overweight, undergunned, and downright dangerous ashore. The chief hazard came from the vehicle's deck-mounted fuel cells filled with 456 gallons of gasoline. Safe enough from direct-fire RPGs, but fatally vulnerable to VC shaped-charge antitank mines. Easily 90 percent of the 300 LVTs lost by the Marines in combat in this war resulted from enemy mines. Every penetration of the fuel cells ignited a crowd-killing fireball.

Here's a typical scenario, etched with acid in this Marine's memory. An armored patrol of tanks and LVTs approaches Liberty Bridge bound for An Hoa with an infantry company embarked. The troops, well aware of the danger, all ride topside on their LVTs. The column proceeds down Route 1, the old "Street Without Joy," then turns west on Route 4, both roads swept every morning by mine-clearing engineers but always susceptible to some VC stuffing a fresh mine in a culvert after the sweep.

There are people everywhere—these are their main roads, too. You watch their hands; you watch their eyes. Most never look at the Marines. One does. An ancient papa-san, squatting on a paddy dike not far away, stares impassively at the column, conical straw hat shading his face, hands tucked into his sleeves. The lead tank passes. Next comes your LVT, covered with twenty-five Grunts. A slight movement from the papa-san. Hands appear, touching two electric wires together. *Wham!* The thirty-four-ton vehicle explodes, lurches into the air, tossing Grunts everywhere, begins burning. In an instant a film of raw gasoline covers every man. In another instant all will be on fire. In rage you swing the machine gun toward the papa-san. Long gone. Your driver, killed instantly by the blast, slumps forward against the vision blocks, the blazing vehicle still rolling mindlessly toward the ditch. Then you tumble out of your turret as the gasoline vapors explode and the real inferno begins. The roadside is utter chaos: screaming, burning Marines and civilians. As hearty souls come running up the ditch to help, someone steps on an antipersonnel mine, ingeniously planted to create even greater horrors. Chaos compounded.

Swarms of medevac choppers come, bless them, but you can hear the screams of the burn victims above the roar of the engines. You'll always hear those screams. Always. Those Marines who live—if enduring third-degree burns is "living"—will be evacuated to stateside burn trauma centers. The stricken vehicle will burn for forty-eight hours, melting the steel hatch covers, warping the hull. No one will ever catch the VC papa-san. Without firing a shot, the enemy has knocked the equivalent of a Marine rifle platoon out of the war.

The rest of the convoy, badly shaken, lurches across the bridge toward An Hoa.

Pipestone Canyon, brought in "Rome Plows" (enormous bulldozers) of the Army Engineers, dug up the whole damned island, and literally turned it into a parking lot. The VC simply migrated west into "Dodge City" territory. A strange war.

For those 1st Marine Division troops hankering for more conventional warfare, there was always Arizona Territory, the rolling wasteland below Charlie Ridge and west of An Hoa. "The Arizona" became a boxing ring for Marine infantry battalions and NVA regiments in the latter years of the war.

Elements of the 9th Marines approach the NVA complex on Tiger Mountain near the Laotian border during Operation Dewey Canyon in 1969. (U.S. Marine Corps)

Here, for example, Lieutenant Colonel William Riley's 1st Battalion, 5th Marines, spent a violent six weeks in mid–1969 trading body punches with the 90th NVA Regiment. Riley's Marines, well supported each day by low-flying A–4 Sky Hawks from Chu Lai, and around the clock by 155mm self-propelled guns at An Hoa, engaged the NVA in full-scale firefights, maintained contact throughout the deployment, sustaining moderate casualties, yet inflicting twelve times as many on their opponent. War as it should be.

In between these pitched battles, Recon Marines kept the pressure on NVA forces in Arizona Territory and the adjacent Que Son Mountains using "Sting Ray" operations. Six-man teams, inserted stealthily, established observation posts along suspected NVA approach routes, ready to direct interdiction missions by Marine air, artillery, or heliborne reaction forces. The NVA, never ones to believe in coincidences, began hunting the Sting Rays.

Extracting a compromised Sting Ray team was dangerous, nerve-wracking work. The NVA in this region had plenty of 12.7mm antiaircraft machine gunners ready to hose down rescue choppers. Mountainous terrain and foul weather added to the hazards.

Such conditions in November 1970 took the life of Lieutenant Colonel William Leftwich, commanding the 1st Reconnaissance Battalion. Leftwich voluntarily accompanied a CH–46 on an emergency mission to extract one of his teams in the Que Sons. The weather was awful, the terrain extremely rugged, but they managed to snake the entire team out of the jungle by harnesses attached to a 120-foot nylon rope. Then their luck soured. The bird crashed in the mountains, killing all fifteen men, including those on the rig. Few Marines ever combined more valor, vision, and intellect than Bill Leftwich. Marines everywhere mourned his death. Many believed he had been on track to become the first Marine Chairman of the Joint Chiefs of Staff.

The 3d Marine Division's war along the DMZ did not end with the razing of Khe Sanh. Major General Raymond Davis, veteran of Peleliu and Chosin Reservoir, now commanded the division, and he untethered his units from their static combat bases for a series of high-mobility strikes into the western mountains. Davis, trained by Chesty Puller in peace and war, applied Puller's hard-hitting tactics from long-ago Nicaragua, using helicopters in place of pack mules. "We were really pushing the lessons I learned from Chesty to another level," said Davis of Operation Dewey Canyon, the most innovative and successful of these campaigns.

Colonel Robert Barrow led his 9th Marines (called by Davis "my Mountain Regiment") into the Da Krong Valley of western Quang Tri Province on January 22, 1969, to launch Dewey Canyon.

The jumble of mountains rising to the Laotian border was virgin territory for the Marines. Although occupied by several NVA regiments, the region's military attractiveness stemmed from its elaborate system of logistic

staging bases along infiltration routes leading from the Ho Chi Minh Trail toward Hue and the A Shau Valley. The place bristled with NVA heavy antiaircraft artillery ("a tip-off that they were protecting something," said Barrow).

Deploying a regiment so far from its combat base and relying totally on helicopters for tactical mobility and logistic support during the final weeks of the northwest monsoon was risky. Barrow did it in stages, reversing the usual Marine deployment sequence of infantry first, artillery second.

Barrow first seized two remote, dominant hilltops with heliborne light security forces and plenty of strong-armed troops with axes and chain saws. In short order, trees felled, brush cleared, the choppers returned with 105mm and 155mm howitzer batteries. Almost overnight, two heavily armed fire support bases ("Razor" and "Cunningham") bloomed deep in enemy-held territory, extending Marine artillery range fans all the way to the border.

Then came the three infantry battalions of the 9th Marines, and Barrow dispatched them west and south, advancing across sheer cliffs and through triple-canopied jungles, the roughest terrain the Leathernecks had yet endured in Vietnam.

One rifle company ran into an NVA ambush, flanked it, and drove the enemy off in savage fighting. But it was a hollow victory for Captain Daniel Hitzelberger. With darkness coming, he had eighteen wounded Marines, and he was miles from a suitable helo-landing zone.

"At this time the stretcher cases were moving up and down slopes in excess of 70 degrees," Hitzelberger said. "We had to use eight, and at times ten men to carry a stretcher, and it would take us over thirty minutes to move one stretcher over one bad area." Getting out of this wilderness took Hitzelberger forty-eight exhausting hours.

Monsoon weather threatened to close down Dewey Canyon, producing one eleven-day stretch of "zero/zero" flying conditions. Barrow pulled in his horns a bit, but kept the pressure on the NVA. Davis kept the resupply choppers on ten-minute strip alert. Any combination of a brief "hole" over the airfield and the distant landing zone thus permitted a quick liftoff.

The Leathernecks scaled and captured towering Tiger Mountain, uncovering a massive NVA headquarters and service facility carved out of solid rock. The Marines also captured several Russian-made 122mm artillery pieces, weapons whose fourteen-mile range and powerful punch had hammered the advancing troops all week.

There were other pleasant discoveries. As Gunnery Sergeant Russell Latona walked warily along a mountain trail, he kicked something unnatural: "Sticking out of a bomb crater I saw the footpad of a mortar bipod." Latona dug it out and found a bonanza, a subterranean NVA armory that yielded a thousand weapons, including recoilless rifles and AA machine guns.

The NVA did not willingly give up their invaluable stockpiles. In a day-long battle on February 22 near Lang Ha, Lieutenant Wesley Fox's Alfa Company fought

357

at close quarters against a reinforced, dug-in NVA company. So closely were the antagonists locked together that Fox could not call in supporting air or artillery.

Painfully wounded three separate times, Fox somehow retained limited mobility and acute presence of mind. His Marines eventually swept the field with the weapons at hand—rifles, machine guns, 60mm mortars. The sustained, point-blank fighting cost Fox eighty-three casualties, including eleven Marines killed. More than a hundred dead NVA littered the underbrush. Fox received the Medal of Honor for this remote battle.

The 9th Marines now moved up to the forbidden border and observed heavy NVA military traffic along Route 922 inside Laos. Nineteen years earlier, Barrow had stood on his captured dike in downtown Yongdong-po free to shoot any North Korean vehicle he could see. He knew this war was different, but he also knew his mission. "Interdiction of the road was clearly essential," he said. "Efforts by B–52 Arc Light strikes . . . had been to no avail." The Marines, far removed from their base, struggling to sustain themselves with what they could carry on their backs, were fighting one-handed.

Barrow asked permission to extend his combat operations into Laos to cut Route 922. In closing, he added one sentence which seemed to capture the essence of this limited war: "My forces should not be here if ground interdiction of Route 922 not authorized."

Ray Davis agreed. So did Army Lieutenant General Richard Stilwell, commanding 24th Corps, and General Creighton Abrams. As the U.S. ambassador to Laos waffled, Abrams gave the green light.

Captain David Winecoff then had the pleasure of leading Hotel Company across the border, establishing a night ambush along Route 922, and blowing away an NVA military convoy with Claymore mines and well-aimed rifle fire. Then they boogied back into Vietnam. A tiny blow, perhaps, in this protracted war of fits and starts, *but my God it felt good!*

Barrow fought his way into the high border country, then fought his way out. Operation Dewey Canyon, seven weeks long, dealt heavy casualties to both sides: 130 Marines killed, 920 wounded; 1,617 NVA killed. The Marines captured enough weapons and equipment to outfit an entire NVA division.

But just when the Marines were getting good at high-mobility operations, the war began to unwind. The 9th Marines would in fact be the first to leave; before the end of 1969 the entire 3d Marine Division was gone.

The buzzword became Vietnamization—letting the ARVN fight its own battles. With peace talks underway in Paris, troop withdrawals occurring steadily, and the American public seemingly willing to forget the whole affair, the spark was gone.

Marines continued to fight and risk, but no Leatherneck wanted the distinction of coming home in the final body bag of this misbegotten war.

In the spring of 1971 the last combat elements of the 1st Marine Division and the 1st Wing departed Vietnam, closing the long chapter. Only 500 Marines

remained, advisers to the South Vietnamese Marine Division. Fittingly, some of these men participated in the last good fight.

The North Vietnamese chose Easter of 1972 for their long-expected offensive to overwhelm the south. No guerrilla war here. No U.S. Marine combat unit in front of them. The NVA swarmed across the borders with tanks and heavy artillery, driving a wedge of terrified refugees before them.

But the Vietnamese Marines and their Leatherneck advisers hung tough. At Dong Ha, Captain John Ripley single-handedly throttled the advance of 30,000 NVA troops and 200 tanks by blowing the bridge over the Cua Viet River at extreme personal risk. Exposed to direct fire for three hours, Ripley made repeated trips to the center of the bridge, handwalking the lower beams, to rig 500 pounds of explosives, crimping detonators with his teeth.

Exhausted, Ripley thought he had failed. The electrical connections produced no spark. At the last minute the backup time fuses kicked in. The explosion flattened troops and refugees, dropped a 100-foot span of the bridge into the river, and set the rest of the structure ablaze. Ripley's brigade headquarters to the south radioed: "We can see the smoke from here—what the hell did you do, nuke it?" No Marine's Navy Cross was ever more dearly won.

Stumped by this unexpected setback, and hammered by U.S. ships and aircraft, the NVA offensive petered out. In Hanoi, the Politburo fired the great General Giap for this fiasco.

The body armor worn by the Marines throughout the Vietnam War saved many lives, but it was hot as hell to wear—along with field pack, gas mask, canteens, and weapon. These exhausted members of the 26th Marines seek relief in a stream after a long patrol beyond Hill 190 northwest of Da Nang.
(U.S. Marine Corps)

359

But in the end Ripley's heroism and the steadfastness of the RVN Marines served only to buy time for war-weary, polarized South Vietnam. Three years later the NVA came back in even greater force, and this time there were no U.S. Marines left at all—no advisers, gunships, attack planes.

Cambodia fell first, then Vietnam. In both Phnom Penh and Saigon, Marines executed complicated mass evacuations of thousands of Americans and endangered nationals by helicopters from amphibious ships of the Seventh Fleet.

In Saigon, Master Sergeant Juan Valdez, senior NCO in charge of the Embassy Marines, was the last man to board the final helicopter that chaotic morning, April 30, 1975. In a plain brown bag he grimly carried the American flag. The antithesis of Iwo. But it was over.

Vietnam was the longest war in U.S. history. In overall terms, it was also the costliest for the U.S. Marines. A total of 13,067 Marines were killed in action or died of wounds; 88,633 Marines were wounded.

Although the number of dead was less, the combined Leatherneck casualties exceeded those of World War II.

Thirty-eight Marines were captured and eventually released; eight died in captivity. Forty-nine Marines are still missing in action.

The Marines lost 252 helicopters and 173 fixed-wing aircraft in combat.

In 1968, at the peak of the fighting in Vietnam, III MAF counted 85,755 Marines on its rolls, a greater number than those who fought at Iwo Jima or Okinawa. Nearly 800,000 Marines served in the Corps during 1965–1972.

The Vietnam War was frustrating, corrosive, maddening—but not without redemptive valor. Otto Lehrack in *No Shining Armor* quoted one of his company commanders in the 3d Marines, Captain Raymond Findlay, who applied this philosophical perspective: "It probably wasn't conducted the way it should have been conducted, but hell, if there was a perfect war, you wouldn't need a Marine Corps."

Historian Robert Moskin contributed a fitting epitaph: "Although Marines made up only one-tenth of all U.S. forces that served in Vietnam, one in every four names carved in the Vietnam Memorial in Washington, D.C. is that of a United States Marine."

The Vietnam War left a long festering scar on the soul of America's military forces that took most of two decades to heal. The Marines suffered just as much in the transition, but got well by going back to the basics.

"We are pulling our heads out of the jungle and getting back into the amphibious business," announced new Commandant General Robert Cushman in 1972.

Getting away from the "second land army" focus and returning to their naval roots was how the Marines had reinvented themselves following World War I. The Marines set out to reestablish themselves as the world's premier amphibious and expeditionary force.

First came the need to purify their ranks, to reassert the high standards of discipline and accountability that had distinguished Marines since the days of Archibald Henderson.

Two tough-nosed Commandants would bridge this gap during 1975-1983—combat veterans Louis Wilson and Robert Barrow. Both men emphasized quality over quantity in recruiting and retention standards. The new Marine recruiting slogans of the 1970s—"We Never Promised You a Rose Garden" and "We're Looking for a Few Good Men"—stood out in startling contrast in the permissive social environment.

The "October War" in 1973 between Israel and her hostile Arab neighbors was the world's first "high-tech" war. In addition to raising U.S.-Soviet tensions to the highest level since the Cuban Missile Crisis, the war provided an eye-opener about the vulnerability of armor and air forces in the modern battlefield. Within three weeks the Mideast deserts were littered with 1,500 destroyed tanks and 500 downed aircraft.

The Marines who deployed to the eastern Mediterranean in event of a wider war—the 4,400-man 4th Marine Brigade—read the tea leaves, considered their own thin stocks of missiles and sparse tactical mobility, and frowned collectively.

Developing and acquiring enhanced firepower and mobility for Marine combat units would take a priority effort over the next dozen years.

In the meantime, the Marines continued to respond to short-fused missions that reflected much of the undesirable baggage of the past war—top-level political micro-management and obsessive fear of failure, flawed intelligence, blind insistence on jointness.

When Cambodian rebels seized the American merchant ship *Mayaguez* in 1975, a joint force of Marines, Navy, and Air Force made a valiant effort to recover the ship and crew by force.

Things worked well at first. Marines embarked on the destroyer escort *Holt*, formed an eighteenth-century boarding party, and manned the rails as the ship came alongside *Mayaguez*. The boarders swarmed over the merchant ship. She was empty. Unknown to any Americans on the scene, the Cambodians had released the crew; even now they were approaching in a small boat.

Meanwhile a company of 179 Marines had landed by Air Force helicopters on Koh Tang Island in the belief that the hostages were held there. Instead the Americans stepped into a buzz saw. Well-armed Cambodians blasted several helicopters out of the sky, scattered the Marines into three small enclaves, and fiercely resisted attempts to reinforce or retrieve the landing party.

Another 100 Marines managed to land at mid-afternoon, and eventually the three forces linked up. Tropical darkness finally enabled the remaining helicopters to return and extract the exhausted force. Forty-one Americans died in the operation; fifty more were wounded. Most galling of all, the confused extraction had left three Marines behind on the island, a bitter, unwelcome flashback to the Makin Raid of 1942. Koh Tang had been an unmitigated disaster. And not the last.

Five years later, another joint force assembled in the Iranian desert in a stealthy, high-stakes attempt to rescue the fifty-two American hostages (including nine Embassy Marines) held in Teheran.

The plan was for Marine pilots to fly Navy helicopters with Army Delta Team commandos into the capital to make the snatch. When three of the eight helicopters crapped out before reaching Desert One, the rendezvous site, the mission had to be aborted. It quickly turned to tragedy when one of the choppers collided with a C–130 and caught fire. Three Marines and five Air Force personnel died in the blaze.

These were troublesome setbacks for all of the services, seemingly jinxed since Vietnam. The Marines studied the

"Peace Keepers." The United States dispatched a Marine Amphibious Unit to Beirut, Lebanon, in 1982 to help bring peace to that divided land. Gradually, however, the Marines themselves became a lightning rod for the various factions. Here Marines fight for their lives against an assortment of terrorists threatening their position around the Beirut airport. (U.S. Marine Corps)

problem, absorbed the lessons, moved on. Quietly, steadily, the Leathernecks under General Barrow, then his successor as Commandant, General Paul Kelley, completed the total overhaul of their war-fighting capabilities, which had atrophied in the previous conflict.

The advent of the Marine AV–8 Harrier V/STOL jump jet, the high-speed air-cushioned landing craft, the family of light armored vehicles, and a whole array of antitank and antiaircraft missile systems injected mobility, firepower, *and confidence* into a Corps now committed around the globe.

Problems of strategic lift were nicely solved by investing in a fleet of maritime prepositioning ships, stuffed with essential heavy equipment, afloat near the most remote and threatened regions.

The Marines also launched a low-profile retraining program in special operations to enable their expeditionary units to more smartly execute missions involving hostage rescue, embassy evacuations, and forcible seizure of ships or oil wells.

Yet the Cold War began to place onerous and increasingly dangerous political restrictions on the ability of forward-deployed Marines to defend themselves. The same "restrictive rules of engagement" decried by the Marines in Spanish East Florida in 1812 left Marines in the 1980s with the decidedly unhealthy regulation of not being able to shoot unless someone else shot them first.

Lebanon, that seething stew of tribal and religious animosities, would demonstrate the absurdity of such policies.

The Marines enjoyed one brief success in 1982. Colonel James Mead's 32d Marine Amphibious Unit (MAU) landed in Beirut, formed a well-armed, no-nonsense cordon, and promptly, peaceably evacuated 6,000 Palestinians and Syrians from an explosive situation. In and out, nicely done.

But then the Lebanese civil war worsened, and President Ronald Reagan ordered the Marines back to Beirut. Fatefully, they would stay ashore 533 days. Static, shackled, increasingly vulnerable, attractive targets.

By the summer of 1983, when Colonel Timothy Geraghty's 24th MAU arrived to take their turn on the firing line, the situation had deteriorated to open combat between an assortment of Muslim militias and Iranian and Syrian guerrillas who perceived the Marines to be unabashed agents of the Christian government.

The Marines in Beirut thus became a lightning rod for U.S. Mideast policy, a small band of amphibians, terribly exposed at an international airport, sniped at by day and shelled at night from the Shouf Mountains.

Marines returned fire, but it was tough to spot the shooter amid the houses and streets thronging with civilians. Navy ships stood ready to provide fire support offshore, but there were few targets. Marines fell, wounded, killed.

On October 23, 1983, a suicidal terrorist drove a Mercedes dump-truck directly into the lobby of the four-story building housing the 1st Battalion, 8th

Marines—and blew himself up. The truck, loaded with six tons of TNT enhanced by pressurized propane gas and primer cord, had the explosive force of eleven Silkworm antiship missiles, roughly the yield of a small tactical nuclear bomb.

The building quartered about 300 Marines and a few sailors and soldiers. The blast killed 241 of them. In that terrible instant, more Marines died than those who had fallen defending Khe Sanh, or recapturing Hue City, or assaulting Eniwetok.

When the anguished reports reached Washington in the middle of the night, General Kelley placed personal calls to notify each of the six living former Commandants. He already knew this was going to be the worst disaster in Marine Corps history.

The only comfort Kelley received throughout the excruciating week that followed came at the military hospital in Wiesbaden, Germany. There, Lance Corporal Jeffrey Nashton, gravely wounded and temporarily blinded by the concrete dust of the explosion, did not believe the officer speaking at his bedside was the Commandant of the Marine Corps. Nashton mustered enough audacity to grope for Kelley's collar in order to count the stars on his rank

Grenada, 1983. A heavily armed Marine patrol advances up a Grenville street during Operation Urgent Fury.
(U.S. Navy)

insignia. Finding, sure enough, four stars, Nashton grinned, then signaled for a pencil and pad of paper. With failing strength, Nashton scribbled *"Semper Fi . . ."*

Four months later, after more Marines had fought and died protecting other peacekeepers and the Embassy, the Reagan administration removed the last of the amphibious troops from Beirut—533 days. . . .

Two other less-than-satisfying military operations, in Grenada and Panama, involved the Marines before the decade of the 1980s finally closed. Both continued to reflect high politics, skimpy intelligence, hasty planning, and the holy grail of fully joint operations.

In Grenada, two days after the Beirut bombing, Colonel James Faulkner's 22d MAU joined the joint task force assaulting several hundred Cubans and restoring a democratic government.

The Marines made multiple amphibious landings, fought with commendable professionalism and restraint, and didn't hang around very long after the shooting stopped. Three Marine helicopter pilots died in the fighting; fifteen other Marines suffered gunshot wounds. American medical students were safely rescued.

In December 1989, the other joint forces intervention occurred in Panama.

The Marines had first landed here in 1856, and had returned on numerous occasions. This time the Army dominated the operation, given their advantage of having 10,000 troops already in the Canal Zone. Heliborne Marines landed to secure the Bridge of the Americas and the westward approaches. One Marine died; three more were wounded. In relative terms, the nineteenth-century landings had been costlier.

Then a funny thing finally happened to the Marines and the protracted Cold War between the United States and the Soviet Union. *We won!* On the day after Christmas, 1991, the Soviet Union officially dissolved. The enormous Soviet war machine came apart at the seams.

The event generated only mild enthusiasm in the Western media—there was ecstasy in Berlin, business as usual in New York—but for two generations of Marines, the Leathernecks who had faced the well-armed surrogates of the Russian bear over so many ramparts, who had spilled their blood in so many remote battlefields to fight Communist aggression, the victory was sweet.

Ironically, for forty-one Cold War years, the Marines had never fired a single shot at a single Russian soldier. But the very excellent military hardware of the Soviet Union had taken a miserable toll. And the Marines, soon enough, would be facing it again in sobering quantity and manned by a huge, battle-hardened Soviet-trained army.

A Marine rifleman guards an outpost in Grenville, Grenada. The terrorist bombing of the Marine barracks in Beirut had just occurred. Marines in Grenada were ready for anything. (U.S. Navy)

367

20: BRAVE NEW WORLD

DURING ONE OF OUR NIGHT COMBINED ARMS RAIDS, I HEARD OVER OUR RADIO THE VOICE OF THE [FORWARD AIR CONTROLLER] PILOT TELLING THE "WOLFPACK" PILOTS: "HURRY UP! THEY ARE ATTACKING OUR MARINES!" AS HE WATCHED MUZZLE FLASHES OF THE IRAQI ARTILLERY FIRING AT OUR GROUND RAID FORCE. THAT WAS ONE OF THE MOST POIGNANT MOMENTS OF MY LIFE. I NEVER TAKE THE AIR-GROUND TEAM FOR GRANTED. . . . BUT THE RESULT IS A MARVELOUS MARRIAGE, MORE POWERFUL THAN THE SUM OF ITS PARTS, WHERE A MARINE'S MOST SOUGHT AFTER PRIVILEGE IS TO BE ABLE TO FIGHT FOR ANOTHER MARINE.

Major General Mike Myatt, USMC, Commanding General,
1st Marine Division, Operation Desert Storm

Marines train for
Operation Assured
Response while en route
to Liberia in 1996.
(Marine Corps Association)

If anything as miserable as war can be said to be the realization of a dream, the Gulf War was it for the United States Marine Corps. A beautifully rebuilt, expensively crafted fighting machine at the peak of its readiness and ferocity was injected into a sudden war with an outrageously evil enemy. The terrain was tailored to the Corps' slashing mobility. Deployment was near flawless, battle planning and performance even more so. Teamwork was beautiful within and without the Corps. Against a huge, veteran, capable military machine they achieved swift, crushing victory in a key sector. And, most gloriously, casualties were astonishingly low. They returned home to the smashing acclaim that had been withheld after Vietnam. If the battle history of the Marine Corps were to end, this would be an ideal place. Of course that would mean the end of war, or rumors of war. Good luck.

Realization that a maverick dictator suddenly sat securely on 20 percent of the world's oil supplies and threatened to double that hegemony prompted President George Bush to declare, "This will not stand."

Iraqi dictator Saddam had launched his invasion of Kuwait on August 2, 1990, in partial belief that neither the United States nor the rest of the free world would do much more than cry foul and wring their hands. In short order, he had seized Kuwait and staged formidable armored forces along the Saudi border.

Closely supported by British Prime Minister Margaret Thatcher, and noticeably unopposed by Soviet Premier Mikhail Gorbachev, the President began to build a coalition of thirty-seven nations willing to oppose Saddam.

The Marines were instantly on the move. While one Marine expeditionary brigade deployed from the East Coast loaded for the traditional amphibious mission, two others marched aboard strategic airlifters to fly directly to Saudi Arabia to marry-up with their maritime prepositioning (MPS) ships.

Desert Storm would be the largest single combat operation in Marine Corps history. Nearly 93,000 Leathernecks took part—men and women, aviators and grunts, amphibians and desert rats, staff pukes and snake-eaters. Lieutenant General Walter Boomer commanded more Marines in combat than did Harry Schmidt at Iwo Jima or Roy Geiger at Okinawa.

As Joint Chiefs Chairman General Colin Powell set out to execute the President's policies, he exacted from the Commander-in-Chief a promise to avoid the "mission creep" and top-level micro-management of the Vietnam War. In this crisis, Powell insisted, "Set a clear political objective, provide sufficient forces to do the job, then keep out of the way."

The 7th Marine Expeditionary Brigade flew from California to Al Jubail on August 14.

The next day their five MPS ships arrived from Diego Garcia in the Indian Ocean. On hand watching the tanks rumble ashore was the campaign's commander-in-chief, Army General Norman Schwarzkopf. Seeing the flow of combat gear coming off the ships "made me feel great," he said. Within five

The New Corps

Gone forever were the days where a municipal judge could offer a young miscreant the option of going to jail or joining the Marines. Insistence on quality over quantity in the lean years of the 1970s had positioned the Marines in the vanguard of the nation's All-Volunteer Force. Recruiters looked diligently for evidence of character and achievement. The Marines of Desert Storm were the smartest, best-trained, most physically fit troops that ever served the Corps. Where only half of Vietnam-era Marines had high school diplomas, the figure approached 100 percent by the mid–1980s. Many enlistees were junior college graduates. While the Marines needed smarter recruits to handle sophisticated new hardware like global positioning systems and laser range finders, the greater need was for self-reliant achievers. Molding this promising raw material into disciplined Marines remained the special province of enlisted drill instructors, the backbone of the Corps. Marine Boot Camps at Parris Island or San Diego never relaxed their standards, regardless of the winds of popular culture. "Making hard people in a soft age," observed columnist George Will about Marine recruit training. Women were not spared:

Twenty-five-hundred women Marines served in the combat zone. Said Brigadier General Charles Krulak of his WMs at the forward logistics base: "Ten of my female truck drivers went through the breach after dark on the first day of the ground attack to bring back enemy prisoners, so they were actually ahead of some hard-charging infantry units."

Having 94,000 highly motivated, free-thinking troops would have little benefited an expeditionary corps if the commanding generals remained rooted in hide-bound, stone-age leadership. Perhaps it was a coincidence, but I MEF's top three ground commanders—Walt Boomer, Bill Keys, and Mike Myatt—each served as advisers (*co-vans*) to the Vietnamese Marine Corps during their second combat tours in that war. Successful *co-vans* listened more than they pontificated, experimented freely, operated independently. It showed twenty years later.

---

days the 7th MEB moved north, ready to fight, 15,248-men strong, fielding 123 tanks, 425 artillery pieces, and 124 tactical aircraft, both helos and fixed-wing.

Saddam missed a golden opportunity to make an early grab for Saudi Arabia's economic center of gravity along the east (Gulf) coast. The 7th MEB and the Army Airborne forces on hand were no match for the hundreds of thousands of first-echelon Iraqi troops stacked up along the Kuwaiti-Saudi border.

Asked whether his initial forces could stop an Iraqi invasion that first month, General Boomer replied, "I don't know how, but we will. This will never be a Dunkirk. We will stop them."

Boomer and Schwarzkopf held their breath as the Allied buildup went forward frantically. Within sixty days Boomer had 42,000 Marines on hand.

As time passed and Saddam failed to respond to diplomatic and economic pressures, President Bush realized that Kuwait would have to be liberated by force from her occupying legions.

For such an offensive against the world's fourth-largest army, Schwarzkopf asked for double the amount of forces, Marines and Army.

Again, the old warhorse, the 2d Marine Division, got the call to combat, its first as a division since Okinawa in 1945. President Bush also called up 23,000 Marine Reservists. These flowed into Camp Lejeune, North Carolina, to be processed and integrated into the division.

Said Major General William Keys, commanding the 2d Division, "Camp Lejeune looked like it must have during World War II, with Marines reporting

A pair of Marine M1–A1 Abrams main battle tanks advance across the Kuwaiti desert during the ground war of Operation Desert Storm, February 1991. (U.S. Marine Corps)

at all hours of the night, then starting out first thing the next morning to train for combat."

By late January, Boomer commanded what was called the I Marine Expeditionary Force (in reality, a Marine expeditionary corps), which included the 1st and 2d Marine Divisions and an enormous 3d Marine Aircraft Wing. More than 17,000 of Boomer's Marines were embarked and combat-loaded on board thirty-one amphibious ships in the Persian Gulf, a larger force than those MacArthur had assembled to seize Inchon forty years earlier.

Marine Corps Commandant General Al Gray spoke the obvious: "We now have four kinds of Marines: those in the Gulf, those going to the Gulf, those who want to go to the Gulf, and those who don't want to go to the Gulf but are going anyway!"

As autumn gave way to winter, the Allied coalition began to stir itself for a massive offensive to wrest Kuwait from the Iraqi forces.

Among the competing strategies being discussed for this mission was the role to be played by the huge American amphibious armada loitering in the Persian Gulf. Meanwhile, the amphib Marines were not exactly idle.

Small units trained in special operations helped enforce the maritime blockade of Iraqi shipping. Whenever an Iraqi ship captain refused to stop and allow a conventional naval boarding party to inspect his cargo holds, the Marines would take the direct approach. With one helicopter gunship hovering nearby with its guns and missiles trained on the ships' bridge, a trans-

port chopper would hover directly overhead while the Marines scampered down ropes like so many armed spiders to conduct a little heart-to-heart talk with the captain.

The Navy and Marines also conducted a series of purposefully publicized amphibious "rehearsals," resulting in dramatic video footage of helicopters and Harriers and air-cushion landing craft converging on the objective. News clips of these active demonstrations proved downright riveting in Peoria. And in Baghdad.

General Schwarzkopf had things he wanted to plant in Saddam Hussein's mind. He wanted Saddam to believe that these Marines would swoop ashore at any minute in the northern Gulf. Saddam bought the stratagem.

Actually, Schwarzkopf had decided against a forcible amphibious assault.

As the North Koreans had so convincingly demonstrated at Wonsan in 1950, the cheapest, most effective way to defend against an amphibious assault is to flood the zone with antiship mines. Saddam had released close to a million of these in the northern Gulf. Two ships of the amphibious task force sustained major mine damage. The Navy and Marines insisted they could still pull it off—but it would take time. And cost casualties.

Schwarzkopf could ill-afford either. He asked Walt Boomer if I MEF could achieve its objectives without resorting to an amphibious assault.

This was a tough call for Boomer. A century of institutional history weighed heavily. But this was no time to be parochial. Yes, we can, Boomer told the CINC, but we've got to maintain the amphib force as an offshore ruse until the last minute. Schwarzkopf agreed. Both men knew that Saddam had committed at least three divisions to defending the coast against the expected landing from the sea.

The grand assault plan took shape.

First, the "air supremacy" advocates would be given the opportunity to prove their claim that a smart air campaign would win the war without the need for a single infantryman to seize any contested ground.

Failing that, the half-million Allied troops would retake Kuwait and punch out the Iraqi military the old-fashioned way.

With the amphibious force posing a major distraction in the Gulf, General Boomer would launch his two Marine divisions through the Iraqi barricades into Kuwait, a "fixing attack" in Army lingo, to further divert Saddam's attention from Schwarzkopf's main effort, the celebrated "Left Hook" around enemy forces on the left flank by two heavily armored Army corps.

Boomer's first plan involved a breaching of the Iraqi defenses by Myatt's 1st Marine Division. The breach successfully accomplished, Keys's 2d Division would execute a passage of lines and lead the attack farther into Kuwait. The plan reflected practical limitations. Breaching equipment was scarce; strategic lift assets were so tight the 2d Division could only dribble a thousand Marines a day into the theater.

373

THE BATTLE HISTORY OF THE US MARINES

Myatt and his staff examined their mission in light of what they learned from the recent Iraqi-Iranian War.

The Iraqis had constructed two belts of obstacles and minefields opposite Myatt's division. "We knew we would have to breach those belts rapidly or face destruction by the Iraqi artillery," he said. More than 1,200 Iraqi artillery pieces confronted the Marines. "We knew the Iraqis were planning on trapping us in two 'fire-sacks' when we attacked."

The air war began at 3 A.M. Baghdad time with a spectacular series of strikes by USAF F–117 Stealth bombers and Navy Tomahawk cruise missiles. Marines flying F/A–18 Hornets out of Bahrain joined, taking out radar sites, power plants, and railroad marshaling yards.

Consistent with Air Force policy in Korea and Vietnam, a Joint Forces Air Component Commander in a light blue uniform called all the shots in the air—at first.

Then, according to Major General Royal Moore, commanding the 3d Marine Aircraft Wing, "We started weaning our own assets, and pretty soon, with General Schwarzkopf's acknowledgment, about fifteen days prior to the ground campaign, we were into battlefield preparation. At that time, if a target didn't do something for the I MEF and battlefield preparation, we weren't going."

Less than 1 percent of Moore's pilots were combat veterans, and the learning curve was immediate—no milk runs. "The Iraqis were real trigger pullers," said Moore. "They filled the sky with flak and SAMs. . . . When a missile, even unguided, goes over the top of your canopy, you get concerned."

Iraqi AAA dominated the lower altitudes where the Marines needed to operate for battlefield preps and close air support. Moore authorized fifty-plane "Gorilla Strikes" in the effort to take out AAA positions in Kuwait.

Desert Storm marked the combat debut of the Marine Corps F/A–18D, the two-seat, all-weather, night-attack version of the Hornet, destined to replace the ancient and honorable A6-E Intruder (the "F/A" designator connotes the dual roles of fighter and attack bomber).

The planes, equipped with forward-looking infrared targeting systems, would operate above the AAA envelope at 10,000 feet, the pilots wearing "Catseye" night-vision goggles and studying the ground below with ten-power binoculars.

Target priorities, according to Captain Rueben Padilla, were "artillery and rocket launchers, armor, troops, and trench lines." Finding some T–72 tank lurking in a revetment at night, the FastFAC (Forward Air Controller) would call in the "Wolfpack" of Harriers, marking their target with a 2.75-inch rocket tipped with a white phosphorous warhead.

The abandoned Saudi frontier town of Khafji seemed an unlikely place for the first major ground encounter of the 1991 Gulf War.

During the night of January 29, 1991, the 5th Iraqi Mechanized Division

swept across the border and seized the town in a surprise, spoiling attack, abruptly disputing claims by Air Force strategists that the Air War had immobilized Saddam Hussein's ground forces.

Arab screening forces retreated south before this sudden onslaught. A handful of Marines stayed. Two recon teams from the 3d Marines hid on the roof of a four-story building. The senior NCO, Corporal Charles Ingraham, calmly reported the invasion by radio to his regiment, offering to direct air and artillery strikes against the Iraqis swarming through the streets.

Ingraham's situation was critical. The Iraqis would surely discover his bypassed outpost. He deployed his troops in firing positions, rigged Claymore mines in the stairwell, and unrolled a large orange panel to alert Allied aircraft that there were "friendlies" on the rooftop. Peeking into the building's courtyard, Ingraham could see the helmeted heads of Iraqi troops searching the floors below. The Marines hunkered down, sweating out a nerve-racking twenty-four hours.

Khafji lay in the Arab sector. As keenly as the Marines wanted to move in and rescue their stranded recon teams, they could only offer assistance and wait for Saudi and Qatari mechanized forces to counterattack.

The Arab task force met stiff resistance from Iraqis as they tried to recapture Khafji. Corporal Ingraham made the difference. From his rooftop perch Ingraham called in air and artillery strikes with masterful precision, some rounds impacting so close that one of his men went down with a shrapnel wound.

Then, as the Arabs forged into town and the fighting became localized, Ingraham took advantage of the confusion and led his teams through back streets toward the Allied lines, rifle in one hand, radio in the other, orange air panel in his teeth, furling out behind. Made it.

The Allied recapture of Khafji revealed in advance two key aspects of the ground war that would soon follow. The Iraqis, for all their vaunted experience and weaponry, were unmotivated and ineffective fighters. And the Marines had junior leaders in their enlisted ranks like Ingraham who, despite their lack of combat experience, were well trained, cool-headed, and lethal. After Khafji, the uneven battles that ensued in late February should have come as no surprise.

Marine pilots had a turkey shoot against the armored columns of the Iraqi 5th Mechanized Division trying to reinforce their toehold in Khafji. In one incident reported by Captain Padilla, a Marine FastFAC with night-vision goggles found and marked an advancing column, and "a section of A–6Es laid a string of Rockeye antiarmor submunitions across the column, stopping it dead in its tracks."

When the air war erupted, Iraqi artillery began shelling Marine positions in northern Saudi Arabia. The fire was not particularly accurate, but the incoming explosives were powerful enough to get everyone's attention.

Most nerve-racking were the 300mm rockets, the equivalent in caliber of the twelve-inch naval rifles of Japanese battleships in the Solomons. "A

375

THE BATTLE HISTORY OF THE US MARINES

300mm rocket makes a crater twelve feet in diameter and three feet deep," said Major Craig Huddleston. "They have a spectacular signature at night, both during launch and impact. The launcher can displace in seconds after launch. We've had trouble killing them."

Generals Mike Myatt and Bill Keys initiated a series of lightning-fast combined-arms raids to gain the psychological edge over the Iraqi gunners. Myatt struck first.

Escorted by a rifle company riding in six-wheel-drive LAVs (light assault vehicles), an artillery battery of self-propelled 155mm guns would take off at night across the desert, stopping just shy of the Kuwaiti border. The battery would rain holy hell on an Iraqi artillery position. Once the startled enemy gunners returned the fire, an airborne FastFAC would mark the muzzle flashes for a loitering Wolfpack to thunder in with Rockeyes. The old double whammy.

"Our aim was to defeat the minds of the Iraqi artillerymen," said Myatt. "We convinced 'em it wasn't smart to man their artillery pieces because every time they did Marine air would come rolling in on them."

The LAVs grabbed a piece of the action as well, conducting highly mobile "drive-by shootings" across the border with their 25mm Chain Guns as further distraction during the artillery "shoot and scoots."

Artillerymen of the 2d Battalion, 12th Marines, man their M198 155mm howitzer in this on-the-scene painting during the ground war in Kuwait. (Sergeant Charles G. Grow, USMC, Marine Corps Combat Art Collection)

The more General Bill Keys studied the ground assault plan for breaching the Iraqi defenses, the less he liked it.

Any passage of lines is a complex military maneuver. To do so on a division level, with both units vulnerably exposed to Iraqi firepower, would court disaster. Plus it would take forever. The trail of vehicles from both divisions trying to get past each other could stretch back thirty miles in the desert. There were better ways to skin the cat.

Keys asked Boomer to change his plans at the last minute to enable a simultaneous two-divisions-abreast breaching farther west. The Marines should approach this breaching just like an amphibious assault, argued Keys. Land on multiple fronts, keep units in assembly areas until cleared to cross the line of departure, avoid stacking up 40,000 Marines at a single landing point. Substitute "breachhead" for "beachhead."

Boomer saw the plan had merits, but worried about timing. Logistics support looked like the long pole in the tent.

Boomer asked Brigadier General Charles Krulak, commanding the Direct Support Command, whether he could support Keys's plan. Krulak thought hard. His troops had just completed the main logistics base at Kibrit on the coast. Moving the 2d Marine Division eighty miles west would render Kibrit useless. "Yes, we can!" he replied, not looking forward to breaking this news to his staff.

Krulak's logisticians, long-inured to the vagaries of the "broad-arrow strategists," shook their heads and went to work. An advance site, Gravel Plains, within sight of the border, seemed right for supporting two parallel divisions. Krulak named the place *Al Kanjar,* Arabic for "The Dagger."

The story of the Gulf War is often told in terms of the grand movements, savage battles, hi-tech weapons. In truth, logistics dominated the campaign. Among many startling American achievements in this unheralded field was Krulak's construction of the Al Kanjar logistics base.

Two weeks after getting the green light from Boomer, Krulak's logisticians had completed a marvelous facility, 11,280 acres in breadth, almost entirely underground, which housed in carefully compartmented sectors, a million tons of ammo, five million gallons of fuel, a million gallons of water, the third-largest Naval hospital in the world, plus two C–130 airstrips, and a helicopter support facility named "Lonesome Dove." "Mind-boggling," said Boomer.

The Marines continued to play ambiguity games against the Iraqis. The amphibious force snorted and huffed; a bogus Marine division seemingly deployed to the east, Operation Troy, with helicopters and staff vehicles cycling in and out, and a lot of phony radio traffic being generated.

Quietly, westward, Keys and Myatt began their final preparations for the Marine ground war. Between them they made several dozen cuts in The Berm, the fifteen-foot wall of sand that paralleled the Kuwaiti border, built years earlier by Japanese contractors for the Saudis.

Through these cuts during the dark of night went Marine combat patrols of considerable strength, clearing the most immediate obstacles, reconnoitering Iraqi positions, calling in more artillery and air strikes. Technically they were "crow-hopping," crossing the international border before the President directed the start of ground hostilities. Their goal was to make the G-Day passage a bit easier, faster, safer for the main forces.

MARINE WEAPONS THAT WORKED

Being few in number and chronically underfunded, the Marines fought many of their earlier battles with hand-me-down weapons of dubious quality.

Things were a lot better in the Gulf War. The Marines fought with the M–16A2 rifle, a weapon so much improved over the M–16 it should be designated the *M–116*, a combat rifle designed, developed, tested, and evaluated by Leathernecks for Leathernecks. They also had TOW and Dragon antitank missiles and awesome, deafening 227mm Multiple Launch Rocket Systems. Even the humble LVT (redesignated AAV, assault amphibian vehicle) was upgunned with M–19 Automatic 40mm Grenade Launchers. AH–1W Cobra helicopter gunships firing TOW and Hellfire missiles added an aerial dimension.

While the Marines went to war with only a relatively few of the highly touted M1–A1 Abrams tanks, their older M–60s were hardly toothless. The M–60s repeatedly fired 105mm discarding-sabot, fin-stabilized, depleted uranium rounds into Iraqi tanks (and *through* Iraqi armored personnel carriers) from extended ranges.

Graced with such an abundance of working weapons, the Marines put together powerful armored columns of tanks, AAVs, and LAVs. Widespread use of laser range finders and thermal imagery sights enabled first-round hits against Iraqi armor despite the abysmal visibility on the battlefield. Still, Marines continued to treasure the eye-guided missile that came out a rifle barrel.

Finally President Bush approved G-Day for February 24. General Boomer sent a message to his huge force poised along The Berm: "May the spirit of your Marine forefathers ride with you. . . . "

Then each Marine took counsel of his private thoughts, waiting for the assault signal. Officers checked their watches. The troops watched their NCOs. It was cold that night. The air fouled by heavy smoke of burning oil wells. Saddam's "Scorched Earth" policy at work. It was time.

General Bill Keys's double-barreled assault strategy would catapult the spearheads of both divisions well clear of the obstacle belts before the demoralized Iraqis could mount serious armored counterattacks.

The 1st Marine Division initiated the Allies' ground war at 0400, surging across The Berm, the ear-splitting noise of artillery and MLRS rockets masking the telltale sound of tank plows, armored bulldozers, and line-charge-firing AAVs grinding through the minefields.

The advance task forces had done their nocturnal clearing and misleading work well. The Iraqis were spooked, slow to react, tentative in their fire missions. Myatt met each outburst of fire with immediate counterbattery fire by his 11th Marines or with "Quick-Fire" calls to Marine Harriers stacked up overhead.

Here was Marine close air support as first envisioned sixty years earlier: on station, responsive, loaded for bear. "This is the time we start earning our flight pay," Royal Moore told his pilots. "Now we have Marines in combat."

A light assault vehicle (LAV–25) with Task Force Shepherd bearing the American and Marine Corps flags pauses during the recapture of Kuwait.

(Sergeant Charles G. Grow, USMC, Marine Corps Combat Art Collection)

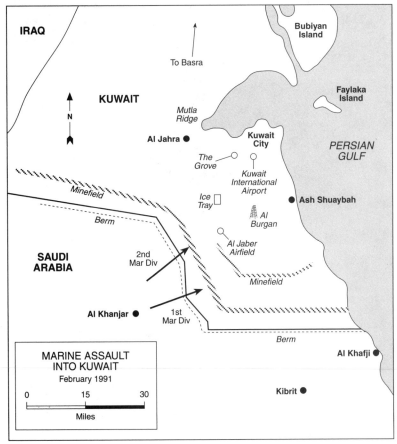

IRAQ

To Basra

KUWAIT

Bubiyan Island

Faylaka Island

Mutla Ridge

N

Al Jahra ●

Kuwait City

The Grove ○

PERSIAN GULF

Kuwait International Airport

Ice Tray ▢

Ash Shuaybah ●

Al Burgan

Minefield

Berm

Al Jaber Airfield

SAUDI ARABIA

2nd Mar Div

Minefield

Al Khanjar ●

1st Mar Div

Berm

Al Khafji ●

MARINE ASSAULT INTO KUWAIT

February 1991

0   15   30

Miles

Kibrit ●

379

Gulf of Oman. Two Marine Corps AV–8B Harriers, attack aircraft with vertical takeoff and landing capabilities, prepare for launch from the amphibious assault ship Nassau during the preliminaries for Desert Storm. (U.S. Navy)

Moore's pilots would not have an easy time of it. The Ground War occurred during the four worst flying days of the entire war.

The weather was bad; the oil well fires made things worse. Four low-flying Harrier jets would fall to Iraqi shoulder-fired infrared missiles. On several occasions Marine Cobras resorted to air-taxiing down highways, searching for their targets at almost eyeball level. Darkness notwithstanding, the 3d Wing flew 671 support missions on G-Day, hitting six different Iraqi divisions.

Things got so dark at one point Mike Myatt said he couldn't see beyond the front of his vehicle. Added an M–60 tank commander, "I couldn't even see the muzzle of the goddamned machine gun in my hand."

If it was dark and ghostly for the Marines, it was doubly terrifying for the Iraqis.

They were being plastered by everything in the books. Their tanks were getting nailed from impossible ranges, even in the smog. Marine infantry appeared out of nowhere, always on the flanks. Even the winds had turned against them, reversing the normal direction, blowing the smoke north into their faces, a bad omen. Iraqi soldiers began to quit. The 1st Marine Division would capture them by the thousands.

General Keys's 2d Marine Division launched its attack ninety minutes later. The PsyOps people had rigged their loudspeakers along The Berm for the occasion. "The Marines' Hymn" burst forth at mega-decibel level.

Each maneuver element of the 2d Division had run through a full-scale replica of the Iraqi defenses at dark in full MOPP (chemical warfare protective) gear. They found no surprises north of The Berm.

The 6th Marines led the way through the cleared lanes. Keys kept them moving. "Contrary to some reports, the Iraqis were still there, waiting for us," he said. "They fired about 300 rounds of artillery as we worked to breach the minefields, but they had no forward observers to coax the fire on target, so we could discount the prospect of heavy casualties from their shots in the dark."

Since one of Keys's three infantry regiments (the 2d Marines) had been assigned to the amphibious role for the duration, General Schwarzkopf had assigned him the Army's Tiger Brigade of the 2d Armored Division.

The Tiger Brigade brought 118 brand-new M1–A1 Abrams tanks and a commendable proficiency to the fight. Keys called them "a first-class outfit." (The Army tankers now wear the 2d Marine Division patch on their sleeves to reflect combat service with the Marines.)

The Tiger Brigade streamed through the gaps in trace behind the 6th Marines, then angled north. The superb M1–A1s began knocking out dug-in Iraqi T–55 tanks from two miles away.

By dark on G-Day, each division had substantial forces beyond both obstacle belts, with forward-deployed artillery battalions readily in range. The cost had been ridiculously low: three killed, seventeen wounded in action. They had taken 16,000 prisoners.

General Schwarzkopf would exult, "I can't say enough about the two Marine divisions. If I used words like brilliant, it would really be an under-description of the absolutely superb job that they did in breaching the so-called impenetrable barrier. It was a classic, absolutely classic, military breaching of a very, very tough minefield, barbed wire, fire trenches-type barrier. They went through the first barrier like it was water. . . . A textbook operation, and I think it will be studied for many, many years to come."

Elated at this progress, Schwarzkopf advanced the launch date for his massive Left Hook by twenty-four hours. Boomer began landing the 5th Marine Expeditionary Brigade from their amphibious ships to a secure beach below Khafji to constitute the I MEF reserve and help police up the unexpected large number of POWs. The 5th Marines began to advance northward.

The second day of the ground war brought more bad weather and scattered, intense fighting in central Kuwait. Both divisions encountered large-scale counterattacks, defeated them in wild slugging matches, and consolidated all elements well north of the obstacle belts.

In the west, the 1st Battalion, 8th Marines, intercepted what became known as "The Reveille Counterattack" by an ambitious column of Iraqi tanks and APCs. Combined arms won the morning—Marine air, tanks, artillery, and missile-firing infantrymen. Thirty-nine enemy armored vehicles lay burning.

Eastward, the roving task forces of the 1st Marine Division collided in the smoke and fog with Iraqi armored units boiling out of the Burquan Oil Field.

This became a real donnybrook, the largest tank battle in Marine Corps history. A hasty radio message from the division reported "Enemy tanks and troops flushed from Burquan area. Much confusion."

Marine attack aircraft circled above the smoke, searching fruitlessly for holes in the soup, clear targets to nail. But the forces were too intermixed. Only the AH–1W Sea Cobras could help, although with the ceiling rarely higher than fifty feet the gunships were as vulnerable as ground combat vehicles.

A swarm of Iraqi tanks and armored personnel carriers attacked the command post (CP) of Task Force Papa Bear at point-blank range.

Marines returned a hot fire, and rounds of all calibers whizzed through the CP. Said Major John Turner, "I remember hitting the deck for the first time during the war and saw tracers going through the CP from east to west at knee height."

Another Iraqi force struck General Mike Myatt's forward CP at "the Emir's Farm," a grove of tamarind trees on the southwest corner of the oil field. Myatt's light security force of LAVs engaged the enemy tanks in unequal battle—but then came a section of Sea Cobra gunships, the cavalry to the rescue. The Cobras uncorked TOW missiles, and the oil field became dotted with burning hulks.

So close were the Iraqi vehicles to Myatt's position that the Cobras hovered directly over his head, drenching the CP in spent 20mm shell casings.

Everyone got into the act that hectic morning. Sergeant Shawn Toney, a member of a Reserve artillery battery from Richmond, spotted a pair of Iraqi

multiple rocket launchers close at hand. The battery swung into action, leveled the long barrels of their M198 155mm guns, and enjoyed the rare artilleryman's delight of destroying enemy targets by direct fire at 800 yards.

Myatt resumed the offensive by mid-day.

Shortly after dark, Lieutenant Colonel James Fulks led his Task Force Grizzly across the valuable Al Jaber Airfield despite a dozen casualties to Iraqi rocket salvos.

The 2d Marine Division advanced rapidly through Kuwait, the 6th Marines capturing Iraqi defenses in "The Ice Tray," the 8th Marines taking "The Ice Cube," both built-up areas laid out in grids that resembled their names.

The third day finished crushing the Iraqis in Kuwait.

The 1st Marine Division engaged in another enormous and lopsided tank battle at Kuwait International Airport, knocking out an incredible 320 tanks, including 70 of the previously feared Soviet-made T–72s. The 2d Division swung farther north, seizing Mutla Ridge, effectively cutting off the escape of Iraqis from Kuwait City.

Many Iraqis had not bothered to wait for this development; the highway north to Basra was clogged with Iraqi vehicles, military and civilian, laden with booty, trying to escape the hell-bent-for-leather Marines. Here was a rich target for Marine attack aircraft.

A–6E Intruders bottled up the "moving parking lot" by dropping

ABOVE: Marines always favor the high ground, though it was hard to come by in the battle to recapture Kuwait from Saddam Hussein's Iraqi forces. These Marines scramble up a man-made sand berm to take up firing positions. (U.S. Marine Corps)

OPPOSITE: A Marine CH–46 Sea Knight from HMM–165 lands on the helipad of the resurrected WWII battleship *Wisconsin* during Desert Storm. The Navy and Marines had by this time assembled an enormous amphibious task force in the Persian Gulf, the largest since the Inchon landing forty-one years before. The well-armed, well-rehearsed striking force hovering just over the horizon tied down several of Hussein's best Iraqi Army divisions along the coast near Kuwait City, distracting attention from the main Marine assault from the south or the great end run by the Army and the Allies to the far west. (U.S. Navy)

CBU–78 Gator aerial mines up ahead. Then the Hornets and Harriers swept in, 300 sorties, all day long.

Hundreds of Iraqi soldiers met a quick end. Thousands more fled across the sands, leaving their loot behind. The Western media quickly dubbed the carnage "The Highway to Hell."

The best flying of the third day belonged to the helicopter pilots, especially Lieutenant Colonel Michael Kurth. With Task Force Ripper needing gunship support beyond Al Jaber Airfield, and with the unholy smoke and fog the worst yet, Kurth took off in a Huey jury-rigged with laser designation gear, leading five Sea Cobras.

Flying low—so low that his skid marks nearly touched the sand, flying *beneath* three sets of high-tension power lines, Kurth led his Cobras to Ripper to deliver their goods. He did this twice.

The 4th Marine Expeditionary Brigade, still afloat off the coast and hankering for action, contributed by executing a series of fake landing demonstrations that fooled the Iraqis into deploying a fourth division near the coast. The last two battleships fighting on earth, *Missouri* and *Wisconsin*, reactivated for this special occasion, came in close and delivered thunderous sixteen-inch volleys into Iraqi troop concentrations below the capital. The Iraqis countered with two Chinese Silkworm antiship missiles. The battleships and their escorts calmly shot both missiles out of the air. Even the American antiques were killing the increasingly discouraged Iraqis.

The Marines deferred the honor of recapturing Kuwait City to their Kuwaiti and Arab allies, but a Marine recon team flew into the U.S. Embassy early and found the American flag still flying bravely. They replaced it with a large flag that had last flown in Vietnam. Honor restored.

No Marine would ever forget the cheers of welcome and gratitude from the Kuwaitis.

Meanwhile, the Allied main effort unfolded to the west; the Republican Guard divisions either fought and died, or fled north across the Euphrates River. President Bush, quickly accused by the media of "piling on," ordered a cease-fire at the 100-hour mark.

The Allies had succeeded gloriously, and the Marines had garnered new accolades for their tactical prowess. In their uneven fight in Kuwait, the Marines knocked out 1,040 Iraqi tanks, 608 APCs, 432 artillery pieces, 5 FROG missile sites. They killed about 1,500 enemy troops and took well over 20,000 prisoners.

All this came at the cost of five Marines killed, forty-eight wounded in action. Five Marine aviators were shot down, captured, abused, and released. There were no Marine MIAs left from this war.

America welcomed home her combat troops with an outburst of love and affection that the country had not seen since World War II.

The 2d Marine Division joined other services in marching proudly through Washington, D.C. The 1st Marine Division returned in triumph to huge crowds in Southern California. American flags fluttered from every bridge and overpass.

Old-guard Marines watching the ceremonies, the unfulfilled veterans of Korea and Vietnam, wept privately—furiously proud of the new Marines, more than a bit envious of their homecoming reception. *Born too soon.* . . .

Was Desert Storm the face of future combat? Or was it rather the smaller, fuzzier conflicts and emergencies "short of war" that seemed to be popping up every other month? What would be the nature of Marine commitments in the post–Cold War era? There were hints—a combination of humanitarian missions and some perilous policework.

Marines en route to the Gulf in 1990 had been diverted to execute Operation Sharp Edge, the emergency evacuation of several thousand U.S. citizens and other threatened nationals from strife-torn Liberia.

Other Marines turned immediately from fighting Saddam's hapless minions to helping people in extreme need: They conducted Operation Sea Angel in cyclone-ravaged Bangladesh. And then Operation Provide Comfort, an international relief effort on behalf of 750,000 starving Kurds in northern Iraq. The Marines labored in Kurdistan three months, 500 miles removed from their sea base. "Food Soldiers," the Kurdish kids called them. . . .

But death is never far from a Marine, even in the dubious duties of peacekeeping, as they learned in Somalia.

The East African nation, rent by fourteen warring clans, had lost a half million citizens to starvation by the time President Bush organized an armed relief force.

The first Marines landed tactically in Mogadishu on December 9, 1992, and secured the port complex, airport, and the abandoned U.S. Embassy. They were the vanguard of more than 17,000 Leathernecks of the I Marine Expeditionary Force under Major General Charles Wilhelm. A dozen other nations pitched in to help.

The Marines set out to break the gridlock on food distribution by establishing "Humanitarian Relief Sectors" in central and southern Somalia. In each case, the Marines traveled in combined-arms convoys, seized urban centers in harness with Belgian paratroopers or French Foreign Legionnaires. Firefights with bandit gangs and heavily armed "Technicals"—careening light trucks mounting automatic weapons—were frequent.

But deadly incidents began to erupt, especially in urban Mogadishu. Hidden snipers shot several Marines, killing two.

A United Nations headquarters took command. Unlike Lebanon, most Marines had departed by the time the mission "crept" from humanitarian assistance to "nation building," with the obvious implications of taking sides in the civil strife. Disaster was expectable. The ambush and killing of eighteen U.S. soldiers in Mogadishu in October 1993 led to the eventual withdrawal of American ground forces.

The Marine Corps greatly improved its ground tactical mobility following the Vietnam War. Here an AAVP–7A1 amphibious assault vehicle—the "great-grandson" of the original LVTs that crossed the reef at Tarawa—rolls through Iraqi positions in southern Kuwait. (U.S. Marine Corps)

Mogadishu, Somalia, 1992. Marines search an abandoned building for snipers. Compared to Lebanon, the Marines had more rewarding and less costly missions in this strife-torn country. They landed, executed relief missions, then sailed off to other assignments before the situation turned ugly. Returning in 1995, the Marines and Navy executed a flawless "reverse amphibious landing" to extract the last embattled United Nations forces. (U.S. Navy)

By 1995 the United Nations Command despaired of being able to turn Somalia around and called for American assistance in disengaging forces literally under siege in Mogadishu.

The amphibious Marines and Navy got the "911 call." Marine Lieutenant General Anthony Zinni took command of the combined task force for Operation United Shield.

General Zinni had his hands full. "These are the most complex of operations," he reported. "Amphibious landings, relief-in-place of one force by another from a different country, amphibious withdrawal under pressure. We did seven of these totally at night."

Ever so carefully Zinni's Marines relieved the Pakistani, Bangladeshi, and Italian forces, phasing them back to the ships. In the process the Marines sustained twenty-seven firefights, "everything from snipers to rocket-propelled grenades." A large armed mob of Somalis threatened the Marines defending the last beach on the last night ashore.

The Marines backed aboard their waiting amphibian tractors, weapons leveled, gunships overhead. They "disengaged" without losing a man—blessed are the peacekeepers.

Meanwhile, Marines had returned to Haiti after a sixty-year absence, this time to intervene against military strongman General Raoul Cédras.

A Marine Expeditionary Unit landed at Cap Haitien on Haiti's northern coast after months of on-again-off-again threats of U.S. intervention. Army troops swarmed into Port-au-Prince.

Cap Haitien with a population of 65,000 people is the second-largest city in the country. General Cédras's "military police" had ruled the place with an iron hand for years. They did not welcome the Marines.

On September 24 a Marine rifle squad patrolling the inner city encountered a group of military policemen outside their barracks. Their leader aimed his weapon at the Marines. They shot him down. His buddies drew their weapons and opened fire. The Marines responded with a brief, well-aimed fusillade. In a moment ten of the MPs lay dead. One member of the patrol, a U.S. sailor serving as an interpreter, was wounded in the firefight.

General Cédras, enraged at this setback, accused the Marines of murder. The Leathernecks ignored the dictator and continued their search for weapons caches in the city. A week later an Army battalion arrived in Cap Haitien, and the Marines returned quite happily to their amphibious ships.

The Marines' future role seemed pointed less toward the vast slugfests of Desert Storm and more and more to the shadowy half-world of urban warfare. The Marines, traditionally first to fight, would need the savvy and wherewithal to fight both kinds of conflicts.

But, then again, "operations short of war" were not particularly new to the Leathernecks.

A half-century earlier, Red Mike Edson, the combat giant of the Coco River patrols, Edson's Ridge, and Tarawa, produced for the Corps his most significant contribution, the marvelously foresightful *Small Wars Manual*. The Marines have rushed it back into print.

General Tony Zinni, already a veteran of such nontraditional missions in Kurdistan, Somalia, Bangladesh, Ecuador, and Rwanda, acknowledged the complexities ahead: "This is the direction the new world disorder is going, and there isn't anybody else to call upon for help. And these are the kinds of operations we will have to do better."

That's one thing Marines have always been able to understand. Learning by doing. Adapting. Doing it better.

RIGHT: Marine sniper team defending the U.S. Embassy in Monrovia, Liberia, in 1996. Rioting factions twice took the Marines under fire, but withdrew with several fatalities from well-aimed fire by the Leathernecks.
(Marine Corps Association)

OPPOSITE: Liberia-bound Marines train in full riot gear on the flight deck of their amphibious ship.
(Marine Corps Association)

*THE BATTLE
HISTORY OF THE
US MARINES*

EPILOGUE

IT'S NOT THE STARS OR BARS YOU HAVE, NOT WHAT YOU WEAR ON YOUR SLEEVE OR SHOULDER, THAT DETERMINES WHAT YOU ARE. IT'S WHAT YOU WEAR ON YOUR COLLAR—THE EAGLE, GLOBE, AND ANCHOR— THAT PUTS YOU IN THE BROTHERHOOD OF MARINES.

Brigadier General Carl Mundy, USMC
Marine Corps Birthday, 1984

Oklahoma City, April 1995

Two United States Marines were among the 168 people killed by the terrorist bomb that destroyed the Alfred P. Murrah Federal Building.

The Federal Emergency Management Agency deployed teams of firemen and police officers from New York City to help search the rubble for survivors and recover the dead. Several of these volunteers were Marine Reservists or former Marines (there are no "ex-Marines").

Police officer Michael Curtin, a Marine first sergeant in the Reserves, discovered a body pinned in the wreckage wearing the blue trousers with distinctive "blood stripe" of a Marine. He knew he had found the missing remains of Captain Randolph Guzman, executive officer of the recruiting station.

Curtin asked permission to retrieve Captain Guzman's body—dangerous, laborious work. He found three other former Marines to lend a hand.

Manny Hernandez, another police officer, said, "It was something I had to do. I had a squad in Nam, and whenever we lost a Marine, he was never left behind. We take care of our own."

The Marines worked five hours with electric jackhammers to free the captain's remains. Someone provided a body bag.

Hernandez knelt and closed the dead Marine's eyes—"for the glory of God," he said, "and the glory of the Corps." Word somehow passed around the site that the Marines were bringing out one of their own.

An Air Force officer provided an American flag. Officer Curtin draped it over the body, and the men worked their way clear of the building with their burden.

Curtin was stunned at what he saw outside. "It was completely quiet. Cranes stopped, rescuers stopped, people lined the street. Everyone was watching in silence as we brought our Marine out." The workers formed a corridor, removed their hard hats, bowed their heads. The veterans in the crowd saluted, tears in their eyes.

Said Officer Hernandez, swept with emotion, "We are a band of brothers."

Captain Guzman was in good, ever-faithful hands.

Semper Fidelis . . .

(Charles Waterhouse)

Appendix A

No photograph better reflects the horrors of the Chosin Reservoir campaign or the abiding spirit of *Semper Fidelis* than this.

(David Douglas Duncan)

Battle Honors Inscribed on the Marine Corps War Memorial, Arlington, Virginia

Revolutionary War, 1775–1783
French Naval War, 1798–1801
Tripoli, 1801–1805
War of 1812–1815
Florida Indian Wars, 1835–1842
Mexico, 1846–1848
War Between the States, 1861–1865
Spanish War, 1898
Philippine Insurrection, 1898–1902
Boxer Rebellion, 1900
Nicaragua, 1912
Veracruz, 1914
Haiti, 1915–1934
Santo Domingo, 1916–1924
World War I, 1917–1918
   Belleau Wood
   Soissons
   St. Mihiel
   Blanc Mont
   Meuse–Argonne
Nicaragua, 1926–1933
World War II
   1941: Pearl Harbor, Wake Island, Bataan, and Corregidor
   1942: Midway, Guadalcanal
   1943: New Georgia, Bougainville, Tarawa, New Britain
   1944: Marshall Islands, Marianas Islands, Peleliu
   1945: Iwo Jima, Okinawa
Korea, 1950
Lebanon, 1958
Vietnam, 1962–1975
Dominican Republic, 1965
Lebanon, 1981–1984
Grenada, 1983
Persian Gulf, 1987–1991
Panama, 1989–1990
Somalia, 1992–1994

Appendix B

Marine Corps Battle Casualties Since 1775

Conflict	Killed in Action / Died of Wounds	Wounded in Action
Revolutionary War	49	70
Quasi-War with France	6	11
Barbary Wars	4	10
War of 1812	46	33
Creek-Seminole War	8	1
Mexican War	11	47
Civil War (Union)	148	131
Spanish-American War	7	13
Philippine Insurrection	7	19
Samoa (1899)	0	2
Boxer Rebellion	9	17
Nicaragua (1912)	5	16
Mexico	5	13
Dominican Republic (1916–1920)	17	50
Haiti	10	26
Nicaragua (1926–1933)	47	66
World War I	2,457	8,894
World War II	19,733	67,207
Korean War	4,267	23,744
Dominican Republic (1965)	9	25
Vietnam War	13,067	88,633
Lebanon	240	151
Grenada	3	15
Persian Gulf (1988)	2	0
Panama	2	3
Persian Gulf War	24	92

Few photographs ever captured the desperate vulnerability of these island assaults more poignantly. Contrary to popular belief, the Japanese riflemen were excellent shots, and their machine gunners disciplined and deadly. Crossing open ground, here in Okinawa, or anywhere, was an exposure to eternity. (U.S. Marine Corps)

Appendix C

The Commandants of the Marine Corps

Samuel Nicholas* 1775–1781
William W. Burrows 1798–1804
Franklin Wharton 1804–1818
Anthony Gale 1819–1820
Archibald Henderson 1820–1859
John Harris 1859–1864
Jacob Zeilin 1864–1876
Charles G. McCawley 1876–1891
Charles Heywood 1891–1903
George F. Elliott 1903–1910
William P. Biddle 1911–1914
George Barnett 1914–1920
John A. Lejeune 1920–1929
Wendell C. Neville 1929–1930
Ben H. Fuller 1930–1934
John H. Russell 1934–1936
Thomas Holcomb 1936–1943
Alexander A. Vandegrift 1944–1947
Clifton B. Cates 1948–1951
Lemuel C. Shepherd, Jr. 1952–1955
Randolph McC. Pate 1956–1959
David M. Shoup 1960–1963
Wallace M. Greene, Jr. 1964–1967
Leonard F. Chapman, Jr. 1968–1971
Robert E. Cushman, Jr. 1972–1975
Louis H. Wilson 1975–1979
Robert H. Barrow 1979–1983
Paul X. Kelley 1983–1987
Alfred M. Gray, Jr. 1987–1991
Carl E. Mundy, Jr. 1991–1995
Charles C. Krulak 1995–

"Crossing into
Kuwait."
(Sgt. Charles G. Grow,
USMC, Marine Corps
Combat Art Collection)

*Nicholas was Senior Officer, Continental Marines;
the term "Commandant" did not come into use until 1800.
Technicalities aside, Samuel Nicholas is considered the first of the lineage.

Appendix D

Sergeants Major of the Marine Corps

Wilbur Bestwick
    May 23,1957–August 31,1959
Francis D. Rauber
    September 1, 1959–June 28, 1962
Thomas J. McHugh
    June 29, 1962–July 16, 1965
Herbert J. Sweet
    July 17, 1965–July 31, 1969
Joseph W. Dailey
    August 1, 1969–January 31, 1973
Clinton A. Puckett
    February 1, 1973–May 31, 1975
Henry H. Black
    June 1, 1975–March 31, 1977

John E. Massaro
    April 1, 1977–August 15, 1979
Leland D. Crawford
    August 16, 1979–June 27, 1983
Robert E. Cleary
    June 28, 1983–June 26, 1987
David W. Sommers
    June 27, 1987–June 27, 1991
Harold G. Overstreet
    June 28, 1991–June 29, 1995
Lewis G. Lee
    June 30, 1995–

Iwo Jima would be the Marines' greatest battle, an opposed assault for thirty-six consecutive days. Here, on D-Day, it began.
(U.S. Marine Corps)

Appendix E

The Marines' Hymn

From the halls of Montezuma
To the shores of Tripoli,
We fight our country's battles
In the air, on land, and sea.
First to fight for right and freedom,
And to keep our honor clean,
We are proud to claim the title
Of United States Marine.

Our flag's unfurled to every breeze
From dawn to setting sun;
We have fought in every clime and place
Where we could take a gun.
In the snow of far off northern lands
And in sunny tropic scenes,
You will find us always on the job—
The United States Marines.

Here's health to you and to our Corps
Which we are proud to serve;
In many a strife we've fought for life
And never lost our nerve.
If the Army and the Navy
Ever look on Heaven's scenes,
They will find the streets are guarded
By United States Marines.

The 1st Marine Division's battle for Seoul in September 1950 was more savage and prolonged than the earlier Marine urban fights in Veracruz, Garapan, or Naha. Not until the battle for Hue in the Tet campaign of the Vietnam War would such desperate house-to-house fighting be matched.
(U.S. Marine Corps)

For Further Reading

IN GENERAL

These four books remain the best of the USMC histories:

Heinl, Robert D. *Soldiers of the Sea: The U.S. Marine Corps, 1775-1962.* Annapolis: Naval Institute Press, 1962.

Millett, Allan R. *Semper Fidelis: The History of the United States Marine Corps.* Rev. Ed. New York: Free Press, 1991.

Moskin, J. Robert. *The U.S. Marine Corps Story.* 3d Rev. Ed. Boston: Little, Brown, 1992.

Simmons, Edwin H. *The United States Marines: The First Two Hundred Years, 1775-1975.* New York: Viking Press, 1976.

USMC-oriented magazines such as *Leatherneck, Marine Corps Gazette,* and *Fortitudine* regularly feature first-rate historical essays.

Readers interested in primary sources are encouraged to visit the Marine Corps Historical Center, Building 58, Washington Navy Yard, 901 M Street SE, Washington, D.C. The center contains a wealth of archives, biographies, muster rolls, personal papers, oral history interviews, a library brimming with operational and unit histories, and an outstanding museum.

SPECIFIC RECOMMENDATIONS

Early History

Metcalf, Clyde H. *A History of the United States Marine Corps.* New York: Putnam, 1939.

Rankin, Robert H. *Small Arms of the Sea Services.* New Milford, CT: Norman Flayderman, 1972.

Shulimson, Jack. *The Marine Corps' Search for a Mission, 1880-1898.* Lawrence: University Press of Kansas, 1993.

Smith, Charles R. *Marines in the Revolution.* Washington, D.C.: History and Museums Division, HQMC, 1975.

Sullivan, David M. *The U.S. Marine Corps in the Civil War: the First Year.* Shippensburg, PA: White Mane, 1997.

World War I

Bartlett, Merrill L. *John A. Lejeune, A Marine's Life.* Columbia, SC: University of South Carolina Press, 1991.

Johnson, Edward C., and Graham A. Cosmas. *Marine Corps Aviation: The Early Years, 1912-1940.* Washington, D.C.: History and Museums Division, HQMC, 1977.

Thomason, John W. *Fix Bayonets and Other Stories.* New York: Scribners, 1925.

Interwar Era

Ballendorf, Dirk A., and Merrill L. Bartlett. *Pete Ellis: An Amphibious Warfare Prophet.* Annapolis: Naval Institute Press, 1996.

Hoffman, Jon T. *Once a Legend: "Red Mike" Edson of the Raiders.* Novato, CA: Presidio Press, 1994.

Krulak, Victor H. *First to Fight.* Annapolis: Naval Institute Press, 1984.

Millett, Allan R. *In Many a Strife: General Gerald C. Thomas and the U.S. Marine Corps, 1917-1956.* Annapolis: Naval Institute Press, 1993.

Strahan, Jerry E. *Andrew Jackson Higgins and the Boats that Won World War II.* Baton Rouge: Louisiana State University Press, 1994.

World War II

Alexander, Joseph H. *Storm Landings: Epic Amphibious Battles in the Central Pacific.* Annapolis: Naval Institute Press, 1997.

_____. "The Turning Points of Tarawa," *MHQ 8* (Summer 1996), 42-51.

_____. *Utmost Savagery: The Three Days of Tarawa.* Annapolis: Naval Institute Press, 1995.

Buell, Thomas B. *The Quiet Warrior: A Biography of Adm. Raymond A. Spruance.* Boston: Little, Brown, 1974.

Canfield, Bruce N. *U.S. Infantry Weapons of World War II.* Lincoln, RI: Andrew Mowbray, 1994.

Frank, Richard B. *Guadalcanal: The Definitive Account.* New York: Random House, 1990.

Gatchel, Theodore M. *At the Water's Edge.* Annapolis: Naval Institute Press, 1996.

Hunt, George B. *Coral Comes High*. New York: Harper, 1946.

Hynes, Samuel. *Flights of Passage*. Annapolis: Naval Institute Press, 1988.

Isley, Jeter A., and Philip A. Crowl. *The U.S. Marines and Amphibious War*. Princeton: Princeton University Press, 1951.

Lorelli, John A. *To Foreign Shores: U.S. Amphibious Operations in World War II*. Annapolis, MD: Naval Institute Press, 1995.

Miller, Nathan. *The War at Sea: A Naval History of World War II*. New York: Scribners, 1995.

Newcomb, Richard F. *Iwo Jima*. New York: Holt, Rinehart & Winston, 1965.

Potter, E. B. *Nimitz*. Annapolis: Naval Institute Press, 1976.

Sherrod, Robert. *History of Marine Corps Aviation in World War II*. Washington, D.C.: Combat Forces Press, 1952.

————. *On to Westward: The Battles of Saipan and Iwo Jima*. New York: Duell, Sloan & Pierce, 1945.

Sledge, Eugene B. *With the Old Breed at Peleliu and Okinawa*. Classics of Naval Literature Edition. Annapolis: Naval Institute Press, 1996.

Spector, Ronald H. *Eagle Against the Sun*. New York: Free Press, 1985.

Tillman, Barrett. *Corsair: The F4U in World War II and Korea*. Annapolis: Naval Institute Press, 1979.

Twining, Merrill B. *No Bended Knee: The Battle for Guadalcanal*. Novato, CA: Presidio Press, 1996.

Wheeler, Richard B. *A Special Valor: The U.S. Marines and the Pacific War*. New York: Harper & Row, 1983.

Willock, Roger. *Unaccustomed to Fear: A Biography of the Late Gen. Roy S. Geiger*. Reprint Edition. Quantico, VA: Marine Corps Association, 1983.

Korean War

Davis, Raymond G. *The Story of Ray Davis*. Fuquay Varina: Research Triangle Publishing, 1995.

Geer, Andrew. *The New Breed: The Story of the U.S. Marines in Korea*. New York: Harper and Brothers, 1952.

Heinl, Robert D. *Victory at High Tide: The Inchon-Seoul Campaign*. Philadelphia: Lippincott, 1968.

Owen, Joseph R. *Colder Than Hell: A Marine Rifle Company at Chosin Reservoir*. Annapolis: Naval Institute Press, 1996.

Parker, Gary W. *A History of Medium Helicopter Squadron 161*. Washington, D.C.: History and Museums Division, HQMC, 1971.

Russ, Martin. *The Last Parallel*. New York: Rinehart, 1957.

Cold War, Vietnam War

Alexander, Joseph H., and Merrill L. Bartlett, *Sea Soldiers in the Cold War: Amphibious Warfare, 1945-1991*. Annapolis: Naval Institute Press, 1994.

Frank, Benis M. *Marines in Lebanon, 1982-1984*. Washington, D.C.: GPO, 1987.

Hemingway, Al. *Our War Was Different: Marine Combined Action Platoons in Vietnam*. Annapolis: Naval Institute Press, 1992.

Lehrack, Otto J. *No Shining Armor: The Marines at War in Vietnam*. Lawrence, KS: University Press of Kansas, 1992.

Miller, John G. *The Bridge at Dong Ha*. Annapolis: Naval Institute Press, 1989.

Pisor, Robert. *The End of the Line: The Siege of Khe Sanh*. New York: Ballantine Books, 1982.

Puller, Lewis B., Jr. *Fortunate Son*. New York: Grove Weidenfeld, 1991.

West, Francis J., Jr. *The Village*. New York: Harper & Row, 1972.

Gulf War / Brave New World

Gordon, Michael R., and Bernard C. Trainor. *The Generals' War*. Boston: Little, Brown, 1995.

Quilter, Charles J. *U.S. Marines in the Persian Gulf, 1990-1991: With the I Marine Expeditionary Force in Desert Shield and Desert Storm*. Washington, D.C.: History and Museums Division, HQMC, 1993.

Schwarzkopf, Norman H., with Peter Petre. *It Doesn't Take a Hero*. New York: Bantam, 1992.

Index

Gouraud, Henri, 45–46

Gray, Alfred M., Jr., 372, 396

Greene, Israel, 14–16

Greene, Wallace M., Jr., 177, 396

Grenada, **365,** 366

Griffin, Charles, 16

Griffith, Samuel, 120

ground control intercept (GCI), 117

"Grumman Ironworks," 96

Guadalcanal, 110–11

　　Bloody Ridge, 101–4, 106

　　close air support at, 93–96, 100, 105–6

　　D-Day, 90–93

　　Ichiki Detachment counterattack, 98–100,
　　　　104–5

　　map, 90

　　planning for, 88–90

　　Sendai Division counterattack, 104–9

Guam, 76–77, 167–68, 186–89

　　map, 166

Guantanamo Bay, Cuba, 317–18

Guardia, 55–58, 62

Gulf of Tonkin Resolution, 319

Gulf War, 370–74, 377–78, 383–86

　　air war, 374–76

　　G-Day, 378, 382–83

　　map, 379

Guzman, Randolph, 393

Haiti, **50–51,** 53–54, 68, 389–90

"half fish, half crazy" (UDTs), 163, 187, 193, 231

Halley, Thomas, 73

Halsey, William "Bull," 77, 106, 114, 120

　　quoted, 118, 193

Hanneken, Herman "Hard Head," 53–54, 105,
　　　　107, 109, 129, 193–94

Hanson, Robert, 115–16

Harbord, James, 35, 38, 41–42

Harpers Ferry, 14

Harris, Field, 294–95, 297

Harris, Harold "Bucky," 193–94, 199

Harris, John, 14, 16–17, 396

Hart, Franklin, 164

Hartman, Edward, 224

Haruna (Japanese battleship), 105

Haskin, John, 82

Hatfield, Gilbert, 57–58

Hawkins, Deane, 144, 151–52

Hayate (Japanese destroyer), 77

Haynes, William "Tex," 82

Headley, James, 216

Hearst, William Randolph, quoted, 220

Heimberger, Albert (Eddie Albert), 152

Henderson, Archibald, 10–14, 396

Henderson, Charles, 12–13

Henderson, Lofton, 84–85, 93

Hennelly, John, 348

Henry House Hill, 16

Henze, Gilbert, 117

Hernandez, Manny, 393

Herr, Michael, quoted, 346

Heywood, Charles, 396

Higgins, Andrew, 67

Hill, Harry, 143, 179

Hill 660 (New Britain), 134

Hindenburg Line, 45–49

Hinsdale, 228

Hitzelberger, Daniel, 357

Holcomb, Thomas, 39, 41, 43, 72, 139, 396

"honeycomb" tactics

　　at Okinawa, 229–30, 233

　　at Peleliu, 192, 194–95, 198

Hopkins, Esek, 2

"Horse Marines," **64–65**

Houghton, Kenneth, 277

Howard, Samuel, 79

　　quoted, 82

Huddleston, Craig, 376

Hue City, Vietnam, 330, 338–40, 343

Hughes, John "Johnny the Hard," 40–41

Hunt, George, 194–95

Hunter, Daniel "Beau," 35, 39

Huntington, Kenneth, 238

Huntington, Robert, 20

Hurst, Hunter, 242

Hwachon Reservoir, Korea, 305–7

Hyakutake, Haruyoshi

　　at Bougainville, 120–24

　　at Guadalcanal, 89, 101, 105, 106–7, 110–11

Ichiki, Kiyono, 98–100

Ichiki Detachment, **86–87,** 98–100, 104–5

Inchon, Korea, 268–74

　　map, 269

Ingraham, Charles, 375

Iwo Jima, 208–10, 220–22, 224–25

    D-Day, **206–7, 209,** 210–15

    flag-raising at, **214,** 215, 221

    map, 208

Jackson, Andrew, 10

Jamestown Line (Korea), 308–12

"Japanese Marines." *See rikusentai*

Japanese units

    evacuation of, 111, 120

    Ichiki Detachment, **86–87,** 98–100, 104–5

    Kure Special Naval Landing Forces *(See rikusentai)*

    Nagoya Division, 110

    Sendai Division, 105–10

    Seventeenth Army, 89, 121

    Thirty-Second Army, 229, 247

    15th Independent Mixed Regiment, 238

    20th Infantry, 79–80

    28th Infantry, 98–100

    36th Infantry Brigade, 101–4

    40th Division, 248

    43d Division, 168

    62d Infantry Division, 242

    65th Brigade, 125

Jarmen, Sanderford, 175

Jefferson, Thomas, 5–6

JOC (Joint Operations Center), 305, 311

Johnson, Bert, 280

Johnson, Louis, 252, 254

Johnson, Lyndon B., 318–19, 327, 332, 341, 344

Johnson, Opha, 49

Johnson, Randall, 130–31

Joint Chiefs of Staff, 114, 139, 167, 255, 267

Joint Operations Center (JOC), 305, 311

Jones, James, 163, 179–80

Jones, John Paul, 3

Jones, Louis, 164

Jones, William "Willie K.," 153, 157, 170, 179

Jordan, Walter, 145, 147, 150

Juneau, 256

Kaido, Chosaku, 217

"Kaiser Coffins," 204

kamikazes. *See* suicide missions

Karch, Frederick, 319

Kawaguchi, Kiyotaki, 101–4

Keleher, Michael "Irish Mike," 214–16, 221

Kelley, John, 263

Kelley, Paul X., 364–66, 396

Kelly, John, 47

Kennedy, John Fitzgerald, 121, 316–17

Ketcham, William, 224

Keys, Bill, 371–73, 376–78, 382

Khe Sanh, Vietnam, 332–37, 341–49

Khrushchev, Nikita, 318

Kidd, Isaac, 73

kikusui ("floating chrysanthemums"). *See* suicide missions

Kisaragi (Japanese destroyer), 77

Kocak, Matej, 42

Koiari, 124

Kongo (Japanese battleship), 105

Korea, 19–20, 254–55. *See also names of specific campaigns*

    map, 253

Korean units, 1st Marine Corps Regiment, 270

Krulak, Charles C., 371, 377, 396

    quoted, xv

Krulak, Victor "Brute," 62, 141, 253–55, 276, 321, 326

    quoted, xiv

    in World War II, 121, 231–32, 243

Kuma Battalion, 102, 105

Kurdistan, 386

Kuribayashi, Tadamichi, 208, 212–17, 220, 222, 224

Kurth, Michael, 385

Kuwait. *See* Gulf War

Kwajalein, 162–63

Kyle, Wood "Woody," 147, 150, 153, 321

Kyushu, 248

Lam, Huang, 339

Lanang, 26–27

landing ships

    LSDs, 146

    LSTs, **112–13,** 142

landing vehicles, 230

    development of, 52–53

    LVTs, 67, 163, **182–83**

        at Tarawa, **136–37,** 141–44, 147

Schmidt, Harry (*cont.*)
    at Tinian, 180, 184, 186
Schneider, Merlin, 186
Schoettel, John, 145
Schwarzkopf, Norman, 370–71, 373, 382–83
Scott, Win, 287, 290–91, 295
SeaBees (Naval Construction Battalion), 124, 198, 224, 347
Seminole War, 10–11
Semper Fidelis, established as Marines' motto, 18
Sendai Division, 105–10
Seoul, Korea, 274–80
  map, 269
Seymour, Sir Edward, 27
Shannon, Harold, 83
Shapley, Alan, 73, 122, 124, 135, 186, 244
Shearer, Maurice, 41
Shepherd, Lemuel C., 41, 177, 253, 255, 276, 396
  at Guam, 186–88
  at New Britain, 125, 130–31, 134
  at Okinawa, 229, 231–32, 237–38, 243–44, 247
Sherrod, Robert, quoted, 137, 238
Shibasaki, Keiji, 140, 142–44, 150–51
Shiga, Yoshio, 73
Shih-lun, Sung, 287
ships, CVEs, 201, 203–4. *See also names of individual ships*
Shoup, David M., 119, 177, 396
  quoted, 138
  at Tarawa, 139, 141–42, 150–53
  D-Day, 143–50
Shu-fly operations (Vietnam), 319–20
Simmons, Edwin, 280
Simms, John, 12–13, 16
Simpson, Ormond, 317
Sino-Japanese War, 62
Sixth Army, 204
Slappey, Wallace, 198
Sledge, Eugene "Sledgehammer," 195, 230–32, 239
  quoted, 193, 226, 238
Small Wars Manual (Edson), 390
Smith, Alvin, 270
Smith, Holland M. "Howlin' Mad," 66–67, 179, 201, 248

and Iwo Jima campaign, 208–10
and Marianas campaign, 167, 169–70, 174–76
and Marshalls campaign, 162–63
quoted, 161, 186, 215
and Tarawa campaign, 138, 141, 147, 159
Smith, Jacob, 25
Smith, John, 93–94, 106
Smith, Julian, 61, 167
  at Tarawa, 139, 142–43, 146–47, 150–53, 157
Smith, Oliver P., 134, 196, 242, 253
  in Korea, 305–8
    Chosin, 282, 284–87, 290–91, 294–97
    Inchon, 268–70
    Seoul, 274–76, 278–79
  quoted, 263, 300
Smith, Ralph, 175
"Smith *versus* Smith Controversy," 175–76
Snedeker, Edward, 245–46
"Society of the Righteous Harmonious Fists" (Boxers), 27–30
Sohoton Cliffs, 26
Soissons, 42–43
Somalia, 386–89
Sommers, David W., 397
Sousa, John Philip, 18
Spanish-American War, 20–21, 25
Special Naval Landing Forces (Japanese). *See rikusentai*
Spruance, Raymond, 84, 138–39, 142, 158–59, 186, 189, 236–37
  and Marianas campaign, 167, 170, 174–75
  and Marshalls campaign, 162–64
Stevens, John, 262
Stilwell, Richard, 358
"Sting Ray" operations (Vietnam), 356
Stout, Robert "Cowboy," 198–99
suicide missions, 228–29, 235–38
suicides, civilian, 176
Sulfur Island. *See* Iwo Jima
Superfortress. *See* aircraft, B–29s
"Super Gaggle" (aerial resupply, Vietnam), 347
Suribachi, 210–15, 221
Sweeney, Thomas, 82
Sweet, Herbert J., 397
Swett, James, 106